1997 EDITION

BRIDAL GOWN GUIDE

Discover
the dress
of your dreams
at a price
you can afford

DENISE & ALAN FIELDS
Authors of the best-seller *Bridal Bargains*

392.54
F 466

Copyright Page and Zesty Lo-Cal Recipes

No actual brides were hurt in the making of this book.

This book was recorded live in Boulder, CO.

Lead guitar, vocals and tuba by Denise Fields
Drums, keyboards and strange sounds by Alan Fields
Wurlitzer electronic piano and maracas by Ben Fields
Cover design, bass guitar and cowbell by Steve Lux, San Diego

Acoustic guitar on "Alfred Sung's Got A Big Tongue" by Ed Robertson
Harmony vocal on "Tangerines and Bridal Magazines" by Cele & Millie
Bass guitar solo on "Can't You See, Mori Lee?" by Benjamin Orr

Alan Fields appears courtesy of Howard and Patti Fields.
Denise Fields appears courtesy of Max and Helen Coopwood.
This book was written to the music of the Barenaked Ladies,
which probably explains a lot.

Thanks to Sew & So, The Button and Bridal Store (619) 573-1853
in San Diego for providing the beaded lace on the front cover.
Special thanks to Alan Zweig for all the help north of the border.

This book is dedicated to Dee Dee McKittrick.

To order this book, check your local bookstore or call (800) 888-0385. Or send $9.95 plus $3 shipping to Windsor Peak Press, 436 Pine Street, Suite G, Boulder, CO, 80302. Quantity discounts are available. Questions or comments? Feel free to contact the authors at (303) 442-8792. Or fax them a note at (303) 442-3744. Or write to them at the above address.

Library in Congress Cataloging in Publication Data
Fields, Denise,
Fields, Alan,
    Bridal Gown Guide: Discover the dress of your dreams at a price you can afford/Denise and Alan Fields. 1997 Edition.
    416 p.
    Includes index.
    1. Wedding costume—United States and Canada. 2. Consumer education. 3. Shopping. 4. Title.

GTI1752.M33   1997

ISBN 0-9626556-9-4

Distributed to bookstores by
Publisher's Group West, 1-800-788-3123.

⇒ OVERVIEW ⇐

Part I: How To Buy a Bridal Gown

How to Buy a Bridal Gown shows you the seven steps to finding the bridal gown that's perfect for you. You'll learn how to pick the right style, navigate bridal retail shops, what to get in writing and more. Each chapter gives you smart shopping tips, scams to avoid and money-saving secrets.

Part II: Bridal Gown Designer Reviews

Meet the Top 40 bridal designers in North America—you'll learn who they are, what they charge and more. Each review gives you our opinion of their quality, plus in-depth sizing information, delivery time-frames, dress descriptions and more.

Part III: How to Buy a Bridesmaid's Dress

How to Buy a Bridesmaid's Dress gives you all the information you need to select a style for your bridesmaids. Learn about all the recent changes with these gowns, plus money-saving tips, advice on picking the right size and rip-offs to watch out for.

Part IV: Bridesmaids Designer Reviews

Check out complete reviews of more than 20 of the hottest bridesmaids dress designers. You'll learn who offers the best deals, the widest variety of sizing, and quickest delivery.

Part V: Canada's Top Bridal Designers

Who are the best bridal designers in the Great White North? You'll learn this, plus tips on cross-border shopping, money-saving advice and other special considerations for Canada. Then we review Canada's top dress makers, including several brands that are available on both sides of the border.

❖ C O N T E N T S ❖

Introduction

Part I: How to Buy a Bridal Gown

STEP ONE

STEP TWO

STEP THREE

Part II: Bridal Gown Designer Reviews

Part III: How to Buy a Bridesmaid's Dress

Part IV: Bridesmaids Designer Reviews

Part V: Canada's Top Bridal Designers

→ICONS←

What the Icons Mean

 Reality Check

 Shopping Tips

 Scams to Avoid

 Self-Defense

 Myths

 E-Mail

 Money-Saving Tips

Stop! Read This First!

Can you name anything that symbolizes a wedding more than the bridal gown?

Okay, well, the wedding cake. Sure, the exchange of wedding rings is important too. The vows? Yeah, they're significant as well.

Hmmm. So, perhaps the bridal gown isn't the most important part of your wedding. But let's be honest: the wedding dress is certainly at the top of the *bride's* list of priorities. If it wasn't so, why would she spend hundreds (thousands?) of dollars on this dress she'll wear for, at most, four hours?

Unfortunately, this is a gender-specific area of the bridal universe. In contrast, let's take a brief look at how grooms approach their apparel for the Big Day. Let's see. Does the groom spend hours pouring through *Groom's Magazine* searching for just the right tuxedo style? Does he visit eight shops and try on dozens of tuxes? Does he worry that this tux will make him look fat? Please. We didn't think so.

Our point (and we do have one) is the bridal gown is much more important to brides than just about any other part of the wedding. Flowers? They'll be dead by morning. Invitations? Just paper. The cake? No one eats it anyway. Photography? Who cares what the pictures look like if you're not wearing a spectacular dress?

The bridal gown is the ultimate gown for a day that's supposed to be one of the key milestones in life. And, theoretically, you're only going to do this once, so you might as well do it right.

All of this would be easy if shopping for a bridal gown was more like shopping for, say, a TV. Wouldn't that be nice? You'd read the rankings of brands in consumer magazines, visit a few of those electronics stores, pick a model that's in the right price range . . . and then take it home that afternoon. No fuss, no muss.

Yeah, right. A recent survey of "Things Likely to Drive Brides Insane" ranked buying a wedding dress second, right behind having a root canal the day before the ceremony. For some reason, the bridal dress industry has decided to turn the process of procuring a gown into some sort of sick torture test. What should be a simple dress purchase often turns into a test of wills between the Bride (wearing white, weighing 120 pounds, in one corner) and the Evil Apparel Industry (wearing black, weighing 320 pounds, in the other corner.)

And that's why we're here. In the next 200 or so pages, we hope to even the odds and smooth the path between You and That Damn Dress. But, before we get to the details, we'll take a minute to introduce ourselves.

The "Satanic Verses" of wedding books

Our interest in this subject can be traced back to a hot, summer night in Austin, Texas. The year was 1988 and we had just flipped on the ten o'clock news. The lead story was about a riot.

As we watched the pictures of the melee, we wondered just what the heck was happening. Was this a student protest at the university that went awry? Did some political activists stage a protest at the state capital that got out of hand?

Nope. This riot was in the parking lot of a *bridal shop*. And the riotors were not student radicals or political activists. No, the folks raising a ruckus were a throng of brides-to-be.

You see, Austin's largest chain of bridal shops had suddenly closed its doors one Friday afternoon in June. With no warning, brides arrived to pick up their dresses for upcoming weddings, only to discover the doors padlocked by security guards. The riot broke out when a UPS truck pulled up to deliver dresses to the shop. The poor, hapless UPS driver (in one of those brown uniforms with the cute shorts) was far outnumbered—brides stormed the truck and snatched the gowns. The cops were called to quell the disturbance.

We sat there on the couch with our mouths hanging open. As an engaged couple planning a wedding ourselves, we had heard all the dress horror stories from other brides-to-be— gowns that arrived late, shops that couldn't care less and other rip-offs and scams. Yet watching the Great Bridal Riot of Austin there on the ten o'clock news made us realize that perhaps all those stories weren't hyperbole.

And we had another reason to watch the proceedings with amazement. As a way to pass the time, we wrote a small paperback guide to planning a wedding in the Capitol City. The book, *Austin Weddings*, introduced us to a subject that would become our life's work: brides, grooms and the general mayhem that surrounds this thing we call marriage.

At first, we thought the blatant consumer fraud with bridal gown shops was unique to Austin . . . or, perhaps at most, limited to Texas. Weddings are big business in the Lone Star State. And, sure, people get married in Montana and Vermont, but we doubt the spectacle of marital theater there could rival the 400-guest extravagances Texas brides and grooms subject themselves to.

After we researched our first national book on wedding, *Bridal Bargains*, we realized that was a wrong assumption. We interviewed over 1000 couples about how they saved money for weddings and receptions. We also published our phone number and address in our books. And what subject do you think brides had as their number one complaint? Gowns, of course. Whether they lived in the Pacific Northwest or the Upper Midwest, brides were united in their displeasure with the gown-buying process.

The success of *Bridal Bargains* and the national exposure we received on shows such as "Oprah" and "Good Morning America" enabled us to pursue consumer advocacy on behalf of brides full-time. This didn't thrill folks in the wedding business, who by now were convinced we were the Salman Rushdie of bridal writers. Most were not too happy to have the industry's dirty laundry aired on TV, radio and (worse of all) in their local newspapers' bridal section.

Yet, even though we have a full chapter on buying a wedding gown in *Bridal Bargains*, the main focus of that book was saving money on the entire wedding and reception, not just the dress. As our research files bulged with information on buying a wedding gown, we realized we had a whole book of info on this subject.

The Ballad of J.R.

So, that's how we got here. And what happened to the owners of that bridal shop in Austin that inspired our crusade to save brides from gown rip-offs and scams? Well, that's an even more interesting story than our biography.

The owner of the bridal shop chain was a colorful fellow whose first name was (and we're not making this up) J.R. Seems like J.R. got himself in a scrape in the early 1980's and was convicted on federal fraud charges. Apparently, our hero bilked some elderly people in Waco out of their Medicaid and other monies and, worst of all, got caught.

After serving nine months in a federal pen, J.R. looked around for something to do. This was news to us, but apparently one of the few jobs you can get if you're a convicted felon is running a bridal dress shop. J.R. and his wife bought an existing bridal shop in Austin.

So, where did J.R. get all the money to buy the shop and expand the chain into seven stores? Why, a savings and loan, of course. By having his wife sign the loan papers, J.R. was able to borrow two million dollars. But the bank wasn't the only clearly intelligence-impaired company in this story—the bridal designers extended J.R. big credit lines to stock his stores with their gowns.

The result of all this wheeling and dealing was we had a convicted felon who bilked old ladies out of their savings running a chain of seven bridal dress shops in Texas' fourth largest city. Even a blind man could see the next chain of events: the economy hits the skids, business slumps ... but the shops continue taking deposits until the day their landlords padlock the doors. And brides are left without money and without a dress.

After this story came out in the press, we realized how few laws protected the dress deposits of brides-to-be. Anyone can print up a business card that says they're a "bridal specialist." The dress designers in New York City will apparently give credit to anyone with a pulse. And when the well-known substance hits the electrical convenience, well, stand back. The brides are out their money. The designers get stuck with unpaid bills. And the bridal shop owner is left laughing at us while sipping a mixed drink on some Caribbean island.

Except, that is, for J.R. from Austin. Seems our boy was not only stupid but unlucky too. Before he could high-tail it out of town, federal investigators put two and two together and arrested the Bridal Shop Owner from Hell. Last time we checked, J.R. was cooling his boots in another federal penitentiary.

Bridal shop bankruptcies have struck every state of the union, according to our research. There was California in 1992, Michigan in 1993, Virginia in 1995 and Colorado in 1996.

And it's more than just sudden shop closings that have many brides hopping mad. Consumers report to us a string of scams and rip-offs, ranging from outrageous overcharges for simple items like bras and shoes to clever bait-and-switch schemes. Our conclusion: Despite its sweet and lacy image, the bridal gown business is one of the sleaziest games in town.

And, yet, for every retail shop we found that ripped off brides, we found others that really cared about their customers. For every bridal designer that charged ridiculous prices for poorly sewn gowns, we found others that were making quality garments at fair prices. The goal of this book is simple: we want to show you how to avoid the bad guys ... and how to spot the good ones.

Come Along for a Ride

To accomplish that, we want to blow the lid off the secrecy that surrounds the bridal gown business. In the first part of this book, we'll show you the seven steps to finding the right gown—learning the lingo of fabrics and lace, how to spot a quality dress, what to get in writing on your dress order and more. Of course, we couldn't resist the temptation to tell you what the bridal shops don't want you to know: how to save money on that dress. You'll find a couple dozen tips that will shave hundreds of dollars off your gown purchase.

Part II is where the rubber meets the road—reviews and ratings of the country's top bridal designers. We'll tell you much more than you'll ever read in the bridal magazines. Does the designer have a free catalog? Do they carry special sizes? How long does it take to get a gown? What special options are available? And, most importantly, how much is this going to cost you?

If that weren't enough, it's on to the dress that's earned its special place in the Bridal Hall of Shame: the bridesmaid's gown. Part III tells the truth about these garments that often earn a special place in the back of the closet. You'll learn money-saving tips, shopping strategies and rip-offs to avoid. Then it's on to the designer reviews—we'll reveal who makes the best bridesmaid's dresses . . . and who doesn't. Again, we'll talk candidly about sizing, delivery and other topics you won't read about in a bridal magazine.

Finally, we can't forget our favorite country north of the United States (okay, it's the only country north of the United States). You'll read about Canada's top bridal gown designers, a low-profile outlet for a famous U.S. designer in Quebec, and the perils of cross-border shopping.

Disclaimer to Appease Our Lawyers

We should point out that there are no advertisements in this book. No company or individual paid us a fee or other form of compensation to appear in the *Bridal Gown Guide*. We don't take bribes. Our publishing company, Windsor Peak Press, derives its sole income from the sale of this book and other consumer-oriented publications.

Another important point: The opinions in this book are our own and merely reflect our own twisted views. While every effort was made to make sure the information inside this book is accurate at press time, hey, we're only human. Mistakes can happen. We'll try to fix 'em as soon as we spot 'em. Of course, prices quoted in this book can change without notice; consult a local retailer for the latest information on pricing, sizing and other details. We'll also post free updates to this book on our web page (www.bridalgown.com). As always, we welcome any comments and feedback you have, as long as it's positive of course. (Just kidding.) Our phone number, fax number, e-mail and regular mail addresses appear at the end of this book.

PART ONE

How to Buy a Bridal Gown

SETTING THE STYLE

Gown basics, silhouettes and the bridal magazines

What's the right style for your bridal gown? What the heck are the basic styles, anyway? We'll help answer those questions in this chapter, plus look at the four basic dress silhouettes and what looks best on different body types. Next, we'll take a hard look at those glossy bridal magazines and reveal a few secrets they don't want you to know.

O PEN UP ANY of those 1000-page bridal magazines and just look at all the gowns. Go ahead, we'll wait right here.

Mind numbing, isn't it?

As a country, the United States may have crumbling highways, a health care crisis, and kids that rank 19# in science (right behind Sri Lanka), but darn it if we don't have the most developed bridal industry in Western civilization. It makes us proud to be Americans.

The sheer number of bridal gowns may renew your faith in the free enterprise system, but it quickly makes the task of actually *selecting* a dress seem like climbing Mount Everest.

What dress would look best on *you*? Should you go for the understated look or a dress that resembles a chandelier? And how do you pronounce those stupid designers' names, anyway?

In order to keep mental institutions from being overrun with brides who mumble to themselves, we'd like to present our five-stage process of picking the right style for your bridal gown. Here goes:

1. Find a groom.
2. Get him to propose to you (or vice versa).
3. Pick a date.
4. Find a place to have the ceremony and reception.
5. When you find the ceremony site is booked on that date, go back to #3 and start again.

Now, we only mention the step of finding a groom as a courtesy reminder. This might seem like a safe assumption in the bridal gown shopping process, but we actually did meet a bride who bought her wedding dress before her groom ever proposed to her. Now, *that's* self-confidence. Or maybe it was just a good sale.

Reality Check

 The selection of a date and place for your wedding sets into a motion a series of events that impacts your gown style decision. Let's take a look at the mess you're in now:

1 DRESS CODES. Churches and synagogues may have dress restrictions on the proper attire for brides and grooms. After all, this is a house of worship and sashaying down the aisle in the Bridal Bikini from the Pamela Anderson Lee Wedding Collection may be a tad gauche. Some ceremony sites actually have written booklets with dress "guidelines." Low-cut necklines, sleeveless or backless gowns may be no-no's. (Of course, the bridal designers have realized this and in some cases may offer a little jacket you can wear during the ceremony).

2 THE TIME OF DAY. Will your wedding be at 2pm with a small reception afterwards in the church hall? Or a 7pm ceremony with a sit-down dinner at a four star hotel? While one might assume that a garden wedding would imply a bridal gown that is less formal, there are no federal laws on the subject. If you want to select a style that is more or less formal, however, we'll go into the differences later in this chapter.

3 THE LOCATION OF THE CEREMONY. Are we talking a majestic cathedral ceremony presided over by your Monsignor or a local civic rose garden ceremony with a justice of the peace? Besides style issues of formal or informal, there are practical issues as well. For example, if you plan on a religious ceremony that calls for you to kneel at some point, you might want to stay away from form fitting skirts like sheath and mermaid designs.

What makes a dress "formal," anyway?

If Congress would just pass a law that says a formal bridal gown is white and an informal gown was some other color, say red, this would greatly simply the whole question as to what makes a formal gown. But given the current mood in Washington, that seems unlikely, leaving brides on their own to decipher the subtle clues that separate a white formal gown from a white *semi-formal* gown.

We have suspicions that this whole issue is a make-work program for the bridal magazines. In every issue, they'll run fancy charts with advice on "what to wear" for various formality categories. Let's see, there's formal, informal, semi-formal, the new age para-formal and our favorite, the dreaded pseudo-formal. And don't forget, demi-formal—any event in which someone arrives dressed (or undressed) as Demi Moore. But that's another book.

If that wasn't chilling, consider that bridal magazines will next offer you advice on what's politically correct for certain times of the day, such as "daytime formal" and "evening semi-formal." While they've yet to invent rules for "informal brunch" and "ultra-formal night-time snack," we assume they're just around the corner.

To simplify this discussion, let's just do the basics:

❦ *Formal.* If a dress has a full, floor length skirt and train, it is considered formal. In general, the longer the train, the more formal the dress. Of course, you can add details like gloves and a fancy headpiece to increase the formality of most dresses.

❦ *Informal.* In the past, wedding dresses that were shorter than floor length were considered informals. Today, some designers offer informal gowns with floor length skirts. The key deciding factor between what makes a floor length dress formal or informal is the train. Most informal gowns don't have a train at all or, at most, a slight brush train (a train with a just a few inches of fabric brushing the floor). A simple hat or headpiece without veil usually completes the look.

Of course, nothing in the real world is so black and white. In your gown search, there's no doubt you'll find examples of gowns that don't seem to fit in either the "formal" or "informal" categories. With the right accessories, these dresses will look equally beautiful at a morning garden wedding or an evening sit-down dinner reception.

Silhouettes: Setting the overall look

Before you get lost in the blizzard of bridal fashion terms for sleeves, necklines and trains, consider the basic outline of the dress. The "silhouettes" (a French term, literally translated as "that damn dress") for bridal gowns fall into four broad categories:

1 BALL GOWN. This is probably the most traditional of all bridal gown silhouettes. The ball gown look is typified by a fitted bodice and waistline that leads to a very full skirt. In recent years, this look has been quite fashionable, as designers try to echo the golden age of Hollywood.

Pictured here is Marisa style 243 ($1300), a classic ball gown silhouette with a simple sleeveless bodice.

2 EMPIRE. A high waistline (right under the bust) which falls to a slimmer skirt width is the hallmark of an empire style gown. This look was hip in the 60's, all but disappeared in the 70's and 80's, only to return with a vengeance in the 90's. This example of an an empire silhouette is Lila Broude's style 479 ($1500). The dress features a scalloped lace bodice and a floor-length chiffon skirt with removable gossamer Watteau train (not pictured).

3 A-LINE OR PRINCESS. This style has vertical seams flowing from the shoulders down to a flared skirt. Unlike the ball gown, the waistline in an A-line/Princess style is not as defined. Because of its versatility, this style is quite popular as a silhouette that fits many different body types. As an example of a A-line dress, we've picked another Lila Broude design (style 478, $1750).

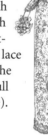

4 SHEATH. As you might guess, the slim skirt is a key attribute of a sheath silhouette, probably one of the more contemporary bridal gown looks. It goes without saying that the body-hugging sheath style isn't for everyone. A variation of the sheath is the mermaid-style gown, which is also form-fitting but flares below the knees. Pictured here is a lace sheath from Country Elegance (style 4488, the "Miriam," $565). This gown comes with a full detachable organza sweep train (not shown here).

Shopping Tips
Fashion in the Real World:
Different styles for different folks

In the recent book, "Woman who have Different Bodies and the Men Who Love Them," a psychologist pointed out that, yes, women *do* have different bodies. This came as a revelation to us. After you spend endless hours looking at bridal magazines, you'd be convinced that every American bride looks just like Cindy Crawford.

But seriously folks, we do realize that there is more out there than size 10. So, let's look at some common body types and possible bridal gown silhouettes that might work with each.

❖ FIVE FOOT TWO AND EYES OF BLUE

"I'm a very petite 5'2". Since bridal shops only carry gowns in sizes several times larger than I am, it's darn difficult to figure out what gowns would look best on me. Any ideas?"

Silhouettes that look best on petite brides include A-lines and sheath gowns. Most small brides should stay away from bouffant skirts, which can swallow up a petite figure. Consider a dress that has beautiful detailing at the neckline to help draw the eye up to the face. Avoid frou-frou detailing like ruffles on the skirt and dangling beads on the sleeves. Another idea: you can also wear a higher headpiece such as a tiara style to add height to your figure (later in the book, we'll go over the various headpiece options).

❖ ONE STYLE FITS ALL

"How can anyone make sense of all those dresses in the bridal magazines? Are there any styles that look great on everyone?"

This may come as a surprise, but there are a few styles that look good on almost every body type. A-line/princess dresses seem to be universally pleasing regardless of your personal plusses or flaws. If you're lucky enough to be one of those tall, thin types (if so, please stop reading this book, go to the kitchen and eat a Twinkie), you can wear just about any style out there.

❖ FULL-FIGURED FAUX PAS

"Being a size 24, I've had incredible problems finding sample gowns to fit. It's so difficult to visualize what will look good on me while I try to hold the dress on. Any fashion do's and don'ts for full figured woman?

As you've probably discovered, most bridal shops only stock sample gowns in size 10 or 12. Isn't that nice? Oh, you happened to be bigger than that size? Well, unfortunately, the attitude of far too many bridal dress shops is "go lose some weight."

Fortunately, there are a couple of solutions. The designer Bridal Originals (call 800-876-GOWN or 618-345-2345 to find a local store) actually encourages its dealers to stock samples in large sizes. What a concept. Another idea: in "Step #4: Money-Saving Tips," we'll discuss several off-the-rack bridal warehouses and other options that carry large sizes in stock.

Once you actually find a place that carries gowns in real world sizes, there are a few do's and don'ts that work better for full figures:

🕯 **Fabrics.** Avoid bulky fabrics like velvets and heavy satins. Instead, consider lighter weight satins, chiffons, crepes and silk shantungs (more on the different fabrics later in this book).

❦ **Finishes.** Glossy fabrics are probably a fashion don't. Skip the shiny satins and instead go for the understated elegance of matte satins or silks and lightweight crepes.

❦ **Necklines.** V-necks, keyholes and scoop necklines help de-emphasize the bust-line.

❦ **Sleeves.** Fitted sleeves are a better choice than puff or full sleeves.

❦ **Silhouettes.** Empire waists and A-lines work well, while mermaid and form-fitting sheath silhouettes should be left on the rack. If you want to de-emphasize your hips, skip the large back bow (derisively called "butt bows" by some brides).

❦ **Accessories.** Bring attention to your face with beautiful jewelry or a stunning headpiece (although skipping the huge pouf veil is probably wise). Carry a small bouquet of flowers rather than a mass of blooms.

❖ WHAT IS EGGSHELL ANYWAY?
"I'm Hispanic and have rather dark skin. With all the different shades of white and ivory out there, what would best compliment my skin tone?

While most gown designers seem to know what a white bridal gown is, there seems to be no agreement on what "ivory" should be. Heck, there isn't even agreement on what to *call* ivory gowns. Depending on the designer, ivory gowns are referred to as "eggshell," "candlelight," "ecru" and a series of other nonsensical names. In terms of color, some ivories are simply a pale off-white, while others are nearly tan.

A bride with a darker skin tone is actually in luck—most fabric colors will look great. The only exception: African-Americans, Hispanics and other brides with dark skin should stay away from ivory colors with yellow undertones, since that hue may not compliment a dark skin tone.

A great option to consider are the pale "rum pink" colors available from some manufacturers such as Mon Cheri and Bridal Originals (later in the designer section we'll note which designers carry different colors).

What if you have pale skin? Stay away from stark white gowns, which tend to wash out already fair skin. Instead, a better bet would be warmer natural and ivory colors. One designer who has one of the best ivory fabrics in the business is Bonny (more on specific designers later).

Whatever color you pick, make sure you see a fabric sample or swatch before you order. Since some shops only stock gowns in white or ivory, you may not be able to try on the dress in the color you want.

Meet the Bridal Magazines

It's darn near a right of passage. As soon as you get engaged, you'll probably be tempted to rush to your nearest newsstand to buy a bridal magazine. At $5 an issue (which works out to a dollar a pound, sort of like rutabagas), they seem like innocent fun . . . cheap dress catalogs . . . and, as a bonus, you get those silly advice articles with breathless titles like "Six sex tips every honeymooner must know now!"

But all is not as innocent as it seems.

Lurking beneath those glossy covers and lace covered ads is a seamy business that has an agenda all its own. Stuffed with ads, each bridal magazine is a cash cow for the big magazine conglomerates that own them. And the publishers will do anything to keep the dollars flowing.

As a result, all the bridal magazines present a somewhat distorted view of the dress buying process. The bias is toward buying a fancy, formal bridal gown—preferably an expensive one. Little mention is made of money-saving tips. Certain thrifty alternatives like renting or second-hand shops (more on this later) are omitted altogether.

While nearly every bridal magazine has lapses of taste, nothing beats the behavior of the two biggest magazines, *Bride's* and *Modern Bride*. Each has schemed to block ads from dress discounters, while confusing brides with articles on dress buying that are at best stunningly naive, and at worst intentionally misleading.

At this point, you may be asking, so what do I care about this? It's easy to dismiss the bridal magazines as useless pap. Yet, the huge dominance of the magazines in bridal advertising should concern every consumer. By virtually controlling the only national media that targets engaged couples, the magazine's publishers can effectively shut out discounters and off-price retailers. When you eliminate low-price competition, prices go up for everyone.

Since the magazines are in the business to make money and sell ads, you may wonder why they'd block anyone from advertising. The answer is simple: open up a bridal magazine and start counting the number of designer dress ads. Gown manufacturers make up the vast majority of advertisers in *Brides* and *Modern Bride*. And the gown manufacturers want you, the bride, to buy a dress at full retail.

The designers not only dictate to the magazines who can advertise, but also what advice the magazines should give on dress buying. (This may come as a shock, but yes, there have been documented cases of editorial articles spotted in bridal magazines. Every 200 pages or so, the publishers throw one in just to break up the monotony of the ads.)

In the eight years we've been researching and writing about the bridal business, we've seen numerous examples of heinous behavior by *Bride's* and *Modern Bride*. Here's our list of the four biggest lies perpetrated by the bridal magazines:

The Four Biggest Lies Told By Bridal Magazines

1 "Only white people get married."

Well, the major bridal magazines would never *say* that, but just take a look at the pictures. Page after page of Caucasian, size 8 models in $2000 dresses. Just try to find a bride who's black, Hispanic or Asian. Go ahead, take as long as you need to search. While you're at, try to discover an ad that features a bride who's a size 22.

To illustrate this point, we poured over the February/March 1996 issue of *Bride's*. Out of 1026 pages of wedded bliss, we found only *seven* black brides. We did see 15 black bridesmaids models (always a bridesmaid, but never a bride?). We found even fewer Asians (one) and Hispanics (none).

Sure, there are specific magazines for black brides (one of the best is *Signature Bride: For Today's Black Woma*n; for subscription information call 312-527-6590), but their limited distribution means black, Hispanic and Asian brides can only guess as to what a dress might look like on someone who looks like them.

We're sure the bridal magazine publishers would wave open palms and just say "we have no control over what type of models the designers want to use in their ads." We say that's a load of bunk. The magazines could start to fix this imbalance with their own editorial spreads, those dress pictures chosen by editors. How about an occasional Hispanic? A person who doesn't look like Kate Moss? By setting a good example, the magazines would go a long way toward establishing a standard for their advertisers to follow.

2 "You must buy an expensive dress from a full-price bridal shop."

When the bridal magazines aren't busy making sure their pages are lily white, they're busy giving out bogus consumer advice. *Modern Bride* is guilty of the most biased article we ever read on this subject. A piece in January 1991's issue titled "6 Tips on Where to Shop for your Dress" should have won the Pulitzer Prize for shameless propaganda.

The article suggests you should "make shopping for your dress a happy experience by following these guidelines." The author then spends the next several paragraphs trying to convince brides they should only buy a dress from a "full service" (read: full price) shop. If that doesn't work, the article then stoops to scare tactics. "Don't be fooled by what appears to be a bargain," it warns, adding that "many discounters order replica gowns from third parties, not from the actual manufacturer. Poor workmanship may be the result."

The whole piece is a thinly veiled attack on Discount Bridal Service (DBS), the country's largest mail order dress discounter (later in "Step #4: Money Saving Tips," we'll discuss them in detail). *Modern Bride* actually had the chutzpah to re-print DBS's contract in the article (although without attribution). The magazine interpreted clauses like "dye lots may vary" to mean the dress "may be very different than your expectations." Ooo, that sounds scary. What *Modern Bride* forgets to say is that every bridal shop (discounter or full-price) has this standard contract language because, quite frankly, dye lots *may* vary. And, for the record, Discount Bridal Service only sells first-quality, designer merchandise—no copies or "replica" gowns.

We have had several heated discussions with *Modern Bride* editor Cele Lalli on this subject. When we've pointed out that articles like this are blatantly deceptive, she's said her priority was to protect full-price shops. That's fine with us. Just change the name of the magazine to *Modern Bridal Industry* and folks can be forewarned.

A more recent example of biased consumer advice came from the April 1996 issue of *Elegant Bride*. In the subtly titled piece, "Shopping for Your Gown at an Outlet (A Real Life Disaster)," the author contrasts her own experience shopping for her bridal gown at a full price shop in 1982 with her sister-in-law's recent trip to a bridal outlet. "The day I bought my wedding gown was magical," the writer opines, recalling the pampered service she received from a full price bridal shop. Fast forward to today, when the author decides to help her sister-in-law go gown shopping. "Visions of my own magical day floated in my head as we headed out of town to help her. But she had other ideas."

The author and her sister-in-law visit a nameless off-the-rack dress discounter (presumably a David's, mentioned later in this book). The shop was crowded, the dresses damaged and the service non-existent, the author claims. Her poor sister-in-law, the writer sighs . . . in order to save a few bucks, she cheated herself out of the magical experience of spending an amount equivalent to the Federal Deficit on a bridal gown.

3 "Women don't want to rent bridal gowns or bridesmaids dresses."

Why don't you see any ads in the bridal magazines for dress rentals? It's not by accident.

In 1992, the *Wall Street Journal* reported that *Bride's* magazine has a policy that blocks ads from dress discounters or companies that rent gowns. Why? The official position of many bridal magazines is that women don't want to rent dresses. And renting is such a low-brow business that it would sully the magazines' glossy, high-dollar image.

We suspect another reason: the magazines' biggest advertisers (dress designers and their allies, the full-price shops) want you to *buy*, not rent for half the price. In an amazingly stupid move, the publisher of *Bride's* actually sent a letter that said as much to full-price retailers. We obtained a copy. There it was in black and white: "*Brides* has NEVER accepted these ads," the publisher said, "[We] believe that these can only hurt your (the retailers') business."

We found this to be highly ironic, because every bridal magazine (not just *Bride's*) has lots of ads from companies that rent tuxes for *men*. But what if you want to rent a bridesmaids dress and spare women the expense of having to buy these taffeta monstrosities? Sorry, that isn't allowed.

This policy has a devastating effect on the gown rental business. After being denied access to this crucial national advertising vehicle, two major gown rental companies have had to close up shop or curtail operations. While a few dress rental shops exist in scattered cities, no company has been able to break-out on a national level. The result: even if you want to, you may not be able to find a shop that rents bridal gowns or bridesmaids dresses.

4 "We're here to serve you, the bride."

Bridal magazines rake in millions of dollars for all those dress ads. In their zeal to line their pockets with ad dollars, the bridal magazines are famous for selling to out to their advertisers, often at the expense of their readers.

A good example: blatantly deceptive "no dress ads" that appear in many bridal magazines. Here's a little known practice the bridal magazines hope you don't discover—just because a gown ad has listings of local shops, it doesn't mean that those shops actually *carry* the pictured dress.

That's right—you might find the perfect dress in a bridal magazine ad and think all you have to do is visit the listed stores to find it. Well, we've discovered a disturbing number of cases where dress designers don't require shops to buy the advertised dress in order to get listed in the ad. (In the business, they're called "no dress ads"). In a way, this is a bridal version of the old bait and switch scheme. You see an ad, go to the store that's listed and then discover the dress isn't in the shop. But the shop would be glad to show you other dresses that are "just like it."

A bride in California e-mailed us with a story about this very practice. A bridal shop in San Jose that bills itself as a "low-price store" takes out ads in bridal magazines that list it as a dealer for several exclusive designers. When brides arrive there, they're told the shop doesn't have the dress but they can find it at their "sister shop"—an expensive boutique across town that works by appointment only. Brides are lured into one shop, only to be switched to the more expensive store in the end. Besides being a colossal waste of time, the bridal industry should be ashamed of this deceptive advertising practice.

And the bridal magazines share part of the blame. That's because the magazine's ad reps actively pitch "store listing" ads to bridal retailers at the industry's wholesale markets. Each store listing costs stores $100 to $200 a pop. Unfortunately, the magazines line their pockets with ad revenue, with little concern as to whether their readers are being led to a shop that doesn't even carry the advertised dress. We think these "no dress" ads should stop—bridal magazines must take a stand on this issue.

ELUSIVE EXCLUSIVES

The flip side of "no dress ads" are designers who run ads in bridal magazines that imply the listed stores have an exclusive on a particular dress. Bridal shop owners love exclusive gowns (sometimes called "confined" dresses) because they're the only shop in their area that carries them . . . and that often means they can charge a huge mark-up on the gown.

But how exclusive are these exclusives? Surprisingly, some designers will quietly sell confined dresses to other shops who order them. Even though the shop is not listed as an exclusive dealer, you may find that special dress hanging in a competitor's shop.

The bottom line: just because a designer lists only two stores in your area that carry a certain dress doesn't mean you won't be a be find it elsewhere.

LEARNING THE LINGO

Bridal fabrics and laces

Just what is charmeuse? If you answered "a tasty, low-fat, non-dairy dessert," you probably need to read this chapter. You'll learn how to decipher all those foreign-sounding bridal fabrics, finishes and laces. Then we'll discuss what separates the good bridal gowns from the bad ones—and how to tell if you're really getting a bargain.

ANYONE WHO'S GONE SHOPPING in the last century is probably familiar with the basic fabrics in woman's clothing. But while you can certainly spot wool, cotton and linen in most stores, you might be stumped by such terms as *crepe de chine* or *peau de soie*. The world of bridal fabrics and laces has its own lexicon, including exotic names concocted to add cachet to dresses. To separate fact from fiction let's first look at the "bridal-speak" you'll run into at retail stores.

Scams to Avoid

 Step into any bridal retail shop and you'll be assaulted with a barrage of Italian and French fashion terms. While this is only fair, since luxury fabric finishes first originated in Italy (and then were refined in France), you almost need a pocket translator to sift through all the jargon. And then, just to complicate matters, you'll hear conflicting stories from bridal retail stores. Some gown salespeople are simply ignorant of basic fashion knowledge, while others may have darker motives, passing off an inferior fabric to an unsuspecting bride. Here's a quick run-down of several stories from actual brides.

❖ SHANTUNG SHELL GAME
"The salesperson at one bridal shop showed me a dress she described as 'shantung.' When I asked her if it was made of silk, she said 'Yes! All shantung is silk.' Is this true?"

No. All shantung is *not* silk; in recent years, designers have rolled out synthetic shantungs—polyester fabric with a "silk-like shantung finish." Tricky, huh?

By the way, what is shantung anyhow? Shantung is a *finish* to a fabric that gives the dress a rougher, nubby texture. Since this term used to exclusively apply to silk fabrics, it's easy to get confused. Thanks to recent advances in weaving technology, however, you might see many synthetic shantungs in your gown search. For example, one designer offered a traditional gown in "satin shantung" for $816. Translation: it's a man-made blend with a silk-like finish. Interestingly enough, the same design is available in *silk* shantung for $1300.

How can you tell the real thing from the man-made substitute? First of all, synthetic fabric with a shantung finish usually costs much less than silk shantung. Also, the synthetic fabric will feel stiffer than real silk. Finally, real silk shantung is usually not available in stark white—the color of natural shantung is actually off-white.

What's disturbing are bridal shops that are attempting to pass off inferior synthetic gowns as expensive silks. While you might think you can just check the tag, it isn't that simple. As you'll learn later in this book, many bridal shops rip the tags from their sample dresses to keep you from comparison shopping.

❖ THE SEARCH FOR SILK
"Since I began my search for the perfect satin wedding gown I have been overwhelmed with terms like Italian satin, silk-faced satin, dull satin, silky satin, polysilk satin and even L'Amour satin. What the heck is all this?"

Satin is just one fabric *finish* that the bridal industry confuses brides with. Normally, we all think satin means a fabric that is tightly woven to create a finish with a sheen on one side. Like many luxury fabrics, satin used to be made exclusively of silk. Today, this may not be the case. For example, "polysilk satin" and "silky satin" are bogus names that are dead giveaways for man-made satins (made of polyester). Some designers even give their man-made satin fabrics their own name like Regal Satin (by Moonlight) or L'Amour Satin. What do these names mean? Nothing.

But what about "silk-faced satin"? Here's an interesting hybrid fabric that is a blend of silk and rayon (or polyester), woven into a satin finish. This type of fabric is also called Duchess satin (also spelled Duchesse satin) just to make it even more confusing.

All these man-made and blended fabrics do have their advantages. We appreciate the fact that you can now buy a dress that looks like silk for a fraction of the cost of the real thing. On the other hand, all this can be quite confusing. And, as you read above, there's a potential for abuse when some dishonest retailers mislead brides as to what they're buying.

❖ DUPIONI DECEPTION

"I ordered bridesmaids dresses in silk dupioni thinking they would be attractive enough for my maids to wear again. But when the dresses came in they looked like they'd been balled up in the corner of someone's closet! And the incredible wrinkles were nearly impossible to get out! I thought expensive silk dresses would be high quality. What happened?"

What you've discovered is that all silk is not created equal. Years ago, silk used to be a special, expensive fabric. In the last ten years, however, silk has become a commodity. The production of silk by China and other countries has soared and the prices (and some say the quality) have declined.

Unfortunately, there is no grading system for silks (at least that a consumer sees). You don't know whether you're buying Grade A or Grade C silk, other than by simply looking at the fabric. Obvious flaws like huge slubs and inconsistent coloring are the hallmarks of cheap silks.

The biggest problem with low quality silks often occurs with bridesmaids dresses, although we suspect this might creep into bridal as well. There are a couple ways to avoid such a surprise. First ask to see another bride's order of the same type of dress. Compare the actual dress to the store sample—you might notice the actual dress is not as attractive as the sample. Also, be sure to inspect the gowns carefully when they arrive from the manufacturer *before* you pay the shop the balance. That way if there are any ugly flaws, you may be able to get the shop to return the dress to the manufacturer for a corrected gown. Or just avoid dupioni silk altogether.

Self Defense

 Given the potential problems involved with bridal fabric and finishes, here are some savvy shopping tips to help navigate the maze.

1 FAMILIARIZE YOURSELF WITH DIFFERENT BRIDAL FABRICS, FINISHES AND LACES. How? First, note the extensive glossary later in this chapter. Then head out to a fabric store to see some actual samples. Ask the store clerk to show you bolts of silks and man-made blends. Check out shantung, satin, chiffon and other fabrics—it's one thing to read about this in a book or magazine and quite another to see it for yourself. You may even want to get some small swatches of fabric to take with you. If you're curious about fabric content, this information is usually clearly noted on top of the fabric bolt.

2 HERE'S A LITTLE KNOWN SECRET OF THE BRIDAL BUSINESS: SOME GOWN DESIGNERS AND MANUFACTURERS WILL OFFER THE SAME DRESS IN *DIFFERENT* FABRICS. If you fall in love with a silk design that you really can't afford, ask if that manufacturer offers fabric substitutions. For example, Carmi Couture offers a beautiful white silk design with draped bustier, net bodice, long sleeves and Guipure lace accents (style #3060) for $1350. But the same design is available in polyester for $1150. Carmi Couture also offers some designs with or without lace and beading. Other designers offer to upgrade the fabric. Later in the designer reviews section we will mention who specifically offers substitutions and upgrades.

3 CHECK FOR QUALITY CONSTRUCTION CLUES. Later in this chapter, we'll go over the tell-tale signs that indicate quality. By spotting these clues, you'll have a better idea as to whether you're getting a great deal . . . or just a cheap dress.

4 LESS DECORATION ON A DRESS MAY NOT NECESSARILY MEAN A LOWER PRICE. In fact, designer dresses that are not ornate may be *more* expensive. Why? Manufacturers can mask fabric and construction flaws on a cheap dress with lots of beading and lace. If a dress doesn't have much decoration, it requires higher quality fabric and construction techniques to impress discerning eyes. Of course, not all dresses with beading and lace are poorly made, but it pays to look beyond flashy decoration.

Glossary

Fabric Content

Silk. This is the premiere wedding fabric for softness, luster and beauty. Silk is made from silkworm cocoons, discovered by the Chinese in 2600 B.C. France became the most famous producer of finished silk fabric, hence the use of so many French names such as *dupioni* and *peau de soie* (later in this chapter, we'll define fabric finishes).

Until recently, silk has always been an expensive fabric and silk bridal gowns have been equally pricey—most used to cost over $1000. In the last five years, however, more affordable silk fabrics (and silk blends) have dropped that price considerably. Today, there are even designers who are churning out all silk gowns for just $600.

Despite increasing competition in silk production, China still makes 70% to 85% of the world's silk. Other countries like Thailand turn out great silk fabric as well; the designer Wallentin brags that it only uses 100% Thai silk in their gowns.

Cotton. Used as thread and fabric as long ago as 600 B.C., cotton is made from the fibers of its namesake plant. Cotton's popularity in everyday clothes has probably contributed to its absence as a bridal fabric—there's little cachet to a cotton bridal gown. While a few designers use the fabric (woven in sheer or embroidered varieties), it's still rare to see cotton on the bridal dress racks.

Linen. Made from flax fibers, this fabric was first utilized for clothing by the ancient Egyptians. Linen is often combined with cotton or other fabrics; by itself it wrinkles badly. As a result, you're more likely to see linen as a fabric in bridal suits and other informal dresses.

Rayon. Invented during World War II when silk was rationed for use in parachutes, rayon is made from plant fibers. An affordable fabric, rayon often shows up in blends of various bridal fabrics.

Man-made fabrics. Nylon, acetate and polyester are those affordable man-made wonders that became unavoidable in 70's fashion. In the bridal world, manufacturers could weave these fabrics into shiny or glossy finishes, giving a special look at a lower price. Most affordably priced gowns (under $600) are made of man-made fabrics. While most brides don't think "Hey, I want a polyester bridal gown," most popular bridal fabric finishes such as "satin" and "taffeta" are made of just that.

Fabric Finishes

It's easy to confuse fabrics with fabric *finishes*. The finish is what the cloth feels and looks like after it's woven. Most bridal fabrics (both natural and man-made) can be woven into the wide variety of finishes described below:

Brocade. This finish is similar to damask (see below) but of heavier weight.

Charmeuse. (SHAR-moose) A tasty, low fat, non-dairy dessert. Just kidding! Actually, charmeuse is a lightweight version of satin with a softer and more clingy look. Charmeuse is a common finish with silk or rayon and has less body than traditional silk finishes.

Chiffon. (SHI-fon) A transparent lightweight fabric finish, chiffon may be made from just about any fabric. It is often layered and has an unusual luster.

Damask. (DAM-ask) The hallmark of this finish are threads woven into a pattern that create a white-on-white or ivory-on-ivory appearance. Often woven in a floral pattern, this fabric finish doesn't need any additional beading or lace.

Duchess (Duchesse) satin. Also referred to as silk-faced satin, this finish weighs less than traditional silk finishes and is usually less expensive as well. Most Duchess satins are a blend of silk and rayon woven into a satin finish.

Dupioni. (doo-pee-OH-nee) Similar to shantung (see below) but with thicker, coarser fibers woven into a taffeta-like fabric, dupioni has shown up quite frequently in recent bridesmaids designs.

Faille. (rhymes with "pail") Faille is a ribbed fabric finish with structure and body. This finish is also seen in bridesmaids styles today. Most faille finishes are woven from silk, cotton, rayon or polyester fabrics.

Net, illusion, or tulle. This mesh-like fabric is most often woven from synthetic fibers. A recent fad saw several designers adding tulle skirts to their gown designs. Varying weaves can increase or decrease the weight of this finish.

Organdy. A crisp transparent fabric finish made from cotton.

Organza. Similar to chiffon (see above), but heavier and with more body.

Peau de soie (skin of silk). (po-DAY-swa) A heavy, smooth satin with very fine ribbing. This finish is actually somewhat dull in sheen compared to traditional silk finishes.

Satin. A tightly woven effect that creates a fabric with a beautiful sheen on one side. Typically made in man-made fabrics like polyester, satin is probably the most common bridal gown fabric finish. While satin is most often associated with a high gloss look, it is also available in a matte finish with a toned down glow.

Shantung. Originally known as wild (or natural) silk, this finish has a rougher, nubby appearance. Once associated exclusively with silk fabrics, shantung is now seen as a finish for man-made fabrics as well.

Taffeta. This crisp finish is often woven from man-made fabrics. A close second to satin, taffeta finishes are not only common in bridal gowns but bridesmaids dresses too. In the latter, you might find taffeta fabrics with woven moiré patterns.

Velvet. Most folks are familiar with this finish, which has a thick nap. Once associated with silks, velvets can be a finish on cotton or rayon blends today as well. A variation of this finish, crushed velvet is made with a high and low nap to give a shimmering effect.

Laces

Boy, if you thought fabric finishes had funny sounding names, just wait till you check out the laces bridal designers use. Here's a wrap-up of the names you'll encounter:

Alencon. (al-ON-son) Probably the most popular of wedding laces, alencon lace has a background of flowers and swags which are re-embroidered along the edges with cording. This lace may be pre-beaded or beaded after it is sewn on the dress.

Battenburg. This type of lace is made by stitching a strip of linen fabric into a pattern of loops, then connecting them with thread. Besides bridal gowns, battenburg is often found on table and bed linens.

Chantilly. (SHAN-til-ee) Flowers and ribbons on a plain net background define chantilly lace. These details are usually edged with fine cording. Feel free to sing the song now.

Dotted Swiss. Small circles of flocked fabric over a background of netting typify this lace, which is often used on necklines or layered over skirts (not pictured).

Eyelet. This lace is usually made of cotton, which has perforated holes embroidered around the edges.

Guipure. This lace has seen a resurgence in recent years—it seems to be the hip lace of the moment. Guipure features a large series of motifs connected by a few threads. Common guipure patterns may be roses, daisies or other geometric designs like ovals. The result is often a retro 70's look.

Ribbon. A random pattern of ribbon that is sewn over a net background. *(right)*

Schiffli. (SHIF-lee) A light-weight lace with an all-over embroidered design on a net background. *(left)*

Venise. (VEN-ees) This type of lace is a needlepoint-type design. An example connects small flowers with irregularly placed threads.

How to tell a quality bridal gown

Walk into any bridal shop and you'll be greeted by a sea of white. This dress is $500, this other one is $900. How about the boutique up the street with dresses sporting $3000 price tags. What's the difference? What makes one design an affordable $450 and another a whopping $5000? Is it the fabric? Or do you pay out the nose for the designer name?

The proof is in the details, as they say. Here's a brief guide to separating the good gowns from the not so good ones:

❦ **Finished seams:** Check out the inside of the gown. Are the edges of the seams unraveling? High quality gowns always have finished seams. Another quality clue: look at the hem. Quality gowns have an interlocking herringbone stitch (also called a horsehair braid or catchstitch hem). Lower quality gowns have a simple straight stitch hem.

❦ **Lining/Built-in petticoats:** Is the dress lined? Is there a built-in petticoat? Once the province of the most expensive gowns, we've recently seen more mid-price dresses ($700 to $900) sporting this quality feature. Dresses that are lined have more body and may let you skip the purchase of an additional slip. Built-in petticoats are also a big plus for the same reason—you won't have to buy or rent one separately. When petticoats are built-in, they are usually designed into the dress for the most dramatic silhouette. A separately bought petticoat may not provide the same effect.

❦ **Sewn-on beads:** Here's a good way to separate the quality gowns from the cheap ones—check to see if beading and detailing is glued on or sewn on the dress. Better gowns have sewn on beading, never glued. Why is gluing inferior? First, beads attached to a dress with glue fall off much easier than those that are sewn on. Second, if you want to have your dress cleaned after the wedding, be aware that some dry cleaning chemicals will permanently discolor the glue. Some brides report that the glue has yellowed or even turned dark brown. (A solution to this problem: dresses like this may have to be hand washed).

❦ **Scratchy details:** When you try on a dress, gauge how comfortable the garment is. Scratchy necklines, sleeves, seams and other details are tell-tale signs of cheap construction. A dress should feel smooth and soft on the inside.

continued

The following chart summarizes good and poor gown construction techniques:

Bridal Gown Construction

	Good	Poor
BEADING	Sewn-on	Glued-on
SEAMS	No visible threads	Threads show through seams
INSIDE OF DRESS	Completely lined; finished seams	Unlined; unfinished seams
FABRIC	Silk or heavy weight satin	Feels like you can tear it
SEWING	Built-in petticoat or slip	Layers sewn together in same seam
HEM	Herringbone-type hem	A simple straight stitch hem
COMFORT	Dress is comfortable to wear	Scratchy lace or itchy detailing

With all these tips, we have to note that the price of a gown is not always related to the quality. In fact, there are many manufacturers who offer high quality designs at affordable prices. Later we'll identify which manufactures have the best quality for the dollar.

THE UGLY TRUTH ABOUT BRIDAL RETAIL SHOPS

Convenient full-service store or retail experience from hell?

What are the three biggest myths about bridal shops?
How about the ten things bridal shops do that will
drive you crazy? You'll learn this, plus five
"self-defense" tips on avoiding scams. Next,
we'll give you six questions you should ask the
shop before you place an order.

HERE'S A SOBERING FACT—there are 12,641 businesses listed under the heading "bridal shops" in the U.S. yellow pages. And far too many of them have romantic names like "Fred's Bridal Castle of Dreams."

Of course, any bride who's looked at the phone book realizes all those listings aren't really bridal shops. Many other wedding companies (such as photographers) like to list under the heading "bridal shops" since that's the first one they think brides look at. Other listings are combo places like "Aunt Emma's Bridal Shop and Lube Stop" which may or may not be full service bridal retailers.

Yet even if you take the more conservative number of 8000, that's still a lot of bridal shops out there. So, where do you start? You have to buy a bridal dress *somewhere*.

That's what this chapter is all about—the wonderful world of bridal retail. First, we'll talk about the things that drive brides crazy about bridal shops. You'll learn all the tricks of the trade that some unscrupulous shops use to separate brides from their money. Later in this chapter, we'll give you more shopping tips and questions to ask. Along the way, we hope to expose several myths that surround gown shopping and even provide a perspective from the bridal shop owner's point of view.

Bridal Retail 101: Understanding how the bridal business works.

The Wedding Industrial Complex. That's how one groom we interviewed described dress shops (and the whole wedding business, for that matter). He told us he and his bride felt pressured to have the wedding the industry wanted, not what they thought would be nice. That giant sucking sound you hear is the money extracted from engaged couples who walk down the aisle, he said.

Well, that's a cynical view. For a more objective perspective on marriage, we turned to our favorite humor columnist, the all-knowing Dave Barry. On the subject of weddings, Dave wrote: "The sentimental motto of the wedding industry is: money can't buy you happiness, so you might as well give all your money to us."

Whether you like it or not, most brides come face to face with the ugly reality of bridal retail shops at some point in their wedding planning. A recent survey by a bridal magazine revealed that about two-thirds of all brides buy their dress at a bridal store. (For the curious, another 12% found their dress at a department store; 11% had a gown sewn by a friend or professional; 3% of brides purchased a dress from a mail-order discounter, 2% wear a family heirloom and another 2% of brides borrowed or rented a wedding dress. More on alternatives to full-price shops later in this book.)

Since two out of three folks reading this will be venturing into bridal shops to find a dress, let's take a moment to discuss the bridal retail business. In short, it's nuts. Talk with any past bride and you'll hear the standard horror stories of dresses that arrived late, salespeople who didn't care and the general games brides and bridal shops have to play.

After interviewing thousands of brides in the past eight years, we have come to the realization that part of the problem here is a failure to communicate. Since you only buy a wedding dress once in your life (Liz Taylor, you're excused), how do you know what to expect when you step into a bridal store?

Much of the confusion is caused by several widely held myths about bridal retailers. As a public service, let's look at these misconception and the truth (as we see it, of course).

Biggest myths about bridal dress shops

Myth #1: Bridal shops are run by sweet old ladies whose only desire is to make you happy. The first thing most folks realize after getting over the shock of having to plan a wedding is that the bridal business is, well, a business. And a big business. Engaged couples spend $10 billion a year on wedding and receptions. Dresses are a $1.2 billion chunk of that market (for the curious, $800 million is spent on wedding gowns, $400 million for bridesmaids dresses).

Surfing the web for a bridal dress

Even if you don't know a Lycos from a Yahoo, you can't escape hearing about this Internet thing. Soon you'll be able to do *everything* on the World Wide Web, the geeks promise. Who needs a groom when you can just download a JPEG graphic of a guy in a tuxedo to a Sony monitor strategically positioned on the altar. With those Java applets, it looks so real!

So, why not buy a bridal gown in cyberspace? Well, hit the hold button on that 28.8K baud modem. While you can buy an array of products on the Web, bridal gowns still have a way to go. Yes, it's true that bridal shop web pages are springing up faster than mushrooms after a heavy rain . . . and some of those shops are actually soliciting business over the Web. But we say whoa—think about the bridal gown buying process before hitting the send key and blasting your credit card number over that phone line.

The main problem with so-called Internet bridal sites is that (at this point) they are all run by *local* bridal shops. And it's hard to tell long distance whether the shop is reputable just by the look of their Web graphics. Mail-order (which is essentially what bridal shops are doing over the web) is a totally different business than retail—you have to deal with shipping logistics, customer service and all sorts of other complications. We'd like to see someone have at least three years experience doing this operation (selling dresses over the Web) before we'd give our hard-earned cash as a deposit. And, as of this writing, no one on the Web who's selling gowns meets this minimum test.

Most bridal retailers want to make you a happy customer. Unfortunately, all of them must also pay the light bill and make a profit. This shouldn't sound difficult, but for some reason, things can get ugly. One common refrain: shop owners tell us they'd run a decent and honest operation if it weren't for that darn-blasted Debbie Does Discount Bridal Gown Shoppe down the street. In order compete with these "nasty" competitors they must do X, Y, and, though they regret it, Z too. We say get a grip—if you can't run an honest business, go into a line of work that doesn't involve fleecing consumers.

Salespeople at bridal shops can be a peculiar breed, too. Most are on commission—hence, they only get paid when you buy something. As long as times are good, this works fine. The salespeople try hard to find you a gown that meets your needs and budget. Yet, when the competition heats up, things can go haywire. An air of desperation sometimes leads salespeople to use tricks honed in their previous job—as a used car salesperson.

Most bridal shops owners aren't stupid (note: we said *most*). They know you're going to shop the competition. Brides visit at least four stores and try on a dozen dresses before ordering, according to a recent survey. And those are conservative numbers—we've interviewed brides who've shopped 10, 15 and even 20 different bridal stores. Bridal shops must be competitive to get the sale, but not give away the store in order to keep paying the bills.

Our biggest gripe is with bridal retailers who use unethical tactics and downright sleazy practices to separate brides from their money. Later in this chapter, we'll tell you how to avoid being a victim.

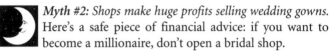 *Myth #2: Shops make huge profits selling wedding gowns.* Here's a safe piece of financial advice: if you want to become a millionaire, don't open a bridal shop.

Let's take a look at the numbers. The average wedding dress sells for $800. What does the shop pay for that? About $400, leaving a $400 gross profit. Not bad, eh? Well, hold it. The shop has to pay all their overhead, advertising, rent, salaries and other expenses from that amount. What's left over is a pittance, on average about 5% to 10% (or $40 to $80).

And that assumes the shop sells the dress for full price. Most don't. In order to meet competition, many discount or have "special sales." In other businesses, discounting might spur demand for items like TV's and VCR's. But no one says, "Hey Honey! Let's get married because that bridal shop is having a sale!" All shops accomplish by discounting is cannibalizing sales from competitors.

Another problem: sample overload. Shops have to invest thousands of dollars in inventory. This not only sucks cash faster than a West Texas dust devil, but at the end of the season, shops are often left with a full inventory of tried on samples. Then it's sale time—most samples sell for steep discounts, up to 50% off retail (or at cost).

But don't cry for bridal retailers. They have found ways to make up for the lack of profit in wedding dresses. They charge a premium for everything else in the store, from alterations to veils and headpieces. The biggest money-maker: accessories. Those bras, shoes, garters, and fake jewelry can bring in fat mark-ups, perhaps three to five times their wholesale cost.

So, that's why when you try on the wedding gown, salespeople are quick to whip out a headpiece, shoes, and necklace to make a "complete look."

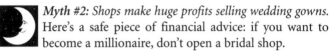 *Myth #3: Gowns are custom-made by the shop.* Wrong. Most bridal retailers don't make anything. Here's how it works in a nutshell: the shops order sample gowns (usually in size 10 or 12) from the manufacturers. That's what you see in the shop—samples or demonstrator models of the various styles. Pick one you like and the shop orders an original in your size. The manufacturer then makes this and sends it back to you, hopefully in time for your wedding.

And at least that's how it's *supposed* to work. One major wrinkle today is that the manufacturers mass produce gowns in plants as far away as Vietnam. Sometimes, the quality of the cheaper gowns leaves much to be desired. When the gown comes in with flaws or damage, it's often the shop that's left trying to correct the problem.

The truth is: bridal retailers are just middlemen. When the dress manufacturer screws up, they are left holding the bag. Of course, some bridal shops are to blame as well—far too many mismanage their business, falling behind in their bills. They "forget" to pay a manufacturer, who then puts them on a credit hold. As a result, your dress is held hostage in the cross-fire.

10 Stupid Things Bridal Shops Do That Will Drive You Crazy

In the eight years we've been researching the bridal business, we've heard just about every scam you can imagine. Sleazy photographers who hold pictures hostage until couples come up with an extra $500. Reception halls who tack on ridiculous fees like "cake cutting charges."

But you have to hand it to the bridal shops. For sheer ingenuity, they can't be beat. Of course, it's important to point out that not all shops employ these tricks and ploys. Fortunately, there are a good number of shops who don't fleece consumers.

Let's not be naive, however: we've encountered these scams personally when we mystery shopped over 200 bridal retailers nationwide. And since then we've interviewed thousands of brides who've told us even more stories. So, under the heading, forewarned is forearmed, here's our list of the Ten Stupid Things Bridal Shops Do That Will Drive You Crazy:

1 Tags? We don't need no stinkin' tags!

"I went to a local bridal shop to look for a particular designer. When I arrived, all the dresses had no tags. And the salespeople refused to tell me who made which dress. What's going on here?"

Here's a typical scenario: you find a dress you like in a bridal magazine and decide you'd like to try it on. So you trot down to the local bridal shop that's listed in the ad. When you walk in, you're warmly greeted by the salesperson. Then you ask to see this particular dress in the picture, the one by Designer X.

"Sorry, honey," the salesperson says. "We don't know which dresses are made by which designers." So you look around and notice something peculiar about the gowns. Apparently, a little gremlin has broken into the bridal shop in the middle of the night and removed all the tags. And we mean *all* the tags—the designer name, fabric content, country of origin, care instructions and more.

Are you looking at a silk gown or a polyester one? Is it a designer label or a cheap knock-off impostor? Who can tell when all the labels are missing?

Of course, many shops will be more than happy to tell you which designer made your gown—that is, *after* you place down a 50% non-refundable deposit.

If this sounds absurd, it is. And it happens everyday. By our estimates, three out of four shops intentionally remove tags out of their dresses. Why? They want to keep you dumb. If you knew who made which dress, you could go down the street to that evil Debbie Does Discount Bridal Gown Shoppe and get it at a 25% discount.

All of this would be fine if it weren't illegal. Yes, there is a federal law that outlaws this practice. The Federal Textile Products Identification Act, Title 15, Sec 70 (for you law buffs out there, the citation is 15-USC-Sec 70 exec) says all apparel sold in this country must include a label with the manufacturer's name, the fiber content and the country of origin. There's no exception for bridal gowns. And it's not a new law either—the law was enacted in 1958 to stop retailers from passing off clothes made of synthetic fibers as natural ones.

It's a great law, except for the fact that it's never enforced. The Federal Trade Commission is supposed to enforce this law, but it's been a toothless watchdog. As a result, bridal shops have nothing to fear.

Sad to say, tag cutting is such a common practice in the business that even the biggest bridal stores do it. Some shop owners make excuses for this practice: one common story we hear is that since they are not actually selling the samples, they don't need to have tags. We say, "nice try." Nearly all bridal shops sell their samples too, but they don't put the tags back in when they put them on the sale rack. Other shop owners simply plead ignorance: they say everyone does it and they didn't know it's against the law. . . blah, blah, blah.

Shops who cut tags not only run afoul of federal law, but also state consumer laws too. Many states have "deceptive trade practices laws" that forbid practices of retailers who obscure the brand name of products they sell.

Solution: We implore you to take a stand on this issue. As a consumer, you'd never shop at a grocery store that removed the labels from the food. Or at a car dealership that refused to tell you whether you're buying a Toyota or a Honda until after you placed a deposit. So we say don't do business with shops that cut tags and hide the identities of gowns.

The best way around this problem is to do your homework up front. Research the different designers and find pictures of

E-MAIL FROM THE REAL WORLD
Tag Slight of Hand & The Zipper Knows All

Removing all those tags from dresses can be such a tough job. Sometimes they miss one or two. Here's an e-mail from a bride in North Carolina with an interesting story on this topic:

 "I just wanted to warn brides about my experience in a 'salon-type' bridal store in North Carolina. I was given several dresses that the consultant picked out based on my verbal description; I never was able to see the entire stock. Initially, only one of the dresses had a manufacturer's tag inside, which happened to be the only one I liked at first glance. After trying on all of these gowns, the consultant suggested I retry the one I liked. When she left us alone, I asked my mother to look at the tag to make certain of the manufacturer and locate a style number. Well, the tag had DISAPPEARED. The consultant or another employee, who I think was the culprit, had gone in the dressing room and REMOVED (i.e. cut out) the tag while I was otherwise occupied. When I confronted them about this ILLEGAL practice I was met with silence. I will NOT be giving them any of my business. You'll be happy to know I found the perfect dress in a consignment shop for $325." ✍

Sue Morris of Pittsburgh, PA writes of discovering a way around the tag problem:

"I'm delighted with myself for figuring this one out and wanted to pass it along. Last night I was left alone in the dressing room wearing yet another gown that had no manufacturer's label. I got ambitious, slipped out of the gown, and lo and behold, found that the store had written "regency" (made by Mori Lee) in small letters, upside-down, in pencil, on the bottom of the inside of the zipper! I know not every store does this—there must be some out there that really do "have to take the time to look up the stock number in the master book to find out," but I was thrilled to have found out how this store squirrels away names. Anything to help a bride feel a little more empowered." ✍

gowns you like in a magazine. Then take the pictures of the magazine into the bridal shop and ask to see these specific gowns.

Of course, as we noted above, some shops will refuse. That's fine, just go elsewhere. On the other hand, some shops that remove tags will tell you who made which dress—if you ask. Don't let the salesperson get away with the line "we can show you something similar."

We should note a related problem with this issue is the "secret codes" game—shops who hide the dresses style number by referring to it with some internal code. While you do have a right to know the name of the manufacturer of the gown, the style number is another issue. Consumer law does *not* require retailers give you the style number of a dress. As a result, shops hide this information as if it were a state secret, assigning special codes to the dresses to hide their identify.

2 The Bridal Inquisition.

"I went to visit a local bridal shop. Before I could even look at dresses, I was given the third degree by a salesperson, who wanted to know my name, address, wedding date, fiancé's name, our ages and more. They even asked for my social security number!"

There's nothing like starting out the gown shopping process by being strapped to a chair and grilled by a bridal shop for intimate details of your life. And bridal shops wonder why so many brides despise this process?

The above story, by the way, is true—the bridal shop actually asked for the bride's social security number. (She smartly refused). We've heard other stories of shops who've asked for annual incomes, parent's addresses and the bride's blood type (just kidding on that last one). Shops are efficient at gathering this info—many have "reception desks" at the door that trap brides before they even get to the racks. In order to see the merchandise, you're asked to fill out an innocent sounding "registration card."

Now, why would bridal shops go to all this trouble? Well, the desire to know your name and wedding date is fine. They need to know how much time you have and that's a legitimate issue, considering how slow some designers are at delivering a wedding gown.

(As a side note: we recommend giving a false wedding date, about a month before your actual date. That way if your gown comes in late, you've got some buffer time before the actual date. Of course, don't outsmart yourself—if you're within six months of the actual wedding, giving an earlier date may result in the shop slapping you with a rush charge to get the dress in on time.)

What about all the other information? What will bridal shops do with your address, phone number, fiancé's name, etc.?

If you answered, "sell your name to other wedding merchants who want to send you a mountain of junk mail," then give yourself a prize. Remember when we said that bridal shops don't make much money on the actual dress? Well, one way they supplement their income is to go into the direct mail business—they'll sell your information to other businesses who'll pay a princely sum to find out your address. Soon, you'll receive little love notes from Bob's Elegante Garter Store and the Love Shack Drive Thru Chapel.

We suggest you only give out an address and phone number once an order is placed. And if you value your privacy, insist the shop not sell the info. You don't have to reveal your age, fiancé's name, or, least of all, your social security number. (The latter can be used by scamsters to get a litany of financial information on you and giving it out is a prescription for disaster.)

3 The Dance of the Delivery Dates.

"I visited three bridal shops and received three different delivery dates for the same dress. One said it would take three months, another said four and the last one claimed six full months. What's up?"

Why would you receive different delivery dates on the same dress? Don't all shops order the dress from the same source, that is the manufacturer?

Actually, the answer is no—and that's why you can get what appears to be inconsistent information from retail dress shops. When a store is an "authorized dealer" of a designer, they can order the gown directly from the manufacturer. What if they don't carry a particular brand name? Are you out of luck? No, most shops can still get the dress through a process called "trans-shipping."

Trans-shipping is when another shop who is an authorized dealer of the gown orders a dress for a shop that isn't. The first shop then ships the dress to the second one—and this takes extra time. That might explain why one shop says the dress will take four months, while another quotes a six month time frame.

Is trans-shipping illegal? No, it isn't—and it happens all the time in the bridal business. Why? All shops can't carry every designer. That's because the designers force their dealers to invest in a certain number of samples each season. These hefty "minimums" can drain cash flow quickly. Hence, most shops only carry 10 to 12 lines of bridal apparel, even though there are 100+ designers out there. If you want a dress from a designer they don't normally carry, they just call up their friend who's in the bridal business in the next town over (or across the country).

Despite the common practice of trans-shipping, we generally recommend you order your dress from an authorized dealer.

(There is one exception: Discount Bridal Service, which we'll discuss in the next chapter).

If you deal with a trans-shipper and there is a problem with the dress, the shop doesn't have a direct connection to the manufacturer to get it fixed. While that doesn't mean you'll be stuck, it just complicates the situation.

What other explanations could account for different delivery dates? Well, new bridal shops might give you an overly optimistic delivery date because they don't know better. Experienced retailers will know which manufacturers run chronically late, despite their "promised delivery dates." Savvy shops will pad the time by a few weeks to account for such stragglers.

Of course, some of the difference can be sheer stupidity. A salesperson who's eager to make the sale may promise a bogus delivery date. Others are simply too lazy to look it up in their programs and just give out a "standard answer."

4 Refundable deposits that aren't.

"I found a great dress at a bridal shop, but still wanted to think about it. The salesperson said I could put down $100 to hold the dress. The next day I had second thoughts, but the shop refused to refund my money!"

Act now! Discount prices good one day only! As a consumer, it's easy to get pressured to buy something you realize isn't in your budget. And bridal gowns are no exception.

We've heard them all; stories of slick salespeople who remove the money from your wallet before you know what hits you. Add in all the emotions of shopping for a wedding gown and it's a volatile mix.

One twist on this rip-off is what we call "contract slight of hand." In this situation, a salesperson promises you that money you've put down to hold a dress is "completely refundable." Then you sign a sales receipt that states exactly the opposite—no refunds, no exchanges, no nothing. If you go to court, you'll probably lose. That's because a written contract (and that's what a signed sales receipt is) always takes precedent over any verbal promise.

We've heard this story enough times to think it's not accidental. It's a clever shell game. The shop thinks if it can get any money out of you, you'll come back to buy the dress. We love the owners that blame "rogue salespeople" for bilking brides. "They should never have told you the deposit is refundable, honey" they say, while still keeping your money. Please. I was born at night, but not *last* night.

Here's the bottom line: never put down money on a dress unless you want to buy it. If you'd like to think about, walk out of

E-MAIL FROM THE REAL WORLD
Disappearing Deposits

Here's a post from alt.wedding (an Internet newsgroup) from a bride who discovered the "disappearing deposit" scam in New York:

 "I found a dress (call it dress #1) at a shop on Long Island, but I was still undecided. The shop said the discounted price was only available *that* night. When I said I needed to sleep on it, they said, 'well, you can put down a $100 deposit just to hold the price and if you change your mind, we'll tear up your check. You can trust us.'

"The next day I went dress shopping like crazy, and found dress #2, which I liked more. When I told the first shop this, they said they could order dress #2 also. But I knew I could find dress #2 through a discounter for even less, and when I did, the first shop refused to give me my deposit back.

"After six weeks of trying to get hold of the owner (who wouldn't return calls; I had to hunt her down on a Saturday in the shop), she told me the store's policy was NEVER TO REFUND DEPOSITS, despite what I was told. Obviously the salesgirl would say anything—lies and all— to get my money. Then they claimed they had another policy of charging $50 for trying on dresses. Six weeks after the fact and NOW they have a policy! Absurd. It was the first I heard of it.

"Basically the shop is ticked off because I bought a dress (that they don't even carry!) through a discounter. C'mon. Welcome to the wonderful world of free enterprise and fair competition!"

A word to the wise: Don't get pressured into putting money down. A verbal promise of a "refundable" deposit obviously means zip. So watch out, keep your cool when the pressure tactics kick in, and hang on tight to your money! ✍

the store without leaving a deposit. If the dress is gone the next day, then it wasn't meant to be. (Of course, you can almost always order another one from the shop, but that's besides the point.)

5 Outrageous mark-ups.

"I was given a bra to try on at a bridal shop. I noticed a price tag that said $28. This was neatly put right over the manufacturer's suggested retail price, which said $22."

If you thought wedding gowns were expensive, wait till you see the price of accessories at some bridal shops. A simple veil and headpiece can top $200. Faux pearl necklaces at real pearl prices. And worse.

It's no secret that bridal shops can make a killing on all the little extras that brides need. Shoes, bras, slips, jewelry, head-pieces, garters, toasting glasses—it's a never-ending parade of merchandising love and marriage.

Here's our favorite: the "lucky six pence." You've probably heard the "tradition:" a bride is supposed to wear this coin in her shoe for good luck. So, how much should this lucky six-pence cost you? Let's see—we checked out the currency exchange rates in the *Wall Street Journal* and found out a six-pence is worth about 10 cents. One dime. And how much do sixpences cost in bridal shops? Try $12. And, no, we're not making this up.

And it's not just companies who take advantage of brides lack of knowledge of European money rates. We also ran across a company at a bridal show that was hawking "lucky pennies" for $5 a pop.

Our advice: get creative. You can find just about every wed-ding accessory at another type of shop for much less money. Those special white "bridal shoes" can be found at the mall for 50% off. Lingerie can be bought mail-order for a fraction of the bridal shop price. Toasting glasses, garters and more can be found for cheap rates at craft stores.

6 Fake Discounts.

"This is it! I found the perfect dress at a local shop for $890. With the 'special sale' that was running, they took 10% off, bring the price down to $801. Yet when I saw the same dress at another shop, I noticed the retail was just $795."

Mark 'em up to mark 'em down. That's the mantra of some less than scrupulous operators. As consumers, we've become so addicted to sales, that some merchants cheat—they secretly mark up dresses before that big sale.

So, how can you find out the real price. You can look at the back of this book, of course. If you can figure out the manufacturer and style number of the dress you're looking at (no small task we realize), then you'll know how much it costs. Another alternative: call a mail-order discounter like Discount Bridal Service (contact 800-874-8794 for a dealer near you). If you find a picture of the dress in a magazine, their dealers can usually tell you the actual retail price. This may take some detective work, but will be well worth it.

7 Salon stress.

"Our local bridal shop doesn't let you actually look at the dresses. Instead, you have to describe what you're looking for and then the salesperson goes into the back to find a gown. What a hassle!"

These bridal shops have what's called "closed inventory." Instead of letting you look through racks of dresses, the salesperson decides what to show you. And that's the problem.

Some salespeople just aren't very good listeners. They bring out what they want to sell, not necessarily what you want to see. If you walk in wearing expensive clothing or have a nice-sized diamond engagement ring, watch the price of the gowns shown go up accordingly.

It helps to know exactly what you want. If you're at the beginning of the shopping process, it may be maddening to deal with a closed-inventory shop. Later, after you've tried on gowns, it will be easier to tell the salon salesperson what *you* like.

We call these shops "salon-style" stores, since they hark back to the old days when bridal salons at department stores offered this kind of service. Most bridal salons today are ritzy establishments that sell top-dollar gowns. The owners of these shops claim they have to keep their inventory closed to keep brides from pawing the merchandise. This keeps the samples more fresh, they claim. Well, they may have a point, but it's such an inconvenience to consumers that the benefits may be outweighed by the hassle factor.

8 Deceptive discontinuations.

"The dress I love is going to be discontinued in the next week. At least that's what the shop said. If I don't order in the next few days, they say I can kiss it good-bye."

Bridal designers roll out new designs two times a year: spring and fall. To make room for the new, out goes the old—many manufacturers will discontinue a large number of gowns twice a year.

And there's the rub: once retailers are notified a gown will be discontinued, they can't order it. So, we're skeptical of shops that claim you can still get a dress that's "going to be discontinued next week." Call another shop that carries the same manufacturer to verify the information.

9 False flattery.

"Here's what got on my nerves while dress shopping—no matter what dress I tried on, the salesperson gushed 'You look sooooo beautiful.' Please."

When we went dress shopping, we couldn't help but notice the number of salespeople and bridal shop owners who needed some serious sedation. Every gown I would try on would bring "oohs" and "ahhs" from the staff. While this was nice at first, it quickly grew tiresome. I felt that if I tried on a potato sack, the salesperson would scream "Oh! That rustic look is so you! It really picks up your skin tones."

While it's certainly nice to have a positive retail environment, some shops just go overboard. Most brides would prefer an honest opinion, not false flattery. Unfortunately, the desire to close the sale and make a commission leads some salespeople to declare every dress "beautiful" or "stunning." As a result, it may make more sense to take one trusted person (a friend or relative) with you while dress shopping. Getting an objective opinion can help cut through the hype.

10 No deposit. No return.

"My fiancé is in the military and has been shipped out to a combat tour. Obviously, we had to postpone the wedding indefinitely, but this seems lost on the bridal shop. They said I have to cough up the money for the dress I special ordered or they'll take me to court!"

When you order a bridal gown from a typical retail shop, you'll sign a receipt that says something like "all sales are final. No deposit. No cancellations."

They ain't foolin'. And we see that bridal shops have a point—if you could easily return a bridal dress for a full refund, some less-than-honest consumers would drop it off on the way to the airport for extra honeymoon cash.

The only problem is that some bridal shops will take this policy to the extreme. If you fall on hard financial times and lose your job, that's tough, say some shops. Most won't even offer you store credit. We've actually heard cases of shops who took brides to small claims court to get them to pay the balance on a dress after their wedding was *canceled.*

The worst cases of this (and an example of a stunning lack of patriotism) occurred during the Persian Gulf War. We heard from quite a few brides whose fiancés were fighting overseas, only to find themselves fighting a local bridal shop who demanded the balance on their wedding gown order.

A word to the wise: realize when you order a wedding dress, it's going to be yours. Even if the wedding is called off, you'll still have to buy the dress.

And that's just the start of the rip-offs and scams that happen with bridal gowns. Later in this book, we'll go over all the things that can go wrong *after* you order the dress. But first, let's look at some basic steps you can take to protect yourself.

How to find a "reputable" bridal shop

Here's one of our favorite pieces of dress-buying advice from bridal magazines: buy a dress from a *reputable* bridal shop.

Duh. I thought I'd just buy a gown from a guy named Joe Bob selling "designer originals" from the back of his Buick Riviera. I never realized you should give your money to a reputable store!

The real question that is never answered in these magazines is *exactly how do you tell which shops are reputable*? Do you just go with the one that has the biggest ad in the phone book? Or the one that's been around since the Eisenhower administration? What about the shop that's advertising a MONSTER ONE DAY ONLY SALE in the local newspaper?

The fact is, there is no easy way to separate the reputable shops from the scamsters—it's not like the shops that want to rip you off will post a big neon sign over their entrance that says "BUY FROM US! WE SCREW YOU!" And, surprisingly, the age of the shop has little to do with its reputation. We've interviewed dozens of brides who felt scammed by long-time shops with ten, 20 and even 30 years of history in the bridal business.

So, as a public service, we'd like to present the Fields' three-step program to finding a reputable bridal shop. Or at least one that won't take your money, skip town, and flee to Bolivia.

❦ *Step 1: Listen to your friends.* Not only should you ask your friends for recommendations, but we also recommend actually *listening* to what they have to say. This might sound obvious, but we're always struck by the number of brides who are warned about a shop and then go there anyway. To be sympathetic, we realize that some brides in small towns don't have a lot of choice in bridal shops. And some may fall into the "it won't happen to me" syndrome. Either way, it's still important to listen to the bridal grapevine. Brides who complain about local bridal shops are rarely hallucinating.

❦ *Step 2: Do a background check.* Bad bridal shops often leave a trail of unhappy customers. While you may have to do some detective work, it's often an easy trail to pick up. First, call the Better Business Bureau. Next, call your local Department of Consumer Affairs (if your city or county has one). Another source: your local district attorney may have a "consumer fraud" division that fields complaints from consumers. If you turn up any record of unresolved complaints, treat it as a red flag.

❦ *Step 3: Run an "honesty test."* When you walk into the bridal shop, check for obvious signs of trouble. Are all the tags cut out of the dresses? Do they insist you give them personal information before seeing dresses? Do they balk at putting an alterations quote in writing? Can you use a credit card for a deposit? Are they asking for more than the standard 50% deposit? Is there heavy pressure to close the sale?

These three simple tests may sound like common sense, but it's easy to ignore red flags when you're distracted by the larger task of planning a wedding. One comment we hear from brides who've been a victim of a bridal rip-off or scam is that "I should have known better. The signs were there." While it's still possible to get burned by a bridal scam even if you take all the above precautions, you'll be greatly reducing the risk by doing some basic research up front.

Self-Defense

 Now that we've really got you paranoid about bridal gown shopping, let's point out that you don't have to be a victim. There are a few simple steps you can take to eliminate most of these rip-offs:

1 USE A CREDIT CARD. Here's a piece of advice that seems out of place. Aren't most consumers suppose to avoid credit cards and the evil debt that they incur at 21% annual interest? Yes, but credit cards have a secret weapon that can save you an incredible amount of grief: it's called Federal Regulation C.

Federal law gives credit card purchases special protection. Basically, the law says that if you fail to receive what you've ordered or the merchandise doesn't live up to your expectations, you can dispute the charge with your credit card issuer. First, you must try to work out the problem with the merchant. If that fails, you then send a written account of the problem to the bank or

institution that issued your credit card. The credit card company contacts the merchant to try to resolve the dispute. And here's
the best part: during this time, the credit card company *reverses*
the charge on your account (and zaps away the money that was
deposited in the retailer's account). At this point, the more documentation you can provide, the better. Written sales receipts, letters you sent to resolve the problem and so on will go a long way
to prove your case.

Of course, there are a couple of limits to this law: you must
make the purchase within your home state, or 100 miles of your
home address. You also have a limited amount of time (60 to 90
days after the purchase) to dispute a charge. (For more details,
check the back of your monthly credit card statement—all the
rules on this law are spelled out quite clearly.) What if you've
already paid off your bill and then a problem develops? It doesn't
matter—you can dispute a deposit or payment on your card at
any time within the time frame mentioned.

So how does this work in the rough and tumble world of
bridal retail? Well, anytime you order a dress, most shops ask for
a 50% deposit. You can pay this with cash, check or (hopefully) a
credit card. What if the shop goes out of business before you
dress comes in? Or the shop orders the wrong dress and refuses
to correct the problem? Or the alterations lady destroys your
dress? If you paid by cash or a check, you're stuck. Kiss your
money good-bye—if the shop wants to play hardball, your only
recourse is to take them to court.

Ah, but let's say you used a credit card. By contacting your
bank or credit card issuer, you should be able to get a full refund
if you can document your case. While this may be little comfort
if your wedding is only weeks away and you don't have a dress, at
least your money is protected.

For a real-life example of how a credit card rescued one
bride, check out the story in the box.

2 GET IT IN WRITING. Verbal promises from a smooth-talking
salesperson are worthless. You'll hear lots of good stories
when you shop at a bridal stores. Free alterations? This small
deposit is 100% refundable? Who can remember what was said
last week, last month or six months ago? Get the clerk to scribble
a note to that effect and sign it. It doesn't have to be a formal
written contract—any scrap of paper will do. Later in this book,
we'll go over what you should get on your order receipt. Don't
order a gown without getting these details in black and white.

3 START EARLY. Many of the rip-offs we mentioned in this chapter have a common ring: you're in a hurry, there's lots of
pressure, you make a snap decision, etc. Leaving plenty of time to
shop for a gown short circuits many of the tactics used by less-

Saved by the VISA

Martha was in a panic by the time she called our office. The tone of her voice told the story—Martha had the unfortunate luck of ordering a dress from a store that went out of business.

Things seemed much brighter eight months ago when she ordered the dress for her October wedding. The shop had been in business for 20 years—how much more established can you get? She placed the order and then went about planning the other million details of her wedding.

The dress was due in late June. Plenty of time for alterations, she thought. Martha's first clue that something was wrong happened when the phone rang one night. "Is that your bridal shop on the news?" her friend asked. "What?" Martha said, reaching for the remote control. There was the shop on the ten o'clock news. The doors were padlocked by a landlord owed three months back rent. Employees refused to answer the phone. Brides outside the entrance were not in a good mood.

The next day, Martha called the shop, only to find the phone disconnected. Her next call was to our office. Did she have any hope of getting her gown? What about her deposit? Since she put the deposit on her VISA, we suggested she immediately contact the bank that issued the card.

Since the charge had occurred nearly four months ago, the bank initially said she was out of luck. Martha didn't give up—she pointed out that the charge was a *deposit* for a dress, not a purchase. Hence, the 60 day limit would not apply since she never actually received the merchandise. After some more wrangling, the bank relented and credited her account. She found a gown at a consignment shop and the story had a happy ending.

While credit cards are not a full-proof method of protection against scammers, they're better than nothing. We've interviewed many brides who found that credit cards gave them extra leverage when a dispute developed with the gown. Stubborn shop owners who refused to fix a problem suddenly become more accommodating when the bride pointed out she could dispute the charge.

than-honest retailers. While we realize no one has the luxury of looking at bridal dresses full-time, procrastination can have its own hazards.

4 LEAVE YOUR WALLET AT HOME. While we know most brides are smart shoppers, there are a few of you out there that need to be restrained with large quantities of sedatives. If you're one of those folks who makes snap decisions you regret later, consider this simple piece of advice: leave your wallet at home during your

Golden opportunity or the business from hell?
Life as a bridal shop owner isn't all lavender and lace.

Pssst. Hey you! Want to make a lot of money? Have we got a business for you: run your own bridal dress shop! It's high fashion! Pure glamour! Big profits! Customers who'll pay anything to get your product!

Many entrepreneurs are attracted to the bridal business with such hype, but the reality of running a retail shop quickly hits them smack in the face. Now, at this point, you might be saying, "what do I care?" While it's easy to dismiss the problems of bridal retailers as much of their own doing, it's also important to recognize what life is like on the *other* side of the cash register. Understanding the pressures that bridal shops face may help explain (if not excuse) much of the behavior, practices and tactics that drive consumers crazy.

One of the biggest and most unpleasant surprises that zaps the novice bridal retailer is the manufacturers themselves. Acting like spoiled children who think retailers are there to serve their wishes, some designers do their best to torture their dealers. Take the issue of minimum orders. The dreaded "minimums" (as they are called in the business) can be draconian—designers demand stores purchase thousands of dollars of sample gowns twice a year. If they miss a season, they're dropped like yesterday's news. And some designers send stores "mystery" samples—dresses that the stores never see in advance, but are expected to stock and pay for. Some of these fashion experiments are best left on the cutting room floor.

And what if there is a problem with a dress order? Some manufacturers have very bad manners. Many ship goods without inspecting them first—and hassle the stores when they want to return damaged dresses. One famous designer has been known to fly into a rage when a store calls with a problem dress. "It's *your* job to fix it," the designer will yell into the phone before hanging up. And that's one of the nicer designers.

Of course, the reality of owning a retail shop, any retail shop, in the 90's quickly leads many bridal shop owners to burn-out. The excitement of opening a store quickly fades into long hours,

initial gown search. That way when you get all excited about a deal that's too good to be true, you'll have a cooling off period to think about it. If you can't take a night to sleep on it, it's not a good deal.

5 MAKE SURE THE SHOP IS LEGIT. Later in this book, we'll give you the phone numbers to every known bridal designer and manufacturer in the universe (well, almost). Use them. Before you order a dress, call the manufacturer to make sure the shop is an

---

weekends spent at work, and hassles with employees. And did we mention the competition? The bridal business may look sweet and innocent on the surface, but talk with any retailer and you'll hear stories of competitors that would run over their mother with a truck in order to make a sale. Shops spread rumors about other stores, battle with each other over bridal fashion shows and try to get manufacturers to drop their competition as dealers.

All this leads to burn-out, and in some cases, a flame-out—a bridal store that goes bankrupt, leaving a trial of unhappy brides bilked out of dress deposits and with nothing to wear for their weddings.

We were surprised at an article in a bridal industry newsletter that revealed many bridal shop owners don't take a salary from their operations! That's right—they put in all those long hours, deal with pesky consumers like us and then walk away in the end with no income. For some women (and the vast majority of bridal shop owners are women), the bridal shop is more like a hobby. In the end, however, a lack of salary usually leads to absentee owners and shops run in a far less-than-professional manner.

And when some shop owners tire of the grind and little pay, they can get nasty. We've got stacks of stories from brides who felt literally tortured by a bridal shop owner from hell. Some owners turn into downright thieves—taking deposits from consumers and then not caring if the bride ever sees her dress.

On the other hand, no one is forced into opening a bridal shop. No government agency assigns you this thankless job. And some people get into the bridal business because they think they can make a fast buck. Brides are such an easy mark, they think. Buying a dress is one shot deal—you won't see her again, so take as much money as you can grab.

As long as anyone can print up a business card that says "Bertha's Bridal Shoppe," there will be good retailers and those who should be locked up for eight to ten years. While it would be nice to think that the industry can police itself, we're not so naive to imagine that these problems will go away anytime soon. As a bride, all you can do is hope your walk down the aisle doesn't also mean a trip to the cleaners.

authorized dealer. (There's one exception to this rule: Discount Bridal Service, who we'll discuss in the next chapter). Obviously, there is a greater risk ordering a gown from a shop that's not an authorized dealer of that designer. Protect yourself and your money by making this simple phone call first.

Shopping Tips

 As Tina Turner once said, we can do this easy. Or we can do it rough. The same goes for gown shopping—make it easy on yourself by following some basic rules of sane shopping:

🐦 **Avoid Saturdays.** Most bridal shops are zoos on Saturdays. Dressing rooms are full, the salespeople are pulling out their hair, tempers can flair. We say forget it—go gown shopping on any other day of the week. Another word to the wise: call ahead to see if you need an appointment. Some shops will make evening appointments after hours.

🐦 **Take along only one trusted person.** Whether it's Mom, a sister or close friend, it's nice to have a second opinion. Also, it's easier to resist sales pressure or other tactics when you have someone to confer with. This person can also take notes on the shop's policies, delivery dates, alterations estimates and so on.

🐦 **Try on expensive gowns.** What? Alan and Denise, have you lost your minds? Why should I waste my time trying on a dress I can't afford? Ah, but there is an important lesson here. The only way to educate yourself about a good quality gown is to try one on—and most expensive gowns have a certain fit and finish that you only see at that price level. This tip is especially important if you plan to shop some of the bargain sources like outlets and discount stores we'll mention later in the book. By trying on a few expensive dresses, you'll know what's a good deal and what isn't. Of course, don't get carried away—two or three dresses is enough. Twenty is overkill.

🐦 **Don't fixate on one style.** Sure, you may fall in love with a particular look in a bridal magazine. But remember, dresses look different in the real world. When you shop, keep an open mind. You may end up deciding you look best in a totally different style of dress than you imagined.

🐦 **Realize your bridal limit.** Shopping for a bridal gown is an exhausting process. If you try on too many dresses in one day, they'll all become a white blur. Try to visit just two or three shops in one day. While it's tempting to get it over with in a short time, it's hard to make a good decision when you've just tried on 34 gowns.

❧ **Don't tear out the pages.** Sure, it's a good idea to single out dresses in a bridal magazine. But don't tear out the pages. Many shops (and discount mail-order services) can get you a price quote if they know the page number of the ad. And that's the rub: most bridal magazines have yet to figure out how to print page numbers on their ads. Hence, if you tear out the pages, it may be more difficult to identify the gown.

Questions to Ask a Bridal Shop

The following questions are reprinted from our first book on weddings, *Bridal Bargains.*

1 WHO IS THE MANUFACTURER OF THIS DRESS? As we previously mentioned, some shops try to hide this from you. Even though they have torn out the tags from the dress (in an illegal effort to keep you from comparison shopping), you can still ask them about who makes the dress. This is important for several reasons. First, you can determine if the store is an authorized dealer for the gown by calling the manufacturer. Second, you know what you are buying—some designers offer better quality than others. If the shop refuses to tell you, or if the salesperson says they just "don't know," go elsewhere.

2 HOW LONG WILL IT TAKE TO GET THE DRESS IN? A critical question since the delivery times for different manufacturers vary greatly. If you choose to fudge your wedding date (moving it forward a few weeks from the actual date), be careful here. If you move the date up too early, the shop may not be able to order the dress in time for the early date. In general, bridal gowns take anywhere from six weeks to six months to special order. Bridesmaids' gowns take about three to four months.

3 WHAT ARE YOUR PAYMENT POLICIES? Can I put the deposit on a credit card? Also, confirm the store's refund policy. Nearly all bridal shops have a "no refunds" policy on special-order dresses—even if the wedding is called off or there is a death in the family. Read the receipt (or contract) carefully before you sign.

4 CAN I HAVE A WRITTEN ESTIMATE FOR ALTERATIONS? Before you order, get this in writing. Remember that you do not have to use the store's in-house alterations department (even though they will strongly encourage you to). If you detect any problems here or can't get a written estimate, consider hiring another seamstress.

5 WHAT FREE SERVICES ARE AVAILABLE? Some stores throw in a free "steaming" with all bridal gown orders. Other freebies might include free delivery and even ceremony coordination

(especially when you place a large order with the shop). Some of these services might be offered quietly. Ask and ye shall receive.

6 WHO IS THE OWNER/MANAGER OF THE SHOP? In case something goes wrong, it's always nice to go to the top to get a resolution. In addition to noting the name of the salesperson, make sure you ask for the name of the store manager or owner. In the case of a small, mom-and-pop-type operation, the owner and manager may be the same person. In a larger chain of bridal shops, you may be able to just find out the store manager's name.

What if the bridal shop takes the fifth when asked these questions? Any time a shop balks at answering these basic questions or refuses to put details like the delivery date in writing, it's a big red flag. What are they hiding? While many shops expect brides to disclose their name, address, phone number, blood type and so on, it's amazing how quiet they can be when the tables are turned. We suggest you continue your gown search until you turn up an honest and forthright retailer.

A Brief History of Bridal Retail

As we mentioned earlier in the book, the white, formal bridal gown as we know it today is a rather recent creation. And the concept of a retail bridal shop is even younger: few if any such stores are older than 10 or 20 years. Here's a perspective on how we got here.

Before World War II: Since most brides wore their nicest dress, there was very little demand for formal bridal gowns and hence very few bridal retailers. Oh sure, the very wealthy could afford a custom-sewn white gown from a couture dress shop in New York, London or Paris, but to the average bride, this was far beyond her means.

In the 1920's, the brief fad of flapper-style dresses spawned a similar bridal trend, yet even the bridal versions of these dresses didn't feature trains. This era of extravagance came to a crashing end with the Depression. Marriage rates dipped to an all-time low as couples postponed weddings so they could try to find something to eat. While a few manufacturers can trace their roots to the 1930's (both Alfred Angelo and Fink Brothers started then), their success was limited at first. Yet mass production of fabrics and detailing sewed the seed for future growth

A formal wedding gown with train cost $15 to $20 in the late 1930's. While that sounds like a pittance, it was an extravagance few could afford. Since the average man earned only a dollar a day (if he had a job), it could take a month's salary to buy his bride a bridal gown.

The 1950's. The decade's prosperity spilled over to weddings, as couples returned to formal nuptial fashions. It was the age of white gloves and pill box hats. After years of rationing and shortages caused by the war (silk was used for parachutes, not wedding dresses), luxurious fabrics came back to the market.

Since folks had more money, a new market for a special occasion wedding dress was born. Brides who grew up reading *Life* magazine accounts of royal weddings wanted to have a fairytale wedding too, complete with a princess-inspired bridal gown. Department stores added "bridal boutiques" and several manufacturers sprung up to meet the demand. In Boston, the designer Bianchi started as a custom house, but soon discovered that department store buyers were clambering for their designs.

Few independent bridal shops existed during this time; most bridal dresses were sold at department stores. It's hard to imagine it today, but department stores actually had *service* back then— bridal boutiques pampered brides and their moms. And it was mom that was calling most of the shots, by the way. Since it was unlikely they wore a white gown for their wedding, moms wanted something special for their daughters.

The 1960's. Synthetic fabrics like polyester satin came on the market and this had a tremendous impact on bridal retail. Now manufacturers could churn out more affordable dresses, and as prices tumbled, the bridal retail market expanded. Of course, another factor was the baby boomers—the generation born between 1946 and 1964 was starting to get married in the late 60's, and this helped bridal retailers post significant sales gains.

Department stores still owned the market for bridal gowns in the 60's and it wasn't just the upper-end stores selling expensive gowns. JCPenney added bridal salons in dozens of stores, enabling more of "Middle America" to buy a bridal gown.

The 1970's. It was this decade that saw the beginning of a major change in bridal retail. Despite the fact that bridal was booming, department stores had a change of heart in selling this specialized apparel.

Now, we're not sure what happened, but we assume the department stores hired some fancy management consultants who determined the stores could make more money by selling polyester disco blouses instead of bridal gowns. Bridal was service intensive (read: high labor costs) and many mainstream department stores decided it was time to give wedding dresses the boot.

As the stores closed their bridal boutiques, many of the salon's employees decided this would be a good time to become entrepreneurs. Independent bridal boutiques opened by the thousands.

These events forever changed the way bridal gowns were sold—instead of walking into a familiar department store, brides had to navigate a bewildering number of mom-and-pop stores. Despite the fact that many of the stores were poorly capitalized, many bridal shops were kept afloat by an expanding wedding market. This would change in the next decade.

The 1980's. The trickle of department stores abandoning bridal became a flood in the 1980's. Even JCPenney decided it was time to get out of bridal retail, shuttering almost all their in-store salons during the mid 80's. (Penney's still sold bridal through their catalog, though).

In 1981, the "wedding of the century" featured Lady Diana wearing a bridal gown that quickly caught the imagination of many brides. While that marriage didn't work out well for Diana and Charles, it did wonders for the bridal business. Almost overnight, formal weddings were back in vogue, after taking an extended vacation through the last decade. Brides wanted that big dress and a booming economy helped them afford it.

The price of a wedding dress soared during the 80's, as giddy manufacturers added 10% to 20% to the prices of their wares each season. The numbers are stark: in 1980, the average dress was $350. By 1990, it cost over $800. That increase was nearly twice the rate of inflation.

As a result, the bridal business became vulnerable on two fronts. First, discounters sprung up as brides began to balk at the high prices. What was once a genteel business turned into a cut-throat market, where shops tried to keep pace with competition.

Second, the entire industry was vulnerable to an economic downturn. The first evidence of this problem came in the Southwest in the mid to late 80's—the oil-related economic crash in states like Texas led to a fierce shakeout of bridal retailers. Dozens of shops closed and declared bankruptcy, although this crisis barely registered on the radar screens of the New York-based designers. Most dismissed the problem as isolated and a one-time blip. They were wrong.

The 1990's. The recession of 1991-93 hit the bridal business especially hard. By knocking out the economies of California and New York, the downturn zapped the bridal business where it hurt the most—in the affluent urban markets that provided the bulk of their profits.

Not only did massive layoffs not help, but the return to "cheap chic" in the early 1990's was a double blow. Brides began rejecting the fancy weddings of the 80's and the big bridal gowns that went with them. Many wanted simpler dresses that cost less than a mortgage payment.

As a result of these events, the bridal business was never the same. Couture designers saw their business shrink; lower-price manufactures could barely keep up with the flood of new orders.

Wave after wave of bridal retailers closed during and after the recession. And it wasn't just the small stores; regional "chains" with several locations declared bankruptcy. The resulting publicity gave the industry a big black eye—when shops closed, brides who couldn't get their dresses complained loudly to the local media.

Oddly enough, despite the bridal bankruptcies, the retail end of the business got even more competitive. Bridal "warehouses" sprung up in many cities, offering a "cash and carry" deal with low prices. Mail-order discounters expanded their business as brides began to wonder if their local bridal retail shop would be there next week.

Even department stores began carrying bridal again. Apparently, the stores hired some more consultants, who concluded the previous consultants were nuts. Gee, bridal is good for business, they said. Apparently, brides who buy a dress from a department store are more likely to register there for gifts, buy housewares and other items. No kidding.

Of course, the department stores quickly realized they couldn't provide the service they once did at their own bridal boutiques (partly because many of those experienced department store bridal managers had gone off to start stores of their own). So they sub-contracted out the new bridal salon to existing retailers. For example, Saks 5th Avenue teamed up with Kleinfelds of Brooklyn to manage bridal boutiques in Saks stores in several states.

The Present. So that's how we got here. As the song goes, it's been a long, strange trip. The result of all this tumult is a mixed bag. On one hand, brides have more choices than ever—you can buy a dress at a fancy retail boutique, order one though the mail or check out the cash and carry bridal warehouses.

The only downside: mass competition can also mean mass confusion. Trying to sort out all the different alternatives is difficult for even the most level headed consumer.

Slash Those Dress Costs!

23 bargain tips for saving on a bridal gown

Question: Does buying a bridal gown have to send you to the poor house? Answer: Of course not! In this chapter, you'll discover the best money-saving tips and advice on buying that dream dress. Learn the inside tricks and bargain hints from brides who refused to pay full retail for their gowns.

HERE'S A SCARY THOUGHT: the average bridal gown in this country costs $800. Even worse, as you'll read later, designer creations can easily top $1000 and $2000. And that average figure just covers the dress—so you want to wear shoes with the dress? And a bra? You're so picky, ma'am.

Check out this chart of average costs for the entire ensemble:

HIDDEN COSTS WITH GOWNS CAN ADD UP
Sample figures for a typical gown—and those necessary extras

GOWN	$800
RUSH CHARGE	50
ALTERATIONS	65
PRESSING	30
DELIVERY TO CEREMONY	50
CRINOLINE/SLIP	45
BRA	30
HEADPIECE/VEIL	150
SHOES	60
JEWELRY	25
GLOVES/STOCKINGS	30
TOTAL	**$1335**

Wow! That's a chunk of change. In this chapter, we'll try to slice and dice those numbers with a series of money-saving ideas, tips and advice.

We've divided this step into two areas—"creative" money saving tips and more "traditional" ideas. The creative tips focus on all the alternatives to buying a dress at a full-price retail shop. We'll discuss discount mail-order options, buying a dress second-hand and a host of other innovative options.

What if you want to go the traditional route, ordering a gown through a retail store? For some, the convenience of a full-service bridal shop may outweigh the time and effort to ferret out bargains through other sources. In this case, we have some advice on how to cut costs when dealing with a full-price store.

With each money-saving tip, we have noted the typical savings and the degree of difficulty—just how feasible is each idea? We divide this into easy (●), moderate (■) and difficult (◆).

Get Me Out of Here!
Creative alternatives to shopping at full-price boutiques.

Discount Bridal Service (DBS)

Discount Bridal Service is the bride's secret weapon in the war on high prices. This Baltimore, Maryland-based mail-order operation enables you to buy a brand new, designer name dress at discounts of 20% to 40% off retail.

Hold it, you say. How can anyone sell a first-quality dress at those prices? Well, first the company's 300 dealers don't have traditional bridal shops with all that fancy furniture and inventory. By cutting out the overhead, the company can pass on those savings in the form of lower dress prices. Dresses are inspected at and shipped from DBS' Baltimore headquarters directly to your house, cutting out the middleman.

In business since 1984, Discount Bridal Service sells bridal gowns, bridesmaids dresses, veils and headpieces, plus a variety of wedding accessories at deep discounts. For example, we priced a $1200 name brand gown at just $847—a 30% discount.

We have to say we are somewhat amazed at DBS' popularity in recent years. We first discovered them in 1987, when they had half the number of dealers as today. In those early days, many of their dealers had home offices (derisively referred to by competitors as "housewives" with little bridal knowledge) and the company operated on a shoe-string. Today, DBS sells over 10,000 dresses a year and also does a booming business in Japan, of all places. The professionalism of the dealers has also increased—many now sell other wedding items like invitations, accessories and the like.

As DBS has grown, they continue to draw the ire of full-price bridal retailers. Never popular in the industry to begin with, DBS has been blocked from advertising in the major bridal magazines and banned from some local bridal shows. Yet the power of getting a bargain can't be denied—DBS is now a major player in the bridal business. The company can get gowns from over 100 designers, including many of the fancy couture houses you'll read about later in this book.

Designers hate this, of course. Most would prefer to go back to the good old days, when brides bought dresses at full price without complaining. Designers openly attack DBS as the scourge of the bridal business—and then secretly sell them mass quantities of their dresses.

All of which means nothing to you, of course. But if you decide to order a gown from Discount Bridal Service, you should be aware of the controversy that surrounds it.

Contact info: Call 800-874-8794 to find a DBS dealer near you.

Typical Savings. Most dresses are discounted 20% to 30% off the suggested retail price, although some styles and accessories can be as much as 40% off retail. And those discounts are off *suggested retail*. Since some shops mark gowns above their suggested retail price (especially on designs for which they have an "exclusive"), the real savings can be even more dramatic.

Reality check. To order a dress from Discount Bridal Service, you have to know exactly which gown you want—and that can be the biggest challenge. Since the company has no catalog and the dealers stock no dresses, most brides have to shop other stores first. And since those stores may conceal the name of the manufacturer (not to mention the style number of the dress), nailing down exactly which gown you've fallen in love with can be a challenge.

A way around this problem is to find a picture (or advertisement) of the dress you want in a bridal magazine. DBS dealers can determine the style number of any gown by simply knowing the magazine name, issue date and page number. While not all dresses out there are advertised, many are, at one time or another.

Another negative: DBS requires full payment in advance. Instead of the 50% deposit that most retail shops require, you have to pay for the entire dress up front—and this is quite a leap of faith. Yet we've found the company to be very reputable, with an excellent track record in customer service.

If you want to go this route, plan in advance. Ordering a dress from Discount Bridal Service can take up to six months (although most styles take four to five months). This can be four to eight weeks longer than ordering from a full-price retailer. One reason for this delay: dresses first go to DBS' Baltimore headquarters to be inspected before shipping to the bride.

What about alterations? DBS dealers don't do alterations, but refer customers to local, qualified seamstresses. While this isn't as convenient as using an in-store alterations service, it can be another source of money savings—most independent seamstresses will charge less for their services than a bridal shop.

Degree of difficulty: ● to ■ If you know exactly what dress you want and you can wait up to six months to get it, Discount Bridal Service is an easy way to save money. Of course, that's a big *if*—on the other hand, if your wedding is too close or you don't have time to play Sherlock Holmes to discover the maker of the dress you see in a bridal store, DBS may not be for you.

Shopping tips

❧ **You have to pay for shipping and handling.** This runs about $30 per dress. Hence, the savings may be partially negated by the shipping charge—this is especially so for lower-priced gowns, say under $500.

❧ **Beware of misinformation about Discount Bridal Service.** As we mentioned above, retailers despise DBS. They don't like anyone who discounts bridal gowns by 20% to 40%. On a positive note, some stores will attempt to match DBS' prices. However, other stores will use scare tactics to dissuade brides from using them. One common lie: DBS sells counterfeit or inferior, knock-off gowns. Please. We'd never refer consumers to a service that didn't deliver what they promises, that is first-quality gowns.

❧ **Designers will tell you they don't sell to Discount Bridal Service.** Which may or may not be true. Yes, in some cases, DBS procures its gowns through "third-party sources," mostly other bridal shops who carry the lines. Other designers sell directly to Discount Bridal Service, but deny this in public. When you call them, they'll swear they've never heard of DBS. Why? They don't want to offend their full-price dealers. Yet the bridal business is a small, cottage industry where everyone knows everyone else's business, so these denials ring hollow to us.

❧ **Some dealers now take credit cards.** In the past, Discount Bridal Service just accepted cash or checks. Recently, however, DBS began encouraging its dealers to accept credit cards.

Off-the-rack discounters

What's the biggest pain about buying a gown? Well, besides the high price, brides complain most about the hassle of waiting months for a special-order gown. As you read earlier in this book, many of the scams in the bridal business stem from the archaic notion that you should wait forever for your dress.

Even if you want to special-order a dress, shopping for it can be a pain if you don't have the body of a supermodel. For some sadistic reason, bridal shops only stock samples in size 10 or 12. If your size doesn't correspond to that magic number, it can be incredibly frustrating trying to figure out what the gown would actually look like on *you*.

Well, coming to the rescue of brides who think this system is nuts is the latest entry in the bridal shop wars: off-the-rack discounters. Instead of all the fancy trimmings of a bridal salon, these operations stock rack after rack of gowns in all sizes. And the prices are generally less than regular retail. Some are called "bridal warehouses" and feature more selection than service— there's no hand-holding sales consultants, for better or for worse.

One of the pioneers of this concept is David's Bridal, an Ardmore, PA-based chain of 39 off-the-rack superstores (call 800-399-2743 or 610-896-2111 for a location near you.) The company opened it's first store in Florida in 1990 (when it was called David's Bridal Warehouse) and since has softened its no-frills image— instead of endless racks, harsh lighting and cramped dressing rooms, the stores' new layout is more customer-friendly.

We recently visited a new David's store in Dallas, Texas and were impressed. Each store stocks up to 2000 dresses (wedding gowns and bridesmaids dresses), in sizes 2 to 24. Prices range from $200 to $1500 (the expensive gowns are made of silk). What you see is what you get—all gowns are sold off-the-rack; there are no special orders. If your town doesn't have a David's yet, you won't have to wait long. The chain is opening 15 to 18 new locations a year (currently they are as far north as Boston and as far west as Arizona).

Of course, David's is just one example of this trend. Open up the phone book, look under "Bridal Shops" and you'll undoubtedly find at least one such operation in your area (if you live in a city). Other such operations may be an easy drive from large metro areas: one example we've received favorable e-mail about is the Bridal Factory Wearhouse near Allentown, PA. (1044 S. Route 100, Briengsville, PA. 610-398-3130).

Typical savings. Well, it depends on what you buy. As you'll read below, off-the-rack discounters sell a wide variety of goods, from discontinued samples to brand new, private label goods. As for the former, you can usually expect prices to be as much as 50% off retail . . . but, the condition of the gown may be an issue. Brand new gowns usually sell for 10% to 15% less than comparable gowns—not a tremendous bargain, but when you add in the convenience of the off-the-rack purchase it may be worth the effort. And petite or large brides take notice: most off-the-rack discounters don't charge extra for such sizes, saving you another $100 to $200 in some cases.

Reality Check. So, exactly what are the off-the-rack discounters selling? Most bridal warehouses sell a variety of goods—overstock dresses dumped by manufacturers, last season's styles that didn't make it, liquidated stock from closed shops, and more. In some cases, the dresses can be virtually new and hence a good deal when discounted 20% to 50% off retail. On the other hand, some dresses may be trashed, with stains, missing detailing, and other damage. Don't forget to calculate in the cleaning costs ($100 to $250) and alterations or repairs to make sure the bargain is all it seems.

David's takes a slightly different tack—it mainly sells brand-new, private-label goods. The dresses are marketed under pseudo brands like Gloria Vanderbilt and Oleg Cassini. (Yes, you too can own a bridal dress with the same name as those 70's era designer jeans hanging in your closet!) Since these dresses really aren't *designer* originals, you might ask just where the heck David's gets these gowns? Well, the answer is: the same factories that churn out the name-brand gowns. It's a little known fact about the bridal business: many of the plants in Taiwan and other Far Eastern countries that churn out name-brand gowns also quietly make knock-off, "clone" dresses. David's buys these dresses cheap, puts on a fake brand name like "Gloria Vanderbilt" and then sells them in their stores.

Which is not to say they're ripping off brides—actually, most of David's gowns are rather good copies of the real thing. But are you getting a good deal? That's where your comparison shopping will come in handy. Before you hit a David's, shop at full-price stores to familiarize yourself with fabrics, laces and construction quality.

Basically, we found David's to be offering slightly good deals. Since the dresses it sells aren't sold elsewhere, it's hard to exactly say what their real retail price would be. But we estimate a $600 gown at David's would be about $700 or so in a full-price shop. Yes, that's just a savings of 10% to 20% in general but don't forget the convenience factor—you find your size, pick a style and you walk out the door with the dress.

Degree of Difficulty: ● If you have such an operation near where you live, it's pretty easy to follow this money-saving strategy. The off-the-rack discounters can't be beat, especially for brides who don't have much time before their wedding or those who need a petite or large size. Of course, what you save in time and money you lose in service—most of these operations have minimal (some say non-existent) service.

Shopping tips
❦ Look for another twist on this concept: coming soon, the bridal superstore. "We Do" started this trend in Dublin, Ohio (6655 Sawmill Rd., Dublin, OH 43017. Phone: 614-799-2933). Their 26,000 square foot store features 600 dress styles with prices ranging from $300 to $3000. Their claim to fame: one-stop

E-mail from The Real World
Some Brides Love David's, Others Can Leave It

Ever since the company began their national expansion, our e-mail on David's has run hot or cold on the concept. Here's a sampling:

A bride in Indianapolis was very happy with David's . . .

"I was at David's Lombard, IL location two days ago and it was wonderful. After two straight days of hitting all of the stores in the area, David's was a breath of fresh air. Many of the other stores had advertised 'thousands of gowns, size 2-28, no ordering.' Unfortunately, most had only tens or hundreds of dresses in stock and only five above a size 14. I was very frustrated because I had driven all the way to Chicago from Indianapolis based on the claims in these ads. I am a size 22 and needed a gown immediately for my wedding which is only a month away.

"When I arrived a David's the difference was clear. There they were, hundreds of dresses in a size 22 and thousands in the store. The store obviously recognized that all brides aren't a size 6. They had all of the latest styles and a wide range of prices in my (and everyone's) size. I tried one ball gown-style that was only $150. The dress I bought is pictured in their national ad and only cost $399."

"My appointment was not only honored, but special. When I told my sales person that I felt I should hurry so she could help another customer, she assured me that she was there to service me until I had made all of my selections (dress, undergarments, headpiece . . . everything at great prices). She catered to all of my needs and made me feel like a princess.

She didn't try to up-sell me or force me to buy their accessories. I found just what I needed at a good price. I walked out feeling like my trip was truly worth it." ✍

. . . While a bride in New Jersey was less than impressed.

"I've just got to add my two cents about David's Bridals in Paramus, NJ. I was not impressed at all. They requested I make an appointment and then when I arrived, one sales clerk was handling about four or five of us. She led me to a rack of dresses and told me to pick which ones I wanted. This was not an easy task. I say this not because they were all so beautiful or too pricey, but many had lipstick smears, dust, lace missing or hanging off, etc. None of the dresses I saw were in any type of protective garment bag, as in most other bridal shops. I finally found four I could live with and, after hunting down my sales clerk, was ushered into the fitting room.

"The dresses I tried on had a few 'workmanship issues' (poor stitching, appliqués ready to slip off) that my mother detected. I thought that maybe these were the ones women just tried on, and that once you were ready to make a purchase, a clean one would be produced from the stockroom. I'm sorry, but $599-$699 was a bit much for a dress I'd have to 'fix' myself (after I had it completely dry-cleaned)." ✍

shopping. Besides having a full selection of dresses, We Do sells wedding accessories and has on-staff bridal consultants to help arrange meetings with local photographers, florists and other wedding merchants. At the time of this writing, We Do has planned a second store in Atlanta, Georgia and five more locations in other cities in 1997. Stay tuned.

❦ **Prepare to line up alterations yourself.** Most of these no-frills operations don't have on-staff alterations departments (David's is the exception—they do have in-store alterations available). You're basically on your own, so check out our tips on this subject later in the book.

Factory Outlets

You can buy just about anything today at an outlet store, so why not a bridal gown?

Unfortunately, there are just a handful of bridal outlets in the U.S. Most manufacturers prefer to dispose of their overstock in quiet ways, in order to avoid raising the ire of their full-price retailers. As a result, you're not going to find a bridal outlet in most so-called outlet malls.

Nonetheless, there are a few out there. After these general tips, we'll give you a round-up of where the best outlets are.

Typical Savings: Discounts can range from 20% to 70% off retail.

Reality Check: Shopping at a bridal outlet is a great bargain *if* (and that's a big *if*) you happen to live near one. Most are on the East or West coasts. If you don't live in one of those locations, you may be out of luck.

And even if you go, you may be disappointed—most outlet stores have dresses that vary widely in condition. In some cases, there may be trashed samples, overstock that never sold or last season's failed styles. While that doesn't mean you can't find an incredible bargain, it may just take some looking. And perhaps a few repeat visits.

Finding a bargain at a bridal outlet is like winning the lottery—you have to show up on the right day and hopefully be the right size to walk away with a gown.

Degree of Difficulty: ◆ Darn difficult. Not only do you have to be lucky to be near an outlet, but you also need to be a savvy shopper—you must have a good knowledge of bridal gowns, a sense of timing as to when the best goods come in and other street smarts. And what about alterations? You're usually on your own.

Shopping tips

❧ **Ask the sales clerks for inside info on shipments.** Most smart shoppers know that the selection at outlet stores can vary widely depending on when you visit—and the best time to visit is when a fresh shipment arrives. Bridal outlets may receive these goods just two times a year, when designers are clearing out for their fall and spring collections.

❧ **Once again, homework counts.** An outlet store should be last on your shopping list. First, go to regular retail stores and familiarize yourself with prices, fabrics and garment quality. As we've mentioned before, this step is crucial. It's easy to be fooled into thinking a dress is a bargain when you haven't comparison shopped first.

Our roundup of the best bridal outlets

❧ **Jessica McClintock** has not one but SIX outlets for her popular line of bridal apparel. The flagship outlet store is the Gunne Sax outlet in San Francisco (415) 495-3326, which not only has 20,000 dresses discounted 20% to 70%, but includes a fabric outlet too. Also in California, the company has "Jessica McClintock Company Stores" in South San Francisco (415) 737-2525, Mont Clair (909) 982-1866 and Huntington Beach (714) 841-7124. If you live in the East, check out the Jessica McClintock outlets in Reading, PA (610) 478-0810 or Central Valley, NY in Woodbury Commons (914) 928-7474. All outlet stores carry past-season styles of bridal gowns, bridesmaids dresses and all kinds of accessories.

We recently visited the Gunne Sax outlet in San Francisco and were impressed. This is a factory outlet in the original sense of the term—on the third floor of an old warehouse in a downtown business district. Outside, there's little parking (search for a space on the side streets). Inside, you'll find concrete floors, open dressing rooms and rack after rack of gowns.

We saw over 1000 bridal gowns (priced from $225 to $500), plus bridesmaids dresses, flower girls, party dresses and more. Most of the bridal gowns were discounted 10% to 25%, but we're told periodic sales offer even better deals. We've heard of brides who found $5 formal bridal gowns (no, that's not a typo). While the deals weren't that fantastic when we were there, we did notice a large rack of informal gowns on sale for just $80. You can then buy a separate train ($20 each) or walk over to the fabric outlet on the other side of the store. There you can find bridal fabrics and laces at incredible prices to help make a train or alteration. Top off this bargain with a pair of white shoes with lace trim, on clearance while we visited for just $5 a pair. Wow.

Most gowns we saw at the Gunne Sax outlet were sizes 8-14, although a few 4-6's and 16-20's were floating around. Surprisingly, the dresses were in pretty good shape—most were in protective bags and had very little damage or wear. Watch for those end-of-season clearances for the best deals (you can put your name on their mailing list to get notices).

Speaking of San Francisco, our readers have spotted a mini-boom of bridal discounters in the same area as the Gunne Sax outlet. One example is the **Proteus' Discount Bridal Store** (415) 495-7922 (not related to Discount Bridal Service, by the way), which is just around the corner from the Gunne Sax outlet at 300 Brannan St. On a recent visit, we saw several large racks of name-brand designer gowns from $200 to $1500 (most average $400). You can buy off-the-rack and save 40% or more—or special order a gown at a 25% discount. Top off that bargain gown with a discounted headpiece for just $25 to $90. Owners Harlan and Yvonne Russell have been in the business since 1986 and we found the staff at the Discount Bridal Store to be quite friendly.

If that weren't enough, walk across the street and check out the **Bridal Warehouse** (625 2nd Street, Suite 218, 415-882-4696). In business since 1992, this second-story warehouse has 600 gowns in stock in sizes 6-20. Prices start at $99 and most average $300. While we were there, they were running a sale with additional discounts of $50 to $250 per gown (which worked out to 20% to 25%). Don't see what you want? Check out the special order gowns on the other side of the warehouse. You can special-order a designer gown (or bridesmaids dress) at a 10% to 20% discount.

We liked Bridal Warehouse too. The staff was helpful and the gowns were well organized—color-coded tags separated the dresses by price level and extra charges for such items as large sizes and rush fees on special-order gowns were clearly spelled out. Alterations are available on site.

Want more bargains? How about a combination headpiece outlet and consignment shop? In the same building as the Bridal Warehouse at 625 2nd Street is the **Bridal Veil Outlet** (415) 777-9531. This small store is the manufacturer's outlet for Chance bridal headpieces. Choose a discounted style off-the-rack for $80 or have them custom design something for you. Hard to believe, but the same shop also houses a consignment bridal gown store, where you can pick up a second-hand designer gown for just $300 to $500.

❧ **Alfred Angelo** sells discontinued styles and over-stock samples at an outlet store in Sawgrass Mills Mall near Ft. Lauderdale, Florida (954) 846-9198. Prices are about 50% off retail, with bridal gowns ranging from $149 to $550. All sales are "cash and carry" (there are no special orders). The outlet also sells bridesmaids dresses.

Alfred Angelo is one of the largest bridal manufacturers in the country and their decision to open an outlet store a few years ago set off a firestorm of controversy. Full-price shops angrily complained about the outlet and the resulting brou-ha-ha scuttled plans for further outlet stores.

❦ **JCPenney** (214) 431-0226 has eight "catalog outlets stores" that carry bridal in a few states. Our readers have praised the selection and prices for both bridal gowns and bridesmaids dresses. Call your local JCPenney store for outlet locations near you.

❦ Arizona brides can find deals on bridal gowns at **Affordable Bridal Warehouse** in Phoenix (602) 279-4933. This shop sells first-quality over-runs from several famous designers from 30% to 70% off. Prices range from $99 to $499. Most gowns are sold off-the-rack (sizes 4 to 34), but special orders are also discounted about 10% to 20% or so off retail. Affordable Bridal Wearhouse also sells brides-maids gowns (by special order), flower girl dresses (starting at $29), shoes, bras, veils and headpieces, and other accessories.

❦ Dallas-based **St. Pucchi** is one of the few "couture" designers with an outlet. Pucchi's "wholesale warehouse" (214) 631-4039, located in a commercial district near downtown Dallas, fails the "truth in advertising" test, however. While it is a warehouse, everything is not priced at wholesale.

True, there is a back room with 100+ samples which range in condition from "brand new" to "torn to shreds." Mostly size 10's, the dresses from Pucchi's lower-priced line ran $50 to $1500, about 45% to 75% off retail. A slim selection of mangled head-pieces and single bridesmaids' dresses were shoved in one corner.

The biggest disappointment was the fact that a whole room of "special order" (read: new) dresses were only slightly discounted. These dresses ranged from $950 to $4700 and delivery takes three months.

It really torques us to walk into a "wholesale warehouse" only to find the nicest merchandise is priced at regular retail—a lesson for outlet shoppers everywhere. Add on top of this the ware-house's non-existent service and you're suppose to pay nearly full price for this? Pucchi's "outlet" is for hard-core fans only—if you can find a sample that's not too trashed, it may be a good deal. But if you're not a size 10 and don't have time to make repeat visits, you may want to skip this one. One interesting note: it appears that the gowns we saw had tags indicating the true style number—a boon for discount mail-order shoppers.

❦ **"1385 Broadway"** is the address in New York City for the Bridal Building, the place where many designers have their show-rooms and sales offices. And here's a little secret of the bridal business: many of these showrooms are open to the public on Saturdays and pass along big discounts to brides. That's right—the same designers who rail against discounting are themselves quietly cutting deals at 1385 Broadway.

We recently visited the non-descript office building and were impressed by the prices. When you enter the building, you're handed a list of which floors are open that Saturday. (This apparently changes from week to week). After a crowded elevator ride, we arrived at the first open floor. We visited several showrooms and came away with the following impressions: designers are selling not only used samples but also are taking special orders for new gowns. Discounts for samples were up to 50%, while special orders were an amazing 20% to 25% off. In some showrooms, the designers themselves were present, showing off their gowns to brides.

Why do the designers do this? One insider told us it's the only way the designers can keep their best salespeople happy—the commissions from "Saturday sales" are a big salary boost.

Service varied widely from showroom to showroom—in some cases staffers were relatively friendly. Other showrooms had little or no service and the attitudes of some salespeople needed adjustment. Alterations is another issue—some showrooms include alterations in the price, while others charge exorbitant fees. One designer was charging a flat $200 fee for alterations, no matter what needed to be done.

So is it a good deal? Yes, with some cautions. Critics contend that the prices on some gowns at 1385 Broadway are lower at places like Kleinfelds in Brooklyn (another bargain source listed in this book). So, like any so-called "discount" option, make sure you shop around first to educate yourself on quality and price.

Don't forget to factor in the price of parking and tolls ($15 a trip) for not only the initial visit but also any follow-up alteration fittings. Selection and which showrooms are open will vary from Saturday to Saturday—it's really a gamble to find the right dress. By using the phone numbers listed in the back of this book, you can contact the designers to see about their public sample sales. (Of course, other New York designers who have showrooms at locations other than 1385 Broadway may also be open to the public from time to time. Call them directly to get schedules on public sample sales).

Our sources say the best pickings are after the twice yearly bridal markets in April and October. Lots of samples are available at these times, but special orders are taken all year round. So, if you live near New York, you may want to venture into Manhattan and check out the bridal building.

Kleinfelds: The Original Bridal Superstore

Kleinfelds (8202 5th Ave., Brooklyn, NY 718-833-1100) claims to be the largest bridal retailer in the country, if not the world. And all that buying power translates into lower prices on their giant selection of bridal apparel—you can choose from over 1200 dress styles on the floor.

In business since 1942, Kleinfelds even has an entire building dedicated to bridesmaids and "special occasion" dresses for moms and guests. The "bridal attendants" store is about two blocks from their main location, at 8209 3rd Ave. in Brooklyn (718) 238-1500.

What if you don't live in or near New York? Well, you can order gowns by phone. Just fax them a magazine picture of the gown, along with your measurements. Kleinfelds will then special-order the gown and have it shipped to your home address. The company even takes credit cards, a big plus in our opinion. Delivery takes about three to six months.

Typical savings. While Kleinfelds claims it isn't a "discount" store, their prices are often 10% to 25% below retail.

Reality Check. What do our readers think of Kleinfelds? The reviews are decidedly mixed. One bride called to rave about their mail-order service, claiming she saved 20% over retail. Others aren't so generous about the store itself. One bride panned the store's selection of sample dresses which were in "terrible condition," she said. "The salespeople were also very pushy." Other brides complain about appointments running two hours late, designer tags torn out of dresses and general rude treatment. "This is a very New York experience," one bride summed up. "Terrible service but great deals."

On the other hand, Kleinfelds is probably the only discount source for hard-to-find couture brands. The store carries upper-end gowns by designers that you can't get through other discount sources like Discount Bridal Service.

Another interesting development at Kleinfelds: the store is reportedly adding private label goods. Apparently, Kleinfelds has approached several small dress manufacturers in the New York area about making goods especially for the Brooklyn store. Hence, you may see name brands of bridal apparel at Kleinfelds that you've never heard of before.

Degree of Difficulty: ● Well, if you live near New York City, a visit to Kleinfelds is quite easy. Critics of Kleinfeld's service and over-crowded aisles, however would probably say this bargain tip isn't for the novice shopper. Of course, you can always order a dress over the phone, which may easier than braving the crowds.

Shopping tips
❧ **Avoid Saturdays.** Kleinfelds always seems busy, but it's even crazier on Saturdays.
❧ **Make an appointment.** It goes without saying, but this is important. Even if you have an appointment, however, you can be kept waiting to see a salesperson.
❧ **If you can't get to Kleinfelds, it's possible that Kleinfelds will be coming to a location near you.** In 1995, the company joined forces with Saks Fifth Avenue to roll out "Wedding Dress" boutiques

nationwide. Located inside Saks Fifth Avenue's department stores, these Kleinfelds outposts carry an "edited" selection of gowns (about 200 styles). While the prices are the same as at the original Kleinfelds store, the alterations charges may vary. At this writing, there are two Wedding Dress boutiques open in Saks (in New York and Atlanta), with more slated for California and Florida.

Go custom! Have a dress custom made for you.

Here's a quick quiz: when looking through the bridal magazines, do you have to fight back that gagging reflex? Does every dress look just, well, wrong? If you answered yes, then you just may be a good candidate for a custom dress.

Hold it, you say. This is going to be expensive, right? It'll take forever to get the gown. And how will I find a dress designer if I don't live in New York or Los Angeles?

Well, let's dispel a couple of myths about custom designing a wedding dress. First, these gowns don't have to be expensive. In fact, you can *save* money by custom designing a dress with a less expensive fabric or detailing. Also, the gown is custom made to your measurements—that means no costly alterations.

As for the time element, yes you do have to allow time to meet with the designer to discuss the dress and then the subsequent fittings (three to six, depending on the design). How long does this take? Surprisingly, going the custom route can be faster than special-ordering a gown. While it obviously depends on the seamstress and time of the year, we've heard of several custom designers who take just two to three months to do a dress start to finish—contrast that to the almost six month wait that some "traditional" designers take to deliver a gown. (And then you've got to add on a few more weeks for alterations!)

You don't have to live in a huge city to find a custom dress maker either. For example, in Boulder, CO, A Formal Affair (303) 444-8294 is a traditional bridal shop that also has a talented, young designer on staff who can create just about any look. The focus for their custom designs is on luxurious silk fabrics, such as silk charmeuse. The styles are kept simple with minimal beading and lace, letting the silhouettes speak for themselves. And the prices! Did we mention that most of these custom dresses are *under* $1000, with the majority in the $700 to $800 range? And that's for a totally custom look with no alterations required. Most dresses take just two months, start to finish.

Typical savings. In some cases, you may be able to save 50% or more by going the custom design route. If you're trying to copy a dress, the best bargains are on dresses that would retail for $1000 or more. Why? On upper-end dresses, you're often paying for the designer label or exotic fabrics. By switching the fabric or using less lace, you may be able to replicate a design for much less than the retail price. However, dresses under $1000 (and especially those under $600) will not be cost-effective to knock-off. That's because these gowns are sewn with very cheap labor in places like China, and your seamstress will probably insist on more than $2 per day.

Reality Check. The only drawback to custom designing a dress is that you must know what you want. And that can be a tall order. Since you've probably never shopped for a wedding gown before, it may be bewildering to make choices about fabrics, laces, styles, and so on.

If you're indecisive, forget this idea. You'll have to make decisions about mundane issues like buttons, zippers, petticoats and other seemingly minor details.

Degree of Difficulty: ■ Well, the actual process of custom designing a dress isn't that difficult, but finding a good dress-maker can add time and frustration.

Shopping tips
❦ **How to find a custom designer.** Not easy, you say? In some cases, they will actually advertise in the Yellow Pages or appear at local bridal shows. Or you may hear about them from friends and colleagues or from the staff at local fabric shops. Be sure to ask for several references and check with the Better Business Bureau as well. Ask the designer to show you examples of work in progress and pictures of completed designs. Many designers will also have extensive sketch books full of dress ideas.
❦ **Once you've found a designer, check out dresses advertised in bridal magazines.** But don't necessarily look at the overall style of the dresses, rather look at necklines, sleeves, back treatments and other details. Cut out pictures that appeal to you and save them to show the custom designer.
❦ **Try on dresses at a traditional bridal shop.** Be sure to choose quite a few gowns in a variety of styles. You might have thought an off-the-shoulder neckline would look great on you only to realize it's difficult to lift your arms above your shoulders. Or maybe a bouffant skirt actually makes your hips look too big and de-emphasizes your bustline. You never know till you try them on.
❦ **Check out fabric stores, especially stores that your custom designer suggests.** Look at the different fabrics and laces up close and compare them. You'll see that even white fabrics have different undertones of yellow, blue and brown. By looking at them together in one place you can find the right tone for your skin type.
❦ **Leave extra time to correct any possible problems.** Occasionally you may find that the neckline is too low or the train is too long. Whatever the case, leave yourself plenty of time to make adjustments.

Sew it yourself

If you have the time and skill, sewing your own bridal gown is a tremendous money-saver. While we realize this option isn't for everyone, it is a possibility if you like to sew as a hobby or have a friend or relative who wants to help out with your dress. What makes this option surprisingly easy is the support network that exists for home sewers. As you'll read below, you can easily purchase a pattern for a stylish bridal gown, even a couture design. And today's advanced electronic sewing machines do much of the hard work.

Despite the time commitment, many brides we've interviewed who've made their own gowns are thrilled with the results. Not only do they save big bucks, but they also end up with a dress that's truly unique.

Typical savings. Up to 75%. Yes that's right, you could save a whopping 75% off the retail price of a popular design by sewing it yourself. As an example, we compared the costs of sewing a gown that retailed for $995. Even with the price of fine fabrics and lace, the total material bill came to a mere $225. Another plus: you can substitute less expensive fabric and other details to lower costs even more. And your gown will be made to fit; no costly alterations.

Reality Check. Working with bridal fabric and laces can be a challenge. Many fabrics like satins are slippery and have unique textures, requiring good sewing skills to achieve the desired result. And the cost of materials can soar if you make mistakes and have to start again.

Degree of Difficulty: ■ to ◆ If you are familiar with bridal fabrics and have sewn other complex outfits, sewing your own bridal gown isn't the world's biggest challenge. But let's be honest: this isn't a project for the meek. The average gown will take hours of sewing and construction. If you don't have the time and doubt your skills, consider a second option: hiring a professional seamstress to custom-make you a dress (we'll discuss this more later in this chapter).

Sewing Tips

❦ A quick guide to pattern books. Just about any fabric store will have a selection of pattern books with a section on bridal gowns, complete with full-color photos. Here's a wrap-up of the more common pattern books:

Butterick. This book had about 12 pages of bridal apparel patterns with a handy "degree of difficulty" rating for each design (easy, average, difficult). Prices for each pattern ranged from $8.95 to $12.95.

Vogue. A subsidiary of Butterick, Vogue offers high-style patterns from famous bridal and formal-wear designers such as Carolina Herrera, Vera Wang and Victor Costa. The downside: these designer dress patterns are quite pricey, about $20 to $25 each. Vogue's "in-house" patterns are more affordable (about $12.50 each) and the book even offers patterns for bridal accessories like headpieces, gloves, garters and the like.

Simplicity. One pattern in this book was billed as the "design your own gown" style. You can choose from nine dress styles, mixing and matching different elements like necklines, sleeves and skirts. Cost: only $8.50. The Simplicity book also carries petite dress patterns and quite a few bridesmaids styles. We even saw a bridesmaid design by Jessica McClintock.

McCalls. This book offers a rather wide selection of bridal styles including some that look like Country Elegance designs (a designer of informal gowns we review later in this book). Another plus: many patterns have petite size options. If you're looking for ethnic or theme-style wedding attire, this is your book—we saw a dress inspired by traditional African customs and another that was perfect for a Western theme. McCalls also includes patterns for accessories and even men's vest/tie/cummerbund sets. Most dress patterns were around $11.

The above dress pattern books are widely available at local fabric stores. Check the phone book for a source near you.

❦ **Customize the pattern.** Why be locked into one dress style? You can customize your dress by combining elements of one pattern with that of another. Most patterns have standardized sizing that makes this option more feasible.

❦ **Get carried away.** Once you delve into the pattern books, you'll notice more than just bridal gowns. Other styles include dresses for bridesmaids, mothers-of-the-bride and even flower girls.

❦ **Buy a book on sewing wedding gowns.** Our favorite pick is *Sew a Beautiful Wedding* by Brown and Dillon ($8.95, Palmer/Pletsch Publishing, call 800-728-3784 or 503-274-0687 to order), which we found at our local fabric shop. The authors are home economists with extensive backgrounds in bridal apparel. Their advice covers the gamut from deciding on styles, colors and fabrics to customizing the dress with useful sewing shortcuts. The book also includes information on custom-making headpieces and veils, mothers dresses, children's formal wear and bridesmaids designs. Considering the potential money-savings, it's a good buy for under $10.

❦ **Sew in extra features.** Since you are making your dream dress from scratch, consider adding a built-in bra and petticoat. Not only will this probably be cheaper than buying these items at retail, but they'll also be designed to fit the dress (and you) just right. You can even add in extra boning in the bodice to hold in your tummy or extra padding in the bust.

❦ **Be prepared.** Before you get started, make sure you have everything you need to make your dress. This includes all notions (thread, zipper, buttons, etc.) as well as extra sewing machine needles and other supplies. Avoid the frustration of stopping in the middle of a project because you forgot to buy interfacing or hem tape. A good fabric shop should be able to give you advice on everything you'll need.

The Running of the Brides
Snagging a Designer Gown for $249 at Filene's

Can you buy a $3000 designer bridal gown for just $249? You can if you brave Filene's Basement sale in Boston and Chicago. Four times a year in Boston (and twice in Chicago), this sale prompts a stampede of brides who strip the racks of designer gowns in mere seconds. Call the stores directly for the latest schedule (Boston 617-542-2011, Chicago 312-553-1055).

There is probably no bridal event more famous in the U.S. than Filene's Basement sale. If you happen to be near Boston or Chicago when the sale is on and think you can survive the scene, this is definitely one event not to miss.

That's because Filene's sale features designer gowns that cost $1000, $2000 and even $3000—all marked down to an amazing $249. Yes, you read right. $249. As you might expect, bargains like this attract a crowd.

After interviewing several brides who braved the sale and got great deals, we'd like to offer our tips to making the most of Filene's Basement Bridal Sale. These tips first appeared in our book, *Bridal Bargains:*

continued . . .

10 Smart Tips for Filene's Sale

1 *Plan in advance.* Filene's Basement does *not* regularly carry bridal gowns. Each year, they collect discontinued samples and other dresses from bankrupt shops and designers. When they've collected enough gowns, they hold the sale at only two locations: downtown Boston (617) 542-2011 and Chicago (312) 553-1055. In Boston, the sale usually is held four times a year—February, May/June, August and November. In Chicago, expect it in May and November. (Call the store directly for the latest schedule).

2 *Brace for bargains.* No matter what the original retail price, all gowns are marked at $249. Patricia Boudrot, Filene's spokesperson, told me she's seen one originally priced at $7000, although most would retail in the $1000 to $2000 range.

3 *Arrive early.* While the doors open at 8 am, brides start lining up as early as 5:30 am to 6 am. Several hundred brides will be in line by the time the doors open.

4 *Bring an entourage.* These gowns are heavy—some brides bring an entourage of friends and family to help them hold dresses. Of course, second opinions are nice too. In addition to bridal gowns, Filene's also sells bridesmaids, mothers-of-the-bride and other formal dresses at the sale.

5 *Dress appropriately.* Sneakers are a must. Forget your purse or let a friend carry it. While dressing rooms are available, most brides just try on the dresses right there in the aisles. "Some women wear leotards or bodysuits," says Filene's spokesperson, "but others are in the underwear they plan to actually wear under the wedding gown—these women are not shy."

6 *Brace yourself.* This is not a sale for the meek—brides can get darn aggressive. Waiting brides have broken down the door at the entrance at least five times over the years in Boston. When the doors open, everyone rushes to the racks. All the gowns are gone in 32 to 46 seconds (this has been timed by more than a few amazed reporters, says Filene's.) In the feeding frenzy, fist-fights have broken out, although Filene's says security is on-hand to keep the event from becoming a melee.

7 *Grab anything.* Here's a bummer: gowns are not separated by size. Everything is mixed together. Hence, the best strategy would be to grab just about anything. Then let the bargaining begin.

8 *Be prepared to haggle.* At many sales, brides will trade with one another to find the style or size they want. That's why you should grab as many gowns as you can—more bargaining power. If you're a size 8 and you've grabbed a size 14, never put it back on the rack. Instead, trade it with another bride for a dress you like. You might have to barter several times before finding "the" dress.

9 *Mix and match.* Here's a smart strategy: mix and match different gowns. Some brides have had a seamstress combine pieces of two or more gowns they found at Filene's sale. Take the lace from one dress, combine it with the fabric and train from another and viola! A designer look at a fraction of the designer price. Remember the cost of embroidered lace and silk fabric today is far more than the $249 cost of each dress.

10 *Cut it down.* You may find the perfect gown at Filene's sale— except it's two sizes too big. Yet at these prices, you may be able to easily afford to have a seamstress cut it down to size. One bride had a size 14 re-made into a size 4.

Buy a consignment gown.

Yuck. Who would want to buy a *used* wedding gown? Second-hand stores are musty places that sell stained dresses from 1972, right?

If that's what you think of buying a bridal gown at a consignment store, then we have two words for you: WAKE UP. Stores that sell "pre-owned" bridal gowns have come a long way in recent years—many have surfaced that specialize in bridal and are anything but musty. In fact, these bridal consignment shops look just like regular bridal shops with one big exception: the prices.

We've been amazed at the deals at second-hand bridal stores. Designer gowns that originally cost $2000 or $3000 selling for as little as $400. These are often the very latest styles, not something out of the 70's. And most bridal consignment shops are very picky about their inventory—most gowns are cleaned before they hit the racks and any damage is repaired.

And bridal gowns are just the beginning at such shops. You can often pick up veils and headpieces along with other wedding accessories at a fraction of full retail.

Typical savings. Some of the best bargains can be found at bridal consignment shops—we've heard from brides who've saved as much as 80% off the original retail price. Prices at most second-hand bridal stores start at 50% off retail, with other deals at 60% or 70% off or more, depending on the condition of the dress, brand name and style.

How to find. Most consignment stores are listed in the phone book under "Bridal Shops," although you might find some listed under "Clothes—Consignment & Resale." Another source: send a self addressed, stamped envelope to the Bridal Consignment Shop Network, c/o PJ's Closet, 432 Garrisonville Rd., Stafford, VA 22554. They'll send you a list of second-hand bridal shops near you. Yet another source: send $3 and a SASE to the National Association of Resale and Thrift Stores, Attention: Bridal Resources, 20331 Mack Ave., Detriot, MI 48236; call (800) 544-0751.

Reality check. Most bridal consignment shops are in larger cities. If you live in a more rural part of the country, you may have to take a drive to find one.

Once you get there, the shop may or may not have something in your size. If you're looking for a petite or a large size, that can be a challenge. It might pay to call before you make a major trek to see what the odds are of finding a dress you'd like.

Of course, like other resale shops, selection will vary from time to time. The best gowns are snapped up quickly, so you may have to make a few return trips if you don't find what you want on a first visit.

While some bridal consignment shops offer alterations, most don't. Hence, you'll be on your own to find a seamstress to make it fit, fix any damage, etc.

Degree of Difficulty: ● With the proliferation of bridal consignment shops, it's pretty easy to follow this money-saving strategy. If you're patient and can make a few return trips, you should be able to find a gown at a tremendous savings.

Shopping tips
🖤 **Remember dresses have already been altered.** Hence the sizes you see may not correspond to reality. You may have to try on several in different sizes, ignoring what the tags say.

🖤 **Ask the owner to call you with new finds.** Most consignment shops are mom-and-pop style operations—you can often find the owner or manager right there behind the counter.

🖤 **Our readers' favorite second-hand stores.** Ever since we wrote our first wedding book, *Bridal Bargains*, we've received dozens of letters from readers with their consignment shop finds. In Boston, **Zazu** (617) 527-2555 is one of the industry's pioneers, featuring perhaps the best selection of second-hand weddings dresses in New England.

A Chicago bride e-mailed her recommendation for **"I Do" Bridal Consignment** in the Windy City. She found a Bianchi dress for just $450—and that included a matching custom headpiece, full length veil, gloves and full petticoat. Now that's a deal. "They were very patient," the bride said of her four hour visit to try on dresses. "I couldn't be more pleased."

In Rockville, Maryland, a bride told us she found a once-worn Christos gown for half the $2500 retail price. The shop? **I Do I Do Consignment** (301) 762-4464. They carry about 500 gowns at 20% to 60% off retail. The gowns average about $400 to $800 but go up to $3000. They are a great bargain find for DC-area brides.

New York brides have to be patient to get an appointment at **Michaels** bridal consignment shop on the upper east end (Madison and 79th) (212) 737-7273. A bride e-mailed us to say the shop has a six week wait for Saturday appointments! Apparently, the bargains must be good—the shop told us they typically carry 80 to 90 bridal gowns, with prices ranging from $800 to $1000. These are fancy label couture gowns that originally cost $2800-$5000.

Also in the Northeast, there's the **Bridal Exchange in Philadelphia** (215) 923-8515. This second-hand source carries only 100% silk bridal gowns and headpieces. Prices range from $400 to $2500. If that weren't enough, you can also special order new gowns from Bridal Exchange at 25% off retail, check out their custom-designed in-house gowns or buy a custom-designed headpiece.

In Glastonbury, Connecticut, we heard good things about **Brides to Be** (860) 633-3639. A bride wrote to us about the great

E-MAIL FROM THE REAL WORLD
Consignment deal surprises bride

A bride in Massachusetts was thrilled at the bargain she found at a Maryland consignment shop. Here's her story:

"The place where I actually bought my gown was called The Vintage Bride, in Clarksburg, MD (301) 540-3540. I would never have thought to stop by if my mom hadn't found them in the phone book. It's a consignment shop, and after my experience there, I heartily recommend at least considering going the consignment route—please don't rule it out like I almost did.

"The dress I ended up getting is great! It fit almost perfectly and is in excellent shape! I found an almost-matching veil and garland headpiece. The price of the whole package? Just over $300.

"The best part about shopping consignment, I think, is that you've got a whole other array of styles than what you see in the boutiques and magazines. Gowns have really gotten more ornate over the years, and I was happy to find a good source of simple, pretty, and inexpensive gowns." ✍

---

deal she found there: a Demetrios (Ilissa) dress at one-third the original retail price. In business since 1981, Brides to Be also carries antique and vintage dresses and offers alterations on site.

And that's just the beginning. There are great second-hand shops in other parts of the country too, from Dallas to Denver, San Diego to Seattle. Check the phone book for local sources.

Hotel gown sales offer quick bargains

If most bridal designers don't have outlet stores, what do they do with all their samples, overstock and discontinued styles? Most prefer to sell these dresses to liquidators, who then go around the country and hold "sample sales" at hotels, bridal shows and other venues.

Hence, you may open up your local newspaper one day and see a big ad for a ONE DAY ONLY SALE! PRICES SLASHED! FIND A BRIDAL GOWN FOR JUST $99!

For some reason, we've seen several of these sales in the Pacific Northwest, especially Portland and Seattle. Occasionally, these dress sales are held in conjunction with a bridal show (that is, trade fair).

In other cases, the liquidators will just rent out a hotel ballroom or convention center. All of which gives the sale the air of a fly-by-night operation and that's what it is—all sales are final, no returns or exchanges and so on. If you get the dress home and decide you don't like it or discover some damage, that's tough. You own it.

Typical savings.
Prices are usually at least 50% off retail.

Reality Check. All the hype often doesn't live up to reality—most of these dresses are trashed. The hems may be dirty, the trains ripped and worse. Hence, you might find a bargain for just $99, but you'll spend $100 or $200 or more to clean it and then maybe another $200 to alter and repair it. Your bargain may cost more than the price of the dress brand new.

And the venue most of these sales choose doesn't make the shopping process very easy. Most hotel sales have cramped dressing rooms, if they have them at all.

On the other hand, some brides have found great deals at these shows. At the end of this tip, we'll relate the story of one bride who was satisfied with her visit to a hotel bridal dress sale.

Degree of Difficulty: ◆ Not only must you be in the right place at the right time, but you also have to find a dress in your size that isn't too trashed. Lightning may strike, but don't bet on it.

Shopping tips
🌿 **Get there early.** Just like Filene's sale in Boston and Chicago, it helps to be the early bird. Check the earlier article on

---

E - M A I L   F R O M   T H E   R E A L   W O R L D
A Steal in Seattle

It's not impossible to find a good deal at a hotel dress sale. This bride from Seattle came away with a bargain she was proud of.

"Even though you rip on wedding shows, the one I went to in Seattle had a sample gown sale in a room nearby with dresses and headpieces from several local shops. There was a huge selection of gowns (luckily I'm a size 10, the majority of the gowns available) and the prices were good. Most were more than 50% off. On the negative side, it was crowded, the gowns weren't in very good shape, and there was an "as is" policy. I found a gown there for $300, but some flowers from the back were missing, some beading was coming apart, the zipper was ripped, the hem of the dress was very dirty and there was a lipstick stain on the train! My mother will be doing the alterations, and said all can be easily fixed, and I'll just get it cleaned before the wedding." ✍

Filene's sale for more tips on shopping hotel sales; most of the same advice applies here as well.

❧ **Once again, comparison shop beforehand.** When confronted with a sea of white bridal gowns at a hotel sale, it may be difficult to separate the good deals from the bad ones. When you comparison shop at full-price stores first, you'll be better prepared to tell the bargains from the trash.

More bargain tips

Want even more money-saving advice on dress buying? Here are six more quick ideas.

1 **Go West!** Western, that is. Western-style wedding dresses are much less expensive than formal bridal gowns. The Cheyenne Outfitters has a Wedding Collection catalog (800) 234-0432 with bridal gowns, bridesmaids dresses, matching flower girl dresses, hats and wedding accessories—all with a western flavor. And prices are hard to beat: "Laramie Lace" is a western wedding dress with all-over lace for $80-$85. Other styles range from $120 to $220. Add a pair of wedding boots ($130) and your ready to ride to the hitchin' post.

2 **Classifieds.** We've found some incredible bargains listed right in the Sunday classifieds. Sometimes weddings are canceled or postponed. In other cases, recent brides who need extra cash are willing to part with their gowns. Most of these gowns are in excellent shape; some have never been worn before! Best of all: the prices we've noticed are often 50% or more off retail. Of course, you'll need to carefully inspect the gown before buying. Other items available through the classifieds: accessories like crinolines or full slips.

3 **Wear Mom's dress or borrow one from a friend.** You'd be surprised how easily a seamstress can inexpensively restore a vintage gown. Even if you spend $100 to $200 to have the gown altered or jazzed up, this will be much less than buying a gown at retail. Borrowing a gown from a friend is another great money-saving option. If the gown needs to be restored, we found Imperial Gown Restoration (800) WED-GOWN to be reputable. (Later in this book, we'll give more tips on how to hire a company who does gown preservation and restoration). Of course, local shops may also be able to help—a bride e-mailed us a recommendation for A Joyful Creation in Rhode Island (401) 724-2154. She said they did a great job in restoring a 56-year old dress to perfect condition.

4 Some vintage clothing shops also carry wedding gowns. If you want something truly different, this is a definite option. A reader in Berkeley, CA found a beautiful 1950's wedding gown in excellent condition for just $200 at a local vintage clothing store. Most large cities have such stores; check your local phone book under "Clothes—Vintage."

5 Don't forget the JCPenney catalog. Let's say you live in the middle of nowhere. The nearest bridal shop is 200 miles away. Can you buy a dress from a mail-order catalog? Try JCPenney's bridal catalog (800) 527-8345. Penney's features affordable bridal gowns from Sweetheart and Alfred Angelo for $175 to $495. Also available: bridesmaids gowns ($89 to $160), flower girl dresses, headpieces, shoes and other accessories. While the prices aren't discounted from retail, they are on the more affordable end of the bridal spectrum.

6 Rent a gown. Guys can rent a tuxedo, but can a bride rent a wedding dress? Actually, the answer is yes—if you're lucky to live in a city with a dress shop that rents wedding dresses. Rental prices for bridal gowns range from $75 for simple dresses to $600 for expensive designer gowns. That's right, you typically can rent one of those exquisite designer gowns dripping with pearls and lace that would retail at $2000 for under $600. Most rental shops require a $100 to $200 deposit. The dresses, which are professionally cleaned after each rental, can be altered to fit.

The only drawback to renting may be the search required to find a good rental shop—there are typically only one or two in each city. For example, while you'd expect to find a rental shop like **Just Once** in New York City (292 5th Ave., 212-465-0960), but what about a smaller city like Kansas City? Even here we found a rental shop, **An Alternative** (800) 995-2338 or (816) 761-8686. A couple of other shops that rent bridal gowns:

> ❦ **Expecting Elegance** 2011 LeMoine Ave., Ft. Lee, NJ 07024. (201) 947-8300. This store rents bridal gowns, mother of the bride dresses and maternity evening gowns. Bridal gowns rent from $200 up.
> ❦ **One Night Affair Rental Shop** (previously known as Dressed to Kill) in Hollywood, CA (310) 652-4334 is famous on the West Coast for their bridal rentals.
> ❦ **One Enchanted Evening** in Pennfield, NY (near Rochester) rents bridal, bridesmaids, mother of the bride and prom dresses. Their number is (716) 385-5550.

The bottom line on dress rentals: check your local Yellow Pages under "bridal shops" for possible sources.

Once you find a rental store, how does the process work? Well, most shops let you reserve a dress as far as a year in a advance. Then the gown is taken off the racks about three to four months before the wedding, to make sure no one else damages the dress. Alterations are an extra expense, running about $50 to $125 at most rental stores.

What about bridesmaids? Some shops will rent these too. An Alternative in Kansas City (see the phone number above) has 400 bridesmaids styles in stock which rent for about $75 (which includes alterations charges). If they don't have the style you want, the shop will order it in and rent it for the wholesale price plus 25%. That's a great deal.

The biggest surprise about many of these rental shops is how fresh the dress styles are. A common misconception is such stores only have styles from 1979. Actually, on our visits to such bridal rental establishments, we saw brand new gowns and other styles that were just a year or two old. And why spend $900 to buy that dress when you can rent it for $350?

Traditional Money-Saving Ideas

Buy a Sample Gown.

The bridal fashion treadmill stops for no one. Each season (fall and spring), the designers crank out more and more samples they insist stores must buy. Unfortunately, the stores are often stocked to the ceiling with last season's fashion experiments. What to do? It's SALE time!

Stores run sample sales not only to clear out old dresses but also to get rid of recent styles that never caught on. Of course, "last season's" bridal style doesn't really look out of date; heck, they all are just white dresses. It's not like the dress designers start rolling out different colors each year and your guests will guffaw when they see you're not wearing an orange bridal gown at your wedding.

While the fashion doesn't change much, the only downside to sample gowns is that they are, well, samples. And, boy, have some of these dresses been sampled. Make-up stains, dirty hemlines, missing beads and other misfortunes can happen in even the best shops. Hence if you see a newspaper ad that says "ONE DAY ONLY! SAMPLE SALE! 50% OFF!," don't get too excited. A trashed bridal gown may not even be worth it's wholesale cost.

Typical Savings. 20% to 75% off retail, although this can vary dramatically. A sample gown in very good condition may only be discounted 20%, while a damaged gown with stains and other problems may be up to 75% off.

Reality Check. Some brides have no choice—their wedding is coming up soon and they don't have the time to wait around for a special-order dress.

The only problem: sample dresses only come in size 10 or 12. If you are smaller, you may have to pay hefty alterations charges to cut the dress down. If your size is larger than a 10, you may be out of luck—while it's possible to make a dress smaller, it's darn near impossible to make it bigger.

Another consideration: repair and cleaning bills can make a sample less of a bargain than it appears at first. Some shops may negotiate on these points (offering to clean the dress for free, for example) but if you're stuck with a $150 cleaning tab, it may negate the savings.

Degree of Difficulty: ■ There are lots of samples out there—the problem is you have to be right size to make this bargain tip work. Since samples may require you to do extra legwork (cleanings, alterations, damage repair), this strategy is definitely not as easy as it may look.

Shopping Tips

❧ **Timing is everything.** Call local shops to see when they hold their sample sales. Most offer sales two or three times a year

❧ **Who needs a sale?** Here's a quiet secret of the bridal business: just about any sample you see in a bridal shop is for sale. While some shops claim they can't sell samples because they need them to take future orders, most are more than happy to unload a sample. The deal you can get depends on your negotiation skills and the condition of the dress.

❧ **Get a second opinion.** If you find a sample that needs repairs, have an independent seamstress check the dress over before you buy it to get an objective estimate of alteration costs. Have the seamstress come to the shop if necessary (call her your dear old Aunt Edith from Poughkeepsie). Tips on finding a good independent seamstress appear later in this book.

❧ **Ask for contingencies.** If the shop promises that stains on the sample will come clean, get it in writing. Ask for references for a good local cleaner. Get a couple of estimates and look for a dry cleaner who has substantial experience with wedding dresses.

Choose one of our "Best Buy" designers

Okay, you want to save money on a dress, but you don't have the time to scour second-hand shops or outlet stores? Is it possible to find a brand new dress without going bankrupt?

Actually, it is—just look for our "Best Buy" designers later in this book (they're noted with a special symbol). Let's be honest: with over 100 designers of bridal apparel on sale in North America, some offer better deals than others.

Take Mon Cherie, for example. This New Jersey-based designer offers incredible deals on gowns which feature stylish accents and quality fabrics. Pictured on this page is style #316—a traditional off-the-shoulder design in 100% silk with a hand-beaded bodice and semi-cathedral train. The price? $798. And that includes a built-in crinoline, which Mon Cherie includes for many of their designs. A silk dress like this from other designers might set you back $1000, $1500 or more. (And Mon Cherie offers many of their designs in satin for even more savings: most are 20% to 30% less than silk prices).

Typical savings. Depending on the brand, you can save 20% to 50% off retail prices by sticking with a "best buy" designer.

Reality check. Although we found several designers that offer good deals on their entire line, what if these designs don't set your pants on fire? There is another twist to this tip: look for "value collections" within a major designer's line. These are sub-lines that offer special pricing.

The best example is Galina, which launched the Galina Bouquet line several years ago as a lower-priced alternative. How much can you save? Regular Galina dresses start at about $1200, while Galina Bouquet has a more reasonable $700 starting point—that's a 40% savings. While the Bouquet gowns are styled more simply and the fabric is less ornate, you'll still get excellent construction quality and a well-known name brand.

Other designers offer value collections, too. Already a good buy in its regular dresses, Eden's "Value" line has four styles that are just $355 to $380—each features traditional styling and a full train. St. Pucchi's ornate gowns start at a whopping $1790, but their special "Alvine Perucci" line begins at just $850. The lower-priced gowns still feature the designer's trademark hand-embroidery.

Degree of Difficulty: ● Most of our "best buy" designers are widely available at retail shops and widely advertised in magazines. You can even see ads for designers like Mon Cherie, who until recently shunned the bridal magazines.

🎁 Shopping Tips

❦ **Educate your self about fabrics, finishes and construction.** As we mentioned earlier in this book, we suggest trying on at least a few expensive gowns so you can familiarize yourself with quality construction, fabric weights, etc. Then when you try on some of our best buy designers, you'll be able to recognize quality features like finished seams, built-in crinolines, herringbone hems and so on.

Bridesmaids in white /informal gowns

At this point, you might be saying, "Are you nuts? You want me to wear a bridesmaids dress as my wedding gown?" Okay, we admit the idea sounds a little preposterous, but think about it. Take away the train and beading from a bridal gown and what do you have? A bridesmaids dress, in white.

And while we admit that some bridesmaids dresses are hideous, there are several manufacturers whose dresses in white could pass as elegant bridal gowns.

Take Watters & Watters for example (see Part IV for more information on this and other bridesmaids designers). Look at any bridal magazine and you'll discover their sophisticated, upscale looks. As an example, we noticed Style #5052 is a beautiful off-the-shoulder design in silk. The bodice has scattered pearls that drop to peplum waist. And the price? $320. Just try to find a silk bridal gown for that price.

A different spin on this tip is to look for "informal" gowns (that is, gowns with less detailing and no trains). They're the little known secret of the bridal business: many manufacturers have informal lines, yet rarely advertise them. And that's the catch—shopping for one may be difficult since most designers don't send out catalogs to consumers. You have to be lucky to happen upon these styles in a retail store.

One of the best informal bridal lines is by Country Elegance by Susan Lane (see Part II for more information on this manufacturer). You can choose from 17 informal dresses from this designer, most priced from $200 to $400. And these are not cheaply made dresses—each are inspired by vintage styles, fully lined, and individually beaded with hand-made trim and appliqués.

Typical savings. As you can see from the prices above, buying an informal bridal gown or a bridesmaids dress in white can save you 50% or more off the typical formal dress price.

® **Reality Check.** Let's be honest: there's a lot of pressure to have a dream wedding, complete with the "big dress." Family and friends may scoff at the notion of buying a bridesmaids dress or informal gown. And, unfortunately, many of these folks may not be tactful enough to keep their mouth shut. Dealing with this pressure may be an unforeseen downside of this tip.

Another slight downside of this bargain advice—you still have to deal with a traditional bridal shop. White bridesmaids styles are almost exclusively available at bridal retailers . . . and that means all the hassles of ordering, alterations and so on. On the upside, ordering a bridesmaids dress is quicker than ordering a formal wedding gown. Most take six weeks to four months to get in (about half the time of a traditional dress).

Informal bridal gowns, on the other hand, can take just as long as a traditional dress to order.

Degree of Difficulty: ● **to** ■ In one sense, it's easy to do this money-saving tip. There are fewer bridesmaids styles and informal dresses to choose from, so the shopping process may be less bewildering. On the other hand, you still have to special order the dress if you go the bridal shop route.

Shopping tips
❦ **Searching out informal gowns.** Identify manufactures in Part II of this book that offer informal lines and call to find a local dealer. Ask to see a catalog if the bridal shop doesn't have the samples in stock. As for designers who make attractive bridesmaids dresses that could double as wedding dresses, check out Galina, Jim Hjelm and Watters & Watters (all reviewed later in this book).
❦ **Have the bridal shop make you a small train.** You can jazz up a bridesmaids or informal (floor length) gown by having the bridal shop's alterations department make a small, detachable train. The cost for this usually is minimal ($50 to $100, depending on the fabric).
❦ **Complement, don't overwhelm.** Make sure the accessories you choose are appropriate to the dress. A headpiece with cathedral-length veiling will look out of place on a tea-length dress. Simple pearl studs will work better than over-the-top, dangling earrings.

Swap the fabric

Fallen in love with a dress but can't afford the price tag? See if you can swap the fabric. Here's a little known secret of the bridal gown business: some designers actually let you substitute less-expensive fabrics. Take Lili, for example (call 800-258-7944 for a local dealer). When you read their information later in this book, you'll note that this designer offers several styles in different fabrics. For example, style #3508 is an off-the-shoulder, long-sleeve gown with cathedral train, lace appliqués, bugle beads and scalloped hemline. In silk, it runs $792. Too much? Try the same style in satin for $632—a 20% savings.

Other designers offer fabric swaps as well. Carmi Couture (call 212-921-7658 for a local dealer) sells several styles in different fabrics. Lila Broude (call 212-921-8081 for a local dealer) is another example on the upper-end. This designer advertised an off-the-shoulder gown with silver bullion embroidery in the August/September 1996 issue of *Bride's* magazine. In Duchesse satin, this runs $2150. But did you realize you can order the same dress in silk shantung for $350 less?

Typical savings. Swapping the fabric can range from $100 to $400 in savings, depending on the manufacturer and the style.

Reality Check. Only a few designers allow you to change the fabric to save money. While some designers officially offer this service (printing up catalogs that show fabric choices), other manufacturers will do fabric swaps "off-the-record." In other words, if your bridal shop has a good relationship with the designer, you can have them inquire about a fabric swap as a special request. Both Jasmine and Galina (two designers rated highly later in this book) will swap the fabric to lower the price on a gown.

Of course, just finding out who does and who doesn't allow you to swap the fabric can be vexing. You need a knowledgeable salesperson to get the low-down and in some shops that can be a tall order.

Degree of Difficulty: ■ to ◆ Since you have to find a shop that knows this information, following this money-saving strategy can be difficult. If the salesperson doesn't know the answer, the store may have to place a long distance to the manufacturer—and some shops will simply refuse this request. Another limiting factor: even designers who offer to fabric swap don't do it on all styles. You may just have to get lucky.

Shopping tips
❦ **Check our reviews.** Later in this book, we'll look at this policy on a designer-by-designer basis.
❦ **Always ask.** It never hurts and information in this book will certainly change after we go to print. Hence, a designer who doesn't offer fabric swaps may change their policy by the time you read this.
❦ **Get a swatch.** If you decide to change the fabric, ask the shop for a swatch of the different fabric. Or try on a different style in that fabric. That way you'll have a better idea whether it will be worth it to make the change.

Buy accessories anywhere but a bridal shop.

A recent survey of brides by a major bridal magazine revealed that about one-third of all brides
buy accessories like shoes and jewelry at a bridal
retail shop. We have two words to say to these women: WAKE UP!
There's a reason that two out of three brides shop elsewhere:
bridal shops take obscene mark-ups on these items. With little
effort, you can find a bra, shoes, jewelry, slip and other bridal
items at much lower prices. In Step #7: The Finishing Touches,
we'll go into specific details on this topic.

Typical Savings. Buying accessories from a non-bridal
source can save brides as much as 50% to 75% off the bridal
shop prices.

Reality Check. You will have to find the time to go shopping
at alternative sources for shoes, undergarments, jewelry,
even gloves and hose. You may also find it difficult to find a local
source for some products like full slips (also known as crinolines
or petticoats).

Degree of Difficulty: ● Except for truly unique items, this tip can
be accomplished when you head to the mall or outlet stores for
your regular shopping.

Shopping Tips.
❦ **Outlet stores are great for bargains.** Look to outlet malls
for items like shoes (even dyeable styles). If you're just looking for
simple pumps in white or ivory, you can even find shoes on sale
at department stores. Bali has many outlet stores throughout the
country where you can find bras and some slips.
❦ **Do it yourself.** If you have your heart set on lavishly decorated shoes, consider buying plain designs and adding bow clips, or
gluing on lace and ribbon to create your own look.
❦ **Jewelry sales.** Department stores and mall jewelry stores have
frequent sales on good quality costume jewelry. You may even
find that regular prices at these sources are still better than the
bridal shops.
❦ **Join frequent buyer clubs.** Many department stores offer frequent buyer clubs for hosiery. You buy a certain number and then
get one free (or at a discount). Use your club membership to buy
hose for all your bridesmaids and moms as well.

Get competitive bids on alterations.

Averages can be deceiving. If you look at the chart at the beginning of this section, you'll discover the average alterations charge for a bridal gown is about $65. Unfortunately, for some brides, those charges can be much higher—running $100, $200 or $300.

Extensive changes to a dress can add to the alterations bill, but even a simple hem can be pricey. If you hem a bridal gown from the bottom, a seamstress must first remove any lace or decoration and then put it back. Some dresses can be hemmed by taking apart the waistline and pulling the skirt up. This involves removing (and then replacing) the bodice decoration. Translation: labor ain't cheap.

Here's the bottom line on alterations: there's no law that says you have to get your dress altered by a full-price bridal shop. While we'll go into more detail on this subject later in the book, you should consider getting competitive bids on your alterations from other sources.

Typical savings. While alteration charges are all over the board, getting your dress altered any place other than a full-price shop can save 50% or more on average. And those savings can be even more dramatic for expensive gowns—a recent survey of bridal shops revealed stores charged more for alterations on pricey gowns, even though they didn't require any more labor or effort! Some shops just think if you can spend $1500 or $2000 on a gown, heck, you can afford more on alterations.

Reality check. It's darn convenient to have your gown altered at the bridal shop—they have seamstresses on hand and the process is (hopefully) expedient. Searching for an independent seamstress, on the other hand, will take some research. Calling around to find sources, checking references and meeting with prospects may not be worth the effort if you're pressed for time.

Of course, another factor here is your comfort level with the bridal shop's in-house alterations department. Some shops are professional, providing written estimates for alterations and giving you a tour of their alterations area. However, other shops inspire less confidence. If you harbor any misgivings about the full-price shop, getting the alterations done elsewhere may be more than a money-saving strategy—it might be the best way to insure your dress alterations aren't botched.

Degree of Difficulty: ■ In some towns, you may find quite a few names of independent seamstresses who do bridal alterations. Yet, in other places, it may be difficult (or impossible) to turn up one name. Hence, you may be better off going with the shop's alterations services.

Shopping tips

How do you find an independent seamstress? Here are a few tips:

❧ **Call fabric stores.** Most places that sell fabric and sewing supplies can usually refer a local seamstress who works on bridal apparel. Check to see if they have a bulletin board where folks may post their business cards.

❧ **Ask Discount Bridal Service.** This mail-order discounter has 300 dealers nationwide (call 800-874-8794). Since they don't do alterations, each dealer has contacts with local seamstresses. Ask for a referral.

❧ **Check references.** Before you hire any seamstress, get references from two or three recent customers. Make sure they have extensive experience altering bridal gowns (not just prom dresses or other garments). Ask to see a "work-in-progress."

❧ **Get it in writing.** Make sure you receive a written estimate and a delivery date.

Avoid rush charges.

Order early and you can avoid hefty "rush charges." Of course, your definition of "rush" and that of the bridal industry may be two different things. Some designers take forever to deliver a bridal gown—up to six months in some cases. Of course, if you want the dress in a mere four months, they suppose they can fit you into their cutting schedule . . . if you pay a "rush" charge.

Rush charges vary from designer to designer. In general, the designers who manufacture overseas charge retail shops about $25 wholesale for a rush order (sometimes called a "rush cut.") The stores then mark this up to about $50 retail (in some competitive markets, stores may offer this service at cost).

Couture designers (especially those who manufacture gowns here in the United States) charge $50-$150 at wholesale, which means you pay the bridal shop $100 to $300.

Designers who offer rush service say they incur extra costs when a dress is "specially cut." That's because most bridal gowns are mass-produced in certain size batches, as we explained earlier. Some manufacturers think rush cuts are such a hassle that they don't even offer this service—out of the 40 largest manufacturers, we count 12 who don't even offer this service. Later in the designer review section of this book, we'll note who does and who doesn't.

Typical Savings. $50 to $300. That works out to a 5% to 10% savings on a typical gown.

Degree of Difficulty: ● Just start early (we recommend ordering your gown nine to 12 months before your wedding) and you won't have to worry about rush charges. If your engagement is going to be short, don't waste your time looking at designers who take six months to deliver a dress and charge big "rush cuts" to get it there sooner. Instead, pick a designer whose delivery schedule fits your timeline. The designer reviews later in this book give you approximate delivery schedules based on manufacturers' policies.

Shopping Tips

❦ **Keep an open mind.** Bridal designers are famous for knocking each other off—you may be able to find a similar design in several manufactures' lines. Hence, if you fall in love with one gown that requires a rush cut, think about finding a similar style from another designer who offers quicker delivery. The only drawback to this approach is finding a knowledgeable bridal retailer who can provide you with different options; some shops simply don't have this expertise.

❦ **Negotiate a better deal.** Just because a bridal shop tells you your dream dress will run another $100 in rush charges doesn't mean you can't negotiate. In order to meet the competition, shops may be more "flexible" on this point than you might think. Mention you plan to buy other items like a headpiece or bridesmaids dresses and you might find that rush charge shrinks dramatically.

❦ **Look for designers with "quick service" options.** The opposite of designers who take forever to produce a gown and then charge rush charges for "fast" delivery are manufacturers who offer "quick service" options. These companies have a limited number of styles of bridal gowns and bridesmaids dresses in many sizes in stock for quick delivery. At the time of this writing, four designers who offered this service include Alfred Angelo, Bari Jay, Bridal Originals and Loralie. For more information on these manufacturers, check out Part II of this book.

PLACING THE ORDER

Getting the details in writing, picking the correct size and avoiding the scams

What are the six details you should get in writing for your dress order? You'll learn this, plus how to decipher all the fine print on those sales receipts. Next, we'll go over the low-down on picking the right size. Learn the three basic dress measurements and seven more you might not think of. Then it's on to the scams— what are the biggest rip-offs with dress orders?

THE SHOPPING IS OVER. After visiting what seems like all of the bridal shops in North America and trying on more bridal gowns than Elizabeth Taylor, you've found *the* dress.

Unless you're lucky enough to find this gown in the right size, it's time for something the bridal industry euphemistically calls "special orders." (Cue theme music from *Jaws*).

Just when you thought it was safe to whip out your shiny credit card and all the problems of gown shopping were over. No, you're only half way there. Welcome to the Special Order Zone.

Slightly longer than a space shuttle mission

A state-of-the-art personal computer can be assembled in just over four hours. An $18,000 car can be built in just 17 hours. Heck, even the average new home takes just 90 days to construct. Yet for some reason, it can take up to SIX MONTHS to order a wedding dress. Is something wrong with this picture?

We say, "yessirree, Bob." You spend weeks (if not a month or two) trying on dresses, only to have to hurry up and wait for your dress to come in. And wait and wait. Seasons come and go and still the dress is not ready.

Of course, designers and manufacturers tell us they must take this long in order to create the *perfect* dress. Besides, lining up all that child slave labor in Thailand isn't as easy as it looks. Just ask what's-her-name.

Perhaps the most frustrating part of this as a consumer is that, during that nice long wait, all sorts of nasty things can happen. Four to six months may be just a drop in the celestial time bucket, but it's like 17 decades in "retail" years. Salespeople come and go, managers come and go—heck, even entire shops come and go in that slim margin of time.

Hence, putting a deposit on a dress is like making a deposit at a bank, except there's no federal deposit insurance. You give them your hard earned money and they give you a piece of paper that *promises* you'll get a dress someday before you turn 65.

Unfortunately, Bertha's Bridal Shoppe Bank & Trust is slightly less stable than Chase Manhattan. As you'll read later in this chapter, there are a multitude of scams, rip-offs and just plain "things that can go wrong" when you special order a gown. Fortunately, most of these tragedies are preventable if you pay attention to the two key parts of special ordering a gown: following the paper trail and ordering the correct size.

The Paper Trail:
Getting all the details of your dress order in writing.

Throughout this book, you've probably noticed our nice admonishments to "get it in writing." At this point, you may be saying, "Okay Mr. & Mrs. Smarty Pants—exactly WHAT do I get in writing?"

We thought you'd never ask.

Notice the sample order contract we've printed below. Here are the basic items you should always get in writing, *before* you place your deposit down:

1 YOUR INFORMATION. Most bridal shops will ask for such basic information as your name, address and phone numbers (home and work).
Warning: If you don't want this information sold to other wedding merchants, make it clear to the shop.

2 THE DATES. Not only should the shop note today's date, but your "wedding date" should also appear on the order form. Should you tell the shop your real wedding date? The answer in most cases is "no." Most brides fudge the wedding date (moving it up from the real date) to make sure the gown arrives in time for alterations, etc. This is such a common practice that savvy bridal shops themselves may move up the date.

You'll notice a third date on the sample order contract: the "last acceptable date." Fill in this date if you need your dress to be in substantially earlier than your wedding date. For example, the

Bertha's
Bridal and Formal Shop

22703

CUSTOMER NAME Paulina Orr ❶

ADDRESS 34 Panorama Dr.

CITY & ZIP Risque, VT   TELEPHONE 843-2277

WEDDING DATE August 19, 1998   ORDER DATE 1/6/98

BRIDES NAME Same / Last Acceptable Date: 7/1/98 ❷

MEASURE	BUST 34"	WAIST 25"	HIPS 35"	HT. 5'11"	Hollow to Hem: 60"

MFG	STYLE	SIZE	XL	XS	COLOR	DESCRIPTION	PRICE
Fink	5114	8			Ivory	Shantung, gathered skirt w/ Flat front, tulip sleeves	$700.00
❸			Y			Extra length	70.00
			❹				❺
					Featured in Modern Bride Aug-Sept. "Fantasy" Ad	
					Promised Date of Delivery: April 27, 1998 (16 weeks)	❻

CHARGE FOR ALL ALTERATIONS ☑ $65 Estimate

I hereby agree that this C.O.D. sale is final and cannot be cancelled. All gowns are ordered in size supplied by customer or by measurements to the closest size available from each manufacturer. No returns or credits. Voluntary prepayments of balance may be made but are not required. Balances are required within 30 days of stores receipt of merchandise or at fitting appointment, whichever is earlier; at which time I may pick up the garment or authorize storage until my wearing date. No checks will be accepted within 2 weeks of delivery. No alterations will be performed until the balance is paid in full. Shop not responsible for dye-lots, goods left over 30 days or circumstances beyond our control. ❼

SUB TOTAL	770.00
SALES TAX	61.60
SERVICE CHARGE	—
TOTAL SALE	831.60
DEPOSIT	
CASH☐ CHECK☐ CHARGE☑	415.80
RECEIVED A/C	
CASH☐ CHECK☐ CHARGE☐	
BALANCE DUE	415.80

CUSTOMER SIGNATURE Paulina Orr
I AGREE TO MY MEASUREMENTS AS STATED AND THE SIZE ORDERED FOR ME.

SOLD BY R.O.

*Any returned check subject to a $25.00 service charge.

ALL SALES FINAL

KEY: *1. Your information. 2. Order dates. 3. Gown description. 4. Special requests (XL=extra length, XS=special size). 5. Price. 6. Delivery date. 7. Fine print.*

last acceptable date is helpful if you plan to have a bridal portrait taken before your wedding. Popular especially in the South, a bridal portrait is a formal picture of the bride that is displayed at the wedding reception. Most photographers need four to six weeks to do a bridal portrait. Now, those of you good with math will realize that means your gown has to be in and altered weeks before your real wedding date in order to do a bridal portrait.

Here's a sample of the schedule for an actual bride's dress in Dallas, Texas:

- ACTUAL WEDDING DATE: First weekend in September
- BRIDAL PORTRAIT: Late July
  (assuming a four to six week turnaround)
- ALTERATIONS TO BEGIN: Late June
  (assuming four weeks to complete)

So, we'd suggest a "last acceptable" date for the dress to get in as mid-June. That means you have to order the dress anytime from December of the previous year (six months) to March of this year (three months), depending on how long the designer takes to deliver the dress. And we'd highly recommend ordering that dress before Christmas. Why? The most popular time to get engaged is December 25th (followed by Valentines Day, for the curious). That means most bridal shops are especially crazy in January; try November and early December for fewer crowds.

Warning: Don't outsmart yourself by moving your wedding date up too far. If your pseudo wedding date is too soon, you may be hit with a rush charge. If your real wedding date is only three to six months away, you should probably tell the shop the actual date.

3 GOWN DESCRIPTION. We strongly recommend getting four key points in writing: the manufacturer's name, real style number for the dress, color and size.

Now, when we say the real style number we mean just that— no fake style number the shop uses to discourage price shopping. Another tip: don't forget to read the section later in this chapter on how to pick the right size for your bridal gown.

Selecting the color of your gown may be more complicated that just noting "white" or "ivory." Some designers are now offering styles in two colors, white with rum pink accents, for example. Since you can often get the dress all white (or ivory) or in a combination of colors, make sure this is clearly denoted on the order form. Be careful to use the words the designers use to describe their colors—some call ivory "natural," and so on. (See the designer by designer review for more info on this quirk).

Warning: Some shops refuse to give you the manufacturer's name and style number when you order a gown. Instead, they'll write something cryptic on your order form like "White gown, #88AG." This is dangerous for one simple reason: if the shop goes out of business or fails to deliver what they've promised, how can you prove what you ordered or track down the dress? The bottom line: if the shop balks at giving you this in writing, don't order the dress there. And as you walk out the door, remind them of the big sale they just kissed good-bye.

4 SPECIAL REQUESTS. Do you need extra length? A special size? A custom change? A rush cut? Make sure all these details are spelled out clearly.

Another key issue is fabric: some gown styles are offered in a choice of fabrics. Some designers also allow you to upgrade the fabric, from satin to silk, for example. As a precaution, you may want to have the fabric noted on the order form, even if you're sure the dress you want only comes in one fabric.

We should note that a few designers do "custom cuts," which means the dress will be made to your measurements. Hence, the order form will have to include your bust, waist, and hips measurements (as well as any other measurements the designer requests). Some shops will include these measurements on the order form whether or not you've ordered a custom cut.

Warning: Many special requests cost extra, so make sure these charges are clearly detailed. Another good idea is to have the shop write a description of your dress on the order form, especially if you've made a few changes to the gown.

5 PRICE. As we mentioned above, you should get a detailed breakdown of all the gown's charges. Ask for an alterations estimate as well (although this might be written on another form). Another alternative: get a written schedule of alteration charges from the shop.

Warning: Be sure you understand the shop's payment policies. Typically, you have to put down a 50% deposit upon ordering. The balance is due when the dress comes in, before the alterations begin. While it may be tempting to pay the balance in small monthly installments, we say resist this urge. That's because you may end up paying for the dress in full before you ever see it. As you'll read later, one bride in North Carolina was a victim of a scam when she pre-paid in full for her gown.

6 DELIVERY DATE. Yes, you should get in writing the date your dress will come in. Since some designers have a range of delivery dates (12-14 weeks, for example), you may have to accept an approximate range for this figure. It's better to get a specific date than a vague estimate of weeks.

Warning: This is a critical detail, since a top complaint we get from brides is late dresses. If the salesperson promises your dress by April but no one puts it in writing, who is to say what was promised when June rolls around and your dress still isn't in? If you're paying for a "rush cut," the shop may have to call the manufacturer in order to get a delivery date. Obviously, if you're paying extra to have the dress early, you'll want to get that date in writing.

THE FINE PRINT:
WATCH OUT FOR DISCLAIMERS

A t the bottom of the order form you get from the bridal shop, you might notice a smudge of ink. No, wait! It's no smudge—it's actually the fine print of your dress order. Grab your electron microscope and let's take a look at the typical "terms, conditions, and disclaimers" of your standard bridal gown order form:

❦ *"I agree to give the bridal shop my first-born child."* Ha! Just kidding. In most cases, bridal shops don't ask for your first-born child when ordering a dress. It just seems that way.

❦ *"I agree to the style, size, and color ordered."* If you're a petite bride, but the bridal shop says "Oh, honey, we should order you a size 14," then by signing the order form, you agree to that size. While that's an extreme example, we hear from brides all the time who feel the shop ordered too large a size for them (which resulted in pricey alterations). If there is any doubt as to what size you are (see later in this chapter for tips on this subject), then write "bridal shop recommends size" on the order form. This way you have some leverage in case of a problem down the road.

❦ *"No refunds, exchanges, cancellations or credits."* That's what it means. If you have the slightest hesitation about the gown or think you can't afford it, STOP! Don't order it. Once you sign this form, you've bought yourself a gown.

❦ *"Dye lots may vary."* What the heck does that mean? If you order an ivory dress, will you get a green gown? No, but you should be aware that "shade variations" can occur, meaning that an off-white dress may be a slightly different off-white when you get it in. Blame this problem on the crazy way the bridal industry works—samples are cut months in advance of the season. Several months later, the designer may have to use a different fabric supplier or contractor to make your gown. While most designers try to match the sample as much as possible, there may be minor changes in color or even the lace and detailing of the dress.

Ordering the Correct Size

On the surface, this seems like an easy task. You wear a size 8 dress, right? So, you just order that size in a bridal gown, right?

Wrong. As we'll explain below, it's more tricky than it looks. And while we do reprint the sizing charts of major bridal designers later in this book, it's important to follow the steps below to make sure you get the right size. That can mean the difference between a gown that fits close to perfect and one that needs extensive alterations.

Five Steps to Choosing the Right Gown Size

Step 1: Remember that bridal sizes don't correspond to real world sizes. For some sadistic reason, the bridal designers of Planet Earth have decided to make sure their dress sizes don't correspond to the sizes of the world's other apparel makers. We're not sure if there was some kind of a falling out between these two groups during the War of 1812, but there is one thing you can count on: your size in "street" clothes probably won't be the same as in a bridal gown.

If you happen to wear a size 8 dress in real world clothes, don't be surprised to look at the sizing charts of your favorite designer and discover you're now a 10. Or a 12. Or, gasp, a 14. Now, for understandable reasons, some brides can get darn emotional when told their official bridal dress size is several numbers larger than they otherwise wear. Don't take this as a sign it's time to diet. Just remember it's the bridal designers who are insane, not you.

Step 2: Don't pay attention to the sample gown. You try on a sample dress and it fits perfectly! So, you just order that size, right? Hold your silk shantung. Odds are the sample dress is NOT your real bridal size.

The reason is simple physics: sample dresses are just that, samples. They've been sampled, trampled, tried on, stepped on and worse. Since dresses are made of fabric and fabric tends to stretch over time, what once was a 10 may now be a 12 or even a 14.

This is a common mistake of lazy bridal salespeople. Instead of taking the time to measure you, the salesperson just recommends you order the sample size, since it fits so beautifully! Then the dress comes in and it doesn't fit so beautifully. And you get stuck with the alterations bill.

Step 3: Get measured with a vinyl tape measure. Why vinyl? The alternative is a cloth measuring tape. The problem with cloth is that it can stretch out and give inaccurate measurements over time. And a mistake of as little as an inch can throw you into a different size category.

Later in this section, we'll tell you what measurements a bridal shop should take before determining your size.

Step 4: *See the manufacturer's sizing chart.* As you've probably realized by now, each manufacturer has its own sizing chart. This is sent to local bridal shops. While you can use the sizing charts we've included in the back of this book, check to see if the shop has an updated size chart. Designers occasionally will make changes to their sizes and those changes may not be reflected in this edition of our book.

If you study the size charts of most manufacturers, you'll realize that this process is quite mystifying. Choose any three designers and the same bride can end up wearing three *different* sizes. For example, a bride with the measurements of 36, 26, 38 (bust, waist, hips) would be a size 8 in a Bianchi, a size 10 in Galina and a size 12 in Demetrios/Ilissa. According to a survey of 35 top manufacturers, this same bride would need to order a size 8 in 3% of the designers, a size 10 in 34% of the designers, a size 12 in 45% of the designers, or even a size 14 in 18% of the designers! Hello? Earth to the bridal designers! Wouldn't it make more sense to agree on a standard of sizing?

Just to confuse you more, we should note that there are actually *two* types of bridal sizing charts: body measurements and garment measurements. What's the difference? A designer who uses a body measurement sizing chart makes gowns to correspond to the actual physical measurements of the bride. On the other hand, a *garment* sizing chart is just that—a measurement of the outside of the dress.

How does this work in the real world? Well let's assume you have a 36" bustline. If a designer offers a size that has a 36" bustline and uses a body measurement sizing chart, you can fit into that dress. However, if the designer uses garment measurements and the dress measures 36" on the outside of the bustline, it'll be too tight and won't fit. In that case, you'd have to order the next largest size.

Crazy, eh?

In the designer reviews section of this book, we'll note whether a designer uses body or garment measurement sizing when this information is available.

Step 5: *Given your measurements, pick a size that closely matches your largest measurement.* Remember that gowns can only be altered in, not out. Make sure the size you pick is clearly marked on the sales receipt.

Brides encounter problems in this area when they let the shop pick the size for them. Instead of measuring you, they'll just guess what your size is (usually over-guessing). Other cases we've seen involve intentional fraud—the shop knowingly orders a size too large in order to make extra money on alterations. Be careful.

If you accept the shop's "advice," write on the receipt that "bridal shop recommends size." If the dress comes in way too big or too small, you have more leverage in negotiating a solution.

Here's a little test: let's assume you have the following measurements: 40 (bust), 29 (waist) and 38 (hips). Now, take a look at a portion of one bridal designer's measurement chart (from Jasmine):

	SIZE			
	10	12	14	16
BUST	36"	37.5	39	40.5
WAIST	26	27.5	29	30.5
HIPS	38	39.5	41	42.5
LENGTH	59.5	60	60	60

(also referred to as "hollow to hem")

So, what size should you order? Well, your hips will fit into a size 10. But wait! That waist needs a size 14. And the topper (pardon the pun) is the bustline, which requires a size 16. So the answer is: you should order a size 16. Yes, that means you'll have to take in the waist an inch and a half—and the hips in a whopping 4.5 inches. But remember that if you ordered the smaller sizes, you would have to let out the top, a near impossibility with most bridal gowns.

And remember that picking the right gown size is part art and part science. A body-hugging sheath gown may require a more exact hip measurement match than a loose-fitting gown with an empire waist. Also, don't forget the hollow to hem (or "length") measurement. If this bride's hollow to hem measurement exceeded 60 inches, she would need to order extra length.

More about Measurements

If you haven't ever made clothes of your own or had a seamstress make them, you may not be familiar with exactly which measurements correspond with what body parts. You may also not realize exactly what are the standard measurements required by the majority of bridal manufacturers and designers. There are three basic measurements every company requires: bust, waist and hips:

❧ **Bust:** This is NOT your bra size. This is the measurement around your chest at the fullest part of your breasts.
❧ **Waist (also know as "natural waist"):** Around the narrowest part of your stomach above your hips.
❧ **Hips:** As it sounds, this is the measurement at the fullest part of your hips. Find your hip bones and measure here.

Not always required, but helpful:

❦ **Hollow to Hem:** Find the hollow at the base of your throat. Then measure straight down to where you want the hem of the dress to fall. Be sure to wear shoes that are the same height as the shoes you will wear at your wedding or the measurement will be inaccurate. If the dress has a full skirt or requires a petticoat, don't forget to include this extra bulk in the measurement—try on a sample with the appropriate undergarments (slip, petticoat, etc.). Then measure the hollow to hem on an angle to allow for the fullness of the skirt,

Although many manufacturers do not show a hollow to hem measurement on their size charts, they may have a "standard" hollow to hem for all their dresses. This is about 58" (petites average around 54"). What if your hollow to hem is more than that figure? Well, additional length is often available (at a price, of course). However, some designers will only allow a maximum of six inches of extra length.

On the other hand, a few manufacturers don't offer extra length at all (at the time of this writing). These include Bianchi, Country Elegance, Eve of Milady, Forever Yours, Jessica McClintock, Jim Hjelm, Lili, and Mori Lee. If you're a tall woman, try not to fall in love with a gown that can't be lengthened.

Other measurements that may be required:

Although the above measurements are all most manufacturers ask for, some designers and custom dressmakers will require additional measurements:

❦ **Low Hip:** Measure 7 inches below the natural waistline. Alfred Angelo is one designer that requests this measurement instead of the standard hip measurement.

E-MAIL FROM THE REAL WORLD
Stick to your guns

Even if you specify an exact size on the gown order form, you can still fall victim to sizing scams. A bride in Vermont was a case in point. The bridal shop told her she was a size 8. The bride insisted they order her a size 6, which was written on the sales slip. When the gown arrived, guess what size it was? An 8—the shop the claimed the manufacturer sent that size based on the bride's measurements. The bride bought this story and was zapped for an additional $240 to cut the gown down to a size 6 (her true size).

What's wrong with this picture? Nearly all manufacturers never see your measurements, unless you pay extra for a "custom cut." Obviously, the shop intentionally ordered the larger size OR tried to pawn off an in-stock sample in size 8. The lesson? Don't accept a gown that arrives in the wrong size. You have a contract with the store to deliver a particular size—if they fail to fulfill their end of the deal, insist on a complete refund. ✍

❦ **Inside Sleeve Length:** Armpit to wrist measurement. This is more typically required when ordering long sleeve dresses.

❦ **Arm Girth:** Measure around the largest part of your upper arm. Once again, if you are ordering a dress with long sleeves, this may be useful to the designer or seamstress.

❦ **Back Shoulder Width:** Shoulder blade to shoulder blade measurement.

❦ **Waist to Hem:** Find your natural waist and measure straight down to the desired hem.

❦ **Center Back:** Base of the neck to natural waist.

Helpful Hint

Wearing the proper undergarments (bustier, bra, control top panties or hose, or whatever you plan to wear on your wedding day) and shoes with the appropriate heel height will ensure proper measurements.

It's a Tall Order:
The Best Gown Designers for Tall Brides

Okay, you're a "statuesque" bride. Well, the bridal industry has a surprise for you! If your hollow to hem measurement is more than 58" (the standard from a majority of bridal designers; see earlier in the chapter for information on this measurement), you will have to order extra length when special-ordering your gown. Here's the surprise: this can range from $40 to $150 or more! Some designers make you pay for a standard six inches of extra length, even if you only need an inch or two. Then you have to pay for extra alterations to shorten the extra long dress! What a rip-off.

There are two solutions to this problem. First, adjust your heel height. Don't wear two-inch heels if this puts you over the length limit—flats might just save you big bucks. If you can't avoid the height issue, consider some of the following manufacturers who have longer standard hollow to hem measurements:

DESIGNER	LENGTH (hollow to hem)*
Alfred Angelo	59" to 61"
Demetrios/Ilissa	60"
Jasmine	59" to 61.5"
Moonlight	58" to 60"
Venus	59"
Montique	58" to 60"
Victoria's	59"

* *Hollow to hem measurements that are given in a range of inches vary according to the dress size. See the designers individual size chart later in this book for details.*

Scams to Avoid

 ❖ The Wrong Dress at the Wrong Time.
"When I went to the bridal shop to pick up my dress, I was shocked to find it was the wrong color—I ordered a white gown, but the dress they said was mine was ivory. When I calmly pointed this out to the shop, they looked at me funny and said, 'Honey, this is your dress. We're not going to fix it.' Now my wedding is only two weeks away and I'm livid!"

It's sounds so simple—you try on a few sample dresses, pick out the one you want and then order it. And then it comes in perfect and you're happy. The only problem with this picture is that there isn't always a happy ending.

We're amazed at the never-ending stream of calls and letters we get from brides who tell a similar story: the dress they special ordered at great expense has come in and something is wrong. Perhaps it's the color, size or style that isn't what was promised. Or it's the wrong dress. Or the gown is damaged.

Now this wouldn't be a problem if you and your dress were in the real world. Then the shop would just fix the problem and you'd move on, one happy customer. But you may forget that this is the BRIDAL WORLD, where the standards of customers service often seem straight out of the Dark Ages.

We're consistently amazed (if not surprised) when we hear from a bride who's got a legitimate problem with a gown and then is victimized twice—first by the defective dress and then by a retail bridal shop that couldn't care less. Some shops can turn downright hostile when confronted with a problem dress. We heard of one bride who was threatened with arrest by the shop owner when the bride said she wouldn't accept a damaged dress.

What causes these problems in the first place? Well, in some cases it is the shop's fault—they ordered the wrong size/color/style from the manufacturer. Let's be honest: bridal shops are run by humans and sometimes they mess up an order. That would be fine if these shops fixed the problems.

Of course, there is another more common explanation: the manufacturer screwed up. Here the shop sent the designer a correct order, only to have the designer ship the wrong gown or a damaged one. Industry insiders tell us this happens because far too many manufacturers have non-existent quality control systems—dresses come in from (insert Third World country here) and then are given only a cursory review before being quickly shipped to the stores. While some designers are more careful than others, the problem of wrong/damaged goods is an epidemic in the bridal industry.

How many dresses come in flawed? One major retailer who sells 10,000 bridal gowns a year told us that, shockingly, two out of every three dresses comes in with a flaw. In about half of those cases, the problem is minor and can be easily fixed. However, the other half include such serious problems as the wrong size or poor workmanship. These must be sent back to the manufacturer to be corrected.

What if the designer balks at fixing the problem? The bridal shop is then left holding the bag with an angry customer. If there is enough time before the wedding, the designer can sometimes do a "rush cut" to get another dress. But it's a long way to China—and sometimes there isn't enough time. Then the well-known substance hits the electrical convenience.

If you're dealing with a good bridal shop, they should do everything in their power to fix the problem. This may involve cleanings, damage repair and other steps to make you happy—at their expense, not yours. Of course, if the dress is the wrong color or has some other unfixable defect, your options are simple: take the dress or go elsewhere to find another gown. In the latter case, the shop should give you back your deposit, no whining.

We wish more shops fell into the "good category." Unfortunately, we hear more about the bad ones. With these guys, you may have to get tough. After this section, we'll list some "self-defense" tips that can hopefully provide a solution without much bloodshed.

❖ WHOOPS! WE FORGOT TO PLACE THE ORDER.
"I was told my dress was to arrive in March. Well, March came and went and no dress. The bridal shop then promised it would arrive in April. Then May. Then June. Now, it's July and my wedding is only three weeks away and there is no dress! Help!"

That's a true story from a recent caller to our office. She was given the royal run-around from the shop, which finally admitted that "they FORGOT to place the order." Whoops! Sorry! The shop suggested the bride buy a dress from their used sample stock. The bride said "no thanks" and called her attorney.

In the legal world, what the shop did is called "breach of contract." In the real world, it's called "you're stuck." Even if you have a written agreement with the shop that says they will order X dress by Y date, if they decide to break their end of the deal, there is little you can do. Sure, you can hire an attorney to send them threatening letters, but this is costly and probably won't get you a dress. The best you can hope for is to get your deposit back (an easy task if you placed it on a credit card; much more difficult if it was by cash or check).

This type of bridal fraud comes in two flavors: shops that never place the order (like the above example) and those shops that *hold* orders. In the latter case, the shop knows your wedding is really not until August, so why get you that dress in March? What do you need if for that early anyway?

Instead of immediately placing your dress order with the manufacturer, the shop holds on to it. Why? Well, financially-strapped stores may be tempted to use your money to pay other bills—ordering the gown immediately means having to pay the invoice that much faster. How common is this problem? Even Vincent Piccione, president of Alfred Angelo, recently acknowledged how widespread the tactic is. "A major problem that concerns us is retailers who hold on to orders. This is one practice that should be eliminated, thereby putting an end to the root cause of so many horror stories that plague the industry," Piccione said in an industry trade journal.

A parallel scam is the "involuntary lay-away" rip-off. In this case, the bridal shop claims it will take much longer than reality to get in a special-order dress. Most designers fill orders within three or four months, with six being the maximum. Yet, some of our readers report shops who claim it will take *eight or ten months* to get in their dress. What's happening? It's the same as the above rip-off. Perhaps the shop is using your money to pay their electric bill or other expenses—and plans to order your dress a few months down the line. In a sense, this is like an "involuntary lay-away" plan, where the shop holds your money for several months longer than necessary.

Be suspicious of retailers who claim they need more than six months to deliver a bridal gown. Also, stay on top of the situation. If your dress is due March 1, don't wait until late April to call the shop to see what's up.

❖ THAT DIET REALLY WORKED! SIZING RIP-OFFS

"I'm a size 10 but the bridal shop suggested I order a size 14! When the dress came in, it was like I was on some miracle diet— the gown was so huge, I swam in it. All this would be funny, except the shop now wants to charge me $200 to cut the gown down. Is this fair? It was the shop that recommended the wrong size in the first place!"

No, it isn't fair, but it happens all the time. Sometimes it seems like an innocent mistake . . . until you receive the bill for alterations.

Why do sizing mistakes happen? Well, there are several reasons, ranging from simple errors to outright fraud. Let's be honest: sometimes shops goof and order the wrong size, perhaps by misreading the size chart. Inexperienced salespeople may suggest you just order the sample gown size, if it fits. As we explained earlier, this is a big mistake—that's because samples stretch out from all those try-ons. Hence, what once was a 10 may now be a 12 or 14. This mistake can be a big screw-up; that's because you may very well end up ordering a dress that's too small. While it's possible to take a dress *in* (making it smaller), it's darn difficult to expand a gown without major surgery. And the result may not look anything like you imagined.

E-MAIL FROM THE REAL WORLD
Installment plans can backfire

This recent bride had an interesting twist on the Sample Shell Game. Here's the story, as told by her groom.

 "My wife ordered her dress in November from a shop in North Carolina and made payments from November until early April. But alas! The company who manufactured the dress went out of business in December. However, the shop never bothered to tell us, even as we continued to make payments. Their solution was to give her a sample dress at a 20% discount. But the dress didn't fit, so after all the alterations there was only a $17.00 difference. They refused to give us a cash refund, only an in-store credit! What the hell are you going to get at a bridal shop for $17.00!

"The worst part was their attitude. It was as if *we* had done something wrong. The owners' son was insulting and rude. Finally, my sister, who is an attorney, had to go down there and get tough with them."

Let's take a look at the above story to see what the bride and groom could have done to protect themselves. First, never pay in full for a dress before receiving it. While it may be convenient to make small monthly payments, you lose critical leverage if you put more than 50% down (the standard deposit for special-order dresses).

Second, the bride should have called the manufacturer to see if the shop was telling the truth. Most gown designers put their phone numbers in their ads; we also print the phone numbers to most of the major dress manufacturers later in this book. (If you still can't find the number, call our office; see the "How to Reach Us" page at the back of this book).

Even if the shop was telling the truth, we would never have accepted the used sample gown at just a 20% discount, and then paid for alterations. The shop had a contractual obligation to get the bride a new dress in the correct size. By failing to do so, the bride could dispute the charge(s) made on her credit card (if she used a card for the payments).

What if she paid cash? Well, the options are more limited, that's for sure. She could sue the shop in Small Claims Court if she's documented the order and problem well. She could also complain to her state attorney general's office, the county district attorney and the Better Business Bureau. What are the odds she'd get justice? Slim, but we'd never accept the solution first presented by the shop. By turning up the heat on the shop (perhaps calling a local TV consumer reporter), she could have received a better resolution. ✍

Some dishonest bridal shops may intentionally oversize a gown (recommending too large a size) in order to profit on alterations. Now this might seem counter-productive, since as you'll read in the next chapter, bridal shops claim they *lose* money on gown alterations. Nevertheless, it seems suspicious to us that the shop that recommends too large a size ends up tacking on big alteration fees. The worst example of this rip-off we heard about was a Dallas bride who ordered a $3000 gown. When the shop recommended the wrong size (two sizes too big), the bride was informed the gown could be cut down—for a $1000 alteration charge.

Of course, there is another explanation for a gown that shows up in the wrong size: the manufacturer. Yes, designers sometimes blow it and ship the wrong size. Some will even put the right size label on the wrong gown—the only way you can spot this problem is to compare the gown's dimensions to the manufacturer's sizing chart. While one would hope that if this happens the shop will send back the gown and the manufacturer will happily ship the correct size, it isn't always smooth sailing. You may have to fight with the shop (or the shop may have to go to bat for you) to fix the problem.

Protect yourself by using the four-step process we mentioned earlier in this chapter. Consumers who take a proactive role in picking their gown size can eliminate most of these rip-offs. If a shop refuses to show you the manufacturer's sizing chart, don't order the gown from them. If you decide to ignore this advice and order it anyway, write on the order form "shop recommends size."

❖ THE SAMPLE SHELL GAME
"I waited over five months for my special-order gown to come in. Yet, when it arrived, the dress looked suspiciously like the sample I first tried on. Have I been scammed?"

Welcome to the Sample Shell Game. So, you thought you ordered a brand new wedding dress? Well, have we got a surprise for you! Instead of delivering you a new gown, your bridal shop has decided to try to pawn off the used sample dress you originally tried on!

This increasingly common scam among dishonest bridal shop owners has been reported to us by brides nationwide. Although it seems rampant at some shops in Chicago and Detroit, it can happen anywhere.

Why would a bridal shop do this? Well, as we mentioned earlier, some retailers are overloaded by sample inventory. Trying to pass off an old gown as a new one solves two problems—first, they get rid of a dress that's been hanging around too long and second, they don't have to use any cash to order a new gown.

Some bridal shops are more savvy scamsters than others.

We've heard of shops that first try to clean up the sample before presenting it to the unsuspecting bride. In other cases, retailers aren't that smart, attempting to pass off an obviously tried-on, damaged and dirty dress as a new one. One bride who called us even told us a more ridiculous story—her shop tried to give her an entirely different gown than the one she ordered!

Of course, at about the time that the Sample Shell Game starts, something miraculous happens—the original sample gown you tried on mysteriously disappears from the shop. That way, you can't try on that gown to compare it to the not-quite-right "new" dress.

Here are some rather ingenious ways to spot this rip-off, as submitted by our readers. First, take a needle and red thread with you to the bridal shop. While you're in the dressing room, sew this thread inside the sample dress in an inconspicuous location. If the shop tries the scam, you can spot the used "sample" by the thread.

Another protection is to take a picture of the gown. But most shops don't allow pictures, you say. Sneak a small camera in your purse and snap a few pictures in the dressing room, after the salesperson leaves. The pictures will help you remember all the details and styling of the sample dress—just in case the shop tries to substitute that used sample or a different gown altogether. One bridal shop employee tipped us off to this scam, saying they often substituted cheaper dresses since the customer could never remember what she ordered several months ago!

❖ STORAGE FROM HELL
"My wedding is not until next year, so I asked the bridal shop if they could store my gown. Without any warning, the shop suddenly closed and now my gown is held hostage! The landlord has padlocked the doors and I can't get my fully-paid-for dress!"

Sure, it's tempting to leave a gown at a bridal shop until your wedding. It looks like a safe place, right? Wrong. Just about anything can go wrong, including all manner of disaster both by nature (floods, earthquakes) and man-made (fires, an employee who accidentally spills something on your dress, etc.). Bridal shops aren't Fort Knox either. We've heard of gowns that were stolen, damaged or destroyed in an arson fire. While you hope the shop has insurance, that's a big leap of faith.

While not as catastrophic as a fire, surprise storage charges can be bothersome as well. We received one letter from a bride in Oregon who was charged a $20 per month fee to keep her gown at the bridal shop. Somehow, the shop neglected to mention this to the bride and demanded payment for six months storage before releasing the dress.

Of course, the biggest nightmare is the shop that suddenly disappears or closes down. If the shop goes out of business between now and your wedding, you could be stuck—most shops have leases that let landlords seize the premises and inventory (read: your dress) in case of default. The bottom line: when your dress comes in, take it home. That rule applies even if you plan to do alterations later; you can always take it back to the shop at that point. Later in this book, we'll pass along some tips on how to store a bridal gown at your home.

❖ COUNTERFEIT GOWNS

"When my dress came in, I couldn't believe my eyes! The gown was poorly sewn, the lace was falling off and the fabric seemed different from the sample. Then I noticed there was no designer tag. What happened? What should I do?"

The shop seemed so nice. The salespeople were friendly . . . and the price was right. You tried on a designer gown, asked all the right questions and then waited patiently for four months for the gown to come in. Then, the excitement of seeing the dress for the first time fades quicker than a flash of lightning. This can't be *your* dress. It's as if the gown was a cheap knock-off of the real thing.

And that's exactly what might have happened—you got a counterfeit gown.

It's an increasing problem in the bridal business: shops that promise designer originals, but then deliver cheap knock-offs that are sewn in back-room sweatshops. What's in it for the shop? Well, they can produce these gowns more cheaply and sell them for a premium price, producing more profits than the legitimate way of doing business.

And spotting these knock-offs might be harder than you think. First of all, how well can you remember the sample dress you tried on four, five or even six months ago? And some brides seem blind to the obvious defects of a knock-off gowns; just like a parent of a not-so-cute newborn baby, they may think their dress is the most beautiful gown in the world.

But what about the designer label? The obvious tip-off to a knock-off dress is a missing tag or label. Yet even this piece of advice can be difficult to follow—some designers intentionally leave tags with their names out of dresses (see box below for more information on how to deal with this problem).

What can be done if this happens to you? If you have any doubts about the dresses' authenticity, ask the shop to provide proof it ordered the gown from the designer—an invoice, packing list or other shipping documents. Most counterfeiters don't think you'd ever ask for such documentation, so it's doubtful they've thought up an excuse for this.

If the shop refuses to prove the authenticity of the dress and still claims the dress is a designer original, then things might get ugly. First, refuse to accept the dress and don't pay the balance. In order get back your deposit, you may have to contact your credit card company immediately (if you paid by credit card, of course).

Can you call the designer directly to report a counterfeit operation? Yes, but don't expect an outpouring of sympathy from them. Most seem inherently suspicious of brides for some strange reason. If the shop is an authorized dealer of the manufacturer, you might ask the designer to check their records to make sure they actually shipped a gown to them. Whether they would cooperate at this point is debatable, however.

The Incognito Bridal Designers

You spend good money for a "designer original" gown, but then the dress arrives and there's no designer tag. How can you tell if you've received the real thing or a cheap knock-off?

Unfortunately, this process can be made more difficult by designers who leave their name tags out of their dresses. Isn't that illegal, you ask? Yes, but the designers get away with it by exploiting a loophole in the federal labeling law (called the Federal Textile Identification Act): instead of putting their name in the dress, they can just put in a tag with their "registered number" (RN). This obscure unique number (which is assigned to every apparel maker who sells goods in the U.S.) is then kept on file with the Federal Trade Commission.

Why would designers do this? Don't they want you to be a proud owner of their name-brand garment? There is one main answer: unions or the fear thereof. The garment industry (and, yes bridal apparel is included) is heavily unionized. In order to lower their costs, some designers will secretly use non-union labor to sew their gowns. In order not to raise the suspicions of the unions, the designers "omit" their names from such garments. One famous bridesmaids dress designer puts its name in some dresses, but not others. Guess which are made by the union?

Another reason designers don't put name tags in their gowns is fear of counterfeits. During the busy season, the designer may use an outside contractor to handle the overflow. If that contractor also handles work for other manufacturers, the designer may fear being copied by the competition. Since there is little trust in these arrangements, the designer usually doesn't permit the temporary contractor to use their name tags.

Complicating this matter are some designers that only use "hang tags." Instead of sewing a label into the gown, they'll attach a "hang tag" with their name or logo to the dress. Since this tag is only attached to the dress by a thread or safety pin, it may come loose in shipping and get discarded in the box.

Still other designers will put only a style number in their gowns. That's why it's important to get this true number when ordering your gown—without the designer sewn-in tag or hang-tag, it will be your only reference number to confirm the authenticity of the gown.

In the designer section of this book, we'll note how most designers mark their gowns (sewn in label, hang tag, both or none).

Self Defense

 While thousands of brides special order gowns each year without any trouble, it's important to take simple steps to protect yourself. There's no Federal Department of Bridal Regulation—it's left up to you to protect yourself and your money in this transaction.

And what if something goes wrong? While some problems are not intentional, a frustrating situation can be made worse by a bridal shop that just doesn't care about you as a customer. While reputable shops take care of their brides, far too many others may want to fight you, for whatever bizarre reason. What are the best ways to solve the problem without resorting to sending your cousin Vinny to visit the bridal shop owner late at night? Here are some basic tips:

1 Remember the golden rule of bridal: She who holds the gold, makes the rules. The more you control the money (your dress deposit and final payment), the better off you'll be. Hence, don't put down more than the 50% deposit, so there's more at risk for the merchant if they screw up. Never pay the balance until you are satisfied with the gown. And put that deposit and final payment on a credit card—bridal shop owners can suddenly become much more accommodating when you casually mention you might dispute the charge. This action on your part will instantly zap the money out of the shop's bank account. If one presumes that dishonest bridal shops are motivated by anything, it will the smell of money that just flew away.

2 Get it in writing. Okay, we've said it before, but we'll say it again. When we hear from a bride that's fighting with a shop about a late gown or a dress that isn't right, one common mistake that's made over and over again is the lack of written evidence. Just when is that dress suppose to come in? Which salesperson promised you free alterations? It's hard enough to remember what you had for dinner last night, much less what was said 20 weeks ago by a salesperson who's now gone on to other career opportunities.

3 Go to the top. If a problem happens, don't waste your time with a sales clerk or cashier—go straight to the top. Ask to speak with the store manager or owner. Sometimes this person may be hidden behind a wall of protective employees and it may take some effort to talk with her. Keep trying.

4 Document the dispute in writing. If you've got a sinking feeling that the bridal shop is going to fight you on that dress that's damaged, the wrong size or (insert other problem here), you need to create a paper trail. Keep a log of phone conversa-

tions (who you spoke to, what was said, etc.). If phone calls get you nowhere, send the shop owner/manager a letter that nicely asks them to fix the problem. If that doesn't work, send a more strongly-worded letter that sets a deadline (say, seven days to fix the problem). These letters will be important evidence if you have to dispute the charge on your credit card—most card companies want you to show you tried to solve the problem first before you resorted to a reversal of the credit card bill.

5 LEAVE A BUFFER ZONE. The worst situation you can be in is trying to solve a problem with your bridal gown while the clock is ticking away toward an impending wedding. The specter of this deadline gives dishonest retailers more leverage over the bride—they know you might have to accept their sorry sample gown because your wedding is next week. The best way to avoid this pressure is to leave a buffer zone. Order your wedding dress at least six to nine months before your wedding (a year is fine, too). Then if a problem develops, you won't be racing the clock to fix it.

6 DON'T LOOK TO THE GOWN'S DESIGNER FOR HELP. Yes, we print the phone numbers of the major bridal designers in the back of this book. Does that mean you can call them if a problem develops with your dress? Are you kidding? The sad fact is that brides can't look to the majority of dress manufacturers for help with a dispute with a bridal shop. Most refuse to get involved. Others will scream at you on the phone. And those are the nice designers.

What happens if the shop goes out of business entirely? We'll look at that nightmare next.

What happens if your bridal shop disappears?

It's the ultimate dress nightmare: you flip on the evening news and the top story is about a bridal shop that has gone bankrupt, leaving an angry mob of jilted brides sans dresses. Then you realize that's *your* shop.

While no one has exact figures on how many bridal shops go out of business each year, the anecdotal evidence suggests the number is staggering. The simple fact is that the bridal business is brutal and the turnover rate among shops is high.

Take for example the city in which we started our research of the wedding business: Austin, Texas. In 1988, this mid-size city had 17 full-service bridal shops. In 1996, only two of those have survived. That's right—the other 15 went to bridal shop heaven. While some closed "responsibly" (they stopped taking special orders and referred their existing customers to other shops to get their dresses), we estimate that three-quarters of the shops that closed did not. That means they just shut down, taking with them the deposits of brides who would never see their gowns.

And that's just one example. In 1995, major bridal shop bankruptcies occurred in New York, Virginia and California. And these weren't always mom-and-pop shops. One regional chain of six stores closed in a hail of bad publicity; one bridal shop owner in Michigan actually drew a jail sentence when a court determined he and his wife bilked customers out of tens of thousands of dollars (this is a rarity—most bankrupt bridal retailers are never prosecuted).

So, what can you do? Here are some tips if you've discovered your trusted bridal dress shop has gone Chapter 11:

❦ **Avoid the surprise.** If you can, keep tabs on the shop to make sure it's still in business. Drive by once a month or give them a call to make sure they're still breathing on the other end of the line. While most shops won't announce that they plan to close forever next Tuesday, we have heard of cases where employees have tipped off brides to an impending disaster.

❦ **Time is of the essence.** If there is a problem, you'll need to take immediate steps to protect your deposit and get your dress.

❦ **Beware of confusing press accounts.** Some bridal shop owners have put out conflicting statements to the media when they have financial problems. At the outset, they usually promise that everyone is going to get their gowns—despite the fact that their landlord has pad-locked their doors and the electric company has cut off the power for non-payment. Don't get sucked into these false hopes— most bridal shops that have financial problems don't rescue themselves. They usually just go bankrupt and close forever.

❦ **Draw up a contingency plan.** If there is time before your wedding (say, at least four months), you may be able to order another gown. If there isn't time, scout out the alternatives: you can buy a consignment gown, have a sample altered to fit, or hit the off-the-rack warehouses mentioned earlier in this book. The best advice is to have a "plan B."

❦ **Contact your credit card company immediately.** You did put that dress deposit on a credit card, right? Well, if you did, it's time to test that federal law that protects credit card purchases. Most banks and credit card issuers will request a written account of what's happened with your dress deposit. Since there may be a time limit on this process, you should do this as soon as possible.

❦ **What about the designer?** Can't you just call up the designer and have them ship your special-order dress to another shop? Fat chance. The sad fact is that most designers turn a deaf ear to brides. That's what's happened over and over again in the past few years when bridal bankruptcies rolled over the industry. Frantic brides who called the designers about their orders were simply referred to other retail stores . . . who were happy to *sell* the bride another gown. At full retail. While there were exceptions to this rule (Bill Levkoff should be given the Bridal Nobel Prize; they worked overtime to get stranded brides their dresses at no additional cost), the rest of the bridal industry should be ashamed of themselves. The designers set up this crazy special-order system to begin with. They buy expensive ads to convince brides to patronize their "authorized dealers." Then when those shops fail, the bridal designers simply shrug their shoulders and say "Whoops! It's not our problem." And then the bridal industry wonders why brides are running for the exits, abandoning the special-order process for bridal gowns?

ALTERATIONS

Getting your gown to fit just right

How much do bridal gown alterations cost? What are the five most common alterations? You'll learn these answers, plus how to spot four rip-offs. Next, we'll discuss some basic self-defense strategies, how to find an independent seamstress and more.

HERE'S A QUICK QUIZ. Name the three most secure jobs in America. Go ahead, we'll wait right here for a few moments . . . Okay, pencils down. What did you come up with? Here's our list:

1. Tax collector
2. Airline baggage complaint officer.
3. Bridal shop seamstress.

Thanks to the world's bridal dress designers, the future employment of bridal seamstresses is virtually guaranteed. For some insane reason, the gown manufacturers have decided to make dresses for women who are 5' 9" tall. What? You're not exactly that height? Well, then that's too bad. Looks like you'll have to have your gown altered.

The average bridal gown is about 58" long (measured from "hollow to hem," as we explained in an earlier chapter). And it doesn't matter whether you are a size 4, 6 or 8—the dress still comes in that same length with most designers. Hence, even if you exactly match the designer's size chart for bust, waist and hip measurements, you'll still be hit with alteration charges to shorten the gown.

And what if you're taller than 5'9"? Well, you won't escape the needle either. Most designers force tall brides to order extra length. And you can't order just the amount you need. Nope, you'll have to get the standard six inches of extra length even if an inch or two would be enough.

So, as you can see, it's almost a given that your bridal gown will need to be altered. Let's start off with the three biggest misconceptions about this process.

Three Biggest Myths About Dress Alterations

 Myth #1 "When I ordered my gown from a local bridal shop, the salesperson took careful measurements which she included on the order form. I guess this means the dress will be custom-made to fit me, right?"

Wrong. It's perhaps the biggest misconception about ordering a bridal gown—that the dress is being made to your measurements. This false impression is fed by erroneous information that appears in bridal magazines. Just check out this quote that appeared in a recent wedding issue of *Martha Stewart Living* : "Sample (dresses) allow a bride to select a designer and a style; each dress is then custom-made to fit the bride."

Earth to Martha! Let's go over this slowly: dresses are NOT custom-made to fit each bride. When a bridal shop takes your measurements, they're only comparing these to the manufacturer's sizing chart. In the end, you get a 6, 8 or whatever size that is *closest* to your measurements. And "close" is the operative word. Often, close means you're still off a couple of inches here and another inch there.

For example, let's say you want to order a Mori Lee gown. Your measurements are 37" bust, 25.5" waist and 36" hips. A quick glance at the Mori Lee chart (reprinted later in this book) reveals that you should order a size 12 (the 37" bust will correspond exactly to that size). However, according to the size chart, the dress would be two inches too large in the waist and 2.5 inches in the hips. The bottom line: it's alteration time!

Why don't manufacturers custom make dresses? The answer is cost. In order to keep prices down, nearly all bridal gowns are mass-produced in batches. The designer waits until it receives a certain number of size 12 orders and then fires up the production line. Large stacks of fabric are loaded onto cutting machines, which use lasers to slice up a batch of size 12's. Other machines bead lace and attach elements like sleeves, decorative trim and the like.

Of course, we should note that a very few couture (read: expensive) designers do "custom cuts," where the dress is actually made to your measurements. Perhaps these are the places where Martha Stewart shops. But it will be helpful to have Martha's bank account when you order such a dress—most are $2000 or more.

 Myth #2 "Help! I'm no sewing expert, but I couldn't help but notice several obvious flaws with my wedding dress. I thought the bridal shop would have caught these problems and corrected them."

A word to the wise: don't assume anything. You'd think the folks who own shops that sell bridal gowns would know how to sew, right? Wrong. One of the most surprising facts we discovered in our research was the number of bridal shop owners who have no clue how to sew! Since 95% of all bridal gowns needs some type of alteration, you'd think this would be a given. Is it any wonder then that dresses that arrive with flaws are never spotted or corrected? How can bridal shop owners hire competent seamstresses if they aren't familiar with sewing basics to begin with? Later in this chapter, we'll go over several tips you can use to protect yourself and your gown.

 Myth #3 "My bridal gown needed some basic alterations. I assume I have to use the bridal shop's alteration department, right? Aren't they specialists in handling these types of alterations?"

Unfortunately, some stores act like there's some kind of federal law that says *they* must do your dress alterations. One look at the prices some shops charge and you can begin to understand why there's pressure to do the alterations "in-house."

Even more troubling are the reports we get from brides who say their dress alterations were botched. Blame it on an inexperienced or careless seamstress—and a bridal shop that doesn't supervise their workers.

How can you protect yourself? First, check out the qualifications of the in-store seamstress. Find out how long she's been altering wedding gowns. Ask for and check references. Finally, ask to see work-in-progress—the work area should be clean and well-organized.

While the convenience of in-store alterations can be tempting for busy brides, consider the alternative of using someone else. An independent seamstress with years of experience may do a better job. And the price may be less than the bridal shop with all its fancy overhead. You can often get a referral to a bridal seamstress from local fabric shops. Or call your local Discount Bridal Service representative for a referral. We mentioned DBS earlier in our money-saving tips chapter; call (800) 874-8794 to find a dealer near you.

The bottom line: don't be pressured into using the bridal shop's in-house seamstress. Check out their qualifications carefully and, if you detect a problem, go elsewhere.

How Much Will it Cost?

The average bridal gown will require $75 to $100 in alterations. Start making significant changes, however, and the bill can soar to two or three times that amount. On the other hand, if all your dress needs is a simple hem and you comparison shop for alteration services, you might spend $50 or less.

The Five Most Common Bridal Alterations

Here's a break-down of the top five bridal gown alterations:

1 **Hem.** As we noted earlier in this chapter, it's almost a given that your dress will need to be shortened. Now this may sound simple, but the way a gown is constructed can complicate matters. For example, a dress with extensive lace on the hemline cannot be easily hemmed from the bottom. Instead, the skirt will need to be shortened from the waist. How? The seamstress will separate the bodice and skirt, pull *up* the skirt, and then re-attach the bodice. The hem is never touched. Another note: dresses that are lined require a "two-layer" hem, which shortens not only the dress, but also the lining.

2 **Side seams.** In order to make the bodice fit comfortably (with .25 to .50 inches of give on either side), the side seams are taken in.

3 **Bustle.** Love that long train, but you also want to dance the night away at the reception? Since you probably don't want to carry that train over your arm all night, most brides will have their train "bustled." This is done by sewing a series of hidden buttons and loops on the train and back of the dress. After the ceremony, the train is then gathered to the waist and secured with the buttons. This "bustle" lets the train fall to the floor, without dragging it's entire length. (Of course, if you choose a gown with a detachable train or no train at all, you can skip this expense).

4 **Sleeve adjustments.** This alteration is common with long-sleeve gowns. Most dress designers leave extra sleeve length so they may be adjusted to perfectly fit the bride. Of course, this alteration can be tricky (read: expensive) if the amount of decoration (lace, beading, appliqués) on the sleeves requires significant labor to remove and then replace. In addition to sleeve length, you may need to adjust sleeve width either at the top or bottom of the sleeve.

5 **Shoulder alterations.** If you have a long waist, the shoulders on your dress may have to raised to give you more room. Other minor alterations to the shoulders may be required depending on the style of the dress.

So, how much is this going to cost you? According to a 1994 survey by *Vows* magazine (an industry trade journal), the price for two of these alterations varied widely, depending on where the shop was. Here's a sample of what shops in five different states charge:

	FL	MN	TX	CO	NH
Hem *(two-layer)*	$45	$55	$35	$50	$35
Side seams	$22	$15	$15	$25	$15

Note: Shops had different methods of determining the cost of a train bustle. Some charge a flat $30 or $40 fee. Others charged by the number of loops/buttons needed (for example, $6 per loop).

For Further Reading

How to Alter a Bridal Gown by Susan Ormond ($15.95, 132 pages, Emrick Enterprises) is an excellent guide to bridal gown alterations. With over 15 years in bridal apparel alterations and custom design, the author gives readers step-by-step instructions for the five most common alterations and several more "special problems." Whether you plan to do your own alterations or just want to know more about this process, this book is a must read. To order, send $15.95 plus $3 shipping to Emrick Enterprises, 6008 Spruce Mill Dr., Yardley, PA 19067.

Can a wedding dress be "let out?"

What if your gown arrives in and it's too tight? Can a bridal gown be let out?

As we noted earlier in this book, the general rule of thumb is to order a gown that's slightly larger than your measurements. Why? It's easier to make a gown smaller (that is, take it in) than the opposite direction. Of course, there are exceptions to this rule. Some designers actually leave room in the seams to enable a gown to be taken out.

What if there isn't any extra fabric? Well, the only solution then is to make a "gusset," a piece of fabric inserted into the dress to give extra room. If that sounds complex, it is—only skilled seamstresses should attempt this alteration. A gusset may change the way a dress looks, sometimes for the worse.

In the end, it's always safer to order a gown slightly larger than your measurements. A professional bridal shop may know which designers have extra room in their dress seams, but that's taking quite a chance.

Scams to Avoid

❖ FREE ALTERATIONS DEALS.
"A local bridal shop offered me what looked like a great deal: free alterations! They said this would save me a hundred dollars or more on my dress. But then I shopped around and discovered the shop had inflated the price of the dress to begin with!"

There's no such thing as a free lunch. While shops occasionally discount dresses, it's extremely rare to find free alterations even on a limited time or promotional basis. Because alterations require a great deal of time (and seamstresses don't work for free), the cost of providing free alterations has to be covered somehow—unscrupulous shops may mark dresses over retail to make up the difference.

A Louisiana bride fell victim to a variation on this scam. She traveled to an off-price bridal store in Houston that offered special-order dresses at incredible discounts. One particular dress caught her eye, but wasn't quite right. "No problem," the salesperson said when asked whether small changes could be made to the gown. The bride alleges that the salesperson said the alterations and changes would be included in the price of the gown.

Guess what happened next? When the bride picked up the dress, she was informed that the changes would be extra. And, to top it off, the discount shop didn't even have an in-house alterations department—the bride was on her own to find a seamstress.

This is a good lesson for all brides: make sure you get any promises about alterations or changes to your dress in writing. Don't let a salesperson make vague verbal promises. Some of these folks are smooth talkers who'll say anything to make a sale. Always get a written quote or list of alteration charges.

❖ INEXPERIENCED SEAMSTRESSES WHO BOTCH ALTERATIONS.
"My dress is a complete disaster! The shop promised they could do a list of simple alterations—shortening the sleeves, adding some lace to the train and so on. After my second fitting, however, it was obvious they didn't know what they were doing! Now I'm stuck with a dress that looks like a bad experiment from a junior high sewing class! Help!"

Bad alterations can ruin your whole day. Don't make a snap decision when hiring a seamstress to do even "simple" changes to your dress. Look for red flags when you talk with a bridal shop's in-house seamstress—a messy work area, late appointments, a seamstress who simply isn't listening to you, etc.

❖ THE MORE EXPENSIVE THE GOWN, THE MORE THE ALTERATIONS.
"The bridal shop's alterations flyer said a simple hem is $45.
Yet, when I ordered my gown, they quoted me an $80 figure for
the hem alteration. The shop owner said my $1800 silk gown
was more 'complicated' to alter. Is this true?"

We doubt it. Here's a not-so-shocking fact from the bridal business: a recent survey of bridal shops revealed that the more expensive a gown, the more they charge the bride to alter it. Why, you might ask? Do these pricey gowns fit badly? Are the expensive dresses so poorly constructed they need extensive alterations and repairs?

Please. The answer is simple: greed. Some bridal shop owners think that if you can afford $1000, $1500 or even $2000 for a dress, then you certainly can afford to pay more than the going rate for alterations.

An article on this very subject in *Vows*, an industry newsletter, confirmed this practice: "Generally shops that have a higher price point (for gowns) charge more for alterations," it said. "These more expensive dresses are not more difficult to alter, nor do they fit badly. It's a matter of what the market will bear."

To prove the point, a survey of 130 bridal shops in the same article revealed dresses that cost $500-$700 required an average of $52 in alterations. However, gowns that were in the $700-$900 range racked up $67.05 in alterations—a 28% difference. (And those average alteration figures were from 1991; prices are certainly higher today).

The worst story we ever heard about this practice was from a bride in Dallas, Texas. Her $3000 gown came in and the bridal shop told her it would require $1000 in alterations! And this wasn't for any extensive dress surgery; just the normal nips and tucks.

Frankly, there's no excuse for price-gouging. Since most alterations departments at bridal shops are at best a break-even operation (at least that's what they claim), it must be tempting to sock well-healed brides with extra charges. As for self-defense, it probably goes without saying that brides who plan to purchase an expensive gown (that is, over $1000) should probably get competitive bids on alterations from one or two outside seamstresses. It may even be possible to negotiate with the bridal shop. While you won't probably talk them down much, a little savings may make it worth the effort.

❖ WE'RE NOT RESPONSIBLE FOR YOUR PROBLEMS!
"The seamstress at my bridal shop totally screwed up my alter-
ations. When I complained to the shop owner about the problem,
they told me the seamstress was an 'independent contractor' and
they weren't responsible for the problem. At first, the shop refused
to fix the dress and then later said they'd correct it, but it would
cost me extra money!"

Some bridal shops subcontract out their alterations services to third-party companies as a way to save money. These "independent operators" hire seamstresses, fit brides and do all the work. In some cases, they may even rent space from the bridal shop or share a common building. As a result of these cozy relationships, it may be difficult to tell whether the alterations are done in-house (by a bridal shop employee) or run by an outside contractor.

What happens when something goes wrong? That's where the problems start. Is the bridal shop responsible or the independent contractor they hired?

Dishonest shops may refer brides to these independent alterations companies, get a cut of the charges . . . then run like mad if a problem develops.

As a result of these scams, it may be smart to ask whether the alterations department is a part of the shop or some other independent company. If there is a problem with the alterations, will the shop take responsibility?

Self Defense

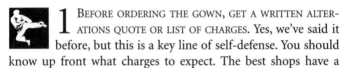 1 BEFORE ORDERING THE GOWN, GET A WRITTEN ALTERATIONS QUOTE OR LIST OF CHARGES. Yes, we've said it before, but this is a key line of self-defense. You should know up front what charges to expect. The best shops have a written list of standard alteration charges. Others will give you a written estimate for your gown before you order.

Unfortunately, some shops wait until the first fitting before giving you an estimate and that's when the problems can start. With your wedding coming up, it may be too late to get a competitive bid.

2 HIRE AN INDEPENDENT SEAMSTRESS. As noted above, most horror stories come from bridal shop's in-house alterations departments. Cut out that possibility by hiring an independent seamstress, preferably one with years of experience altering bridal apparel. Look for independent seamstress referrals from some of the sources listed earlier in this chapter. Be sure to ask for references, check the Better Business Bureau and see their works-in-progress.

3 PAY A SMALL DEPOSIT. Some shops will want a deposit on alterations, which can range from 20% to 50% of the estimated charges. Our advice: put down as little as possible and put it on a credit card.

4 AVOID PROM SEASON. If your wedding is in June, make sure all alterations are done before April. Once prom season starts (the height of which is May and early June), many bridal shop

alterations departments are swamped. In all the excitement of prom season, your gown may get ignored.

5 FIND OUT WHO IS RESPONSIBLE FOR THE ALTERATIONS DEPART-MENT. As we mentioned above, some stores use independent operators to run their alterations departments. Find out up front who is responsible in case a problem develops.

6 INSIST ON A FINAL FITTING. Most bridal alterations departments schedule two to three fittings for each dress. In order to cut corners, however, some don't schedule a "final" fitting after all alterations are completed. Since you have to sign a release that says all the alterations are done to your satisfaction when you pick the dress, it's in your best interest to have a final fitting before you walk out the door. Without the final fitting, you may get the dress home only to discover something wasn't done correctly—and the bridal shop may refuse to fix the problem at that point.

Shopping tips

 ❦ **If you want to add fabric or lace to your dress, you may be locked into using a bridal shop.** Yes, some bridal designers sell extra fabric or lace. No, you can't just call up the designer's 800-number and order it over the phone. Designers only sell their precious fabric to authorized retailers (read: bridal shops).

❦ **Ask for the left-over lace/fabric.** No matter who does your alterations, always ask the seamstress to keep any extra lace or fabric. What can you do with this stuff? How about a custom headpiece that matches your dress? Or even a simple garter? Another idea: you can put the lace in a bridal scrapbook. Or use the lace to decorate champagne glasses for a toast at the reception. (Glue gun, anyone?)

❦ **Insist the on-staff seamstresses do your alterations.** If you have the bridal shop do your alterations, beware of shops that subcontract out work during the busy season. If the alterations department looks swamped, you may want to insist that your dress be handled by the in-house crew (and not some untried stringer brought in at the last moment).

THE FINISHING TOUCHES

Headpieces, veils, accessories, gown preservation and more

How can you save money on a veil and headpiece? What are the best mail-order sources for bridal jewelry, hosiery and shoes? Discover these gems, plus advice on how to store and ship your bridal gown. And what to do with your dress after the wedding? The last section of this chapter looks at the surprisingly controversial topic of gown cleaning and preservation.

IF BUYING A BRIDAL GOWN is a marathon, then the finish line must be in sight. Before you get to the end, however, there are a few details to consider: the headpiece and veil, for example. This pricey accessory can top $200 or more at some shops. Then it's on to the other extras: shoes, undergarments, jewelry, gown preservation and more.

Headpieces and Veils

What the heck is a headpiece, anyway? Is this different from a veil? Before we get rolling here, let's go over some basic definitions.

A *headpiece* is typically a frame, clip or headband that is covered with bridal fabric and lace. Some have silk or real flowers. A headpiece can be worn alone or with an accompanying veil, which brings us to that second term. A *veil* is simply flowing, see-through fabric (illusion, tulle, organza and so on) that is attached to a headpiece. As you'll read later, veils can be of varying lengths and more than one layer.

Although the white bridal gown tradition can be traced back to the 1800's (Queen Victoria started the trend), bridal veils and headpiece have a much hazier beginning. We don't know exactly who started this trend. The Bible mentions wedding veils briefly and anthropologists have evidence of the use of bridal veils among ancient Greek and Roman societies.

Today, you can choose from several basic headpiece options. Let's take a look at the most popular styles.

The Nine Most Popular Headpiece Styles

What's the best-selling headpiece design? Designers tell us crowns and headbands make up more than half their business. The next most popular options are backpieces and wreaths, followed by sprays. What do these styles look like? Here's an overview, with pictures from the Betty Wales Bridal Veil company (call 212-279-8895 for a dealer near you):

1. Crowns. A fabric, lace or bead covered circlet that sits high atop the bride's head.

2. Crescent/headbands/bandeaus. A fabric or bead-covered strip that arcs over and fits close to the head.

3. V-bands. Usually a thin, beaded band that encircles the top of the bride's head and dips down to a V over the forehead. It may have fabric flowers or lace at the back of the band.

4. Backpieces. Most often a bow or cluster of flowers (such as fabric roses) that attach to the hair at the nape of the neck. Veiling flows from the bottom of the bow.

5. Halos/wreaths/garlands. Less formal than crowns, wreaths are also circles that sit on top of the head. For a more informal look, some wreaths are made of silk or real flowers.

6. Sprays. Composed of beading and flowers, sprays are smaller, less ornate headpieces that do not include veiling. Sprays typically clip to the hair.

7. Tiaras. This very formal style sits tall on a brides head in the same position as a headband.

8. Caps. *(not pictured)* A headpiece that is fitted closely to the bride's head. A cap is either positioned forward on the forehead or placed back on the rear of the head (also called a Juliet cap).

9. Picture hat. *(not pictured)* This type of hat has a very wide brim that may have lace, flowers and tulle surrounding the crown. Picture Scarlet O'Hara in *Gone With the Wind*.

Veils

Veils can be just as varied as the headpieces they're attached to. Some are plain, while others have satin ribbon edging, scattered pearls or even lace appliqués. Most bridal veils are described by their length. Here's a breakdown:

Blusher/illusion. In addition to the main veil, a blusher is a short, chin-length veil. It is pulled over the bride's face when she walks down the aisle, then pushed back during the wedding ceremony by the groom or father of the bride.

Pouf. *(not pictured)* In the '80's this was an incredibly popular veil style. A pouf veil rises up from the bride's head at least six inches and is usually worn with a longer veil in back.

Fly-away. Shoulder-length veil.

Fingertip. The most common length, this one reaches to your fingertips.

Ballet/waltz. Extends to knee length.

Sweep. This style is the same length as the dress skirt.

Chapel. 1.5 feet long from waist.

Cathedral. 2.5 feet long from waist.

Royal. *(not pictured)* A veil three or more feet long from the waist, matching the length of a cathedral train.

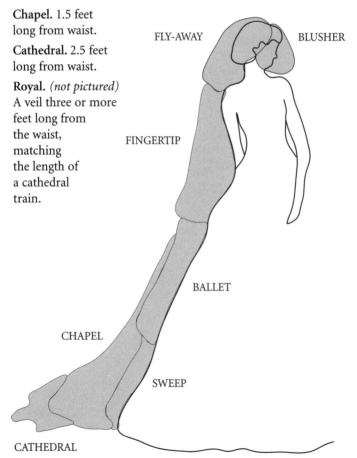

FLY-AWAY   BLUSHER

FINGERTIP

BALLET

CHAPEL

SWEEP

CATHEDRAL

How much will it cost?

A small fortune is the quick answer. That's because bridal shops have a virtual monopoly on the sales of headpieces and veils. It's not like you can pop down to K-Mart and pick one up. And forget about mail order—nearly all headpieces are sold through retail shops.

And just wait until you see the prices. For what seems like a few small pieces of fabric, beads and lace, you'll see price tags that start at $125 and quickly soar above $200. We've even seen styles that cost over $300 and $400.

What makes something as simple as a bridal headpiece so expensive? Well, retailers say "spoilage" accounts for part of the problem. Delicate headpieces get damaged from repeated try-ons, requiring shops to carry a big inventory in samples.

Of course, good old-fashioned greed is another explanation. Bridal shops look to make big profits on all kinds of accessories, and headpieces are one good example. Since they have a monopoly on headpieces, most bridal retailers routinely add 200%, 300% or even 400% mark-ups. Hence, a simple headpiece that wholesales for $75 might retail for nearly $300. Next up, we'll go over some money-saving tips that can lower this bill.

To be fair, we should note that some ornate headpieces may be worth their price tags. Some styles are delicately hand-beaded with Austrian crystal and seed pearls. These will definitely cost more than simple headbands wrapped in satin fabric. But whether or not you want to shell out $400 for such a fancy headpiece is an open question.

Money Saving Tips

%1 TRY DISCOUNT BRIDAL SERVICE (CALL 800-874-8794 FOR A LOCAL REPRESENTATIVE). In the money-saving tips chapter earlier in this book, we cited Discount Bridal Service as a fantastic mail-order source for bridal apparel. Not only can you order name-brand bridal and bridesmaids gowns, but you can also buy headpieces and veils at a 20% to 30% discount. And those discounts are based on a single-mark-up retail price—as we mentioned above, many shops do double, triple or even quadruple mark-ups on these items.

Here's an example of the savings. Let's take a basic headpiece that wholesales for $50. A standard (one-time) mark-up on this item would mean a retail price of $100. DBS would discount this headpiece down to $70 to $80. Yet, walk into a bridal shop, and you could see the same item for $150 or even $200. Hence, using DBS to buy the headpiece and veil might be more of a dramatic savings than at first glance.

The biggest challenge to buying a headpiece from DBS is simply identifying it. Headpieces don't come with tags like bridal gowns and a verbal description won't be much help. Your best bet is to find a picture of the headpiece in a bridal magazine.

2 MAKE YOUR OWN. Let's be honest. Making a bridal headpiece isn't exactly rocket science. A simple headband, some bridal fabric, a few beads and sequins and voila! Instant headpiece. Add some veiling (available at any fabric store for a whopping $5 per yard) and you've got the complete look for 90% less than the bridal shop price.

You can visit a local craft store for many of the supplies you need (see below for some ideas). In many cases, a glue gun will be your major investment.

Another tip: save your fabric and lace scraps from your wedding dress alterations. These can be used to create a matching headpiece. What about the veiling? Many fabric stores stock pattern books like the ones we mentioned earlier (McCalls, Simplicity and Butterick). These books have headpiece/veil patterns as well as bridal gown patterns. Veiling can be attached to the headpiece by thread or glue. Or use Velcro.

Mail order suppliers are also a good source for headpiece and veiling supplies. The book *Wholesale by Mail* by The Print Project (HarperPerennial, $17, available in bookstores) is a wonderful source for finding mail order companies. Edited by Prudence McCullough, this 600+ page paperback is a must for

---

E-MAIL FROM THE REAL WORLD
Custom-Designed Headpieces Can Be a Bargain

Tired of the high prices and look-alike designs of headpieces at bridal shops? Consider a creative alternative: small, local stores that specialize in custom designed bridal headpieces and hats. Surprisingly, these sources can be much more affordable than a retail shop. Here's an e-mail from a bride in Detroit who found just such an establishment:

 "The best tip I have is a little shop in Sterling Heights called Bridal Veils Unlimited and More (810) 795-4700. They have over 700 veils in the shop and an extremely friendly staff! I had difficulty in finding the veil I wanted at the store where I purchased my gown, even after going there three times. At Bridal Veils Unlimited, I described what I was looking for, and they had many choices for me. The owner, Kathy Thomas, custom designs headpieces as well as selling other brands. You can even borrow the veil to try on with your dress. They also have wedding accessories at very good prices. I can't say enough good things about this store." ✍

any serious mail-order shopper. Some of the mail order companies that carry sewing supplies include:

- ❦ Atlanta Thread and Supply (800) 847-1001 or
  (770) 389-9115
- ❦ Clotilde (800) 772-2891
- ❦ Home-Sew (610) 867-3833
- ❦ Newark Dress Maker Supply (610) 837-7500

What about craft stores? The Michaels Arts & Crafts national chain (call 972-409-1300 to find a location near you) has all sorts of supplies for do-it-yourselfers. One of our favorite craft stores for wedding supplies is MJDesigns (with locations in Texas, New York, Virginia and other states; call 972-304-2200 for a location near you). Check the phone book under "crafts/hobbies" for more ideas.

3 RENT A STYLISH HEADPIECE AND VEIL. We visited one rental shop that offered as many as 20 styles of headpieces and veils for well under $100. That's a price that's hard to beat. In the money-saving tips section of this book, we listed a few local rental shops or look in the phone book under "Bridal Shops" or "Wedding Services." Don't forget about consignment shops: many have headpieces and veils at a fraction of retail prices.

4 DON'T BUY THE DESIGNER'S MATCHING HEADPIECE. Some designers offer matching headpieces for their gowns. We say "don't do it." Why? These items can cost a small fortune. For example, the *wholesale* prices of headpieces from Bianchi range from $65 to $190. Diamond has one headpiece that wholesales at $485. When you add in that hefty retail mark-up (200% to 400%), you've got a decent size mortgage payment here.

Instead, if you want to buy a headpiece or veil at a bridal shop, go with a headpiece from a company that specializes in them. These manufacturers make only headpieces—and they do it for 50% to 85% less than the designer's fancy brands. Here's a round-up:

- ❦ **Betty Wales.** This designer has an extensive collection of headpieces. Call (212) 279-8895 for a dealer near you.
- ❦ **Edward E. Berber.** This designer's headpieces are often featured in dress ads by famous designers. Call (212) 594-0400 for a dealer near you.
- ❦ **Illusions of the Heart** is a Colorado-based manufacturer of headpieces. Call (800) 443-9102 or (970) 858-0220 for a dealer near you.
- ❦ **Juliet Veils/Chicago Bead Works Ltd.** Call (800) 5-JULIET or 708-795-6000 for a dealer near you.

❦ **Marie Bridal Millinery.** Call (212) 768-0880 for a dealer near you.

❦ **Marionat.** Call (212) 921-5046 for a dealer near you.

❦ **Regalia Veils.** This company is probably most famous for the headpieces they make for Galina gowns (they're pictured in their dress ads). Call (617) 723-3682 for a dealer near you.

❦ **T&G Bridal** is a subsidiary of Sweetheart Gowns that makes headpieces. Call (800) 223-6061 for a dealer near you. Internet: http://www.gowns.com

A reminder: the above companies don't sell directly to the public. Call them to find a retailer near you who carries their headpieces.

5 FORGET IT ALTOGETHER. Instead of wearing a traditional headpiece and veil, look into a floral wreath designed by your florist or buy a dressy hair clip. This will cost a fraction of retail prices. Fancy hats at department stores (available around the holidays) may be just the right touch for your wedding without breaking the bank.

Of course, there is no rule requiring a headpiece, hat, veil or clip. Who needs something to mess up that stunning hairstyle anyway?

Accessories

While you can't buy a headpiece and veil through the mail, there are other bridal accessories that are definite mail-order possibilities. Here's a wrap-up of our favorite catalog sources for bridal jewelry, hosiery and shoes. (If you happen upon other mail order companies that supply wedding items, please call us at our office at 303-442-8792 or e-mail us at adfields@aol.com).

Mail-Order Bargains

JEWELRY . . . .

❦ Claire R. Willett Jewelry: This Colorado-based company offers the "Wedding Party Collection", a selection of earrings, necklaces, and bracelets that would make great bride and bridesmaids gifts. The jewelry is customizable, with pearls, onyx and crystals in 29 different colors. All of it is very affordable. Call (800) 315-1615 for a catalog and price sheet.

❦ Eloxite (307) 322-3050: If you're looking for jewelry-making supplies (called findings), Eloxite offers earrings, pendants and pins made to be fitted with a variety of stones. They also sell the stones, from opals to garnets. Discounts on findings and stones are up to 75% off retail. The minimum order is $15; the catalog is $1 and credit cards are accepted.

HOSIERY AND UNDERGARMENTS . . . .
🐦 Lovely Lady Slips (800-319-1199 or 908-341-1864): With six different slip styles including an extra-full option (#S-975, $42), this small mail order company in New Jersey offers savings of up to 50% off. They also carry two strapless "merry widow" style bras from $16 to $29.
🐦 L'eggs Outlet Catalog/One Hanes Place (800-300-2600): This catalog supplies both first-quality hosiery and undergarments, as well as slightly imperfect items with savings up to 60% off retail. They carry Hanes, Bali, Playtex and more. If you want to supply all the bridesmaids with matching hose, here's a great way to do it for very little money.
🐦 No Nonsense Direct (800-677-5995): Another hosiery catalog, No Nonsense carries their own name brand as well as Burlington and Easy Spirit brands at up to 60% off retail. Some items are noted as "practically perfect." Most items are sold as three packs.

SHOES . . . .
🐦 The Next Step (800-575-7837): Based in Brooklyn, the Next Step offers custom appliquéed or dyed-to-match shoes in sizes from 5 to 12, narrow to extra wide.

How to Store a Bridal Gown

At this stage in your wedding planning process you may have already received your wedding gown and, if you ordered early as we suggested, you've got a month or two before your wedding. What to do with your dress now? How do you store it? Here are a few tips:

1 **Lay the dress flat in a cool, dry place.** Climate control is essential; you don't want it in a hot or humid environment like an attic or basement. Be sure the dress is not exposed to direct sunlight—this might cause fading and yellowing.

2 **Stuff the sleeves and bodice with acid-free tissue paper** (available through some crafts stores as well as art supply shops). Stuffing the sleeves and bodice will help you keep these areas as wrinkle free as possible.

3 **Cover the gown with a clean, white cotton sheet.** Plastic bags are a no-no; plastic doesn't let fabrics breath and can collect moisture.

4 **Do not hang the dress on a hanger for more than a day or two.** Bridal gowns are heavy; the sheer weight of the fabric, lace, beading and train can stretch a dress when hung on a hang-

er for a long period of time. A day or two before the wedding you can safely hang it to avoid excess wrinkles.

5 **Do not press the dress with an iron.** If it does have wrinkles, consider taking the dress back to the bridal shop or to a local dry cleaner to have it professionally steamed (some bridal shops will do this for free). Irons are not intended to be used on delicate fabric and detailing.

Dress on the Go
Five Tips for Shipping Your Gown

What if you need to transport your gown to another city, state or country? Here are some tips on moving that gown from point A to point B:

1 **First, consider double bagging the dress.** When you buy a dress from a full-service shop, they give you one of those heavy plastic bags made especially for bridal gowns. Consider buying a second bag (they cost from $10 to $20 each) to protect against any rips, tears or splits in the first bag.

2 **If you're taking the dress on a plane, don't check it!** Take it along as a carry-on. See if you can hang it in one of the garment compartments. If not, lay it as flat as possible in the overhead compartment (you'll have to have the wrinkles steamed out anyway).

3 **Consider UPS.** If you can't take the dress on a plane or don't want to be bothered with the hassle, ship it via United Parcel Service. UPS offers reliable shipping service to any domestic address. (While UPS also ships internationally, you may want to play it safe and bring your dress on the plane if you're planning an overseas wedding). Here's how you do it:

- Leave yourself at least seven working days (double in December) for shipping time.
- Insure the gown for full value.
- Make sure the person you're sending it to is going to be home during the day.
- Ask UPS what normal delivery time is to your friend's/relative's house. Tell the person on the receiving end when the dress will arrive.
- Packing: NEVER use newspaper; stuff bodice and sleeves with acid-free tissue paper; wrap the entire dress in the same paper; fill the box with peanuts.
- If you can afford it, go "second day air." UPS handles air

packages more gently than "ground" shipments, plus you'll know exactly when it will arrive (the cost is two to four times more expensive than regular ground service).

❦ Here's a potential problem with shipping silk gowns: rust spots. We've heard a few reports of silk dresses that have developed small spots (which look like rust stains) when shipped UPS. What's the problem? When silk garments are shipped in air-tight containers (especially in hot summer months), a chemical finish on the silk fabric may have a reaction to the heat and lack of oxygen. The good news is the spots aren't permanent—a professional dry cleaner or bridal shop can usually remove them. But you may have to leave extra time to deal with this problem.

4 **When it gets there.** Find a competent cleaner or bridal shop in your wedding city that can steam out the wrinkles in the dress. Ask friends and family for suggestions or look in the Yellow Pages. If you ship your dress to arrive several weeks before your wedding, follow the storage instructions above.

Gown Cleaning, Preservation & Restoration

You've invested a small fortune in this darn dress. You've bought the headpiece and veil, the bra, slip, shoes, jewelry and other miscellaneous accessories. And, don't forget about those pricey alterations.

So, are you done with that bridal shop? Are you kidding? It's time for the pitch for "gown cleaning and preservation services."

"What are you going to do with that dress after the wedding, honey? Don't you want to preserve the gown for your future daughter to wear?"

Fortunately, your friendly bridal retailer has this all figured out. They've contracted with some "national" gown cleaning company in a far-away state. Just drop off the gown after the wedding and they'll take care of it. After a few weeks, you'll get back the gown, hermetically sealed in a box that supposedly can survive a nuclear war. A little plastic window lets you see your perfect dress, waiting there for that future daughter's wedding.

What's wrong with this picture? Well, the first thing is the cost: getting your dress "cleaned and preserved" via this route will set you back $200 to $300. And what if we told you a little dirty secret about the gown cleaning business—they aren't actually cleaning the gowns.

That's right. We first discovered this rip-off when we got reports from bridal consignments shops suggesting things were not quite right with the gown preservation business. How would they know? Well, second-hand shops just so happen to open these boxes and inspect the gowns. And, surprise, many gowns (as many as 80%) are not only not "preserved," but never cleaned in the first place!

So, what are these bridal gown companies doing for all that money? Check out the story of recent bride Shelley Brown-Parish of Hampton Falls, NH. On the advice of the bridal shop where she bought the gown, she paid $250 to Nationwide Gown Cleaning Service of Flushing, NY to clean and preserve her $3800 Scassi wedding gown with their so-called "Zurcion" process. The allegedly clean gown was returned to her in a sealed box, along with a written warning saying if the box was opened, the company would not guarantee the gown.

Four years later, Brown decided to sell the gown and took it to a local consignment shop. When the box was opened, she was horrified. "The entire gown had changed color from white to ivory," she said, noting it had "large yellow stains all over the dress, blue ball-point pen marks on the front and on the train, and also had blood stains where the gown had been fastened to the tissue in the preservation box." Nationwide Gown Cleaning (which also goes under the names Continental Gown Cleaning and Prestige Gown Cleaning) said they'd re-clean the gown and have it back to her in two weeks.

One year later, the company still hadn't returned the gown.

After complaining to the Better Business Bureau and bringing her story to the *Boston Globe*, the company still refused to return her dress. So, she sued them. After a local TV station picked up the chase, she finally got the gown back, which was *still* dirty and now smelled of cigarette smoke! The dress is now so famous it was featured on a recent NBC's "Leeza" show on wedding scams as an example of what can go wrong with these gown preservation companies.

So what lessons does this have for other brides? What if you want to simply clean a gown you found at an outlet store? Or restore mom's dress to it's original condition? The obvious answer: be careful. For advice on this subject, we spoke to Steve Saidman, the owner of Imperial Gown Restoration (800) WED-GOWN, one of the few reputable gown cleaning companies. Steve has seven questions brides should ask any company who cleans, preserves or restores bridal gowns:

1. Do I have to sign a damage release or disclaimer? Some companies ask you to sign a document that says they are not responsible for damage to the dress, even while it's in their care!

2. Do you guarantee there will be no damage to beads, sequins, appliqués and any glued on or sew-on trims? Be careful on this point—harsh dry cleaning chemicals can destroy cheap sequins or beads. Glue can also discolor, turning a dark color.

3. Do you guarantee that invisible stains like perspiration or champagne will be removed? If they don't, these stains may become visible in a few years. Some dry cleaning methods can miss this type of stain.

4. What are your box and packing materials made of? Insist on only acid-free or pH-neutral boxes and materials. A moisture absorbent desiccant (a small packet of absorbent material) should be included with the dress as well.

5. How long have you been in business? Here's a good tip: ask a local ballet company or museum who they use to clean their costumes. Think about it—what is a ballet costume or antique clothing item made of? Tulle? Silk? Detailed beadwork? These institutions must rely on reputable cleaners, and are usually more than willing to give you a referral.

6. Does your warranty have any limitations on my right to unseal the box and inspect the gown? While this sounds like an obvious red flag, we've been shocked at the number of gown cleaning companies who REFUSE to let you open the box to make sure the gown is clean! If you do, the warranty is voided. The best warranties have a "full replacement value" clause that entitles you to compensation if the dress is damaged within a specific number of years.

7. Do you have one price? Watch out for companies that charge one price for any gown. They can't be giving individual attention to different fabrics and trims with a one-price-fits-all strategy. Reputable companies should be willing to give you a free quote with no obligation to use their service.

The above questions are reprinted with permission from Imperial Gown Restoration (800-WED-GOWN or 888-GOWN-888).

Alternatives to Gown Preservation

Of course, there are a couple of other options besides preserving your gown. Here's some advice:

1 DON'T. If you're saving the dress for your daughter, you're assuming the dress will fit her, not have yellowed or gone out of style. That's a slim shot at best.

2 WE RECOMMEND CONSIGNING YOUR DRESS AT A LOCAL RE-SALE SHOP AS SOON AS POSSIBLE AFTER THE WEDDING. Why? Styles change and dresses start to age quickly. Take the money and put it towards a savings account for your first child or a new refrigerator.

3 CLEAN AND PRESERVE IT YOURSELF. Most bridal gowns are made of synthetic fabrics (satin, taffeta, organza and tulle) that can be cleaned in a washing machine. Cold water, a gentle cycle and a pure detergent (no fabric softeners or bleach) is best. Some bridal shop owners first spray the inside and outside of the dress with Shout or Spray 'N Wash. Hang dry on a plastic hanger. Note: before washing, you should first test the beading or pearls. Place one bead/pearl in cold water for 10 minutes and see if it disintegrates (some designers use very cheap pearls). If it passes the test, you can clean the gown at home.

After the dress is clean, wrap it in a clean, white cotton sheet. If you want to stuff it with tissue paper, make sure it's acid free paper (available from local arts supplies or craft stores or call the Container Store at 1-800-733-3532). Put it in an acid-free box (also available from the source above) and store it in a cool dry place—no attics or basements.

Bridal
Gown
Designer
Reviews

*What the heck is a "keystone" mark-up?
How can you decipher all those aliases
the designers use? We'll unravel these
mysteries, plus look at how we put
together the ratings and reviews of
the top bridal designers.*

B<small>EFORE WE LAUNCH HEADLONG</small> into the designer reviews, it might be helpful to take a minute to explain what some of this information means. Here's an overview:

The Reviews

We divide each designer's review into 12 sections: contact info, also known as, internet, background, our view, outlet stores (if any), delivery, tags, sizing charts, sizing notes, extra charges for options/changes, and gown descriptions. Let's take a brief look at each part:

1 Contact info. For each designer, we print their address and phone number. Does this mean you can call them up and order a dress over the phone? Are you kidding? Most designers only sell to authorized retailers. With the exception of outlet stores and special sales like the Saturday bridal markets in New York City (check out Step 4 earlier in this book for information), you cannot buy a dress directly from the manufacturer.

Besides that, most gown designers/manufacturers have very bad phone manners. While you can call them to find the location of a dealer near you, don't expect them to give up any additional information about their dresses. This isn't L.L. Bean—some designers have been known to yell at brides over the phone, throw hysterical fits and worse. If you're having problems with a store or can't get a question answered, however, you can always contact the designer as a last resort.

What about a catalog? As you'll read in a following box, most designers have catalogs—they just don't send them out to consumers. (We'll note the few that do in their individual reviews).

2 Also known as. Designers sometimes have a plethora of pseudonyms, advertising sub-names and separate division monikers. For example, you might see a dress ad for "Regency Bridal by Madeline Gardner." Then, you'll look up Regency in our book and find no listing. Why? Regency is part of Mori Lee, a major gown manufacturer that also advertises gowns under their own name (just to confuse you). Madeline Gardner, by the way, is the designer of *all* Mori Lee's gowns.

Here's how we address this issue: first, later in this section we'll have an "alias pocket translator," which cross-references all these names with the designers they belong to. Then, in each designer's review, we'll note any aliases ("also known as") they use.

Of course, designers are always one-step ahead of our efforts to make sense of this. Since this book has gone to print, you'll probably notice new names in the bridal magazine ads. We'll post updates to this information on our web page (www.bridalgown.com).

The Catalog Chase

With all the designer phone numbers listed in this book, you might think that you can call and get a catalog, right? Wrong. Most bridal dress designers do not send out catalogs to consumers—and some can be downright hostile on the phone when you ask. Instead, designers dole out glossy four-color catalogs to bridal shops, hoping they'll use them as sales tools.

Fat chance. Most shops horde the catalogs and reprints of ads from bridal magazines, afraid that if they pass them out, their customers would use them to comparison shop competitors. Interestingly enough, several shops debated this topic in a recent issue of *Vows*, a bridal trade magazine. "(Catalogs are) just putting a tool in (the bride's) hands to price shop you to death," an Ohio bridal shop owner said. "I think catalogs are wonderful," said a Wisconsin dress shop manager, who uses them as a resource—not for brides, mind you, but for her *salespeople.* She added: "I don't think they should be finding their way into the hands of consumers."

Of course, not everyone has such an anti-consumer attitude. "I don't worry that the bride is going to shop around," said another shop owner who does hand out the catalogs. "We know they are going to shop around. I feel that if they have something with our name on it, they are going to remember us." And even shops who refuse to give out catalogs will relent and give them to customers—that is, *after* a deposit is placed. Another exception to the catalog chase: bridesmaids dress catalogs. Most shops will hand these out so you can show an out-of-town bridesmaid a picture of the dress.

All this debate may be moot in the coming years—the Internet will soon let brides see those hoarded catalogs after all. At the time of this writing, several designers are scrambling to set up web sites with complete color catalogs online. (We print designers' web addresses in each review when available). Some sites even give out style numbers and prices on dresses. Of course, our web site (http://www.bridalgown.com) will also be a treasure trove of information and updates on designers. Given advances in technology, the days when bridal retail shops could strangle the distribution of dress catalogs may be numbered.

3 **Internet.** As mentioned earlier in this chapter, many designers are in the process of putting together web sites. Some are already up and running; others are in development. When available at press time, we'll note each designer's web site in our book. Of course, updates (and links to these sites) can be found on this book's web page (www.bridalgown.com).

What can you find on these sites? Some offer color catalogs, with dress pictures, style numbers and even suggested retail prices. Others will offer less information, perhaps a designer profile and only a partial catalog on-line.

What will the future hold for these sites? Well, the bridal industry is buzzing with rumors that some designers (particularly those who do bridesmaids dresses) are considering taking orders over the Internet. Stay tuned.

4 **Background.** What's the designer's history? How long has the company been around? This brief section gives you a background on the designer.

5 **Our view.** This is our review and rating of the designer.

We should discuss a few caveats to this information. First, there is no scientific test that determines what is a good or bad bridal designer. The grades we assign are purely our opinion.

That said, we should point out we've been full-time consumer advocates for brides since 1988. In that time, we've interviewed over 1000 engaged couples about their dress buying experiences. We attend the bridal wholesale markets to see the dresses firsthand. In addition, we interview bridal retailers and look at surveys of shop owners on this subject. Our opinions on gown designers and manufacturers are based on these experiences and research, plus the all-important feedback from readers of our bridal books.

You'll note that no designer received a grade lower than a C. That's because even the designers with the lowest grades still do an average job at delivering dresses. (There were a few designers in the past we would have given an F, but they have long since gone out of business. In a way, the free market often flunks these losers before we get a chance to). Designers who get a B do an above-average job, while those with A's are our picks as the best of the bunch.

In determining our reviews, we look at the following four factors:

❧ *Quality.* Let's be honest—no bride wants to spend hard-earned cash to get an inferior gown. In this area, we consider gown construction and the quality of fabrics, laces and finish. Obviously, many big designers produce dozens (if not hundreds) of different styles. As a result, our judgment of their quality is an average of the entire line.

❦ *Value.* Some designers are "best buys." Others expect you to pay a premium for their brand name. When we consider a designer's overall value, we judge them compared to their competition—are the dresses a great buy? Or do you merely get what you pay for? Just because a cheaply made dress has a low price tag doesn't mean the designer is providing value. We'll note the "best buys" with a special symbol at the top of each review.

❦ *Delivery/Service.* How prompt is the designer with deliveries? Some designers take forever to deliver a dress. A late gown may set off a panic, not only for the bride but also the retail store. We should note this issue is a moving target—designers are constantly juggling their production between far-flung countries. A political crisis (Tienanman Square, anyone?) can complicate matters, throwing a reliable designer into a tail-spin on deliveries. As a result, this area can change at any minute. We'll try to note any drastic changes on our web page (see the end of this book for more info).

This category also includes customer service, that is the service the designer gives the retail store. Some designers have fantastic reputations for fixing problems like defective gowns, damaged merchandise, etc. Other manufacturers couldn't care less. While this is a difficult attribute to gauge nationally, we try to raise the grades of designers whose customer service is exemplary. Take Alfred Angelo, for example. Say what you will about the quality of their gowns, but everyone agrees that Alfred Angelo's customer service is among the best in the business.

❦ *Fashion.* Is the designer a style leader? How innovative are the dresses? Does the designer set the trend or merely copy the competition?

How fashionable a designer's gowns are is the least important factor in our ratings. The simple fact is that nearly every designer copies dresses from other designers. If someone has a hot-selling look, you'll be sure to find it copied in no time. Since "duplication" and "inspiration" are ingrained in the bridal gown business, we didn't penalize designers who simply duplicate looks from more expensive manufacturers. Besides, if the dress looks good on you and the price is right, who cares whether the designer thought of the idea first?

Nonetheless, we gave bonus points to designers who were at least trying to do something different.

6 **Outlet stores.** While they are few and far between, we'll tell you about the designer's outlet store, if applicable.

7 **Delivery.** This figure (quoted in weeks) is the "official" delivery time stated by the designer. Warning: this is the *average* time the designer promises to deliver a dress. Actual times may vary depending on the time of the year, how backed up the designer is, etc. Make sure to ask the bridal shop for the latest update on the designer's delivery estimates.

Another consideration: some dresses within a designer's collection may be delivered quicker or slower than the average delivery time. In the former case, the designer may stock a select number of dresses in certain sizes in anticipation of demand. (These are often called "quick service" styles.) On the other hand, "exclusive" gowns (or pricey creations) within a designer's collection may take *longer* than average.

What if the designer you love says it will take 16 weeks (that's about four months) to deliver the gown, but your wedding is sooner than that? Don't forget that some designers offer "rush cuts" on any style or quick service on a limited number of styles. You'll pay extra for the privilege, but it's good to know. We'll note which designers offer rush service, custom changes, special sizes, catalogs and more in a chart at the beginning of the designer reviews.

8 **Tags.** How can you tell if you have a designer original? We'll note how most designers identify their gowns. Some use sewn-in tags, while others use "hang tags," small identifying cards attached to the dress by a string. Others don't use any name tags at all—a few just put the style number in the dress, while others do nothing.

9 **Size charts.** These measurements are reprinted from the designer's "official" information. Of course, measurements are subject to change, so be sure to confirm this info before ordering.

When available, we will note whether the designer uses "garment" or "body" measurement charts. As we mentioned earlier in this book, there are actually *two* types of bridal sizing charts: body measurements and garment measurements. What's the difference? A designer who uses a body measurement sizing chart makes gowns to correspond to the actual physical measurements of the bride. On the other hand, a *garment* sizing chart is just that—a measurement of the outside of the dress.

How does this work in the real world? Well, let's assume you have a 36" bustline. If a designer offers a size that has a 36" bustline and uses a body measurement sizing chart, you can fit into that dress. However, if the designer uses garment measurements and the dress measures 36" on the outside of the bustline, it'll be too tight and won't fit. In that case, you'd have to order the next largest size.

THE KEYSTONE EXPLAINED
How bridal shops set gown retail prices

Who sets suggested retail prices for bridal gowns? The answer may be surprising: no one. Manufacturers simply sell the dresses to the stores at their "wholesale" price (also referred to as "cost").

Most retail stores double the wholesale price. This is referred to as a keystone mark-up, named for a key on an old cash register that used to do this calculation automatically. Hence a $400 gown at wholesale would end up with an $800 retail price, a $900 dress at wholesale would be $1800 retail and so on.

Of course, no law says all retail stores must keystone their dresses. Some may use a lower mark-up to begin with, while others may mark-down merchandise that isn't moving. On the other hand, if a store has an "exclusive" on a certain dress or designer, they may mark the dress at *more* than a keystone mark-up, taking an $800 wholesale dress and marking it at $2000 retail, for example. It's a free market and some shops may think they can get away with higher mark-ups for whatever reason.

As a result, you should approach the "suggested retail prices" in this book with caution. Remember that when you get out in the real world, you may see dresses that are marked above (or below) these prices. One factor: some stores take advantage of "early payment" options designers offer. If they pay their bills within a certain period of time, the shops are granted an additional 10% off the wholesale price (in some cases). The result: the shops may pass on these savings in the form of slightly lower retail prices. Or maybe not.

What about headpieces? Where applicable, we'll note the suggested retail prices for a gown's matching headpiece. Once again, we use the standard keystone markup. The only problem: most shops take much bigger markups on these items. We've seen cases of triple and even quadruple markups on headpieces.

The bottom line: regard suggested retail prices as approximate guidelines. We hope you can use these figures to determine if a shop is truly offering a discount deal. Or to spot stores that may be asking far more than the approximate retail price.

Be sure to ask the bridal shop to clarify any sizing questions before the order is placed.

10 **Sizing notes.** With different designers, there always seem to be a few quirks when it comes to dress measurements. We'll note any special considerations in this section.

11 **Extra charges for options/changes.** Want a "special" size? Extra length? Shorter sleeves? A custom change? This section will run down the extra charges (which you add to the retail price of the dress).

12 **Gown descriptions.** When available, we reprint basic gown descriptions that include the following info: style number, dress description and suggested retail price. If applicable, we'll note where the dress was advertised and whether it has a matching headpiece (and it's retail price).

Speaking of suggested retail prices, we base this information on a standard "keystone" mark-up. We explain this more in detail in the preceeding box.

Designer Name Translator

Flip open a bridal magazine and you'll see a plethora of names. With over 200 active bridal gown manufactures in North America, it's no wonder that this can get confusing.

Adding to the mess, however, is a common problem—designers who use all kinds of aliases to advertise their dresses. Why? Well, some designers assign a different brand name to a series of gowns for a couple of reasons. For lower price dresses, the designer might not want to sully their "prestigious" name with more affordable goods. Hence, they hide these dresses under a separate name (or division) only known to industry insiders. The same goes for fancy, exclusive gowns made by more mainstream manufacturers—a separate name adds cache and helps stores get a premium mark-up.

All of which is darn confusing, of course. As a smart shopper, it helps to know what brand you are really buying. While this happens with other products (cars come to mind, such as Toyota's Lexus division), it's surprising the length that bridal designers go to confuse consumers.

So let's blow the lid off all these pseudonyms, aliases and code names. In the following chart, we give you the name, what it means and to whom it really belongs. We define these terms in three categories:

❦ *Ad names.* Some designers have so many dresses that they group their gowns into various ad names. Demetrios/Ilissa is a designer who's famous for this. At press time, these guys had 18 different advertising names, including such similar sounding names as "Sposabella" and "Sposaeuropa." (For the record, Ilissa is the company name and Demetrios is the designer. In our book, we list them as Demetrios/Ilissa because they tend to emphasize the designer's name in ads.)

Most of the time, a dresses' parent designer is referred to in the advertisement. In a few cases, the source is less obvious. For example, Bianchi advertises gowns under the "Poetry" name, but omits its own name in those ads.

❦ *Designer name.* Occasionally, a designer's name may be more famous than the company's moniker. As a result, they may get top billing. An example: "Scaasi Bride for Eva Forsyth." Scaasi is the designer; Eva Forsyth is the manufacturer. We'd list these gowns under the former heading.

❦ *Gown collection.* We define a "gown collection" as a separate line or division of a manufacturer. These dresses are separately identified in the designer's review. While some designers associate their main name with these collections (for example, "Galina Bouquet" is a lower-price collection within the Galina line), others are more cagey. Nowhere in an ad for Amalia Carrara's gowns does it say the line is manufactured by Eve of Milady. Likewise, Regency Bridals makes no mention of the line's relationship to parent Mori Lee.

Here's a pocket translator for all the names you'll encounter in the bridal magazines. If you don't see a name you're looking for here, check out the index at the back of the book.

Name	What it is	Whom to look up
Academy Awards	Ad name	SEE Demetrios/Ilissa
Ada Athanassiou	Designer's name	SEE Diamond
Amalia Carrara	Gown collection	SEE Eve of Milady
Ashley Love	Gown collection	SEE Jasmine
Avine Perruci	Gown collection	SEE St. Pucchi
Bouquet	Gown collection	SEE Galina
Boutique Collection	Gown collection	SEE Demetrios/Ilissa
Camelot Collection	Gown collection	SEE Wallentin
Crown Collection	Gown collection	SEE Wallentin
Carole Hai	Designer's name	SEE Moonlight
Classics	Ad name	SEE Demetrios/Ilissa
Crystal	Ad name	SEE Impression
DE Collection	Ad name	SEE Demetrios/Ilissa
Emerald	Ad name	SEE Demetrios/Ilissa
Emotions	Ad name	SEE Demetrios/Ilissa

Name	What it is	Whom to look up
Essence by Esther	Gown collection	SEE Bonny
Eternity	Ad name	SEE Ange D'amour
Evolutions	Gown collection	SEE Bonny
Eva Forsyth	Designer's name	SEE Scaasi Bride
Fantasy	Gown collection	SEE Forever Yours
Ginza Collection	Gown collection	SEE Private Label by G
Glamour by Eden	Gown collection	SEE Eden
Grand Traditions	Ad name	SEE Demetrios/Ilissa
Great Performances	Ad name	SEE Demetrios/Ilissa
Illusions	Ad name	SEE Demetrios/Ilissa
Ilissa	Company name	SEE Demetrios/Ilissa
Impact	Ad name	SEE Bianchi (The House Of)
Inner Circle	Gown collection	SEE Jim Hjelm
Innovations	Ad name	SEE Bianchi (The House Of)
Inspirations	Ad name	SEE Bianchi (The House Of)
JH by Jim Hjelm	Gown collection	SEE Jim Hjelm
Lazaro	Gown collection	SEE Jim Hjelm
Madeline Gardner	Designer's name	SEE Mori Lee
Masterpiece	Ad name	SEE Demetrios/Ilissa
Michele Piccione	Designer's name	SEE Alfred Angelo
Mirella	Designer's name	SEE Carmi Couture
Now and Forever	Gown collection	SEE Forever Yours
Pallas Athena	Gown collection	SEE Venus
Platinum Collection	Ad name	SEE Demetrios/Ilissa
Poetry	Ad name	SEE Bianchi (The House Of)
Princess Collection	Ad name	SEE Demetrios/Ilissa
Private Collection	Gown collection	SEE Jim Hjelm
Pure Romance	Ad name	SEE Jim Hjelm
Randy Fenoli	Designer's name	SEE Diamond
Regency Bridals	Gown collection	SEE Mori Lee
Renaissance	Ad name	SEE Demetrios/Ilissa
Riccio	Gown collection	SEE Richard Glasgow
Romantique	Ad name	SEE Demetrios/Ilissa
Rumors	Gown collection	SEE Lili
Sabrina	Gown collection	SEE Bonny
Scaasi	Designer's name	SEE Eva Forsyth
Showcase	Ad name	SEE Demetrios/Ilissa
SL Signature	Ad name	SEE Victoria's
Sposabella	Ad name	SEE Demetrios/Ilissa
Sposaeuropa	Ad name	SEE Demetrios/Ilissa
Susan Lane	Designer's name	SEE Country Elegance
Timeless Traditions	Gown collection	SEE Impression
Ultra Sophisticates	Ad name	SEE Demetrios/Ilissa
Victorian Collection	Ad name	SEE Demetrios/Ilissa
Young Sophisticates	Ad name	SEE Demetrios/Ilissa

THE NAME GAME

Are famous label bridal gowns couture originals or designer frauds?

Flip open any bridal magazine and you'll see the names—some of the fashion industry's top designers have their monikers splashed across ads. But are they really designing these gowns or merely licensing out their names to the highest bidder?

Evidence suggests the latter is closer to the truth. This debate has raged for years in many fashion circles, not just bridal: what role does the designer really play in the design process? When you shell out big bucks, are you really getting a designer original?

Let's get real: Calvin Klein probably doesn't design every polo shirt. And Donna Karan isn't personally slaving over the design of that DKNY skirt. So why should bridal be any different?

We'll tell you why: because bridal manufacturers intentionally use fancy designer names to add cachet to their designs, even going as far as picturing the designer's smiling mug in their ads. Yet, you'd be shocked by how little involvement the name designer has in the gown's design. Some merely approve sketches done by underlings, while others do nothing more than cash the royalty checks.

A few bridal manufacturers are honest about their "designer's" true involvement. Alfred Angelo quietly admits that its designer Michele Piccione designs their "Christian Dior" bridal line (it pays a fee to license the name), although this isn't mentioned in the Dior ads. Other manufacturers are less than honest. One Canadian gown manufacturer touts a fancy designer's name in its ads, even going as far as sending out the designer's personal biography when requested. The only problem: the designer has nothing to do with the actual design (or manufacture) of the gowns.

How can you tell if you're getting a designer original instead of a fraud? Unfortunately, there is no easy answer. Most bridal gown manufacturers closely guard their private agreements with licensed designers. It's hard to tell who really has input and who's shamelessly selling their name for a few bucks. The best advice may be to forget the designer name and to simply look at the gown. The fabric, construction and detailing are more of a quality indicator than a designer label.

All these shenanigans tarnish the reputation of the bridal gown business, which is sleazy enough as it is. Manufacturers shouldn't use designers' names and pictures in ads when they have nothing at all to do with the designs. A little truth in advertising would be helpful.

Top Dress Bargains for 1997

What are the best deals on bridal gowns? We've sat through dozens of fashion shows and poured over hundreds of bridal gowns to find the best deals for brides. Here's our list of the best bargains for 1997 (in alphabetical order by designer):

❖ Eden

Style #	Dress Description	Suggested Retail
385	Silk shantung. Princess line gown with empire bodice detailed in beaded floral lace with short sleeves and sweetheart neckline. Plain skirt.	**$538**

❖ Fink

Style #	Dress Description	Suggested Retail
5161	Italian satin princess line gown with detachable train. Asymmetrically placed Venice lace on bodice and skirt. Sleeveless illusion neckline. Venice lace scallop edges the hem. *Available in white or ivory.* *Advertised in Modern Bride Feb/Mar 1997*	**$750**

❖ Galina Bouquet

Style #	Dress Description	Suggested Retail
1571	White Italian satin band sleeve at the shoulder. Bodice over tulle skirt is scattered with satin roses. *Advertised in Brides magazine Dec/Jan, Feb/Mar 1997 "Page II"*	**$800**

❖ Jessica McClintock

Style #	Dress Description	Suggested Retail
21179	"Grace." Silk dupioni in ivory. Off-the-shoulder sweetheart neckline, basque waist and bodice decorated in lace and beadwork. Plain full skirt.	**$480**

❖ Justine

Style #	Dress Description	Suggested Retail
2431	Royal satin gown, off-the-shoulder, short sleeve, delicately beaded lace bodice, pleated skirt and train accented with streamers of beaded lace. *Available in white or ivory.*	**$530**

❖ Marisa

Style #	Dress Description	Suggested Retail
802	Imported satin beaded lace tulle. An on shoulder t-shirt of satin with a raglan sleeve and elongated torso. Beaded lace encircles the neckline and waist. The multi-tulle skirts are fully circular. *Advertised in Modern Bride magazine Feb/Mar, Apr/May 1997*	**$700**

❖ Marisa

STYLE #	DRESS DESCRIPTION	SUGGESTED RETAIL
804	Silk face satin organza/ imported satin. A youthful sleeveless gown features an open neckline and fitted shaped waist. The waistline is adorned with a contrasting satin sash which streams down the train.	
		$900

*Advertised in Modern Bride magazine
Feb/Mar, Apr/May 1997*

❖ Mon Cheri

STYLE #	DRESS DESCRIPTION	SUGGESTED RETAIL
800	Italian silky satin fabric, alencon lace with pearls and clear sequins, semi cathedral train with sheer inset, trimmed with satin streamers. Available in white, ivory or ivory/rum pink. Also available in large sizes up to size 44.	
		$518

❖ Mori Lee

STYLE #	DRESS DESCRIPTION	SUGGESTED RETAIL
R-232	"Regency by Madeline Gardner." Harmony silk and venise lace. Silk halter neckline accented by venise lace. The slight basque waist leads to plain full skirt with chapel train. Bare back has covered buttons and self fabric roses on a ribbon-layered bow at waist. *Natural only.*	$620

This dress is shown on the cover of Mori Lee's Spring 1997 catalog.

❖ Nancy Issler

STYLE #	DRESS DESCRIPTION	SUGGESTED RETAIL
712	Beautiful linen gown with vertical Venise lace bands.	
		$990
	• Option (712X): with train.	$1200

We hope to feature pictures of these dresses on our home page at www.windsorpeak.com. Note: designers can (and do) discontinue styles with little notice. If you find that one of these dresses is already discontinued by the time you read this, consider other gowns in that designer's collection. (For more information on each designer mentioned above, see their individual review later in this book. Consult the index to find specific pages.)

NAME	RATING	COST	CATALOG	DELIVERY STANDARD
Alfred Angelo	B	$ to $$$	•	14 to 16
Alfred Sung	B+	$$ to $$$	•	12
Amsale	B	$$$		13
Ange D' Amour	B+	$ to $$	•	12 to 16
Bianchi	A-	$$ to $$$	•	8 to 12
Bonny	A-	$		10 to 12
Bridal Originals	C+	$		6 to 12
Carmi Couture	A	$$ to $$$		14 to 16
Christian Dior	C	$$$		10 to 16
Country Elegance	A	$	•	8 to 10
Cynthia C	A-	$$$		12
Demetrios/Ilissa	C+	$ to $$$	•	12 to 14
Diamond	B	$$$		14 to 16
Eden	A	$		11 to 12
Eve of Milady	C-	$$$		16
Fink	A-	$ to $$		12
Forever Yours	B-	$		12 to 14
Galina	A-	$$ to $$$		12
Janell Berte	A	$$$		12
Jasmine	B+	$$		12 to 14
Jessica McClintock	A	$	•	2 to 6
Jim Hjelm	B+	$$ to $$$	•	10 to 12
Lila Broude	B+	$$$		12
Lili	C+	$		14 to 16
Marisa	A	$$ to $$$		12 to 16
Mary's	C	$ to $$		10 to 12
Mon Cheri	A	$		12
Monique	B	$ to $$		10 to 12
Montique	B-	$	•	6 to 14
Moonlight	B	$ to $$$	•	12 to 14
Mori Lee	B+	$		10 to 12
Nancy Issler	A	$$ to $$$		8 to 12
Priscilla	A-	$$ to $$$		8 to 12
Private Label by G	B+	$		10 to 12
Scaasi/Forsyth	B+	$$$		12
St. Pucchi	B	$$ to $$$		16
Sweetheart	B-	$		10
Tatiana of Boston	A	$$$		8
Venus	B+	$ to $$$		12 to 14
Vow & Vogue	C+	$ to $$		12
Wallentin	B	$$ to $$$		12

Notes: RATING: Our opinion of the designer's quality, value and fashion. COST: This symbol indicates how expensive a designer is. In some cases, the figures are estimated. $=under $800, $$=$800 to $1200, $$$=over $1200. CATALOG: Does the designer have a catalog that's available for consumers? **DELIVERY**—STANDARD: The average number of weeks a designer takes to deliver a bridal gown. This figure is the designer's official estimate. Actual delivery times can vary. RUSH CUTS: Some designers offer rush service, a special cutting for quicker delivery. There is usually a fee for this option. Some designers don't offer rush cuts, but have certain in-stock styles for quicker delivery. **SIZING**—PETITE: Designers who offer special petite sizes. Some offer petites for all styles, while others only do petites on a selected number of designs. LARGE: Nearly all designers offer gowns in sizes 4-20. We classify any size larger than a

Key: •=YES

...USH CUTS?	SIZING		OPTIONS		
	PETITE	LARGE	EXTRA LENGTH	CUSTOM CHANGES	CHARGE FOR COLOR
	•	•			
•					
•			•	•	
•		•	•		
•			•		
•		•			
•			•		
•		•		•	
			•		
			•	•	
	•	•			•
•				•	•
•			•	•	
•		•	•	•	•
•		•	•	•	
•				•	
•		•		•	
•				•	•
•		•	•	•	
		•	•		
•			•		
•	•		•		
•		•	•	•	
•		•	•	•	
•		•	•	•	
		•	•	•	
•			•		
•	•	•		•	
•		•	•		
•		•		•	

20 as a "large size." Some designers just offer sizes 22 and 24, while others go up to a 44. As with petites, only selected styles may be available in larger sizes. Most designers charge extra for large sizes. EXTRA LENGTH: Some designers offer extra skirt length for taller brides. In a few cases, the exact amount of extra length can be specified by the bride, although most designers merely offer a fixed amount. This option almost always incurs an extra fee. **OPTIONS**—CUSTOM CHANGES: Some designers let you customize a dress by ordering a longer train, swapping the fabric, etc. Other designers offer "custom cuts," dresses that are made to your exact measurements. COLOR CHARGES: Most designers offer dresses in white or ivory for the same price. The few that charge extra for ivory (or for any other color or color combination) are noted here. **Consult the designer's individual review for more details.**

Helpful Hints

1 With all the gown descriptions in this section, you may encounter a term that's not familiar. Check out the glossary at the end of this book for help.

2 The gown information is subject to change. When available, we try to print gown descriptions for individual designers. We gathered this information at the wholesale bridal markets, which are held in late September and early October for the spring season. Of course, it's a long way between then and when the gowns actually come out—and all this info can change. Here are some examples:

> • *Designs that are not "cut."* Some samples shown at the bridal market are never cut, meaning they didn't garner enough interest to be put into production. As a result, you may read a few gown descriptions in this book that never made it to the retail store.
> • *Price changes.* On the basis of feedback from retailers, the designers sometimes adjust the prices of certain gowns after the wholesale markets. Sometimes a rise in the prices of fabric or lace can trigger an increase in the final gown price. While we make a great effort to make sure the information in this book is accurate, remember that the prices we quote are preliminary.
> • *Late arrivals.* Occasionally, a designer will add to his or her collection one or two styles that are not shown at market. Because of production deadlines, we probably won't be able to get this information in the book.

Of course, we post updates on this book on our web page (www.bridalgown.com). As we become aware of changes, we plan to make them available to you on the web.

We should note that the reviews in this section are broken into two parts. First, we have the full reviews of the industry's top players. After that, we have smaller reviews of the "best of the rest," smaller designers whom are still worth mentioning.

⋆ A L F R E D   A N G E L O ⋆

Contact info. Alfred Angelo, 791 Park of Commerce Blvd., Boca Raton, FL 33487. For a dealer near you, call (800) 531-1125, (800) 528-3589, (407) 241-7755. For a catalog, send $3 to the above address.

Also known as. Michele Piccione (she's Angelo's main designer).

Internet. This designer does not have an official web site yet. Our web site (www.bridalgown.com) will have updates on this designer.

Background. Alfred Angelo is one of the country's largest bridal designers, selling more than $60 million of bridal gowns and bridesmaids dresses each year. Founded in 1935 in Philadelphia by Alfred Angelo Piccione and his wife, Edith, the company is still a family-run business. Alfred's son, Vincent is president and Alfred's daughter, Michele, is the designer. Alfred Angelo has production facilities in Pennsylvania and Florida, although most of the gowns are made in Mexico and other countries in Central America.

Designer Michele Piccione has 20 years of experience in the bridal business. She holds a college degree from the Italian Academy of Fashion and Costume Design in Rome, Italy. Piccione has created gowns seen in various movies, such as "Rocky II" and "True Confessions."

Here's a little known fact about Alfred Angelo: the company has a separate division that turns out gowns under the Christian Dior label. Michele Piccione also designs these gowns, although they are marketed and distributed separately from Alfred Angelo's dresses. (For that reason, we separately review Christian Dior dresses later in this section.)

Our view. What can one say about Alfred Angelo? They're like the Gap of bridal—you can find them everywhere and there's something for everyone. Yet, like the Gap, it's obvious Angelo is not on the cutting edge of bridal fashion.

With over 100 active bridal gown styles, you can find Alfred Angelo gowns in practically every bridal shop in the country . . . even the JCPenney catalog. And, yes, there is practically a style for every bride—traditional dresses, contemporary silhouettes and even a few experiments that should have been left on the cutting room floor.

Alfred Angelo's gowns range from $320 to $1600, although most gowns are in the $600 to $800 price points. What about the quality? Well, you get what you pay for—the higher the price, the better the quality. Conversely, the cheap gowns are just that.

Despite its mammoth size, Alfred Angelo risks becoming a dinosaur in the bridal business. It's no longer the price leader, with a slew of competitors like Mori Lee and Eden offering brides better gowns (silk fabrics, hand embroidery) at much lower prices. And Angelo is hardly a leader in fashion, letting upstarts like Mon Cheri run circles around them in styling. Increasingly, Angelo is left to play the only card left in its deck: relying on mass ad campaigns and hefty distribution to push a series of look-alike styles into the market.

Whatever you think about Alfred Angelo's quality and fashion sense, however, you have to give them bonus points on customer service and deliveries. Every source we talk to in the bridal industry is unanimous: Angelo has the best reliability and service in the business.

We also like that Alfred Angelo offers gowns in a wide variety of sizes—every gown is available in sizes up to 44. Even better, the designer offers a small number of both petite-sized and "woman's" size gowns with no up-charge. **Rating: B**

Outlet store. Sawgrass Mills Outlet Mall, 12801 W. Sunrise Blvd., Sunrise, FL 33323. Phone: (954) 846-9198.

Delivery. 14-16 weeks. Alfred Angelo does not offer "rush cuts." However, "quick service" (6-8 week delivery) is available on a selected number of styles. Check with your local retailer for more information.

Tags. Alfred Angelo dresses have sewn-in labels and hang tags. The style number is noted inside and outside the dress.

SIZING CHARTS

Type: Alfred Angelo uses a GARMENT measurement size chart. For information on this subject, refer to the introduction of the designer review section of this book.

All gowns are available in sizes 4-44. For sizes 4-20, see the average size chart. For sizes 38-44, see the large sizes chart. A selected number of styles are available in petite sizes (sizes 3-13, see petite size chart) and woman's sizes (sizes 16W to 28W, see the woman's size charts).

Average Sizes

	4	6	8	10	12	14	16	18*	20*
Bust	34"	35	36	37	38.5	40	41.5	43.5	45.5
Waist	25	26	27	28	29.5	31	32.5	34.5	36.5
Low Hip	36.5	37.5	38.5	39.5	41	42.5	44	46	48
Length	59.25	59.5	59.75	60	60.25	60.5	60.75	61	61.25
Sleeve	17.5	17.5	17.5	17.5	17.5	17.5	17.5	17.5	17.5

Sizing notes:
• *Low hip is the measurement seven inches below the waist.*
• *Length is the hollow to hem measurement, from the base of your throat to the desired dress hem.*
• *Sleeve is the inside sleeve measurement, from the armpit to wrist.*
• **For sizes 18 and 20, add $20 to the gown price.*
• *For extra length, add 5% to the gown price*
(available on sizes 4-20 only).

A L F R E D   A N G E L O

Large Sizes

	38	40	42	44
Bust	46"	48	50	52
Waist	37	39	41	43
Low Hip	48	50	52	54
Hollow	61.25	61.5	61.75	62
Sleeve	17.5	17.5	17.5	17.5

Sizing notes:
• *For sizes 38-44, add 10% to the gown price.*

Petite Sizes

	3	5	7	9	11	13
Bust	34"	35	36	37	38.5	40
Waist	25	26	27	28	29.5	31
Low Hip	36.5	37.5	38.5	39.5	41	42.5
Hollow	55	55.25	55.5	55.75	56	56.25
Sleeve	16.5	16.5	16.5	16.5	16.5	16.5

Sizing notes:
• *A limited number of styles are available in petite sizes. These dresses have style numbers followed by a "p," such as style 1161P.*

Woman's Sizes

	16W	18W	20W	22W	24W	26W	28W
Bust	43"	45	47	49	51	53	55
Waist	35	37	39	41.5	44	46.5	49
Low Hip	46	48	50	52.5	55	57.5	60
Hollow	61.5	61.5	61.5	61.5	61.5	61.5	61.5
Sleeve	17.5	17.5	17.5	17.5	17.5	17.5	17.5
Shoulder*	16.5	17	17.5	17.88	18.25	18.5	18.75

Sizing notes:
• *A limited number of styles are available in woman's sizes. These dresses have style numbers followed by a "w," such as style 1102W.*
• **Shoulder measurement is measured across the back from shoulder to shoulder.*

Extra charges for options/changes:
1. For sizes 18 and 20, add $20 to the gown price.
2. Extra length is available on sizes 4-20 only.
Add 5% to the gown price for this option.
3. For sizes 38-44, add 10% to the gown price.

NEW BRIDAL GOWNS FOR SPRING 1997

Notes: Alfred Angelo's spring collection contains no new styles available in petite or woman's sizes as described earlier. Such styles are available in Angelo's "carry-overs" (gowns from previous seasons). For space reasons, we have not included a listing of carryovers here. We hope to have

*basic carryover information (style number, price) for many designers
available on our web page (www.bridalgown.com).*

STYLE #	DESCRIPTION	SUGGESTED RETAIL

1201 Satin • back bodice features V-back • basque waistline with roses at back waist • built-in crinoline • elaborate Monarch train features rose to rose bustle • full satin skirt • princess line bodice of satin embellished with hand-beaded schiffli embroidery and pearl clusters • Renaissance sleeve trimmed with schiffli embroidery • sweetheart neckline
Color: White $550

1202 Satin • basque waistline accented with peplum at back waist • cathedral train • full satin skirt • Madeira embroidery, built-in crinoline • princess line bodice of satin encrusted with hand-beaded Madeira embroidery • scalloped V-neckline • short shirred sleeve
Color: White $595

1203 Satin • back bodice features v-back with satin covered buttons • bateau neckline • chapel train. • curved waistline with bow and streamers at back waist . . . shirred tulle skirt adorned with bands of satin • princess line satin bodice • tulle, built-in crinoline
Color: White $398

1204 Satin • a-line satin skirt • detachable satin train, chapel length. • pearl encrusted empire waistline • princess line bodice accented with embellished schiffli medallions • scalloped neckline encrusted with pearls • schiffli embroidery, pearls • short shirred sleeve with scalloped trim
Colors: White, Ivory $498

1206 Satin • back bodice features cut-out lace inset • bodice embellished with hand-beaded venise lace • built-in crinoline • princess line gown of satin • scalloped v-neckline • sweep train. • venise lace
Colors: White, Ivory $398

1207 Re-embroidered lace, organza • basque waistline trimmed with scalloped lace • full organza skirt • high-low hem line • long fitted lace sleeve • princess line bodice of hand-beaded re-embroidered lace • sabrina neckline
Colors: White, Ivory $350

1209 Shantung • basque waistline • princess line bodice of hand-beaded re-embroidered lace • re-embroidered lace, built-in crinoline • scalloped hug-the-shoulder neckline • shirred shantung skirt accented with bows on back skirt • sweep train. • tunnel sleeve of lace
Colors: White, Ivory $478

A L F R E D   A N G E L O

1211 Shantung • back bodice features draped V-back accented with hand-rolled roses and loops • chantilly-type lace • chantilly-type lace flounce • chapel train • princess line bodice of shantung embellished with hand-beaded soutache embroidered lace • rounded basque waistline • shirred shantung overskirt • short shirred sleeve accented with lace • soutache embroidered lace • sweetheart neckline
Colors: White, Ivory $478

1236 Satin • basque waistline encrusted with pearls • built-in crinoline • chapel train • off-the-shoulder neckline encrusted with pearls • pearls • princess line bodice of satin embellished with scattered pearls • scalloped tunnel sleeve of satin and pearls • shirred satin skirt
Colors: White, Ivory $398

1237 Satin • back bodice accented with hand-rolled satin rose bouquet with loops • built-in crinoline • curved basque waistline • princess line bodice of satin accented with asymmetrically draped bands of satin • scalloped semi-cathedral train. • scoop neckline • shirred satin skirt • short pleated sleeve features scalloped edge
Colors: White, Ivory, Ivory-Rum Pink $398

1238 Satin, beaded chiffon • chapel train • hand-beaded chiffon jacket with jewel neckline • princess line satin gown with scoop neckline and spaghetti straps • short sleeve • two-piece ensemble
Colors: White, Ivory $518

1239 Satin • built-in crinoline • cathedral train • curved waist-line with bow at back waist • detachable gauntlets of English net accented with soutache embroidered lace • halter neckline • princess line bodice of satin encrusted with hand-beaded soutache embroidered lace • shirred satin skirt trimmed with lace • soutache embroidered lace
Colors: White, Ivory $498

1240 Satin • back bodice features buttons and loops • basque waistline with rose centered bow at back waist • built-in crinoline • chapel train • princess line bodice of satin embellished with hand-beaded re-embroidered lace • re-embroidered lace • scalloped neckline • shirred satin skirt trimmed with re-embroidered lace • short shirred satin sleeve with scallop
Colors: White, Ivory $478

1241 Satin • bodice encrusted with re-embroidered lace • built-in crinoline, waistline ribbon fastener • chapel train • lingerie straps • long fitted satin sleeve embellished with re-embroidered medallions • princess line satin gown • re-embroidered lace • skirt accented with cascades of lace

and scattered pearls • sweetheart neckline trimmed with hand-beaded re-embroidered lace
Colors: White, Ivory   **$598**

1242   Silk shantung • A-line skirt trimmed with hand-beaded re-embroidered lace • built-in crinoline • chapel train • empire waistline with bow at back waist • princess line bodice embellished with hand-beaded re-embroidered lace • re-embroidered lace • scoop neckline • short sleeve accented with beaded lace
Colors: White, Ivory   **$650**

1243   Satin • ball gown bodice of satin embellished with hand-beaded Madeira embroidery • ball gown sleeve of satin accented with tufts of pearls • basque waistline with hand-rolled rose bouquet at back waist • built-in crinoline • cathedral train • Madeira embroidery • shirred satin skirt adorned with hand-beaded Madeira medallions and trimmed with Madeira lace
Colors: White, Ivory   **$598**

1244   Satin • basque waistline with Madeira embellished bow at back waist • built-in crinoline • long fitted sleeve of hand-beaded Madeira lace • Madeira embroidery • modified V-neckline • monarch train. • princess line bodice of satin encrusted with hand beaded Madeira embroidery • shirred satin skirt accented with hand-beaded Madeira embroidery
Color: White   **$650**

1245   Satin • basque waistline accented with embellished loops at back waist • built-in crinoline • monarch train • princess line satin bodice encrusted with hand-beaded schiffli embroidery • schiffli embroidery • shirred satin skirt adorned with hand-beaded schiffli medallions • short fitted sleeve of beaded schiffli embroidery • sweetheart neckline
Color: White   **$630**

1246   Tulle • basque waistline • built-in crinoline • halter neck-line • princess line bodice of soutache embroidered lace • semi-cathedral train • shirred tulle skirt accented with hand-beaded soutache medallions • soutache embroidered lace
Colors: White, Ivory   **$650**

1247   Organza • basque waistline accented with embellished organza bow and streamers • built-in crinoline • long fitted lace sleeve • princess line bodice of hand-beaded re-embroidered lace • re-embroidered lace • scalloped neck-line • semi-cathedral train • shirred organza skirt embellished with scattered re-embroidered medallions • waistline ribbon fastener
Colors: White, Ivory   **$698**

A L F R E D   A N G E L O

1248   Chiffon, satin • chapel train • curved waistline trimmed
with scalloped lace • lingerie straps • princess line bodice
of satin encrusted with hand-beaded soutache embroidered lace • rounded neckline • shirred chiffon skirt •
soutache embroidered lace • waistline ribbon fastener
Colors: White, Ivory   **$598**

1249   Venise lace, organza • back waistline features elaborate
organza bow and streamers • detachable semi-cathedral
train • natural waistline accented with organza cummerbund • scalloped bateau neckline • Venise lace bodice
Colors: White, Ivory, White-Pink   **$598**

1250   Re-embroidered lace • built-in crinoline • cap sleeve •
hand-beaded re-embroidered lace princess line gown •
sheer lace chapel train • sweetheart neckline
Colors: White, Ivory   **$698**

1251   Re-embroidered lace, satin • detachable chapel train • halter
neckline • natural waistline accented with satin cummerbund and satin bow at back waist • princess line bodice of
hand-beaded re-embroidered lace
Colors: White, Ivory   **$550**

1252   Satin • back bodice embellished with satin bow and streamers • built-in crinoline • curved sweetheart neckline • lingerie
straps • princess line satin gown embellished with satin
bands encrusted with hand-beaded soutache embroidered
lace • semi-cathedral train • soutache embroidered lace •
waistline ribbon fastener.
Colors: White, Ivory, White-Rum Pink   **$598**

1253   Silk Shantung • built-in crinoline • chapel train • halter
neckline • pearl trimmed basque waistline with pearl
studded bow and streamers at back waist • princess
bodice of silk shantung accented with Venise lace and
pearls • shirred silk skirt • venise lace
Colors: White, Blush   **$898**

⋗ A M S A L E ⋖

Contact info. Amsale Aberra, Inc., 347 West 39th Street, Suite 11-N, New York, NY 10018. For a dealer near you, call (800) 765-0170 or (212) 971-0170. (By the way, Amsale is pronounced "am-SAL-a." It rhymes with Marsala, as in veal Marsala.)

Internet. This designer does not have an official web site yet. Our web site (www.bridalgown.com) will have updates on this designer.

Background. Amsale Aberra's first wedding dress design was her own. The Ethiopian-born designer was married in 1985 and just plain didn't like what she saw in the bridal market. "Gowns from other designers were too overdone," she told *New York Newsday* in a recent interview. Amsale's simple dress design was a hit and she started custom designing bridal gowns in 1986, placing a small ad in a bridal magazine.

Amsale has a degree in political science from Boston State College (see, you *can* get a job with a poly sci degree) and worked for designer Harvey Benard before striking out on her own. Compared to other bridal manufacturers, Amsale is a small operation. The designer turns out about ten new dresses a season.

Our View. If you like your bridal gowns plain, then you'll love Amsale. The emphasis here is on the quality of fabric and construction, not how much lace can be heaped on the dress. A typical Amsale dress features an unadorned skirt and a bodice with a few simple lace appliqués. Among the more unique fabrics in the line is a "silk gazar," which features a matte finish and crisp texture.

Amsale is easily the bridal market's most talked about newcomer and we've heard from quite a few brides who ask about her dresses. Unfortunately, most are taken aback at the prices. How much? Are you sitting down? The least expensive gown is $1600. Most are $2200 to $2500.

If you're still with us, you might be wondering if Amsale is worth the price. Well, the fabrics are of the highest quality. And the dresses we previewed featured excellent construction and finish. All gowns are made to order in Amsale's New York office. While that's nice, the prices still seem somewhat high. The luxury bridal gown market is flooded with similar looks (albeit without the same fabric perhaps) at prices that are 20% to 30% below Amsale's. If this designer had dresses that were closer to $1000 than $2000, we'd be more excited. **Rating: B**

Retail store. In October 1996, Amsale opened her own retail store at 625 Madison (at 59th). You can order a bridal gown there or preview Amsale's new evening collection.

Delivery. 13 weeks (90 days). Rush cuts are available on a case-by-case basis.

A M S A L E

Sizing chart

	4	6	8	10	12	14	16*	18*	20*
Bust	32	33	34	35	36.5	38	39.5	41.5	43.5
Waist	24	25	26	27	28.5	30	31.5	33	35
Hips	35	36	37	38	39.5	41	42.5	44	45.5

Sizing notes:
• *Gown length (as measured from hollow of the deck to the desired dress hem) is 59" for full skirts and 58" for sheaths (unless otherwise specified).*
• *For off-the-shoulder gowns, skirt length should be specified on the order.*

Extra charges for changes/options:

1. Sizes 16, 18 and 20 incur an additional charge; consult a retailer for more information.
2. For extra skirt length, add 10% to the gown price.
3. For shorter skirt length, add 5% to the gown price.
4. Changes in fabrics, train length and lace are available, as are "custom cuts" made to your measurements. Consult an Amsale retailer for more information.

NEW BRIDAL GOWNS FOR SPRING 1997

Notes: These gown listings do not include "carryovers" (dresses from previous seasons still available). We hope to have a basic listing of Amsale carryovers (style number and price) available on our web page (www.bridalgown.com).

STYLE #	DESCRIPTION	SUGGESTED RETAIL

A235   Oft the shoulder fitted bodice with panels of silk faced satin and gazar. Short cap sleeve. Full gazar A-line skirt with chapel train. **$2700**

A236   Barely on the shoulder fitted bodice. Small cap sleeve. Slightly dropped waist with full silk gazar skirt and sweep train. Bias band at neck and hem line with hand rolled flowers on sleeve and back waist. Note: sample color shown in "blush." **$2500**
Featured in Bride's magazine editorial Feb/Mar 1997

A237   Square neckline with narrow straps. Empire style, silk faced satin bodice. A-line gazar skirt. Attached organza panel train with satin piping. **$1850**

A238   Closed bateau neckline. Sleeveless silk organza yoke. Floor length silk satin organza skirt. Inset with satin trim on skirt. **$2200**
Featured in Modern Bride magazine editorial Feb/Mar 1997

A M S A L E

A239   Strapless. Fitted waistline with beaded lace appliqué.
        Bell-shaped floor length skirt of silk faced satin.   **$2800**
        Featured in Bride's magazine editorial Feb/Mar 1997

A240   Off the shoulder sweetheart neckline in duchess satin.
        Basque bodice with ruched cap sleeves. Chapel train. **$2100**

A241   Open portrait neckline with lace and crystal detail.
        Full A-line gown in silk faced satin. Sweep train.   **$2400**

A242   Off the shoulder wide scoop neckline. Short cap sleeve.
        Very full duchess satin skirt. Tiny pleats and crystals
        at waistline. Chapel length train.   **$2550**

A243   Ribbon lace bodice with jewel neckline and cap sleeve.
        Full floor length skirt in silk-faced satin. Box pleats. **$2550**

A244   Scoop neckline. Short sleeve. Dropped waistline with
        beaded alencon lace appliqué'. Full floor length skirt
        in silk faced satin.   **$2500**

⇢ A N G E   D ' A M O U R ⇠

Contact info. Ange D'amour, 230 Grand St., 2nd Floor, New York, NY 10013. For a dealer near you, call (800) 288-3888 or (212) 219-2283. For a catalog, send a check or money order for $3 to the above address.

Also known as. Voluptuous Brides by Ange D'amour and Petite Brides by Ange D'amour.

Internet. No official web site. However, our web site (http://www.bridalgown.com) will have updates on this designer.

Background. Ange D'amour's niche is larger-size gowns. Owner Yvonne Greene told us she came up with the idea for their separate Voluptuous Brides collection in 1994 after receiving numerous requests from bridal shops for plus size gowns. To insure a good fit, Ange D'amour uses special patterns for full-figured women.

Of course, this manufacturer also makes regular size gowns. Russian-born designer Mila Steiner whips up a variety of silhouettes, drawing on her experience with such top designers as Eve of Milady.

Our view. "Plus size brides never looked so good" is Ange D'amour's motto. For brides who aren't a size 10, this line is a godsend. Where else can you find a bridal gown in a size 64?

Ange D'amour offers good (if not spectacular) values. Most gowns are in the $750 range, with prices starting at $520. One fancy Scaasi knock-off style with gold embroidery and bugle beads topped $1000, but that was the exception. Most of the gowns have more modest prices and styling.

Ange D'amour has two collections: their regular line and the Voluptuous Brides collection. Despite the not-so-subtle name, the latter features quite traditional silhouettes like ball gowns and tulle skirts. Don't like the shiny polyester satin? You can swap the fabric for a modest surcharge (silk is one option; see below for details). All gowns are available in white or ivory, but a few designs have a blush pink option. **Rating: B+**

Delivery. 12-16 weeks. At press time, rush cuts were not available.

SIZING CHARTS

Type: Ange D'amour uses a GARMENT measurement size chart. For information on this subject, refer to the introduction of the designer review section of this book.

For Ange D'amour's regular gowns, use the standard size chart. For Voluptuous Brides by Ange D'amour, use the women's size chart. For Petite Brides by Ange D'amour, use the petite size chart.

A N G E   D ' A M O U R

Standard Sizes

	4	6	8	10	12	14	16	18	20
Bust	33"	34	35	36	37	38.5	40	42	44
Waist	24	25	26	27	28	29.5	31	33	35
Hips	36	37	38	39	40	41.5	43	45	47
Length	58	58	59	59	59	59	60	60	60

Petite Sizes

	2P	4P	6P	8P	10P
Bust	32.5"	33.5	34.5	35.5	36.5
Waist	24	25	26	27	28
Hip	34	35.5	36.5	37.5	38.5
Length	55	55	56	56	56

Women's Sizes (Voluptuous Brides)

	16	18	20	22	24	26	28	30
Bust	40"	42	44	47	49	51	53	55
Waist	31	33	35	38	40	42	44	46
Hip	43	45	47	50	52	54	56	58
Length	60	60	60	60	60	60	60	60

Sizing notes:
• *For sizes 32 to 64, contact a local dealer for measurement details. Add 25% to the gown price for these sizes.*
• *Length is the measurement from hollow of the neck to the dress hem.*
• *Any regular Ange D'amour dress can be made in a women's size. Add 25% to the dress price for this option.*

Extra charges for options/changes:

1. For a shorter skirt length, add $50 to the gown's price.
2. Extra skirt length is also available. For three extra inches, add $80 to the gown's price. For four to six inches, add $120.
3. To lengthen or shorten sleeves, add $30 to the gown's price.
4. Many dresses are available in custom cuts (made to order to your measurements). Add 25% to the gown's price for this service.
5. Fabric changes are also available. To change the fabric to satin or taffeta, add $200 to the gown's price. To change the fabric to silk, add $300 to the gown price. To change from embroidered satin to embroidered silk, add $600 to the gown price.

NEW BRIDAL GOWNS FOR SPRING 1997

Ange D'Amour styles (available in sizes 4-20, petites by special request)

STYLE #	DESCRIPTION/FABRICATION	SUGGESTED RETAIL
1001	Italian satin	**$598**
1003	Jeweled Venice lace/organza	**$698**
1005	Italian satin/beaded/full skirt	**$750**

A N G E   D ' A M O U R

1006	Alencon lace/organza	$650
1008	Italian satin/alencon lace	$650
1009	Satin/alencon lace	$598
1011	Lace sheath/tulle	$698
1012	Venice lace/tulle	$650
1013	Satin/alencon lace	$650
1014	Italian satin/alencon lace	$578
1015	Italian satin/beaded	$750
1016	Italian satin/cap sleeve	$598
1017	Jeweled Venice lace/full skirt	$638
1018	Satin sheath	$518
1020	Satin	$598

❖ **Carry-overs** ....
(Dresses from previous seasons still in production)
Available in sizes 4-20, petites by special request

STYLE #	DESCRIPTION/FABRICATION	SUGGESTED RETAIL
9316	Satin	$638
9431	Italian satin	$658
9438	Italian satin	$698
9543	Silk organza	$750
9548	Italian satin	$598
9550	Satin	$638
9555	Satin sheath/off shoulder	$510
9662	Satin sheath	$598
9664	Italian satin	$498
9669	Italian satin	$498
9670	Italian satin	$598
9671	Italian satin	$590

❖ **Voluptuous Brides styles** ....
(available in sizes up to a size 64)

STYLE #	DESCRIPTION/FABRICATION	SUGGESTED RETAIL
V3308	Italian satin	$418
V3310	Satin	$638
V3314	Satin/alencon lace	$570
V3316	Satin/cut-out embroidery	$598
V3319	Jewel alencon lace/tulle	$599
V3322	Italian satin/full skirt	$678
V9438	No description available	$838
V9543	No description available	$790
V9555	No description available	$550
V9664	No description available	$538
V9671	No description available	$630

❖ B I A N C H I ❖

Contact info. Bianchi (House of), 1 Brainard Ave., Medford, MA 02155. For a dealer near you or to request a free catalog, call (800) 669-2346 or (617) 391-6111.

Also known as. Impact, Innovations, Inspirations, Poetry. Bianchi advertises under several names, such as "Bianchi Inspirations." On the other hand, some Bianchi gowns (such as the Poetry dresses) omit the Bianchi name from the ads.

Internet. http://www.bridalnet.com/andy/bianchi/bianchi.htm is Bianchi's official site, although it was under construction at the time of this writing. It appears Bianchi plans to have its catalog on-line, as well as a list of local retailers. Of course, our web site (http://www.bridalgown.com) will also have updates on this designer.

Background. In the bridal universe, there are two centers of power. One is New York City, the home of most of the country's fashion industry. The other one is not so obvious—Boston, largely on the strength of two bridal pioneers, The House of Bianchi and Priscilla of Boston (more on the latter designer later in this book).

Bianchi is the Boston bridal juggernaut that churns out 50,000 bridal gowns a year from their recently built factory in Medford. In business since 1950, Bianchi has often dressed several generations of brides in the same family.

There isn't one designer for the House of Bianchi; a design staff of several people is responsible for the line's 50+ bridal styles. Surprisingly, the line also has a good selection of informals (bridal gowns without trains) as well, with nearly 20 at last count.

Our view. If you can't find a dress you like in the Bianchi line, you're just not trying hard enough.

Besides traditional silhouettes, you can find designs that are cutting edge . . . and others that are, well, politically incorrect. For fall 1996, Bianchi offered a bridal gown trimmed with real (dead) Norwegian fox on the neckline. For those who prefer not to have animal rights protesters hurling epithets at them during the ceremony, Bianchi thoughtfully offers the style *without* fur. (For the curious, it's $1740 for fur or $900 sans fur.)

Speaking of prices, Bianchi gowns ain't cheap. The least expensive dresses start at $800 and prices soar to $3000 for an all-over Lyon lace ball gown with satin detachable train. Most average $1000 to $1500.

Are you still with us? If those prices haven't scared you to death, let us telling you what you get for those bucks. First, consider the fabric. Bianchi's offerings are among the most luxurious in the business, with Italian silk satins, crepes, "Parisian tulle" and even a few velvets. Bianchi even lets you swap the fabric on a few styles, which is a nice feature if you like the style but hate the fabric.

The overall construction quality for Bianchi is top-notch and its deliveries are among the industry's most reliable. All gowns have matching headpieces/veils, although these can be quite pricey (some top $300 retail). You can even order a bridal gown in a petite size, a rarity these days. On the downside, there are no custom changes available. At this price point, you should be able to make a few changes here and there.

Nonetheless, we like Bianchi. The styling is innovative and the quality excellent. If you want to splurge, this would be as good as any choice. **Rating. A-**

Delivery. 8-12 weeks. Some dresses may take longer due to lace availability, etc. Rush cuts (four week delivery) are available on some styles.

Tags. Bianchi uses hang tags to identify their gowns. Occasionally, the company will put a sewn-in tag inside the gown.

SIZING CHARTS

Type: Bianchi uses a BODY measurement size chart. For information on this subject, refer to the introduction of the designer review section of this book.

Bianchi offers both an average and petite sizing chart, although only a few of the designer's gowns are available in petites. We'll note which gowns are available in petites later in this review.

Average Sizes

	2	4	6	8	10	12	14	16
Bust	33"	34	35	36	37	38.5	40	41.5
Waist	24.5	25.5	26.5	27.5	28.5	30	31.5	33
Hips	35.5	36.5	37.5	38.5	39.5	41	42.5	44
Center/Back*	15.38	15.63	15.88	16.13	16.38	16.63	16.88	17.13

	18	20	22	24
Bust	43.5	45.5	47.5	49.5
Waist	35	37	39	41
Hips	46	48	50	52
Center/Back*	17.25	17.38	17.38	17.38

Sizing notes:
• **Center back measurement is from the back of the neck to the natural waist.*
• *Bianchi changed its sizing charts in Fall 1996. All new gowns will follow the above chart. Older gowns (carryovers) will use an older sizing chart; contact a local retailer for more information.*
• *Depending on the gown style, Bianchi's gown lengths are 57.5" to 58" (as measured from hollow to hem).*

B I A N C H I

Petite Sizes

	1	3	5	7	9	11	13
Bust	33"	34	35	36	37	38.5	40
Waist	24.5	25.5	26.5	27.5	28.5	30	31.5
Hips	35.5	36.5	37.5	38.5	39.5	41	42.5
Center/	15	15.25	15.5	15.75	16	16.5	16.5
Back*							

Sizing notes:
• **Center back measurement is from the back of the neck to the waist.*
• *You'll note the petite sizing chart is similar to the average sizes.*
In fact, the bust, waist and hips are the same. What's different?
The center back measurement is shorter and the skirt length is 2.88"
shorter than average size gowns.

Extra charges for options/changes:

1. For sizes 18-24, add $80 to the gown price for informal gowns,
$100 to the gown price for regular gowns.
2. For petite sizes 11-13, add $100 to the gown price.

NEW BRIDAL GOWNS FOR SPRING 1997

(Note: Most Bianchi gowns have matching headpieces. In order to caluclate a headpiece's suggested retail price, we double the manufac-turer's wholesale price. Please note that this suggested retail price is our opinion; some shops will take a bigger mark-up on headpieces).

STYLE #	DESCRIPTION	SUGGESTED RETAIL

400   Parisian Tulle, open neckline, petite sleeves,
Venise lace, basque bodice, tulle skirt and train
edged with satin cording.   **$1100**
Advertised in Modern Bride magazine Dec/Jan, Feb/Mar
1997 "Look of Love"
Also available in petite sizes
• Matching headpiece (2-400): Half moon band in beaded
Venise lace, double tiered veil edged in
satin cording.   **$158**

401   Silk shantung, V-neckline front and back that bares shoulders, beadwork on tight fitting bodice and mini-shoulder
sleeves, glittering buttons,
circular skirt.   **$998**
Advertised in Modern Bride magazine Dec/Jan, Feb/Mar
1997 "Look of Love"
Also available in petite sizes
• Matching headpiece (2-401): Beaded bun-wrap,
waterfall veil edged with beading.   **$178**

B I A N C H I

402 Pure silk organza, ballerina neckline with see-through
Venise appliqués, veed back, short sleeves,
full skirt and train. **$998**
Advertised in Modern Bride magazine Dec/Jan, Feb/Mar
1997 "Look of Love"
Also available in petite sizes
• Matching headpiece (2-402): Beaded lace crown
with three-layer illusion fingertip veil. **$168**

403 Satin peau fabric, Ballerina neckline, v-back,
sleeveless, beaded basque bodice. **$780**
Advertised in Modern Bride magazine Dec/Jan, Feb/Mar
1997 "Look of Love"
Also available in petite sizes
• Matching headpiece (2-403): Beaded headband,
two-tier waterfall veil with pearl edge. **$192**

404 Cameo satin, ballerina neckline, v-back, princess bodice,
short tulip sleeves, Venise lace appliqués pair in roses and
leaves outlining the complete
neckline and sleeves, a-line skirt and train. **$998**
• Matching headpiece (2-404) **$160**

416 Pure silk shantung, halter neckline, cami bodice with rose
buds of alencon lace, v-back, princess
silhouette. **$980**
• Matching headpiece (2-416) **$150**

423 Parisian tulle, sweetheart neckline, deep open back, fitted
midriff, tulip cap sleeves, Alencon lace, tulle
skirt and train, lace border. **$1092**
• Matching headpiece (2-423) **$180**

426 Pure silk satin peau, bateau neckline, square back, sleeveless, princess silhouette, Alencon lace scallops
with beading above the hem line. **$1398**
• Matching headpiece (2-426) **$160**

429 Satin Peau, bateau neckline, deep v-back, empire
bodice, short sleeves, a-line skirt, alencon lace. **$1292**
• Matching headpiece (2-429) **$138**

437 Pure silk satin and Lyon lace in a fitted bodice with open
neckline all-around, cap-slit sleeves centered with petite
bow, floor-length skirt, lace on skirt
in a Beauvior pattern. **$1798**
• Matching headpiece (2-437) **$272**

443 Parisian tulle, ballerina neckline with deep scoop back,
fitted bodice, beaded alencon lace appliqués, tulle skirt
with alencon lace border. **$ N/A**
• Matching headpiece (2-443) **$ N/A**

444   Illusion tulle, jewel neckline on lingerie bodice, Venise
        lace appliqués, sleeveless, tulle skirt and
        train with appliqués.   **$1300**
        • Matching headpiece (2-444)   **$146**

457   Lace/pure silk Cor De Soie in "butter cream" color, halter
        bodice, ivory alencon lace re-embroidered with gold
        thread, peach soutache roses, column
        (sheath) skirt, detachable train.   **$1300**
        • Matching headpiece (2-457)   **$150**
        Advertised in Modern Bride magazine Feb/Mar and
        Apr/May 1997 "Innovations"

458   Satin peau, sabrina neckline, low back, cap sleeves, princess
        seams, gathered skirt and train with porcelain
        finish, basket weave detailing at hem.   **$860**
        • Matching headpiece (2-458)   **$N/A**

459   Pure Silk Cor De Soie, empire bodice, round
        neckline, V-back, cap sleeves, ivory/pink/sage
        floral ribbon lace, princess waistline, box pleated
        skirt and train.   **$1360**
        • Matching headpiece (2-459)   **$166**

461   Parisian tulle, basque bodice, v-back, front scalloped
        neckline, short sleeves, Venise lace appliqués, tulle skirt
        and train in white and pink with
        matching lace pyramids.   **$1280**
        • Matching headpiece (2-461)   **$160**

474   Silk Cor De Soie, basque bodice, cap sleeves, full skirt and
        sweep train, detailed with Renaissance
        beadwork pattern.   **$1798**
        • Matching headpiece (2-474)   **$194**

480   Parisian tulle, open neckline, basque bodice, long fitted
        sleeves with Venise lace daises and pink beading.
        White and pink Parisian tulle skirt
        and train.   **$1580**
        • Matching headpiece (2-480)   **$172**
        Advertised in Modern Bride magazine Feb/Mar
        and Apr/May 1997 "Inspiration"

491   Lyon lace, open neckline, sleeveless, basque bodice,
        all-over beaded lace, ball gown skirt.   **$2790**
        • Matching headpiece (2-491)   **$240**
        Featured in Bridal Guide magazine editorial Nov/Dec 1996

495   Embroidered organza, sweetheart neckline, camisole
        bodice, sleeveless, low back, pink beaded Venise lace on
        bodice, embroidered organza skirt
        and train. In Ivory/Pink.   **$1798**

• Matching headpiece (2-495)   **$160**
Featured in Modern Bride magazine editorial Dec/Jan 1997

❖ **Informal Bridal Gowns** ....

All Bianchi informal bridal gowns have matching headpieces.
Prices were not available at press time).

2601	Soufflé chiffon, scalloped open front neckline, deep back, empire bodice with Venise lace, circle skirt.	
		$580
2621	Pure silk De Chine, V-neckline, draped bodice with jewel clip at shoulders, empire bodice, cowl back neckline, straight skirt.	**$398**
2622	Venise lace, sheath gown in all-over Venise lace, short sleeves, tiers of Venise lace on skirt with border of filigree.	**$598**
2626	Silk georgette, knotted halter neckline with empire bodice, princess skirt.	**$N/A**
2627	Gold venise lace sheath with sheer jewel neckline, fitted bodice.	**$N/A**
2628	Swede satin, princess bodice with one shoulder decorated with Venise lace.	**$N/A**
2631	Crepe backed satin, wrapped front veed halter neckline, bare back, empire bodice, A-line skirt trimmed in rosettes.	**$598**
2632	Satin peau, halter bodice decorated in Venise lace daises, sheath skirt.	**$N/A**
2633	Silk georgette, fitted bodice, Queen Anne neckline, short sleeves, cascade of Alencon lace sheath skirt.	**$N/A**

N/A=not available. Some Bianchi prices were
not available at press time.

✦ BONNY ✦

Contact info. Bonny MT Enterprises, PO Box 9369, Brea, CA 92622. For a dealer near you, call (800) 528-0030 or (714) 961-8884.

Also known as. Essence by Esther, Evolutions, Sabrina.

Internet. No official web site. However, our web site (http://www.bridalgown.com) will have updates on this designer.

Background/Our view. Don't blink when you look through a bridal magazine or you might miss Bonny. This small manufacturer doesn't advertise much and that's a shame; many brides may not realize Bonny turns out some of the best quality bridal gowns in the business.

Looking at Bonny's pedigree, you might dismiss them as just another California-based importer of cheap gowns sewn in Taiwan. In business since 1983, Bonny is owned by Jerry and Esther Lu. It's Esther (together with a team of designers) who helps design the line and a few of their collections bear her name.

Yet unlike the gazillion other bridal importers who have flood the market in recent years with low price (and low quality) gowns, Bonny actually gives brides tremendous value for their hard-earned money. Beads and sequins are sewn on, not glued. The overall construction quality is excellent. Bonny's ivory fabric is one of the most beautiful in the market. All this for formal gowns that *start* at $430 and top out at $790.

Bonny offers four gown collections. The basic Bonny line is mid-price ($550 to $660) and features traditional styling. In contrast, the more ornate and upscale Essence by Esther gowns are still a good value at $670 to $790. Several of these designs are made in silk.

Bonny's lowest price line is Sabrina, which go for an amazing $430 to $490. There's even an informal collection (called Evolutions) which are in the $320 to $390 range. Bonny offers matching headpieces for many of its gowns at affordable prices, too.

"Ornate but not overdone" is probably the best description of the fashion of Bonny's dresses. The company has kept pace with the times by offering more matte satin options recently (instead of shiny fabrics) and there are several polyester shantungs in the line. If you like color, you'll find more than just the basic white and ivory: Bonny offers a pink color for its informal dresses and "champagne" (a darker ivory) for other gowns.

Not only are the prices, quality and fashion impressive, Bonny also has real-world sizing. Large sizes up to 44 are available for a very small up-charge (see below for details).

Since Bonny doesn't advertise much (nor offers a catalog for consumers), your best bet is to call the designer directly and find a store in your area who carries their gowns. **Rating: A-**

Delivery. 10-12 weeks. Rush cuts are available.

BONNY

Tags. Bonny dresses have sewn-in labels and hang tags. The style number is noted inside and outside the dress.

SIZING CHART

Type: Bonny uses a GARMENT measurement size chart. For information on this subject, refer to the introduction of the designer review section of this book.

	4	6	8	10	12	14	16	18	20
Bust	33"	34	35	36	37	38.5	40.5	42.5	44.5
Waist	23	24	25	26	27	28.5	30.5	32.5	34.5
Hips	35	36	37	38	39	40.5	42.5	44.5	46.5

	38	40	42	44
Bust	46.5	48.5	50.5	52.5
Waist	36.5	38.5	40.5	42.5
Hips	48.5	50.5	52.5	54.5

Sizing notes:
• *Gown length is 58", as measured from hollow to hem.*
• *Extra length is available. See below for pricing information.*
• *Sleeve length (underarm to wrist measurement) is about 17".*

Extra charges for options/changes:
1. For sizes 18 and 20, add $30 to the gown price.
2. For sizes 38 and 40, add $50 to the gown price.
3. For sizes 42 and 44, add $60 to the gown price.
4. Gown length changes (up to four inches longer or shorter) are $80 extra.
5. Sleeve length changes (up to three inches longer or shorter) are $40 extra.
6. While sleeves can be lengthen or shortened, Bonny cannot make a short sleeve gown into a long sleeve design (and vice versa).

NEW BRIDAL GOWNS FOR SPRING 1997

Note: Most gowns are available in white or ivory. Some styles are available in "champagne;" consult a local retailer for more information.

❖ **Essence by Esther** ....

STYLE #	DESCRIPTION	SUGGESTED RETAIL

8974   Georgette shantung. Alencon lace and pearls highlight this sweetheart neckline gown, with short sleeves and a basque waistline. Full skirt and a "V" back, with a fully decorated royal train, topped by a bow.   **$790**
         Two tone color combination also available.

B O N N Y

8976   Georgette shantung. Alencon lace, decorated with sequins and pearls, accent this scalloped, scoop neckline gown, with long sleeves to point and a basque waistline. Full skirt, and a key-hole back, with dangling pearls and a fully decorated cathedral train. **$700**

8977   Georgette Shantung. Pearled and sequined cutout lace, highlight this off-the-shoulder gown, with long sleeves to point. The full skirt and cathedral train are fully decorated. **$770**

8978   Georgette Shantung. Schiffli lace, accented with sequins and pearls, decorate this sweetheart neckline gown, with long sleeves to point and a basque waistline. Sheath skirt, with a detachable cathedral train, edged in Schiffli lace. **$730**

8979   Matte Satin. Thick Venise lace and pearls decorate, this sweetheart neckline gown, with long sleeves to point and a basque waistline. Full plain skirt, with a cathedral train, edged in Venise lace and pearls. **$690**

8980   Italian Satin. Alencon lace, sequins and pearls, accent this scalloped, scoop neckline gown, with long sleeves to point and a basque waistline. Double key-hole back, with a full skirt, topped by a peplum and a beautiful royal train. **$690**

8981   Italian Satin. Alencon lace, highlighted with sequins and pearls, decorate this modified Queen Anne neckline gown. Long sleeves to point and a basque waistline. Key-hole back, with a full skirt, and an exquisite royal train. **$710**

8982   Italian Satin. Pearled and sequined appliqués, adorn this "V" neckline gown, with long sleeves to point and a Basque waistline. Full skirt, with a "V" back and a royal train, topped by a bow. **$790**

❖ **Bonny Bridal Gowns** ....

STYLE #   DESCRIPTION   SUGGESTED RETAIL

6336   Matte Satin. Venise lace and pearls, accent this high scoop neckline gown, with short sleeves, and an empire waist-line. Plain full skirt, with a low back, and a cathedral train, surrounded by pearled Venise lace. **$550**

6337   Matte Satin. Pearled Venise lace, adorns this off-the-shoulder gown, with short cap sleeves and a Basque waistline. Full two-tiered skirt and a cathedral train. **$610**
        Also available in a two-tone color combination.

B O N N Y

6338   Matte Satin. Alencon lace and pearls, decorate this scoop
       neckline gown, with long sleeves to point. Appliqués adorn
       the skirt and cathedral train, of this princess line gown.
                                                            $570

6339   Italian Satin. Appliqués accented with sequins and pearls,
       adorn this high scoop neckline gown, with long sleeves to
       point and a basque waistline. "V" back, with a decorated,
       full skirt and cathedral train, topped by a bow. $560

6340   Italian Satin. Pearled cut-out lace, accents this scoop neck-
       line gown, with short tulip sleeves and a basque waistline.
       Full skirt, with a cathedral train, topped by a bow. $550

6341   Italian Satin. Lace appliqués, with pearls and sequins
       highlight, this modified Queen Anne neckline gown,
       with long sleeves to point and a basque waistline.
       Key-hole back with dangling pearls, a full skirt and a
       royal train, topped by a bow. $650

6342   Matte Satin. Pearled and sequined Venise lace decorates,
       this sleeveless, scoop neckline gown, with a basque waist-
       line. Open heart back, full plain skirt and a cathedral
       train, edged in Venise lace. $510

6343   Italian Satin. Alencon lace, sequins and pearls, adorn this
       modified "V" neckline gown, with short sleeves and a
       basque waistline. Key-hole back with dangling pearls, dec-
       orated full skirt and a royal train, topped by rosettes.
                                                              $650

6344   Italian Satin. Pearled alencon lace and sequins, accent this
       modified Queen Anne neckline gown, with long sleeves to
       point and a basque waistline. Key-hole back, with dan-
       gling pearls and a sheath skirt, detachable cathedral train.
                                                              $670

6345   Satin and Satin Peau. Alencon lace, pearls and sequins
       highlight, this off-the-shoulder gown, with short sleeves, a
       satin bodice and a basque waistline. Full satin peau skirt
       and cathedral train, surrounded by pearled Alencon lace.
                                                              $590

6346   Shantung and Tulle. Schiffli lace, with pearls and sequins,
       adorns this off-the-shoulder gown, with short sleeves and
       a basque waistline. Tulle skirt and cathedral train, dusted
       with appliqués. $500

6347   Shantung. Pearled and sequined Schiffli lace accents, this "V"
       neckline gown, with short sleeves and a basque waistline.
       Plain full skirt and cathedral train, edged in Schiffli lace.
                                                              $650

B O N N Y

6348   Shantung. Cut-out lace, pearls and sequins, highlight this
        sweetheart neckline gown, with short cap sleeves. Princess
        line, with a decorated cathedral train, edged in cut-out lace.
                                                                $650

6349   Shantung. Venise lace, pearls and sequins, adorn this "V"
        neckline gown, with long sleeves to point and a basque
        waistline/ "V" back, full plain skirt and a cathedral train,
        edged in Venise lace.   **$610**

6350   Italian Satin. Pearled and sequined alencon lace decorates,
        this "V" neckline gown, with long sleeves to point and a
        basque waistline/ "V" back, full decorated skirt
        and cathedral train, topped by a bow.   **$510**

6351   Italian Satin. Appliqués accented with pearls and sequins,
        adorn this off-the-shoulder gown, with cap sleeves and a
        basque waistline. Full skirt, with a tiered cathedral train,
        highlighted with tulle.   **$510**
        Two-tone color combination also available.

6352   Shantung. Alencon lace, sequins and pearls, decorate this
        off-the-shoulder gown, with long sleeves to point and a
        basque waistline. Sheath skirt, with a detachable cathedral
        train, topped by rosettes.   **$660**

6353   Satin and Tulle. Alencon lace, pearls and sequins, adorn
        this scoop neckline gown, with short sleeves and a basque
        waistline. Full tulle skirt and cathedral train, accented
        by a bow.   **$530**

❖ **Sabrina Bridal Gowns** . . . .

STYLE #   DESCRIPTION   SUGGESTED RETAIL

7883   Satin. "V" neckline, short sleeves, basque waistline,
        full skirt, "V" back, cathedral train.   **$480**

7884   Satin. Wedding band collar, long sleeves, basque waistline,
        full skirt, button down back, cathedral train.   **$430**

7885   Satin. Scoop neckline, short sleeves, basque waistline,
        full skirt, keyhole back with dangling pearls,
        cathedral train.   **$420**

7886   Satin. Sweetheart neckline, short pouf sleeves, basque
        waistline, full skirt, keyhole back with dangling pearls,
        cathedral train.   **$460**

7887   Satin. Modified "V" neckline, short sleeves, basque waist-
        line, sheath skirt, double key-hole back with dangling
        pearls, detachable cathedral train.   **$410**

7890	Matte Satin. Off-the-shoulder, short sleeves, basque waistline, full skirt, cathedral train.	$420

7891	Satin. Off-the-shoulder, short sleeves, basque waistline, full skirt, cathedral train. *Two tone color combination also available.*	$450

7892	Matte Satin. High scoop neckline, short sleeves, empire waistline, full skirt, keyhole back, cathedral train.	$330

7893	Jacquard. High scoop neckline, sleeveless, sheath skirt, low back, detachable cathedral train.	$390

❖ **Evolutions** ....

Note: Evolutions gowns are available in white or pink.

STYLE #	DESCRIPTION	SUGGESTED RETAIL

9141	Satin. Modified Queen Anne neckline, short pouf sleeves, full ruffled skirt, double keyhole back.	$330

9142	Satin. Wedding band collar, short pouf sleeves, full ruffled skirt, double keyhole back, with dangling pearls.	$320

9143	Satin. High scoop neckline, long sleeves, basque waistline, "V" back, full ruffled skirt.	$390

9144	Satin and Chiffon. Off-the-shoulder, short ruffled sleeves, basque waistline, full satin skirt, with a chiffon overlay.	$350

⟶ B R I D A L   O R I G I N A L S ⟵

Contact info. Bridal Originals, 1700 St. Louis Rd., Collinsville, IL 62234. For a dealer near you, call (800) 876-GOWN or (618) 345-2345.

Internet. No official web site. However, our web site (http://www. bridalgown.com) will have updates on this designer.

Background/Our view. Founded in 1947, Bridal Originals is one of the country's largest bridal manufacturers in the moderate price point. The company was started by a St. Louis family and is still family-operated today.

Bridal Originals gowns retail for $358 to $800, although most are in the $500 to $700 range. That's not a bad deal, except most of these dresses are made of polyester satin. When compared to other designers who do silk gowns with hand beading for under $800, Bridal Originals value looks somewhat thin.

Don't expect over-the-top fashion statements from Bridal Originals, either. Despite the name, Bridal Originals fashion isn't that original. Most gowns are conservatively styled (some say they're plain vanilla). To their credit, we should note Bridal Originals has recently tried to freshen up the line with newer fabrics (polyester crepes, shantungs), hipper silhouettes (a-lines, off-the-shoulder looks) and even different colors (rum pink, gold accents).

What is most laudable about Bridal Originals is their large size options. The designer offers many gowns in sizes up to 30, and actually encourages its dealers to stock large size samples. A spokesperson told us large size gowns make up 12% of Bridal Originals business, more than typical designers.

We also liked Bridal Originals large selection of informal gowns, which range from $150 to $400. You can even find an extensive collection of flower girls dresses, mother-of-the-bride gowns and more.

Despite the lackluster value and average quality, Bridal Originals does get very good marks for service and deliveries from bridal retailers. **Rating: C+**

Delivery. Six to 12 weeks, although Bridal Originals stocks quite a few styles for quicker delivery. No rush cuts are available.

Tags. Bridal Originals identifies its gowns with the style number inside and outside the dress. No sewn-in tags or hang tags are used.

SIZING CHARTS

Type: Bridal Originals uses a BODY measurement size chart. For information on this subject, refer to the introduction of the designer review section of this book.

All gowns are available in sizes 4 to 20. Selected styles (noted below) are also available in sizes 22 to 30.

B R I D A L   O R I G I N A L S

Average Sizes

	3/4	5/6	7/8	9/10	11/12	13/14	15/16	17/18	20
Bust	32.5"	33.5	34.5	35.5	36.5	38	39.5	41.5	43.5
Waist	23	24	25	26	27	28.5	30	32	34
Hips	34	35	36	37	38	39.5	41	43	45

Large Sizes

	22	24	26	28	30
Bust	46	48.5	51	53.5	56
Waist	36.75	39.5	42.25	45	47.75
Hips	47.5	50	52.5	55	57.5

Sizing notes:
• Extra length (five inches) is available on certain styles. Contact a local retailer for more information.

Extra charges for options/changes:
1. For sizes 22 to 30, add $50 to the gown's price.

NEW BRIDAL GOWNS FOR SPRING 1997

❖ "Limited Edition" dresses ....

(The following gowns are in "limited distribution." That is, not every store who carries Bridal Originals will have these styles.)

STYLE #	DESCRIPTION	SUGGESTED RETAIL

P3702   Duchess Satin long sleeve gown with modified Queen Anne neckline and semi-cathedral train. A keyhole back and heavily beaded Alencon Lace also enhance the style. Built-in hard tulle crinoline.
Colors: Ivory, White.   **$778**
Advertised in Bride's Magazine Dec/Jan 1996/97

P3746   Elegant beaded Alencon Lace enhances this Duchess Satin gown with peek-a-boo sleeves, pearl strand draping in the V-back, and a cathedral train complimented with a folded sash bow. Built-in hard tulle crinoline.
Colors: Ivory, White.   **$678**
Advertised in Bride's Magazine Dec/Jan 1996/97

❖ Regular Bridal Gowns ....

3700   Scalloped triple bias strips outline the neckline and cathedral train of this Duchess Satin gown. Hand-cut beaded Alencon Lace and a rose loop bow complete this romantic style. Built-in hard tulle crinoline.
Colors: Ivory, White.   **$378**

3705   Beaded Embroidered Satin Cut Lace edge the spectacular
        imperial train, bodice, and long sleeves of this 'Italian
        Satin traditional gown. Built-in hard tulle crinoline.
        Colors: Ivory, White   **$858**

3707   Pearl accented fabric loops outline the skirt, neckline and
        tunnel sleeves of this Crepe gown with delicate Venise
        Lace detailing in the bodice. Padded flowers enhance the
        understated chapel train.
        Colors: Ivory, White.   **$550**

3710   A sophisticated princess line Light Italian Satin gown
        featuring Embroidered Cut Satin Lace and pearl etching
        at the sweetheart neckline, back and short sleeves. Floral
        accents with long streamers flow over the court train.
        Colors: White, Ivory.   **$650**

3715   A Light Italian Satin short sleeve gown with triple layered
        peplum over cathedral train. This style has a V-neckline
        and is accented with Schiffli Embroidered Lace.
        Colors: Ivory, White.   **$578**

3719   Classic lines, romantic heart shaped keyhole back with
        hand rolled roses and folded sash over a court train
        emphasize the understated elegance of this Italian Satin
        gown. Built-in hard tulle crinoline.
        Colors: Ivory White.   **$358**

3720   Small Satin petals accentuate the beaded Alencon Lace
        throughout this romantic 'Duchess Satin gown featuring
        a layered peplum over a royal train. Built-in hard
        tulle crinoline.
        Colors: Ivory/Rum Pink, Ivory, White.   **$678**

3724   This Italian Satin gown features an A-line skirt with
        inverted box pleating. Pearls and bugle beads enhance the
        delicate Venise Lace in the empire bodice and hemline of
        the court train.
        Colors: Ivory, White.   **$470**

3728   Satin trim outlines the court train and delicate pearl and
        bias pleated diamond theme bodice of this Organza gown
        with hand rolled Satin rosette back accents and a built-in
        hard tulle crinoline.
        Colors: White Ivory.   **$498**

3732   Elegant pearl etching and beaded Schiffli Lace combine
        for a demure Crepe gown with padded cap sleeves and
        chapel-length train.
        Colors: White, Ivory.   **$598**

BRIDAL   ORIGINALS

3736   Bias trim at the sleeves and sweetheart neckline define
        this Light Italian Satin princess gown with trailing beaded
        Alencon Lace details and a court train with a floral
        sash peplum.
        Colors: White, Ivory, Ivory/Rum Pink.   **$518**

3748   A romantic empire waistline gown of all-over Silky Lace with
        tapered three-quarter sleeves, V-neckline and court train.
        Colors: White, Ivory.   **$538**

3750   Sophisticated Italian Satin sheath with detachable chapel
        train. Short sleeves and back accented with folded bows
        and hand-rolled roses.
        Colors: White/Silver, Ivory, Ivory/Rum Pink.   **$598**

→CARMI COUTURE←

Contact info. Carmi Couture, 1375 Broadway, 14th Fl, New York, NY 10018. For a dealer near you, call (212) 921-7658.

Internet. No official web site. However, our web site (http://www. bridalgown.com) will have updates on this designer.

Background. Libyan-born designer Mirella Naim started Carmi Couture in 1980 and quickly established herself as a trend-setter. "Timeless, yet at the same time, tuned to the mood of contemporary brides" is how Naim describes her gowns. Carmi Couture's innovative use of top-quality laces is the line's hallmark.

Our view. If you're a traditionalist, you might as well skip this review. Carmi Couture's designs are anything but run-of-the-mill.

Typical of this designer's style is their all-over guipure lace sheath—elegant, tailored and understated. There are no huge puff sleeves or over-the-top beading on these gowns.

For a small line (about 70 gowns), Carmi Couture offers some impressive custom options. Want a longer train? Shorter sleeves? Beaded or unbeaded lace? No problem. Carmi even offers fabric swaps on a dozen or so designs, enabling you to substitute a less expensive option.

Sheath-style gowns are a Carmi mainstay, but you can also find princess silhouettes and even a halter top dress.

If we had one complaint about Carmi Couture, it would have to be their prices. Starting at $790, Carmi's dresses can top $2400. Also, some of the dresses are "confined," which means their distribution is limited to just a handful of retail shops. Sizing is also limited (only 4 to 20), although Carmi does have a separate line of dresses available in petites sizes only.

Despite the drawbacks, the quality of Carmi's dresses is excellent and if contemporary is what you want, you'd be hard pressed to name a better designer. **Rating: A**

Delivery. 14 to 16 weeks. Rush cuts are available.

Tags. Carmi Couture uses hang tags to identify their gowns, and, sometimes, a sewn-in label.

SIZING CHARTS

Type: Carmi Couture uses a BODY measurement size chart. For information on this subject, refer to the introduction of the designer review section of this book.

All Carmi Couture dresses are available in sizes 4-20. A selected number of styles are available in petites (sizes 3-13). This option is mentioned in each dress description when applicable.

C A R M I   C O U T U R E

Average

	4	6	8	10	12	14	16	18xs	20xs
Bust	33"	34	35	36	37.5	39	40.5	42	44
Waist	23	24	25	26	27.5	29	30.5	32	34
Hips	33	34	35	36	37.5	39	40.5	42	44

Sizing notes:
• *All orders must include measurement of the hollow to hem (described earlier in this book).*
• *Standard gown length for average sizes (as measured from the hollow of the neck to the desired dress hem) is 58", except for sheath styles (which are 57").*
• *Sleeve length is 18".*

Petites

	3	5	7	9	11xs	13xs
Bust	33"	34	35	36	37.5	39
Waist	23	24	25	26	27.5	29
Hips	33	34	35	36	37.5	39

Sizing notes:
• *All orders must include measurement of the hollow to hem (described earlier in this book).*
• *Standard gown length for petite (as measured from the hollow of the neck to the desired dress hem) is 54", except for sheath styles (which are 53").*
• *Sleeve length is 17".*

Extra charges for options/changes:

1. For sizes 18xs and 20xs, add $100 to the gown's price.
2. For sizes 11xs and 13xs, add $100 to the gown's price.
3. For longer length, add $100 to the gown's price.
4. For shorter length, add $60 to the gown's price.
5. Extra sleeve length adds $30 to the gown's price.
6. Shorter sleeve length adds $100 to the gown's price.
7. For buttons over zipper on dress back, add $50 to the gown's price.
8. For buttons and loops (no zipper) on dress back, add $50 to the gown's price.
9. For buttons and loops on sleeves, add $30 to the gown's price.

NEW BRIDAL GOWNS FOR SPRING 1997

Note: Many gowns are available in petites sizes. Unless otherwise noted, there is a $150 additional charge for petite sizes. (A few new styles this season have no upcharge for petite sizes).

Certain dresses are termed "confined." These gowns have limited distribution; hence, not every shop that carries Carmi Couture gowns will have these dresses.

C A R M I   C O U T U R E

The following information is for new styles only. Carmi Couture also has quite a few carryovers, dresses from previous seasons still in production. We hope to have basic information on carryovers (style number, price) listed on our web page (www.bridalgown.com).

All gowns available in white or ivory.

Many Carmi Couture gowns have matching headpieces. The style number of these items is the same as the bridal gown with the letters "HP" added after it. All headpieces are available with tulle or chiffon veiling. Retail prices for most headpieces range from $170 to $300.

Style	Description	Suggested Retail
4071	Italian satin gown. On the shoulder scooped neckline and short cap sleeves. Slightly dropped waistline, edged with braided pearl trim. Box pleated full skirt with sweep train.	**$650**
4073	Satin and Guipure lace bodice. Sculptured neckline, basque waist and cap sleeves. Tulle skirt with scattered appliqués and unusual satin banded back skirt and train.	**$870**
4074	Mini skirt bridal gown of Guipure lace and shantung Modified "v" neckline and cap sleeves. Removable overskirt with chapel train.	**$850**
4075	Italian satin, Weskit effect bodice and long fitted sleeves created of Alencon lace. Panel front full skirt and chapel train.	**$900**
4076	Organza, Guipure lace and satin. Draped capelet sleeves and sculptured neckline. Basque waist, full skirt and chapel train.	**$790**
5001	Guipure lace bodice and cap sleeves. Swiss embroidered cotton featured at bateau neckline and on floor length dirndl skirt, Back accented with bow, and silk flowers. *Featured in Brides Magazine Editorial - Feb/Mar '97*	**$800**
5002	Chantilly type lace with organza Dropped torso with cuffed cap sleeves. Draped apron skirt accented with cabbage roses. Floor length. *Featured in Modern Bride Editorial - Feb/Mar '97*	**$790**
5003	"Elizabethan" gown of pure silk shantung Notched loose basque waist and separate puff sleeves accented with gold braided ribbon. Floor length. *Featured in Elegant Bride Editorial - Winter '97*	**$790**

5004   Luxurious Guipure lace in a leaf and floral pattern, forms
        a beautiful princess sheath with sculptured neckline and
        off-the-shoulder cap sleeves. Lace trimmed removable
        full tulle train. $1300

5005   Geometric patterned Guipure lace bodice with square
        neckline and sleeveless armhole. Full flowing tulle skirt
        and sweep train edged with ribbon piping. $850
        Advertised in Modern Bride Feb/Mar '97
        Available in a petite at no additional charge.

5006   Italian satin princess sheath, with re-embroidered lace
        accenting the bodice sides. Detachable chapel train with
        self fabric roses. $750

5007   Guipure lace bodice, Satin piping edges the scoop neck-
        line and sleeveless armhole. Swiss embroidered organza
        featured beneath softly flowing tulle skirt. $1390
        Advertised in Brides Magazine Feb/Mar '97
        Available in a petite at no additional charge.

5008   Silk Organza and Alencon lace. Strapless gown with bias
        folds at neckline and around bolero jacket. Galloon
        scalloped border at hemline.
                                                             $1250

5009   Floral patterned Guipure lace, dropped torso with bateau
        neckline and off-the shoulder cap sleeves. Full skirt and
        chapel train of silk shantung edged with wide border
        of lace. $1200

5010   Princess line sheath of re-embroidered Alencon lace
        with scalloped Bateau neckline and off-the-shoulder
        cap sleeves. Removable wrap around poly taffeta chapel
        length train. $850
        Available in a petite at no additional charge.

5011   Silk Shantung gown with basque waist and off-the-shoul-
        der cap sleeves. Mini box pleats form a full skirt flowing
        into a chapel train. Bodice and hemline accented with
        leaf patterned Guipure lace. $1190
        Available in a petite at no additional charge.

5012   Bias banded Empire gown of Italian satin. Mini circle
        patterned Guipure lace bodice with bateau neck and
        sleeveless armhole. Butterfly back highlights the
        chapel train. $1000

5013   Princess fit and flair. Italian satin gown with sheer yoke
        and long fitted sleeves. Soutache ribbon embroidery
        outlines the neckline, bodice and skirt. Removable train.
                                                             $720

CARMI COUTURE

5014   Italian satin, long torso gown with dirndl skirt, featuring
        a banded inset of Art-Deco Guipure lace. Floor Length.
                                                            $700

5015   Guipure lace, draped bodice with scoop neckline and cap
        sleeves. Layered tulle skirt with sweep train beautifully
        accented with lace appliqués. All lace studded with
        rhinestones.
                                                            $1050

5016   Silk shantung and re-embroidered Alencon lace. Bias
        banding at top of bodice, and edging bolero jacket.
        Removable silk shantung cathedral train.
                                                            $1200

5018   Guipure lace, sleeveless sheath with sheer English net
        yoke and back bow. Removable, appliqué studded,
        tubular tulle train.
                                                            $1200

5019   Princess line silk shantung sculptured scoop neckline and
        long fitted sleeves of Guipure lace. Flattering vertical
        rows of lace flowing Into skirt. Chapel train.   **$1170**

5020   Guipure lace princess line flowing into a flared tulle
        trumpet skirt. Removable tulle train.
                                                            $1200

5021   Flattering Empire princess line with Alencon lace bodice,
        Sculptured neckline and off-the-shoulder cap sleeves.
        Removable train.   **$1190**

5040   Fit and flair "A" line. Floral patterned Guipure lace and
        silk shantung with wide banded hem and chapel train.
        CONFINED   **$1700**
        Advertised in Bridal Guide Magazine - Jan/Feb '97

5041   Pure Silk shantung and imported Alencon lace. Princess
        line with scalloped neckline and cap sleeves. Inverted box
        pleated skirt and chapel train beautifully detailed with lace.
        CONFINED   **$1850**

5042   Duchess satin princess panel front with neckline and
        waist embellished with situate embroidery. Redingote
        effect skirt with chapel train.
                                                            $1450

5043   Swiss embroidered tulle, with three dimensional stars. Fan
        pleating on bodice and hem. Bolero jacket of organza
        with matching embroidered edge. Floor length.
        CONFINED
                                                            $1950

C A R M I   C O U T U R E

5044   Duchess satin combined with re-embroidered Alencon
        lace to form a classic floor length gown. Scalloped sweet-
        heart neckline and short cap sleeves. Beautiful box pleated
        skirt with wide galloon lace bordered hem.
        CONFINED   **$2100**

5045   Modified princess line gown of silk shantung with inset
        "bustier" and cap sleeves of beaded Alencon lace. Lovely
        apron back cascading into a chapel train.   **$1500**
        Featured in Bridal Guide Magazine Editorial - Jan/Feb '97

5046   Empire "A" line Duchess satin gown trimmed with a
        unique scalloped, jeweled and re-embroidered Alencon
        lace. Silk chiffon draped "pull through" effect bodice, free
        flowing panels and removable train.
        CONFINED   **$1450**

5047   Duchess satin and Swiss embroidered tulle. "V" neckline
        bodice with vertical piping around fitted midriff Apron
        skirt draped at left side and accented with cabbage roses.
        Chapel train.
        CONFINED   **$1850**

→ CHRISTIAN DIOR ←

Contact info. Christian Dior, 791 Park of Commerce Blvd., Boca Raton, FL 33487. For a dealer near you, call (800) 531-1125, (800) 528-3589, or (407) 241-7755.

Internet. This designer does not have an official web site yet. Our web site (www.bridalgown.com) will have updates on this designer.

Background. Alfred Angelo licenses the Christian Dior name for this line of bridal apparel. Although Dior is designed by Angelo's designer, Michele Piccione, the line is separately manufactured and marketed. For more information on Alfred Angelo, see their review earlier in this book.

Our view. If you want to see some truly expensive wedding gowns, check out the Christian Dior line of bridal gowns from Alfred Angelo.

With prices that *start* at $1200, Dior gowns can top out at (sit down before you read this) $6000. Heck, the average is $3500.

A typical gown in this collection is a ball gown style in silk duchesse satin. Pastel roses accent the cap sleeves and are scattered along the train. For $3500, it's no bargain.

For this price range, there is surprisingly little use of innovative laces. When lace is used at all, you'll see such standards as alencon, venise and chantilly. At least the fabrics are somewhat interesting—one design in Dior's collection is made in swiss-dotted cotton and another in embroidered cut velvet.

We're not sure if we're missing something here, but we just don't get the Dior gowns. For this money, we expect more. We realize Angelo's designer Michelle Piccione is trying to go toe to toe with such couture designers as Vera Wang and Christos, but the styling just isn't there.

One small consolation: the extremely limited distribution of Dior gowns means you won't be seeing your dress on another bride. **Rating: C**

Delivery. 10 to 16 weeks is the average delivery time.

SIZING CHARTS

Type: Christian Dior uses a GARMENT measurement size chart. For information on this subject, refer to the introduction of the designer review section of this book.

	4	6	8	10	12	14	16	18	20
Bust	32"	33	34	35	36.5	38	39.5	41.5	43.5
Waist	24	25	26	27	28.5	30	31.5	33.5	35.5
Low Hip	33.5	34.5	35.5	36.5	38	39.5	41	43	45
Length	59	59.25	59.5	59.75	60	60.25	60.5	60.75	61
Sleeve	18	18.5	19	19.5	19.5	19.5	19.5	19.5	19.5

Sizing notes:
* Low hip is the measurement seven inches below the waist.
* Length is the hollow to hem measurement, from the base of your throat to the desired dress hem.
* Sleeve is the inside sleeve measurement, from the armpit to wrist.
* This sizing chart was accurate as of press time. However, Alfred Angelo has changed their sizing charts, effective in Spring 1997. Since Alfred Angelo owns the Christian Dior line, there may be changes in this sizing chart after we go to press. As always, check with your local retailer for the latest sizing information.

Extra charges for options/changes:
1. For size 16, add $100 to the gown price.
2. For size 18, add $150 to the gown price.
3. For size 20, add $200 to the gown price.

NEW BRIDAL GOWNS FOR SPRING 1997

STYLE #	DESCRIPTION	SUGGESTED RETAIL
51702	Cotton Pique' • back waistline trimmed with bow, streamers, and pique flowers • basque waistline • court neckline • full box-pleated skirt • princess bodice • short sleeve • sweep train. *Colors: White*	**$1650**
51703	Silk Duchesse Satin • basque waistline • full silk satin skirt • princess bodice of silk satin • semi-cathedral train • short sleeve • v-neckline draped with soft pleats and flower accent *Colors: White Ivory*	**$2800**
51704	Silk Shantung • asymmetrically draped floor length sheath • back waist accented with elaborate bow, streamers and roses • detachable chapel train • sweetheart neckline *Colors: White Ivory, White-Red, White-Yellow, White-Pink, Ivory-Red, Ivory-Yellow Ivory-Pink*	**$2400**
51705	Silk Organza • bateau neckline • cap sleeve • dropped back waistline accented with silk roses • princess line gown of silk organza • semi-cathedral train. *Colors: White, Ivory, White-Yellow, White-Pink, Ivory-Yellow, Ivory- Pink*	**$2300**
51706	Silk-wool shantung, silk Duchesse satin • floor-length princess line silk-wool shantung sheath • one-shoulder fichu collar of silk satin accented with hand-beaded floral lace. *Colors: White, Ivory*	**$1800**
51707	Silk Organza, Silk Duchesse Satin • bateau neckline	

accented with satin piping • dropped waistline accented
with satin band and tiny bows • full box-pleated organza
skirt • sleeveless princess bodice of silk organza • semi-
cathedral train.
Colors: White, Ivory   **$2200**

51708   Silk Duchesse satin, re-embroidered Alencon lace • basque
waistline • full shirred silk satin skirt with hem line of
hand-clipped re-embroidered Alencon lace • semi-cathedral train • short sleeve with re-embroidered lace accent •
v-neckline, princess bodice of silk satin
Colors: White, Ivory   **$3900**

51709   Embroidered Silk Brocade, Silk Antique Satin • chapel
train • empire bodice of embroidered silk brocade • full
shirred skirt • scooped neckline • short sleeve • waistline
accented with wide sash and streamers of silk antique
satin and tulle.
Color: White-Yellow   **$2800**

51710   Silk satin organza, silk Duchesse satin • dropped waistline
accented with silk satin band and front bow • full box
pleated organza skirt • scooped neckline • sleeveless
princess bodice of silk satin organza • sweep train.
Colors. White, Ivory   **$1600**

51711   Silk gazar, net • basque waistline • full tiered silk gazar and
net skirt accented with silk satin piping • pearl-encrusted
bustier bodice • semi-cathedral train.
Color: White   **$5000**

⟶ COUNTRY ELEGANCE ⟵

Contact info. Country Elegance by Susan Lane, 7353 Greenbush Ave., North Hollywood, CA 91605. For a dealer near you, call (818) 765-1551. For a catalog, send a check or money order for $4 to the above address.

Internet. This designer does not have an official web site yet. Our web site (www.bridalgown. com) will have updates on this designer.

1997 BRIDAL GOWN GUIDE BEST BUY

Background. "Period-inspired gowns" and "sophisticated informals" are the specialty of Country Elegance.

Founder Susan Lane has dressed 300,000 brides since starting the business in her garage in 1967. Lane's first foray into fashion was a series of hand-made patch-work skirts marketed under the name Mother Hubbard. As the business evolved, Country Elegance moved into special occasion apparel and, eventually, bridal gowns.

In a recent phone interview, Susan Lane said her main passion has "always been her love affair with the romance of past eras" and her gowns reflect this. Manufactured in North Hollywood, California, Lane's dresses have graced such celebrities as Jamie Lee Curtis and Susan Lucci, as well as 20 "heroines of the silver screen" at a recent Hollywood birthday bash.

Susan Lane's Country Elegance is more than just dresses. The company offers a complete line of coordinating accessories, including hats, veils, purses and even shoe clips.

Our view. If you want a more informal dress, our top pick would be Country Elegance.

The looks are pure Victorian. A typical style features a high, wedding-band collar, gibson sleeves and fitted bodice, echoing the fashion of the 1890's. The emphasis is often on the lace and appliqués, not the fabric (which are typically man-made options like polyester satins, chiffons and organzas).

Susan Lane's dresses start at $230 for the "Rose Collection," available in ivory, peach and rose colors. These "budget bridal gowns" offer a great value and are also available in two-tone looks (ivory over blush colors).

A separate line of ten informal styles features no trains and shorter (than floor length) skirts. Country Elegance's regular bridal gowns (with trains) range from $378 to $740. Gorgeous colors like antique ivories and rose beiges are options for brides who don't want to get married in stark white.

The quality of construction is what most impresses us about Country Elegance. Each gown is fully lined, individually beaded and trimmed. The appliqués are hand-made, hand-painted or custom-dyed. New this season are several hand-painted venise lace appliqués of pastel and gold colors. That's amazing quality for this price range.

Our only past criticism about Country Elegance was their sizing, which tended to run small. However, in the past year, the manufacturer has corrected this problem; all their dresses are available in sizes 4 to 20 and a few styles are available in sizes up to 24 for an extra charge. **Rating: A**

Delivery. Eight to 10 weeks. Rush cuts are available.

Tags. Country Elegance identifies their gowns with hangs tags and a sewn-in label.

SIZING CHARTS

Type: Country Elegance uses a BODY measurement size chart. For information on this subject, refer to the introduction of this section.

	4	6	8	10	12	14	16	18	20	22*	24*
Bust	32"	34	35.5	37	38.5	40	41.5	43.5	45.5	47.5	49.5
Waist	24	25	26.5	28	29.5	31	32.5	34.5	36.5	38.5	40.5
Hips	34	35.5	37.5	39	40.5	42	44	46	48	50	52

Sizing notes:
• **Only a selected number of styles are available in sizes 22 and 24 (also referred to as Grand Silhouette sizes). We'll note these styles later in this review.*
• *Standard gown length is 44" (as measured from the waist to the floor). Special cuts for longer or shorter lengths are available for about a $40 fee; check with your local retailer for more information.*

Extra charges for options/changes:
1. For sizes 18 and 20, add $40 to the gown price.
2. For sizes 22 and 24, add $100 to the gown price.
3. All dresses are available in ivory over "Angel Satin" colors (rose beige, bambi, champagne/ivory, and peach). There is no extra charge for these colors.

NEW BRIDAL GOWNS FOR SPRING 1997

Note: Since Country Elegance has a catalog for consumers that features pictures of most of their gowns, we have only noted the dress style number, name and suggested retail price.

STYLE #	GOWN NAME	SUGGESTED RETAIL
2000	June	**$240**
2002	April	**$242**
2003	May	**$226**
2005	September	**$270**
3002	Gwendolyn	**$238**
3004	Francine	**$278**
3024	Tricia	**$292**
4256	Diahann	**$380**
4356-0	Diahann (original)	**$450**
4257	Gabriella	**$390**
4258	Lynette	**$390**
4259	Daphne	**$390**
4262	Mary Helen	**$580**
4264	Margherite	**$440**
4265	Gloria	**$382**

C O U N T R Y   E L E G A N C E

STYLE #	GOWN NAME	SUGGESTED RETAIL
4266	Irene	$370
4406	Evann	$398
4409	Elena	$416
4410	Cecelia	$526
4415	Laura	$398
4420	Carlotta	$588
4421	Jessica	$494
4422	Savannah	$476
4423	Nanette	$460
4456	Amelia	$430
4457	Barbara	$390
4458	Roberta	$684
4473	Elizabeth	$590
4477	Christina	$550
4478	Valentina	$570
4481	Alicia	$388
4482	Anabella	$482
4483	Katrina	$480
4486	Sabrina	$520
4487	Krystal	$570
4488	Miriam	$540
4490	Juliana	$530
4491	Lydia	$460
4492	Paloma	$540
4493	Kyla	$484
4494	Leanna	$390
4495	Lorraine	$430
4496	Lillian	$398
4497	Cathleen	$388
4498	Jeannie	$330

✦ C Y N T H I A C ✦

Contact info. Cynthia C & Company, 4414 W. Broadway, New York, NY 10012. For a dealer near you, call (212) 966-2200.

Internet. This designer does not have an official web site yet. Our web site (www.bridalgown.com) will have updates on this designer.

Background/Our view. Cynthia Corhan designed her first wedding gown while still a student at the Fashion Institute of Technology in New York. She described her style to us a "sophisticated, but still retaining a bridal feel." Many dresses feature clean or simple silhouettes with just a touch of silver embroidery or delicate beading.

With ten-plus years of custom bridal manufacturing under her belt, Cynthia C is one of our favorite (if somewhat obscure) designers. The fabrics are all silks (satins, organzas, etc.) and feature some unusual touches. The "satin plaid fabric" is a stand-out, as is the silk charmeuse and "silk chiffon stripe." All the dresses are hand-made in New York City and cut to order.

Prices for Cynthia C's two dozen or so styles range from $1250 to $3200; most average $2500. Yes, that's darn expensive, but you're really getting your money's worth—top-quality fabrics and hand-embroidery and beading. If you want to splurge, this designer is a great choice.

Cynthia C has limited distribution (only 20 stores carry her gowns nationwide), but it may be worth the effort. The dresses are advertised in *Martha Stewart's Weddings* magazine. **Rating: A-**

Delivery. 12 weeks. Rush cuts are available for an additional 10% of the dress price.

SIZING CHART

Sizing chart

	2	4	6	8	10	12	14	16	18
Bust	33	34	35	36	37	38.5	40	41.5	43
Waist	24.5	25.5	26.5	27.5	28.5	30	31.5	33	34.5
Hips	35	36	37	38	39	40.5	42	43.5	45

Sizing notes:
• *Standard gown length (as measured from hollow of the neck to the desired dress hem) is 58".*
• *Sleeve length (as measured from armpit to wrist) is 17".*

Extra charges for changes/options:

1. Fabric substitutions can be made, depending on availability.
2. Custom changes are available for $150 extra.

CYNTHIA C

New Bridal Gowns for Spring 1997

Style #	Description	Suggested Retail

1786   This scoop neck, short sleeve dress is detailed with scallops on the drop waist and hem. A band of hand embroidery on illusion netting rings the hem line. Each scallop is detailed with appliqué flowers to match.
Available in white and ivory.

$2600

1766   The jewel neck bodice and sleeves of this drop waisted dress are made of a stretch georgette. The ball gown skirt is of a silk charmeuse and silk chiffon stripe. The waistline is finished with a soft belt with bow.
Available in white, ivory, and black. $1600

1544   Ivory satin A-line dress has a scallop, scoop neckline, long sleeves, and contrasting cuff and hem bands, in a darker ivory.
Available in white, ivory, and black with or without contrast.

$2300

1736   This Princess line dress is of a flock dot illusion netting. The neckline, sleeves and low back are sheer, giving this dress a very light and Summery feeling. Neckline, cuffs and hem are finished with a silk charmeuse binding, while the waistline is detailed with a silver and pearl beaded trim. The chapel length train bustles up in back.
Available in white and ivory. $1900

1756   The jewel neck and low V back of this drop waisted dress is done in a silk organza which has been finished with a binding on neckline and armholes. The full skirt is banded with three rows of nine inch cotton lace which has been detailed in back with buttons and small bows.
Available in white and ivory. $1650

1816   The bodice and sleeves of this short sleeve, jewel neck dress are made of a cotton lace of which pattern is highlighted by re-embroidering it with a gold cord and pearl heading. The ball gown skirt is of Duchess satin with Cathedral length train and pearl trim at the hem.

$2400

1746   This organza Princess line dress has a graceful open neck and long sheer sleeves. The front princess panels are detailed with chantilly lace inserts which at the center back flows into a Chapel length train.
Available in white and ivory. $2000

C Y N T H I A   C

1473   A-line dress of satin-faced organza, has train and back bow detail. Chantilly lace bodice and sleeves are lightly beaded and trimmed with self binding. Button back sleeves.
Available in white and ivory.   **$2950**

1403   Silk organza dress with square neck, short sleeves and drop waist bodice is hand beaded and embroidered in a lattice pattern with floral border. Organza skirt is box-pleated and finished with pearl trim.
Available in white, ivory, blush pink, and black.   **$2900**

1594   Short sleeve, scoop neck, drop waisted dress is hand embroidered with a vine pattern design in a satin stitch. Organza skirt is box pleated with pearl trim at hem.
Available in white and ivory.   **$2400**

1405   Off-shoulder cap sleeve dress in silk organza, has scalloped detailing on neckline, waistline, and hem, which has been headed and embroidered within the scallops with silk chiffon rosettes.
Available in white, ivory and black.   **$3200**

1726   This boat neck, sleeveless organza dress is styled as a princess line dress with a fitted sheath underskirt. The front and hem of the dress is banded in a filigree style embroidery and beadwork of pearls, and silver thread.
Available in white, ivory, and black.   **$2400**

1796   This boat neck, sleeveless, dropped waist dress has an elaborately beaded bodice which has been done on illusion net and silk chiffon. The ball gown style skirt is make of layers of illusion netting.
Available in white, ivory, and black.   **$2750**

1694   Off-shoulder organza dress has satin bands on the cuff of the sheer sleeve, trimming the dropped waist and hem of the skirt. Button back and satin bows.
Available in white and ivory.   **$2100**

1826   This cap sleeve organza dress is styled as a princess line dress with a fitted sheath underskirt. The front and hem of the dress is banded in satin.
Available in white, ivory, and black.   **$1600**

1465   Double-silk organza sheath has a jewel neck and empire waist detailed with a pearl trim. The sheer train is detachable.
Available in white, ivory, and black.   **$1250**

1475   This sleeveless cage dress is created with charmeuse ribbon and heading on illusion net. The slip dress underneath is silk charmeuse.
Available in white, ivory, and black.   **$3000**

C   Y   N   T   H   I   A   C

1395   Off-shoulder, drop waisted, cap sleeve dress, has beaded
        and embroidered bands, which trim the neckline and
        skirt. The bands begin side by side at the front waist and
        run down and around the skirt hem, meeting again at
        back. The organza underskirt forms a train in the back.
        Available in white and ivory.   **$2800**

1445   Short sleeve, square neck dress of silk shantung, is
        embroidered on bodice, sleeves and hem band, in a daisy
        pattern. Wide rouched waist drops to a V in back.
        Available in white and ivory.   **$2500**

1504   Scoop neck, low back, rouched drop waist dress, has a full
        skirt trimmed with ivory satin bands. The dress is of a silk
        satin plaid pattern and has bows on the cuffs and skirt back.
        Available in ivory and black.   **$2500**

1484   Satin dress with Basque waist, is detailed with hand bead-
        ed and embroidered collar and skirt border.
        Available in white and ivory, with matching or
        contrasting handwork.   **$3000**

✦ DEMETRIOS/ILISSA ✦

Contact info. The Ilissa Group, 222 W. 37th St., New York, NY 10018. For a dealer near you, call (212) 967-5222. In Canada, Demetrios goes under the name "Sposabella"; see below for more information. In Canada, call (514) 385-5777.

Magazine. Demetrios/Ilissa has a quarterly magazine called "For the Bride by Demetrios" that functions as their catalog. It's available on newsstands nationwide for $4.95 per issue.

Also known as. Academy Awards, Boutique Collection, Classics, DE Collection, Emerald, Emotions, Grand Traditions, Great Performances, Illusions, Ilissa, Masterpiece, Platinum Collection, Princess Collection, Renaissance, Romantique, Showcase, Sposabella, Sposaeuropa, Ultra Sophisticates, Victorian Collection, Young Sophisticates.

Internet. The designer has a web site at http://sgi.computek. net/apparel/bridal/webpages/demetrious/index.html. At this writing, the site included an on-line catalog and store listing. Our web site (www.bridalgown.com) will have updates on this designer.

Background. Just who the heck is Demetrios, anyway? When this prolific designer's first name is splashed across a zillion ads, it's hard to escape seeing his bridal gowns.

Demetrios James Elias (known to his friends by the less pretentious name Jimmy) was born in Pireas, Greece and came to the US as a young boy. Demetrios' parents owned a bridal retail shop in Warren, Ohio, where the young Elias worked as a boy. Bitten by the bridal bug, Demetrios purchased Ilissa, an existing bridal manufacturer in New York, in 1980. The designer set off on an ambitious expansion plan in the 80's, signing up dealers worldwide and plastering the bridal magazines with his now familiar name. By 1991, Demetrios had so many ads in bridal magazines he figured he might as well start his own; "For the Bride by Demetrios" was born as the first (and so far, only) designer-owned bridal magazine that year. Today, Demetrios publishes his magazine quarterly and has over 3000 bridal shops worldwide who carry his gowns.

Our view. The trademark Demetrios look is the all-over lace sheath. Decked out in alencon from head to toe, the dress usually features enough flashy beading and sequins to light up a small town.

If you don't like that look, Demetrios has a few hundred other designs you can try. The designer is probably the most prolific bridal manufacturer today. At the end of last year, Demetrios had a whopping 150 active bridal gown styles, and each season, there are another 50 brand new Demetrios designs added to the collection.

In order make sense of this chaos, Demetrios tries to organize his line into several different collections. Unfortunately, the result is a byzantine flood of aliases and "advertising names" that tend to confuse brides more than help clarify the offerings. (What the heck is the difference between Grand Performances and Grand Traditions, anyway?).

At last count, there were six basic gown collections. The "Ilissa" line is probably the most expensive, with gowns from $1000 to $3500. Most of these dresses are made of silk and feature cathedral trains.

Demetrios' "Young Sophisticates" have more down to earth price tags, running $650 to $800. These slightly less ornate gowns feature several sheath styles and shorter trains.

Even more bewildering are the collections of Sposabella and (its evil twin sister) Sposaeuropa. The latter features many all-over lace sheath styles for $650 to $900. And, just to confuse you Canucks, Sposabella is the name Demetrios operates under in Canada (see below for more detail).

The designer's least expensive line is the Princess collection, traditional silhouettes in polyester satins, taffetas and organzas. The price? $530 to $800.

And it's dresses like the Princess collection that probably explain why Demetrios' popularity peaked several years ago. While Demetrios has just about something in every price range, the designer hasn't kept up with the competition. Most Demetrios dresses fall into the $700 to $1000 range and while there are a few silk gowns in that range, most are polyester. Meanwhile, other designers are turning out beautiful silk designs for that price. As a result, the value for the dollar you get from Demetrios is disappointing.

Perhaps what is more important, Demetrios' fashion has also fallen behind the times. The designer hit his stride in the 1980's, when big dresses with big sleeves and over-the-top beading and lace were the rage. In the 1990's, however, the fashion changed. Simple dresses with little or no beading are what's popular now. In what was a surprise to us, it seemed as if Demetrios failed to react. Look through his magazine and you'll see the company is still churning out those over-the-top, encrusted designs.

As a result of these disappointments, we have continued to lower our rating of Demetrios. The quality of the gowns and deliveries/customer service are merely average. **Rating: C+**

Outlet store. Demetrios/Ilissa does not have an outlet store in the United States. However, the designer recently opened a "Sposabella" sale outlet in Quebec City, in Quebec, Canada (418) 622-3262. That store sells gowns at discounts up to 70% (only sizes 10 to 20 are available). Elsewhere in Canada, Demetrios has full-price stores (which also go under the name "Sposabella") in Toronto, Montreal, and Edmonton. These stores do not regularly discount dresses. For a location, call the Sposabella headquarters in Canada at (514) 385-5777.

Delivery. Average delivery is 12 to 14 weeks. Rush cuts (four week delivery) are available.

Tags. Demetrios/Ilissa identifies its gowns with hang tags. These appear only on some dresses, however.

D E M E T R I O S / I L I S S A

SIZING CHART

Type: Demetrios/Ilissa uses a GARMENT measurement size chart. For information on this subject, refer to the introduction of this section.

	4*	6	8	10	12	14	16	18	20
Bust	32"	33	34	35	36.5	38	39.5	41	42.5
Waist	23.5	24.5	25.5	26.5	28	29.5	31	32.5	34
Hips	35.5	36.5	37.5	38.5	40	41.5	43	44.5	46

Sizing notes:
• *Standard gown length (as measured from hollow of the neck to the desired dress hem) is 60".*
• *Sleeve length (as measured from armpit to wrist) is 18.5".*
• **Most Ilissa gowns (style numbers beginning with a "1") are available in sizes 4 to 20. For these dresses in sizes 18 and 20, add $100 to the gown's price. For extra length in these dresses, add $150 to the gown's price.*
• *All other Demetrios/Ilissa gowns (those starting with style numbers 2, 3, 5, 6, 7 or 9) are available only in sizes 6 to 20. For these dresses in sizes 18 and 20, add $60 to the gown's price. Extra length in these dresses is available only on certain styles. Contact a local retailer for more information.*

NEW BRIDAL GOWNS FOR SPRING 1997

❖ Ilissa Gowns ....

STYLE #   GOWN DESCRIPTION   SUGGESTED RETAIL

1868   Sleeveless form fitting sheath made of beaded and rhine-
           stoned venise lace. Removable tulle cathedral train.
           Color: White Only   **$1500**
           Advertised in "For the Bride" Winter 1997 issue.
           The gown is featured on the magazine's cover.

1869   Modified open neckline with short sleeves in silk shan-
           tung. Beaded cutout lace on bodice and throughout front
           skirt. Removable cathedral length train elaborately
           finished with open cutout lace.
           Color: White Only   **$1190**
           Advertised in "For the Bride" Winter 1997 issue.

1870   Silk shantung with off-the-shoulder neckline and short
           sleeves in a Princess silhouette. Beaded embroidered lace
           adorns empire bodice, front skirt and train.
           Color: White Only   **$1150**
           Advertised in "For the Bride" Winter 1997 issue.

1871   Traditional scalloped square neckline of pure silk.
Elaborately done with beaded appliquéed lace on bodice
and long tapered sleeves. Cascades of lace on skirt and
down entire removable cathedral length train.
Color: White Only $1390

1873   Traditional organza Contessa neckline with embellished
alencon lace on bodice, front skirt and throughout
removable cathedral length train. Long tapered sleeves.
Color: White Only $1190

1874   Romantic traditional embroidered lace on organza with
sweetheart neckline and long fitted sleeves. Cathedral
length train.
Color: White Only $1390

1875   Traditional organza with a wedding band neckline and
long tapered sleeves. Beaded embroidered appliqués
enhance entire front skirt, bodice and cathedral length
train. Scalloped pearl hem lace.
Color: White Only $1300

1876   "CLASSICS"-V-Neck with short sleeves. Elaborately
beaded appliquéed.
Color: White Only $1450

1877   "ULTRA SOPHISTICATES"-Draped sleeveless silk chiffon
halter neck. Empire bodice of beaded venise lace.
Full skirt. Flowing scarf train.
Color: White or Ivory $1100

1878   "ULTRA SOPHISTICATES"-Sleeveless V-neck, all venise
lace sheath. Removable crystal pleated tulle sweep train
accented with venise lace hem.
Color: White Only $1590

1879   "EMERALD"-Open sweetheart neck with beaded venise
lace and lycra sleeves. Full tulle floor length skirt. Beaded
venise lace appliqués throughout. Removable floor length
train with ribbon hem line.
Color: White Only $1500

1880   "MASTERPIECE"-Silk organza jacquard with empire
sweetheart neck and cap sleeves of imported alencon lace.
Pink ribbon trim accents empire bodice. Removable
chapel train.
Color: White Only $1300

1881   "PLATINUM"-Sleeveless silk satin Princess silhouette
with bugle beaded empire bodice. Floor length.
Removable satin chapel train.
Colors: White or Ivory $1500

1882   "PLATINUM"-Silk satin sleeveless jewel neckline with a
        beaded ribbed tulle bodice. Apron front skirt with dotted
        tulle insert. Cathedral length train.
        Colors: White or Ivory   **$2200**

❖ **Young Sophisticates Bridal Gowns**................................

2442   Square neckline with short sleeves on matte satin with
        Leaded venise lace. Full tulle skirt with ribbon hem line.
        Cathedral train.
        Colors: White Only   **$790**
        Advertised in "For the Bride" Winter 1997 issue.

2443   Matte satin princess silhouette with halter neckline.
        Imported cut-out embroidered lace bodice. Front skirt
        and cathedral length train embroidered with roses
        throughout. Floor length. Removable train.
        Colors: White or Ivory   **$900**
        Advertised in "For the Bride" Winter 1997 issue.

2444   Silk shantung sheath with U-neckline. Bodice and long
        sleeves of beaded embroidered lace. Pyramid of appliqués
        of lace on front skirt. Removable cathedral train with
        appliqués of beaded lace.
        Color: White Only   **$990**
        Advertised in "For the Bride" Winter 1997 issue.

2445   Traditional matte satin with jewel neckline and long fitted
        sleeves. Beaded cut-out lace on bodice, sleeves and scat-
        tered through-out front skirt. Appliquéed royal cathedral
        length train with scalloped hem lace.
        Color: White or Ivory   **$990**
        Advertised in "For the Bride" Winter 1997 issue.

2446   Scalloped V-neckline princess silhouette in silk shantung
        with long sleeves. Beaded alencon lace on bodice and
        cascades down front skirt and back of cathedral train.
        Color: White Only   **$900**

2447   Floor length traditional open neckline in matte satin with
        long fitted sleeves. Beaded appliquéed lace on bodice, sleeves
        front skirt and removable royal cathedral length train.
        Color: White Only   **$900**

2448   Matte satin Princess silhouette with sweetheart neckline
        and cap sleeves. Beaded venise lace accents and bodice
        and front skirt. Rosebuds adorn sleeves and front skirt.
        Cathedral train.
        Color: White or Ivory   **$700**

2449 Silk shantung sleeveless slip bodice with beaded embossed venise lace. Appliqués of beaded lace cascade down front skirt. Cathedral length train.
Color: White only. **$790**

2453 Princess silhouette of pure silk shantung with Contessa neckline and long sleeves. Beaded embroidered appliqués on bodice, sleeves and on front skirt and cathedral length train.
Color: White only. **$950**

2454 Sleeveless chiffon empire bodice of beaded venise lace. Floor length princess silhouette. Dramatic draped chiffon back. Removable cathedral length train.
Color: White or Ivory **$790**

2455 Sleeveless 3-dimensional beaded venise lace floor length mermaid with tulle flounce. Removable tulle cathedral length train scattered with beaded appliqués.
Color: White only. **$790**

2456 Chiffon Princess silhouette with Contessa neckline of venise lace and tapered sleeves. Cathedral length train.
Color: White or Ivory. **$850**

2457 Sleeveless sheath of dulcie silk satin with jewel neckline of organza illusion and beaded and embroidered venise lace. V-Back. Removable organza train with beaded venise appliqués.
Color: White or Ivory. **$900**

2458 Halter dulcie silk satin floor length Princess silhouette gown. Beaded embroidered embossed lace on halter bodice with criss-cross straps. Removable tulle cathedral train.
Color: White or Ivory **$990**

❖ **Sposaeuropa Bridal Gowns** ....

Note: Sposaeuropa gowns are ONLY available in sizes 6-20 unless otherwise noted.

5408 Traditional satin wedding band neckline with elaborate cut-out lace on bodice and front skirt. Cathedral plus train.
Color: White only **$700**
• Also available in sizes 4, 22, 24 and 26

5409 Matte satin, V-neck princess silhouette with three-dimensional beaded venise lace on bodice and long tapered sleeves. Appliqués of beaded venise lace on front skirt and along hem line. Cathedral train.
Color: White only **$650**

D E M E T R I O S / I L I S S A

5410   Sleeveless matte satin sheath with three-dimensionally
        beaded venise lace on bodice and front skirt. Removable
        cathedral length train.
        Color: White only   **$700**

5411   Sleeveless silk shantung with beaded alencon lace on
        bodice and fully skirt. Sweep train.
        Color: White only   **$650**

5412   Matte satin sheath with scoop neckline, bustier bodice
        and long fitted sleeves. Pyramids of cut-out lace on front
        skirt. Removable cathedral train.
        Color: White or Ivory   **$650**
        • Also available in sizes 4, 22, 24 and 26

5414   Matte satin traditional with scalloped V-neckline and fit-
        ted sleeves. Bodice, skirt and train elaborately finished
        with beaded cut-out lace. Cathedral train.
        Color: White or Ivory   **$650**
        • Also available in sizes 4, 22, 24 and 26

5415   Matte satin halter sheath with an elaborately beaded
        bodice and front skirt. Criss-cross back and removable
        cathedral length train.
        Color: White or Ivory   **$650**
        • Also available in sizes 4, 22, 24 and 26

5417   Sleeveless princess silhouette of matte satin. Beaded
        embroidery accents front and back bodice. Cathedral
        length train.
        Color: White or Ivory   **$650**

5418   Elaborate traditional hi-neck made of matte satin and
        cut-out lace. Floor length gown with deep border hem
        lace. Removable cathedral length train.
        Color: White or Ivory   **$750**

5420   Traditional matte satin sweetheart neckline with cut-out
        lace on bodice and long beaded sleeves. Elaborate cut-out
        lace adorns front floor length skirt. Removable elaborate
        cathedral length train with cut-out lace.
        Color: White or Ivory   **$750**
        • Also available in sizes 4, 22, 24 and 26

5421   Queen Anne neckline on a matte satin sheath with long
        fitted sleeves. Heavily beaded cut-out lace on bodice and
        pyramid on front skirt. Hi-back of beaded cut-out lace.
        Detachable cathedral length train.
        Color: White only.   **$650**

D E M E T R I O S / I L I S S A

❖ **Princess Collection Bridal Gowns** ....

(Note: Princess Collection bridal gowns are only available in sizes 6-20 unless otherwise noted.)

9408 Matte satin scoop neckline with heavily beaded alencon lace bodice and long fitted sleeves. Full floor-length gown with beaded hem lace. Keyhole back. Removable cathedral train with bustle.
Color: White only. **$700**

9409 Matte satin sheath with scalloped V-neckline and short sleeves. Beaded embroidered lace rosebuds adorn bodice and hem lace. Removable cathedral length train with elaborate appliqués throughout.
Color: White or Ivory **$650**

9411 Matte satin princess silhouette with scoop neckline. Beaded appliqués of lace trimmed with rosebuds. Scalloped hem lace, cathedral length train.
Color: White or Ivory **$590**

9412 Traditional matte satin scoop neck with elaborately beaded alencon lace on bodice and sleeves. Appliqués of beaded alencon lace accents hem line. Floor length. Removable cathedral length train with open beaded alencon lace.
Color: White only. **$700**
• Also available in sizes 4, 22, 24 and 26

9413 Matte satin traditional with pearled V-neckline. Beaded cutout appliqués on bodice. Scalloped hem lace on floor length gown. Scalloped removable cathedral train accented with cutout beaded appliqués.
Color: White only. **$670**

9414 Sleeveless halter mermaid adorned with beaded alencon lace. Removable matte satin cathedral train.
Color: White only. **$590**

9415 Traditional Contessa neckline with heavily beaded and sequined alencon lace bodice. Pyramids of beaded lace on front skirt of matte satin. Cathedral plus train elaborately accented with cutout lace appliqués.
Color: White only. **$350**
• Also available in sizes 4, 22, 24 and 26

9416 All beaded and sequined halter sheath. Removable organza train accented with beaded appliqués.
Color: White Only **$550**

D E M E T R I O S / I L I S S A

9417   Sleeveless princess silhouette with beaded and sequined
        empire bodice. Beaded hem lace on matte satin floor-
        length gown. Removable watteau train.
        Color: White or Ivory   **$550**
        • Also available in sizes 4, 22, 24 and 26

9418   Matte satin scoop neckline with short sleeves. Delicately
        beaded venise lace on bodice and cascades down inverted
        pleats. Cathedral length train.
        Color: White or Ivory   **$590**

✦ DIAMOND ✦

Contact info. Diamond Collection, 1385 Broadway, Suite 1701, New York, NY 10018. For a dealer near you, call (212) 302-0210.

Also known as. Ada Athanassiou, Randy Fenoli. (These are the names of Diamond's designers).

Internet. This designer does not have an official web site yet. Our web site (www.bridalgown.com) will have updates on this designer.

Background. Diamond was founded by Paul Diamond and designer Frank Masandrea in 1983. The company was an innovator on several fronts: Diamond was first to do all silk wedding gowns, translating ready-to-wear looks into bridal fashion. The designer also took a daring approach to advertising, shaking up the bridal world with its innovative dress ads that often saw gown models plunked down on a bale of straw and other unique settings.

Diamond reached a crossroads when designer Masandrea died of AIDS in 1988. Never quite able to replace Masandrea's incredible vision and style, Diamond went through several designers, including such big names as Bob Mackie and Robert Legere, before settling on its current line-up. Young designer Randy Fenoli joins veteran Ada Athanassiou (who was Richard Glasgow's initial partner) as Diamond's current dress designers.

Our view. Diamond's designers each have their own collections, and, as you might expect, each has a slightly different personality. Randy's gowns are more traditional, with moderate amounts of lace and beading. The ball gown is a popular silhouette.

Ada's dresses, on the other hand, are more refined and somewhat European in flavor. The sleek and streamlined silhouettes rely less on lace and more on the fabric to make a statement.

Diamond is a small collection, debuting about 20 new styles each season. All in all, about 50 dresses are available. The prices? Well, all this couture styling doesn't come cheap—dresses start at $1100 and top $3600. Most are in the $2000 to $2500 to the range.

What do you get for that money? Everything is in silk, as you might expect. And the fashion is stunning. While some of Diamond's thunder has been stolen by other designers with better publicity machines (Vera Wang, please take a bow), we still like these guys. Unlike other couture designers who tried to cheapen their image with low-price (and lower-quality) dresses, Diamond has stayed true to its mission. **Rating: B**

Delivery. 14 to 16 weeks. No rush cuts are available.

Tags. Diamond identifies their gowns with hangs tags and a sewn-in label.

SIZING CHART

Type. Diamond uses a BODY measurement size chart. For information on this subject, refer to the introduction of this section.

	4	6	8	10	12	14	16	18	20
Bust	32"	33	34	35	36.5	38	39.5	41.5	43.5
Waist	23	24	25	26	27.5	29	30.5	32.5	34.5

Sizing notes:
• *Gown length (as measured from the hollow of the neck to the desired dress hem) is 57".*

Extra charges for changes/options:
1. For sizes 18 and 20, add $100 to the gown price.
2. For extra length, add 10% to the gown price.
3. To shorten the length of a gown, add 5% to the gown price.
4. Unless specified, all gowns are available in both white and ivory.

NEW BRIDAL GOWNS FOR SPRING 1997

❖ Randy Fenoli Bridal Gowns ....

STYLE #	DESCRIPTION	SUGGESTED RETAIL

400   White silk satin organza gown, sweetheart cut bodice, floral beaded sheer net yoke, short sleeves, beaded full gathered skirt, ball gown length.
Colors: White, Ivory   **$1900**

401   White silk satin bodice beaded and pearled floral appliqués, off the shoulder, short sleeve, full gathered tulle skirt, chapel train.
Colors: White, Ivory, Rum Pink   **$1850**
Advertised in Brides magazine Feb/Mar 1997

403   White silk satin gown, rests at tip of shoulder, dropped waist, skirt of Lyon lace, satin band at hem line, back detailing of pressed roses and satin loops, ball gown length.
Colors: White, Ivory, Rum Pink   **$3450**

404   White silk satin sheath, satin piped sleeveless stretch tulle yoke with boat neckline, silk satin organdy floor length train trimmed with hand rolled satin roses and bias bands of silk satin.
Colors: White, Ivory   **$1900**
Advertised and featured in an editorial in Modern Bride magazine Feb/Mar 1997

405   White silk satin organza, sweetheart cut princess line, stretch tulle halter style yoke, satin bands and bows, floor length.
Colors: White, Ivory   **$1350**

408 White re-embroidered beaded alencon lace bodice with stretch tulle, halter style yoke, full gathered tulle skirt with 3 rows of satin piping at hem line, chapel train.
Colors: White, Ivory   **$1500**

410 White heavily beaded and pearled alencon lace bodice, on the shoulder, V-neckline, short sleeves, basque waist, full gathered taffeta skirt, pressed silk roses in back, chapel train.
Colors: White, Ivory   **$2500**

412 White silk satin princess line halter gown, back interest of silk orchids, roses and crystals, chapel train.
Colors: White, Ivory, Rum Pink   **$1750**
Advertised in Modern Bride magazine Feb/Mar 1997

414 Rum Pink silk satin gown with thread embroidered floral appliqués and pearl trim, off the shoulder, short sleeve, gathered skirt, chapel train.
Colors: White, Ivory, Rum Pink   **$1990**
Advertised in Brides magazine Feb/Mar 1997

416 White organza bodice with crystals, pearls, gold and silver beads and tiny flowers, on the shoulder, sleeveless gown with boat neck, scooped waistline, full gathered skirt of silk taffeta, ball gown length.
Colors: White, Ivory   **$1990**
Beading: Available in gold and silver, all silver
Advertised and featured in an editorial in Brides magazine Feb/Mar 1997

417 White silk satin sweetheart under-bodice with sleeveless re-embroidered lace overlay with satin bows, full gathered silk satin organdy skirt with wide lace hem line, ball gown length.
Colors: White, Ivory   **$1650**
Featured in an editorial in Modern Bride magazine Feb/Mar 1997

418 White sweetheart cut silk satin bodice with stretch tulle yoke and short sleeves trimmed with crystal beaded collar and cuffs, full gathered silk satin organdy skirt with wide satin banded hem line.
Colors: White, Ivory   **$2390**
Advertised in Modern Bride magazine Feb/Mar 1997 Featured in an editorial in Elegant Bride magazine Feb/Mar 1997

419 Rum Pink silk satin princess line gown with re-embroidered and beaded alencon lace trim, spaghetti straps, back interest of hand rolled roses and long lace-trimmed tails, floor length.
Colors: White, Ivory, Rum Pink   **$2390**
Advertised in Brides magazine Feb/Mar 1997

421   White silk satin on the shoulder bodice with low cut
       neckline, V-back, long sleeves of beaded schiffli lace, full
       gathered skirt of beaded schiffli, ball gown length.
       Colors: White, Ivory   **$2150**
       Advertised in Brides magazine Feb/Mar 1997

422   White silk organza bodice beaded and stoned, on the
       shoulder, sleeveless, scooped neckline, natural waistline,
       flared silk satin organza skirt, chapel train.
       Colors: White, Ivory   **$1990**
       Featured in an editorial in Brides magazine Feb/Mar 1997

423   White silk satin bodice with beaded floral appliqué trim
       continuing to back straps, jewel neckline, sleeveless, full
       gathered tulle skirt with satin bows trailing down to
       chapel train.
       Colors: White, Ivory   **$1500**
       Advertised in Brides magazine Feb/Mar 1997

425   Ivory silk satin organdy princess line sleeveless gown,
       gathered skirt at sides and back, trimmed with bias silk
       satin bands and bows. chapel train.
       Colors: White, Ivory   **$1450**
       Advertised in Brides magazine Feb/Mar 1997

427   White silk satin off the shoulder princess line gown, heav-
       ily beaded empire style scoop neckline, short sleeves, hand
       rolled roses and loops in back, chapel train.
       Colors: White, Ivory   **$2300**
       Advertised in Modern Bride magazine Feb/Mar 1997

429   White four-ply silk crepe trumpet style gown, sweetheart
       neck with stretch illusion yoke, long sleeves, crystal
       beaded collar and cuffs, chapel train.
       Colors: White   **$1990**

430   Ivory silk satin organdy, off the shoulder with short
       sleeves, dropped waist, full gathered skirt trimmed with
       bias bands and bows of silk satin, ball gown length.
       Colors: White, Ivory   **$1590**
       Advertised in Modern Bride magazine Feb/Mar 1997

431   White four-ply silk crepe trumpet style gown with low
       neckline and V-back, long beaded and stoned net sleeves,
       chapel train.
       Colors: White   **$1850**
       Advertised in Elegant Bride magazine Feb/Mar 1997

432   Ivory silk satin 18th Century inspired gown with alencon
       lace trimmed boned corset like off the shoulder sweet-
       heart cut bodice, and lace trimmed, chapel train.
       Colors: White, Ivory, Rum Pink   **$3990**

Advertised in Brides magazine Feb/Mar 1997
"Designer's Showcase"

❖ **Ada Athanassiou Bridal Gowns** ....

7051   White silk satin ball gown skirt. Corded ballerina bodice,
        off shoulder cap sleeve, basque waist, pleated skirt, hand-
        made silk flowers in back, chapel train.   **$1990**
        Colors: White, Ivory
        Advertised in Brides magazine Feb/Mar 1997

7052   White silk taffeta ball gown skirt. Halter gown with fluted
        bodice, dropped waist, shirred skirt, chapel train.
        Colors: White, Ivory   **$1990**

7053   Ivory silk organza ball gown skirt. Halter bodice with
        dimensional beaded leaf design lace, sleeveless, shirred
        skirt, chapel train.
        Colors: White, Ivory   **$2390**
        Advertised in Brides magazine Feb/Mar 1997

7054   White re-embroidered alencon lace sheath. Halter gown,
        sleeveless, beaded illusion front and back yoke, detachable
        silk organdy bow, gauntlets included.
        Colors: White, Ivory   **$2500**

7055   White silk wool dupioni ball gown. A-line halter gown,
        sleeveless, neckline is decorated with a 2" beaded band,
        sweep train.
        Colors: White   **$1990**
        Advertised and featured in an editorial in Modern Bride
        magazine Feb/Mar 1997

7056   White silk twirl ball gown. Silk twirl halter gown, beaded
        bodice, dropped waist, 2" gold and white beaded band at
        neckline and hipline, shirred skirt, chapel train.
        Colors: White, Ivory   **$2500**
        Advertised in Brides magazine Feb/Mar 1997

7057   White silk satin gown with tulle skirt. Silk satin with all
        over corded ballerina bodice, spaghetti straps, neckline
        and hipline are decorated with narrow beaded band
        and beaded flowers, tulle skirt with beaded appliqués,
        sweep train.
        Colors: White, Ivory   **$2990**

7058   White silk satin ball gown. Silk satin bodice with 2" wide
        beaded straps, neckline and hipline are decorated with
        beaded bands, shirred skirt, chapel train.
        Colors: White, Ivory   **$2590**
        Advertised in Brides magazine Feb/Mar 1997

7059   White silk satin ball gown. Silk satin halter, beaded
        alencon lace bodice, shirred skirt adorned with beaded
        alencon motifs, chapel train.
        Color: White, Ivory   **$3590**
        Advertised in Brides magazine Feb/Mar 1997 "Images"

7060   Rum Pink silk satin ball gown. Silk satin off the shoulder,
        sweetheart neckline, cap sleeve, bodice is decorated with 3
        dimensional beaded appliqués, shirred skirt, chapel train.
        Colors: White, Ivory, Rum Pink   **$2390**
        Advertised in Modern Bride magazine Feb/Mar 1997

7061   Ivory silk satin gown with tulle skirt. Silk satin bodice is
        decorated with 3 dimensional swirl design heavily beaded
        motifs, off the shoulder, cap sleeve, full tulle skirt, sweep
        train.
        Colors: White, Ivory   **$2190**
        Advertised in Modern Bride magazine Feb/Mar 1997

7062   White silk shantung ball gown. Silk shantung princess line
        gown has cap sleeve, pleated draped band under bust-line
        ending on waist of center back bodice, 3 dimensional
        swirl design motifs on chapel train.
        Colors: White, Ivory   **$2300**

7063   White silk satin organdy ball gown. Swirl design halter
        bodice, beaded collar, princess line skirt, sweep train.
        Color: White, Ivory   **$2700**
        Advertised in Brides magazine Feb/Mar 1997

7064   White beaded bodice with tulle skirt. Gold and white
        beaded bodice with dropped waist, wide criss-cross front
        and back straps, tulle skirt, sweep train.
        Color: White, Ivory   **$1990**

7065   White silk twirl ball gown. Silk twirl empire style princess
        line gown, silk organza on the shoulder, sleeveless, yoke
        decorated.
        Color: White, Ivory   **$2250**

7066   Ivory silk satin with tulle skirt. Silk satin bodice with trio
        beading, off the shoulder, cap sleeve, basque waist with
        decorated beaded alencon lace, tulle skirt, sweep train.
        Colors: White, Ivory   **$1950**
        Advertised in Elegant Bride magazine Feb/Mar

7067   Ivory silk satin ball gown. Silk satin bodice with trio bead-
        ing, halter, sleeveless, draped overskirt with motifs of
        beaded alencon multi-color lace, sweep train.
        Colors: White, Ivory   **$3390**

7068   White silk crepe gown. Four-ply silk crepe trumpet style
sheath with bias folded bands draped over bust-line,
1" wide beaded straps.
Colors: White, Ivory   **$1650**

7069   White/Ivory silk satin ball gown. Silk satin white full
gored skirt with inserted ivory bank, off the shoulder,
waisted bodice with ivory fluted cummerbund, ivory bow
with wide streamers decorated with handmade silk flowers, sweep train.
Colors: White/Ivory, White, Ivory   **$1990**
Advertised in Bride's magazine Feb/Mar 1997

7070   Rum Pink silk satin ball gown. Silk satin gown with
decorated Venice lace bodice, off the shoulder, cap sleeve,
pleated skirt, chapel train.
Colors: White, Ivory, Rum Pink   **$2390**
Advertised in Modern Bride magazine Feb/Mar 1997

7071   White silk twirl ball gown. Silk twirl gown, off the shoulder, stand-up portrait collar, bodice adorned with re-
embroidered lace, full gathered skirt with border of
re-embroidered lace at hem line, chapel train.
Color: White   **$2990**

7072   White silk charmeuse and organza stripes ball gown. Silk
charmeuse, off the shoulder, sweetheart neckline, bodice
crisscrossed with charmeuse stripes, silk hand rolled flowers over shoulders, draped peplum over waistline, hand
rolled silk flowers at back waist, ball gown length.
Colors: White, Ivory   **$2390**
Advertised in Modern Bride magazine Feb/Mar 1997

→ E D E N ←

Contact info. Eden, 230 Pasadena Ave., S. Pasadena, CA 91030. For a dealer near you, call (818) 441-8715.

Also known as. Glamour by Eden, Eden Premiere, Eden Elegance, Eden Collection, Eden Value, Eden Princess, Eden Enchantments.

Internet. This designer does not have an official web site yet. Our web site (www.bridalgown.com) will have updates on this designer.

Background/Our view. If you want a wedding dress but don't want to go bankrupt in the process of buying one, you'll want to make sure this designer is on the top of your shopping list.

Eden has probably the best deal in the market—eight bridal dresses in their "Eden Value" collection for $386 to $408. And these aren't informal tea-length dresses without trains. Nope, we're talking formal gowns with full-length trains.

If one of those styles doesn't do it, Eden has a couple dozen other designs that range from $400 to $700. While most of the line uses synthetic fabrics like polyester satin, there are a few silk shantung gowns in the $600 range. Surprisingly, the fashion is often right on the mark. The gowns are stylish, but not over done. You won't see much beading on Eden dresses; cut-work (where lace is cut out on the sleeves or train) is a more common decoration.

In business since 1989, Eden also has a good selection of informals and even offers gowns in both large and petite sizes. The quality is above average, as are the deliveries and custom service. **Rating: A**

Tags. Eden identifies its gowns with hang tags and a sewn-in label.

Delivery. 11 to 12 weeks, although in-stock styles/sizes are available for immediate delivery. No rush cuts.

SIZING CHARTS

Type: Eden uses a GARMENT measurement size chart. For information on this subject, refer to the introduction of this section. Eden has three sizing charts: average, petite and large.

Average Sizes

	4	6	8	10	12	14	16	18	20*	22*
Bust	33"	34	35	36	37.5	39	40.5	41.5	42.5	45.5
Waist	23	24	25	26	27.5	29	30.5	31.5	32.5	35.5
Hips	35	36	37	38	39.5	41	42.5	43.5	44.5	49

Sizing notes:
• *Gown length (as measured from the hollow of the neck to the desired dress hem) is 58".*

• *For sizes 20 and 22, add $30 to $50 to the gown price (depending on the style). Ask a local retailer for more information on exact charges.

Petite Sizes

	3	5	7	9	11
Bust	32"	33	34	35	36
Waist	24	25	26	27	28
Hips	33.5	35	35.5	36.75	38

Sizing notes:
• Gown length (as measured from the hollow of the neck to the desired dress hem) is 54".
• For sizes 3 to 11, add $200 to the gown price.

Large Sizes

	24	26	28	30	32
Bust	47"	49	51	53	55
Waist	37.5	39.5	41.5	43.5	45.5
Hips	49.5	51.5	53.5	55.5	57.5

Sizing notes:
• Gown length (as measured from the hollow of the neck to the desired dress hem) is 58".
• For sizes 24 to 32, add $200 to the gown price.

Extra charges for changes/options
The following four options are only available on Eden Bridals and Eden Informals:
1. Extra gown length (up to six inches additional) adds $200 to the gown price.
2. Extra train length (up to 106", without additional appliqué) adds $200 to the gown price.
3. Extra sleeve length (up to three inches) adds $200 to the gown price.
4. Change of fabric (not including silk shantung) adds $200 to the gown price.
5. For colors other than standard white, add $20 to the gown price.

NEW BRIDAL GOWNS FOR SPRING 1997

Note: A limited number of styles are available in petites and large sizes. Consult a local retailer for more information.

❖ Eden Informal Bridal Gowns ....

STYLE #	COLORS	FABRIC	SUGGESTED RETAIL
108	White/Ivory	All-Over Lace	**$398**
125	White/Ivory	Shantung	**$318**
137	White/Ivory	Matte Satin	**$318**

E D E N

Style #	Colors	Fabric	Suggested Retail
141	White/Ivory/Pink	Taffeta	**$278**
143	White/Ivory	All-Over Lace	**$318**
148	White/Ivory	Matte Satin	**$318**
150	White/Ivory	Matte Satin	**$318**
151	White/Ivory	Organza	**$378**
152	White/Ivory	Crepe	**$338**
153	White/Ivory	Matte Satin	**$358**
154	White/Ivory	Matte Satin	**$318**
155	White/Ivory	Shantung	**$358**
156	White/Ivory	Matte Satin	**$358**
181	White/Ivory	Matte Satin	**$298**
182	White/Ivory	Matte Satin	**$338**
183	White/Ivory	Matte Satin	**$338**
184	White/Ivory	Lace/Tulle	**$358**
185	White/Ivory	Matte Satin	**$318**
186	White/Ivory	Matte Satin	**$318**
187	White/Ivory	Matte Satin	**$298**
188	White/Ivory	Shantung	**$338**
189	White/Ivory	Matte Satin	**$318**
190	White/Ivory	Matte Satin	**$358**
960	White/Ivory/Pink	Satin/Tulle	**$298**

❖ Eden Bridal Gowns ....

Style #	Colors	Fabric	Suggested Retail
200	White/Ivory	Italian Satin	**$798**
225	White/Ivory	Shantung	**$498**
242	White/Ivory	Matte Satin	**$638**
251	White/Ivory	Matte Satin	**$558**
252	White/Rum Pink	Lace/Organza	**$598**
253	White/Ivory	Matte Satin	**$518**
256	White Only	Organza	**$458**
258	White/Ivory	Matte Satin	**$498**
260	White/Ivory	Matte Satin	**$538**
261	White/Ivory	Satin/Organza	**$538**
262	White/Ivory	Matte Satin	**$558**
263	White/IvoryRumPink	Matte Satin	**$598**
264	White/Ivory	Chiffon	**$478**
265	White/Ivory	All-Over-Lace	**$598**
267	White/Ivory	Shantung	**$498**
269	White/Ivory	Matte Satin	**$478**
272	White/Ivory	Matte Satin	**$598**
274	White/Ivory	Matte Satin	**$558**
275	White/Ivory	Crepe	**$458**
280	White/Rum Pink	Matte Satin	**$458**
283	White/Rum Pink	Satin/Tulle	**$518**
286	White/Ivory	Matte Satin	**$458**
290	White/Ivory	De-lustered Satin	**$438**

E D E N

291	White/Ivory	Shantung	$438
292	White/Ivory	De-lustered Satin	$438
940	White/Ivory	Shantung	$458

❖ **Glamour By Eden Bridal Gowns (Pure Silk Shantung)** ....

STYLE #	COLORS	FABRIC	SUGGESTED RETAIL
301	Natural	Silk Shantung	$798
302	Natural	Silk Shantung	$798
303	Natural	Silk Shantung	$558
304	Natural	Silk Shantung	$658
321	Natural	Silk Shantung	$558
322	Natural	Silk Shantung	$558
323	Natural	Silk Shantung	$538
324	Natural	Silk Shantung	$538
325	Natural	Silk Shantung	$798
329	Natural	Silk Shantung	$898
332	Natural	Silk Shantung	$898
368	Natural	Silk Shantung	$1398
369	Natural	Silk Shantung	$898
371	Natural	Silk Shantung	$578
372	Natural	Silk Shantung	$558
373	Natural	Silk Shantung	$578
374	Natural	Silk Shantung	$558
375	Candlelight	Silk Shantung	$598
376	Candlelight	Silk Shantung	$598
377	Candlelight	Silk Shantung	$578
378	Candlelight	Silk Shantung	$598
381	Natural	Silk Shantung	$598
382	Natural	Silk Shantung	$578
383	Natural	Silk Shantung	$598
384	Candlelight	Silk Shantung	$538
385	Candlelight	Silk Shantung	$538
386	Candlelight	Silk Shantung	$578

❖ **Eden Value Bridal Gowns** ....

STYLE #	COLORS	FABRIC	SUGGESTED RETAIL
501	White/Ivory	Satin	$338
502	White/Ivory	Satin	$358
503	White/Ivory	Satin	$338
504	White/Ivory	Satin	$358
505	White/Ivory	Satin	$358
506	White/Ivory	Satin	$338
507	White/Ivory	Satin	$338
508	White/Ivory	Satin	$358
509	White/Ivory	Satin	$357
510	White/Ivory	Satin	$378

E D E N

511	White/Ivory	Satin	$378
512	White/Ivory	Satin	$358
513	White/Ivory	Satin	$358
514	White/Ivory	Satin	$378
515	White/Ivory	Satin	$378
516	White/Ivory	Satin	$358
517	White/Ivory	Satin	$338
518	White/Ivory	Satin	$398
519	White/Ivory	Satin	$338
520	White/Ivory	Satin	$358

❖ Eden Collection Bridal Gowns ....

STYLE #	COLORS	FABRIC	SUGGESTED RETAIL
614	White Only	Matte Satin	$598
621	White Only	Matte Satin	$598
622	White Only	Matte Satin	$598
623	White Only	Matte Satin	$598
624	White Only	Matte Satin	$598
625	White Only	Matte Satin	$598
626	White Only	Matte Satin	$598
630	White Only	All-Over Lace	$598
631	White Only	Matte Satin	$598
632	White Only	Matte Satin	$598
708	White/Ivory	All-Over Lace	$500
730	White/Ivory	Satin	$590
733	White Only	Satin/Tulle	$538
736	White/Ivory	All-Over Lace	$598

❖ Eden Premiere Bridal Gowns ....

STYLE #	COLORS	FABRIC	SUGGESTED RETAIL
801	White/Ivory	Matte Satin	$518
802	White/Ivory	Matte Satin	$518
803	White/Ivory	Matte Satin	$518
804	White/Ivory	Matte Satin	$538
805	White/Ivory	Matte Satin	$518
806	White/Ivory	Matte Satin	$518
807	White/Ivory	Matte Satin	$558
808	White/Ivory	Matte Satin	$558
809	White/Ivory	Matte Satin	$518

❖ Eden Elegance Bridal Gowns ....

STYLE #	COLORS	FABRIC	SUGGESTED RETAIL
851	Ivory Only	All-Over Lace	$598
852	Ivory Only	All-Over Lace	$698
853	Ivory Only	All-Over Lace	$698

❖ E V E   O F   M I L A D Y ❖

Contact info. Eve of Milady, 1375 Broadway, 7th Fl., New York, NY 10018. For a dealer near you, call (212) 302-0050.

Also known as. Amalia Carrara is a separate collection of dresses made by Eve of Milady.

Internet. This designer does not have an official web site yet. Our web site (www.bridalgown.com) will have updates on this designer.

Background/Our view. An established designer who manufactures all their gowns in the U.S., Eve of Milady is a style leader whose designs are often copied by lower-price manufacturers. A typical Eve of Milady dress is big on drama, with lots of lace and a big tulle skirt. Appliqués are a common adornment. However, Eve of Milady is also a microcosm of what's wrong with the bridal business.

So, what's their problem? First, consider the prices. A dress from this designer will set you back a minimum of $1000. And some designs top $4000. Want a matching headpiece? Eve sells these for up to $250—and that's the *wholesale* price. Mark it up to retail and you've got a headpiece that's more than many bridal gowns go for with other manufacturers.

Yet, the most disturbing thing about Eve of Milady is their attitude toward customer service. Secretive to a fault, Eve refused to answer any of our questions about their background. In a long conversation with owner Eve Muscio, the designer in so many words told us that if we didn't write something nice about them, they'd sue us. Not a way to win friends and influence people.

While the fashion of Eve of Milady's gowns is renowned, their deliveries and customer service is just average. **Rating: C-**

Delivery. 16 weeks is an approximate estimate. Rush cuts (eight week delivery) are also available.

SIZING CHART									
	4	**6**	**8**	**10**	**12**	**14**	**16**	**18***	**20***
Bust	33"	34	35	36	37.5	39	40.5	42.5	44.5
Waist	22.5	23.5	24.5	25.5	27	28.5	30	32	34
Hips	34	35	36	37	38.5	40	41.5	43.5	45.5

Sizing notes:
• **For sizes 18 and 20, add $100 to the gown price.*

Extra charges for options/changes:
1. For gowns ordered in ivory, add $100 to the gown price.
2. Matching headpieces must be ordered at the time of the gown order.

Basic dress information (style number, price) on this designer will be available on our web page (www.bridalgown.com).

→ F I N K ←

Contact info. Fink, 1385 Broadway, 11th Fl., New York, NY 10018. For a dealer near you, call (212) 947-4140.

Internet. This designer does not have an official web site yet. Our web site (www.bridalgown.com) will have updates on this designer.

Background. Fink is one of the oldest bridal manufacturers in business today. Co-owner Lenny Fink told us his grandparents went into bridal manufacturing after tiring of the retail end of the business (they owned three bridal retail shops in New York City). That was 1939. In those days, a formal wedding dress with full train retailed for about $30 to $40. "Today you can't even buy buttons for $20," Lenny said.

Fink's designer of 32 years, Robert Work, recently retired, handing over the reins to Gus Marinelli. Gus is a veteran in the business and has worked for Sweetheart, among other bridal designers. As always, Fink tries for a traditional, mainstream look.

Our view. Fink is another one of those bridal designers who fly under the radar of most brides. To keep costs down, Fink rarely advertises its dresses in bridal magazines. But don't let a lack of exposure keep you from looking at this wonderful line.

This is a small collection. Fink rolls out a half dozen new styles per season and has a total of 40 or so dresses overall. What money Fink saves in advertising is apparently invested in the quality of their dresses. The fabrics are excellent (Italian satin, silk shantung) and the quality of construction is among the industry's best.

Prices range from $500 to $1300, which doesn't rank Fink as a tremendous bargain but the designer still offers strong value. Deliveries are among the industry's most reliable. **Rating: A-**

Delivery. 12 weeks. Rush cuts are available.

SIZING CHARTS

Type: Fink uses a GARMENT measurement size chart. For information on this subject, refer to the introduction of this section.

	4	6	8	10	12	14	16	18*	20*
Bust	31"	33	34	35.5	36.5	37.5	38.5	40.5	42.5
Waist	22.5	24	25	26	27	28.5	30	32	33.5
Hips	32	34	35	37	38	39	40	41.5	43.5

Sizing notes:
• *Standard gown length is 58" as measured from hollow of the neck to the desired dress hem.*
• *Standard sleeve measurement is 17.5" (armpit to wrist).*

Extra charges for options/changes:

1. *For sizes 18 and 20, add 10% to the gown price.

2. Extra gown length (five inches) is available; add 10% to the gown price for this option.

3. Extra sleeve length is available for $40.

New Bridal Gowns for Spring 1997

| STYLE # | DESCRIPTION | SUGGESTED RETAIL |

5152   Organza gown with Basque waist and off the shoulder short ruffle sleeves, full gathered skirt and chapel train. Venice lace with taffeta buds accents the bodice.
Available in white or ivory with white, ivory or pink buds.
$900

5153   Italian satin sheath with detachable chapel train. Basque waist bodice with jewel neckline and net yoke, short sleeves highlighted with re embroidered lace. Slim skirt and train edged with re-embroidered lace scallop.
Available in white or ivory. **$770**

5154   Venice lace bodice, scoop neckline, short sleeves and Basque waist beaded with clear sequins. Gathered full tulle skirt with detachable chapel train accented with Venice lace appliqués.
Available in white or ivory. **$750**
Advertised in Modern Bride Magazine Feb/Mar 1997

5155   Italian satin princess line gown with inverted pleats. Venice lace highlights the off the shoulder neckline, short sleeves and bodice. Venice lace scallop encircles the hem line.
Available in white or ivory. **$840**
Advertised in Modern Bride Magazine Feb/Mar, Apr/May, June/July 1997

5157   Silk shantung sheath with detachable chapel train. Venice lace sleeveless dropped torso with sabrina neckline. Slim skirt bordered with Venice lace.
Available in white or ivory. **$1150**
Featured in an editorial in Modern Bride Feb/Mar 1997

5158   Silk shantung gown, V neckline and short raglan sleeves with princess line dropped torso. French alencon lace beaded with crystals and pearls accents the bodice. Gathered full skirt and chapel train.
Available in white or ivory. **$990**
Advertised in Modern Bride magazine Feb/Mar 1997

5159   Silk shantung gown, Basque waist, off the shoulder neckline and short cap sleeves accented with Venice lace. Floor length A-line skirt.
Available in white or ivory. **$650**

FINK

5160   French re-embroidered alencon lace highlights the dropped torso, long sleeves and jewel neckline. Ankle length chiffon handkerchief skirt.
Available in white or ivory   **$550**

5161   Italian satin princess line gown with detachable train. Asymmetrically placed Venice lace on bodice and skirt. Sleeveless illusion neckline. Venice lace scallop edges the hem.
Available in white or ivory.   **$750**
Advertised in Modern Bride Feb/Mar 1997

5162   Silk shantung princess line gown. French alencon lace with crystal and pearl beading accents the sweetheart neckline, bodice and short sleeves. French alencon lace scallop en-circles the hem and chapel train.
Available in white or ivory.   **$1170**

5163   Italian satin bodice, pearl and soutache daisies accent the off-the-shoulder Bateau neckline and short cap sleeves. Gathered full tulle skirt with sweep train.
Available in white or ivory.   **$520**

5164   Silk shantung pleated A-line with Basque waist. Re-embroidered lace highlights the bodice, jewel neckline and short sleeves.
Available in white or ivory.   **$900**
Advertised in Modern Bride magazine Feb/Mar, Apr/May, June/July 1997

5166   Italian satin princess line gown, re-embroidered lace accents the empire bodice, V neckline and long net sleeves. Lace appliqués highlight the back skirt and chapel train.
Available in white or ivory.   **$790**
Advertised in Modern Bride magazine Feb/Mar 1997

5168   Italian satin gown, headed re-embroidered lace highlights the off the shoulder neckline, long fitted net sleeves and Basque waist bodice. Flat front full gathered skirt and chapel train appliquéed with lace motifs and satin roses.
Available in white, ivory or pink with white or ivory lace.   **$790**

5169   Italian satin gown, French alencon lace headed with crystals and pearls highlight the Basque waist bodice, portrait neckline and short off the shoulder sleeves. Full gathered skirt with flat front and chapel train.
Available in white or ivory.   **$800**

5170   Italian satin gown, headed re-embroidered lace highlights the Basque waist bodice, off the shoulder neckline and long net sleeves. Flat front gathered skirt with chapel train

appliquéed with beaded lace motifs.
Available in white or ivory.   **$790**

5171   Silk shantung gown, asymmetrically placed Venice lace on
       sleeveless dropped torso. Venice lace accents the pleated
       A-line skirt and chapel train.
       Available in white or ivory.   **$900**

5172   Italian satin gown, scoop neckline, short raglan sleeves
       with princess line dropped waist accented with pearl and
       crystal band. Box pleated skirt and chapel train.
       Available in white or ivory.   **$598**

❖ **Fink Carry-over Bridal Gowns** ....
(Dresses from previous seasons still available)

4870   Organza full skirt with off shoulder long fitted sleeves.
       Silk Venice lace accented with taffeta buds on bodice,
       sleeves, skirt and train.
       Available in white or ivory with white, ivory or
       pink buds.   **$810**
       Advertised in Modern Bride magazine Feb/Mar 1997

5057   Informal gown in chiffon and pearl and sequin trimmed
       re-embroidered alencon lace. Circular skirt is a handker-
       chief bottom.
       Available in white or ivory.   **$520**
       Advertised in Modern Bride magazine Feb/Mar 1997

5111   Italian satin princess floor length with removable chapel
       train. Pearl and sequin trimmed re-embroidered alencon
       lace on jeweled neckline, bodice, short fitted sleeves and
       scattered on train.
       Available in white or ivory.   **$720**

✦ F O R E V E R   Y O U R S ✦

Contact info. Forever Yours International Corp., 93 Marcus Blvd., Hauppauge, NY 11788. For a dealer near you, (800) USA-BRIDE. (In Canada, call 1-800-801-7202 for a dealer).

Also known as. Forever Yours Bridals, Now and Forever, Fantasy.

Internet. This designer does not have an official web site yet. Our web site (www.bridalgown.com) will have updates on this designer.

Background/Our view. In business since 1991, Forever Yours is a young manufacturer that concentrates on the lower to moderate price points of the bridal gown market.

The company divides its gowns into three collections. The "Now & Forever" line features silk gowns at very attractive prices: $538 to $700. "Fantasy" is what the company calls their "couture" designs ($500 to $800) and the regular "Forever Yours" gowns run $400 to $800. Besides the silk gowns, most of the other dresses are made of matte satin and Italian satin. While we give Forever Yours good marks on price, their fashion is mostly "inspired" by other designers. A little creativity would have helped some of the dresses we viewed, several of which looked reminiscent of Demetrios designs (all-over lace sheaths, etc.) Forever Yours is a surprisingly large line (60+ dresses) and most feature traditional silhouettes and conservative styling.

While some of the Now & Forever and Fantasy gowns have built-in crinolines, the quality of the company's gowns overall is just average. On the other hand, we like that they offer extensive sizing, with both petites and large sizes with no extra charges. **Rating: B-**

Delivery. 12 to 14 weeks, although in-stock sizes can ship much quicker. No rush cuts are available.

SIZING CHARTS

Type: Forever Yours uses a BODY measurement size chart. For information on this subject, refer to the introduction of this section.

	1	2	4	6	8	10	12	14
Bust	33.5"	34.5	35.5	36.5	38	39.5	41	43
Waist	24	25	26	27	28.5	30	31.5	33.5
Hips	34.25	35.25	36.25	37.25	38.75	40.25	41.75	43.75

	16	18	20	22	24	26	28	30
Bust	45"	47	49	51	53	55	57	59
Waist	35.5	37.5	39.5	41.5	43.5	45.5	47.5	49.5
Hips	45.75	47.75	49.75	51.75	53.75	55.75	57.75	59.75

Sizing notes:
• *Gown length is 59.5", as measured from the hollow of the neck to the desired dress hem. Extra length is not available.*

F O R E V E R   Y O U R S

• *Forever Yours is one of the few designer that does NOT charge extra for large sizes.*

<hr>

NEW BRIDAL GOWNS FOR SPRING 1997

(Note: For this designer, we have prices both in U.S. dollars and Canadian dollars. The first price is in U.S. dollars; the second is in Canadian dollars, noted as "CA").

❖ **Fantasy Bridal Gowns** ....

STYLE #	DESCRIPTION	SUGGESTED RETAIL
4014F	Italian Satin. "Off the shoulder" empire gown in Italian Satin. Heavily beaded bodice and short sleeves. A large design of individually beaded pearls, oats, sequins and clear bugles highlights the front skirt and is repeated in the train. *Colors: White and Ivory.*	$578 US, $820 CA
4015F	Italian Satin. Fit and flare halter gown in Italian Satin. Horizontal beaded bands accent the bodice and double halter straps. *Colors: White and Ivory.*	$458 US, $650 CA
4016F	Italian Satin. Bouffant gown in Italian Satin. Embroidered bodice and see-through short sleeves are heavily beaded with pearls and oats. Cut-out embroidered band circles the skirt 3" above the hem and follows the apron back. Cut-out appliqués and rosettes dot the train. The flat bow in back has twin streamers. *Colors: White and Ivory.*	$578 US, $820 CA
4017F	Italian Satin. Bouffant gown in Italian Satin. Bodice, short sleeves and back bow are covered with see-through embroidery, lightly beaded. High scoop neckline. Beaded, diamond shaped band circles the hem. *Colors: White Only.*	$538 US, $770 CA
4018F	Italian Satin. "Sophisticated" sheath in Italian Satin. The lightly beaded bodice and short sleeves are trimmed with a see-through embroidery. V-front neckline is complemented with pearls dangling in the key-hole back. Beaded, cut-out band edges the hem and circles the detachable train. *Colors: White and Ivory.*	$558 US, $790 CA
4019F	Italian Satin. "Off the shoulder" bouffant gown in Italian Satin. Pearl beaded cut-out embroidery accents the bodice and forms the short sleeves. Beaded see-through appliqués trim the front skirt and circle the train. The gown features a swag back that is slightly covered with an embroidery edged peplum. *Colors: White and Ivory.*	$538 US, $770 CA

4020F   Italian Satin. The ultimate bouffant gown in Italian Satin. Basque bodice and long sheer sleeves are heavily pearl beaded. Scalloped V-neckline front and back. Beaded alencon appliqués adorn front skirt and cathedral train. Graduated streamers trim the back waist.
Colors: White and Ivory.   **$700 US, $998 CA**

4308F   Organza. Sleeveless bouffant gown in Organza. Dainty rows of seam binding trim the collar, armholes, basque waist and hem. Dainty, lightly beaded venise appliqués trim the neckline and waist. A group of rosettes accents the back waist.
Colors: White and Ivory.   **$538 US, $770 CA**

❖ **Now & Forever Bridal Gowns** ....

4021N   100% silk. Bouffant gown in silk shantung. All lace bodice and short sleeves are lightly pearl and sequin beaded A bow and double loop streamers highlight back waist. Full chapel train.
Colors: Natural Only.   **$650 US, $918 CA**

4022N   100% silk. "Off the shoulder" bouffant gown in silk shantung. Entire bodice and short sleeves beautifully beaded with seed pearls and clear sequins. Full chapel train.
Colors: Natural Only.   **$598 US, $850 CA**

4023N   100% silk. Halter, princess in silk shantung Beaded venise lace covers the bodice, stand-up collar, and halter straps. Fabric rose and streamers accent the back bodice. Full chapel train.
Colors: Natural Only.   **$598 US, $850 CA**

4024N   100% silk. Halter, princess in silk shantung Horizontal rows of pearls cover the bodice and halter straps. Full chapel train.
Colors: Natural Only.   **$598 US, $850 CA**

4025N   100% silk. Princess panel sheath in silk shantung. Hand beading embroidered directly on silk trims the bodice and short sleeves. Detachable overskirt features rosettes at front waistline. Shaped V neckline.
Colors: Natural Only.   **$590 US, $838 CA**

4309N   100% silk. Bouffant gown in silk shantung. Pearl beaded re-embroidered lace covers front bodice, forms the square neckline, and extends over the sleeve caps mid way down the long fitted sleeves. A large beaded lace appliqué trims the front skirt and lace bands the hem and train. Flat bow trims the back waist.
Colors: Natural Only.   **$650 US, $918 CA**

F O R E V E R   Y O U R S

4501N   100% silk. Bouffant gown in silk shantung. A tastefully
        beaded, light airy embroidery highlights the bodice and
        short sleeves. A rosette centered double flat bow is at back
        waist. Full chapel train.
        Colors: Natural Only.   **$750 US, $1070 CA**

4502N   100% silk. Bouffant gown in silk shantung. Lightly beaded
        cut-out embroidery trims the V-neckline and short sleeves.
        A graceful, double tiered embroidered peplum rests under
        a rose centered, double flat bow. Full chapel train.
        Colors: Natural Only.   **$790 US, $1118 CA**

4503N   100% silk. Bouffant gown in silk shantung. Pearl beaded,
        peek-a-boo embroidery accents the bodice, forms the
        bateau neckline and long fitted sleeves. The back waist
        features a trimmed bow waterfall streamers.
        Colors: Natural Only.   **$900 US, $1278 CA**

4504N   100% silk. Bouffant silhouette in silk shantung Lightly
        beaded embroidery covers the bodice, forms the sweet-
        heart neck and long fitted sleeves. Trimming the back
        waist is a flat bow and beaded embroidered streamers.
        Colors: Natural Only.   **$850 US, $1198 CA**

❖ **Forever Yours Bridal Gowns** ....

4000   Alencon Lace. Sleeveless halter sheath in all-over beaded
        alencon lace. Stand-up collar, matching lace gauntlets.
        Detachable tubular Italian Satin train.
        Colors: White and Ivory.   **$598 US, $850 CA**

4001   Tulle. Sleeveless, halter, bouffant gown in frothy tulle.
        Lightly beaded venise lace bodice and standup collar.
        Bouffant tulle skirt is dotted with sparkling lace
        appliqués. Lace banded hem and chapel train.
        Colors: White Only.   **$578 US, $820 CA**

4002   Tulle. Bouffant gown in frothy tulle. Beaded venise lace
        trims the bodice, sweetheart neckline and long pointed
        sleeves. Sparkling appliqués highlight the front and back
        skirts. Detachable, cathedral train is all lace appliquéed.
        Colors: White and Ivory.   **$598 US, $850 CA**

400   Italian Satin. Princess gown in Italian Satin. Bands of
        graded pearls edge the scoop neckline that dips to a deep
        V-back. Long pointed sleeves are lace trimmed and pearl
        edged. Sparkling alencon accents the bodice and a wide
        band circles the hem and chapel train.
        Colors: White and Ivory.   **$538 US, $770 CA**

4004   Italian Satin. Sleeveless, sheath in Italian Satin. Sparkling
        alencon lace bodice has a high scoop neckline and basque

waist. Beaded alencon highlights the front skirt. Detachable train is accented with see-through lace appliqués.
Colors: White and Ivory.   **$518 US, $738 CA**

4005   Italian Satin. Bouffant silhouette in Italian Satin. Hand-sewn seed pearls adorn the bodice, short sleeves, and edge the heart-shaped neckline. White and spice piping outline the neckline, sleeves and basque waist. Full circular skirt and chapel train.
Colors: White/Spice and Ivory/Spice.   **$388 US, $480 CA**

4006   Italian Satin. Bouffant gown in Italian Satin. Sparkling alencon lace trims the bodice, sheer yoke, collar and long pointed sleeves. See-through lace appliqués cover the front skirt and are repeated in the chapel train. Beaded rosettes trim the double flat bow and streamers. Lace banded hem.
Colors: White and Ivory.   **$558 US, $790 CA**

4007   Tulle. Bouffant gown in airy tulle. Dainty venise edges the sweetheart neck, cap sleeves and basque bodice. Keyhole back neckline. Rose centered bows trim back waist. Full chapel train.
Colors: White and Ivory.   **$398 US, $570 CA**

4008   Organza. Princess gown in organza. Beaded venise accents the scoop neckline and cap sleeves. Lace trimmed bow at back waist complements the chapel train.
Colors: White and Ivory.   **$298 US, $420 CA**

4009   Italian Satin. Classic silhouette in Italian Satin. Beaded lace covers the basque bodice, V-neckline and long sleeves. Dangling pearls enhance the front waistline, sleeves and key-hole back. Heavily beaded, full chapel train done in checkered fashion.
Colors: White and Ivory.   **$650 US, $918 CA**

4010   Italian Satin. "Off the shoulder" gown in Italian Satin. Beaded alencon trims the bodice and cap sleeves. Oat edged rosettes accent the shoulders. Wide lace banded hem circles the chapel train.
Colors: White and Ivory.   **$578 US, $820 CA**

4011   Italian Satin. "Off the shoulder" gown in Italian Satin. Scattered pearls and clear sequins trim the bodice and cap sleeves. A 1" braid edges the neckline and waist. A beaded window appliqué draws attention to the front skirt and is repeated in the center back train. Flat bow at back waist.
Colors: White and Ivory.   **$538 US, $770 CA**

4012   Chiffon. Understated bouffant gown in chiffon High
scoop neck, raglan sleeves, full circular skirt and
chapel train.
Colors: White and Ivory.   **$458 US, $650 CA**

4013   Tulle. Bouffant gown in tulle. Alencon bodice has a scalloped beaded band that edges the V-neck and waistline.
Long pointed lace sleeves. Lace cascades over the waistline
onto the top of the tulle skirt. Same detail is repeated in
the cathedral train. Pearl edged bow is at back waist.
Color: White Only.   **$650 US, $918 CA**

4301   Italian Satin. Fit and flare gown in Italian Satin. Pearl
bands edge the modified sweetheart neck and notched
cap sleeves. Alencon lace covers the entire bodice.
Appliqués accent the princess skirt and are seen throughout the chapel train.
Color: White Only.   **$518 US, $738 CA**

4302   Organza. High neck beauty in organza. Stand-up lace collar over a sheer yoke. Sparking lace trims the bodice and
Tong fitted sleeves. Beaded appliqués dot the bouffant
skirt and cathedral train. A flat bow and multi-streamers
trim the back waist.
Color: White Only.   **$578 US, $820 CA**

4303   Italian Satin. Traditional, bouffant gown in Italian Satin.
Pearl beaded lace edges the Queen-Anne collar, bodice
and long pointed sleeves. See-through appliqués in front
skirt. The back neckline features a large keyhole with dangling pearls. Cut-out appliqués cover the entire train.
Butterfly bow covers a lace edged peplum.
Color: White Only.   **$558 US, $790 CA**

4304   Italian Satin. Bouffant silhouette in Italian Satin.
Scalloped V-neckline and long lace trimmed sleeves
emphasize the beauty of the lace appliquéed bodice. The
lightly appliquéed front skirt beautifully coordinates with
the diamond tiered train also sparsely appliquéed. Double
flat bow trims back waist.
Color: White Only.   **$518 US, $738 CA**

4305   Satin. Sophisticated sheath in Italian Satin. Softly beaded
alencon lace covers the modified V neckline, the bodice
and comes 3/4 way down the princess line skirt. Long
pointed sleeves. Back neckline features a large key-hole
with swag-strung and dangling pearls. Detachable chapel
train is lace banded and appliquéed.
Color: White Only.   **$538 US, $770 CA**

4306   Italian Satin. Beautiful princess in Italian Satin. Beaded
alencon covers the bodice, surrounds the sheer yoke and

forms the collar and long pointed sleeves. Large keyhole back leads into a rosette centered flat bow that is over a tiered waterfall train.
Color: White Only.   **$538 US, $770 CA**

4307   Italian Satin. Beaded alencon bodice and sleeves over a bouffant Italian Satin skirt. Square front neckline, V-back. Twin bands circle the hem. Sunburst chapel train.
Color: White Only.   **$538 US, $770 CA**

4401   Italian Satin. Sleeveless sheath in Italian Satin. Dainty venise flowers accent the bodice. Detachable sweep train.
Color: White and Ivory.   **$298 US, $420 CA**

✦ G A L I N A ✦

Contact info. Galina, 498 7th Ave., 12th Floor, New York, NY 10018. For a dealer near you, call (212) 564-1020.

Also known as. Bouquet.

Internet. This designer does not have an official web site yet. Our web site (www.bridalgown.com) will have updates on this designer.

Background/Our view. Galina was one of the first upper-end bridal designers to realize that not every bride can spend $1000 or more on a wedding gown. A few years ago, Galina did something that set the industry on its ear: a lower-price line called "Galina Bouquet" that offered top-quality styling at a more down to earth price.

Now, many manufacturers talk about doing a "couture look at a lower price" but few have pulled it off like Galina. The Bouquet line features classic styling and fabrics (silk shantung in some styles) for $700 to $1100, earning our "best buy" rating. Regular Galina gowns run $1300 to $3500 and feature more opulent fabrics (silk-faced satin, etc.).

What most impresses us about the Galina line (both Bouquet and regular Galina) is their fashion. Founded in 1959, this U.S.-based manufacturer produces beautiful silhouettes with subtle touches like box pleats or a basket-weave hemline. The shape of the dress overshadows its individual components; you won't see gobs of lace or beading on these gowns. The colors are also outstanding. Besides white and ivory, Galina makes one of the most beautiful blush pink colors available in the market. **Rating: A-**

Delivery. About 12 weeks. Rush cuts are available.

Tags. Galina identifies its gowns with only a style number inside and outside the gown.

SIZING CHARTS

Type: Galina uses a BODY measurement size chart. For information on this subject, refer to the introduction of the designer review section of this book.

	4	6	8	10	12	14	16	18xs	20xs
Bust	33"	34	35	36	37.5	39	40.5	42	44
Waist	23	24	25	26	27.5	29	30.5	32	33
Hips	36	37	38	39	40.5	42	43.5	45	47

Sizing notes:
* *Gown length is 58" as measured from the hollow of the neck to the desired dress hem.*
* *Sleeve length is 18" as measured from armpit to wrist.*

Extra charges for options/changes:

For regular Galina gowns:
1. For sizes 18xs and 20xs, add $150 to the gown price.
2. For longer gown length, add $150 to the gown price.
3. For shorter gown length (on dresses with lace-bordered hem only), add $100 to the gown price.
4. For extra sleeve length, add $40 to the gown price.
5. For shorter sleeve length, add $30 to the gown price.
6. To add buttons over a zipper, add $70 to the gown price.
7. To add buttons and loops (with no zipper), add $70 to the gown price.
8. To add buttons and loops on sleeves, add $30 to the gown price.
9. Any two-tone color combination adds $50 to the gown price.

For Galina Bouquet gowns:
1. For sizes 18xs and 20xs, add $100 to the gown price.
2. For longer gown length, add $100 to the gown price.
3. For extra sleeve length (three inches), add $40 to the gown price.
4. To add buttons over a zipper, add $70 to the gown price.
5. To add buttons and loops (with no zipper), add $70 to the gown price.
6. To add buttons and loops on sleeves, add $30 to the gown price.
7. Long sleeve extensions are available. For sleeves with lace on net, add $300 to the gown price. For sleeves with lace on fabric, add $300 to the gown price. For sleeves with plain fabric, add $150 to the gown price.
8. Any two-tone color combination adds $50 to the gown price.

NEW BRIDAL GOWNS FOR SPRING 1997

❖ **Galina Bouquet Bridal Gowns** ....

STYLE #	DESCRIPTION	SUGGESTED RETAIL
1570	White silk shantung sheath with basque waisted tank bodice trimmed in beaded alencon lace, detachable chapel train	$950
	Advertised in Brides magazine Feb/Mar 1997 *"Spring Bouquet II"*	
1571	White Italian satin band sleeve at the shoulder bodice over tulle skirt scattered with satin roses.	$800
	Advertised in Brides magazine Dec/Jan, Feb/Mar 1997 *"Page II"*	
1572	Pearl studded empire sleeveless bodice over Italian satin princess line skirt	$900
	Advertised in Brides magazine Dec/Jan, Feb/Mar 1997 *"Page II"*	

1573   White silk shantung off the shoulder princess line gown with venise appliqués

$900

Advertised in Brides magazine Dec/Jan, Feb/Mar 1997 "Page II"

1578   White embroidered organza gown, sleeveless dropped waisted bodice with sheer neckline, full skirt, bow in back

$900

Advertised in Brides magazine Feb/Mar 1997 "Spring Bouquet I"

1579   White over pink lattice embroidered cotton gown, sundress bodice over full skirt, white satin banding.

$770

1580   White satin square neck bodice with rose embroidered encrusted sleeves over full organza skirt banded in satin

$950

Advertised in Brides magazine Feb/Mar 1997 "Spring Bouquet I"

1581   White beaded embroidered organza empire waistline sheath with detachable train.

$950

1583   Short sleeved venise bodice with basque waistline over tulle skirt with venise appliqués and hem.

$770

Advertised in Brides magazine Feb/Mar 1997 "Spring Bouquet II"

❖ **Galina Bridal Gowns** ....

4061   Pin-tucked at the shoulder band sleeve bodice in white silk petal satin over pleated full skirt with chapel length train. $1700
Advertised in Brides magazine Dec/Jan, Feb/Mar 1997

4062   White silk faced satin ballerina bodice with basque waistline over embroidered tulle skirt with satin back bow, sweep train. $1500
Advertised in Brides magazine Dec/Jan, Feb/Mar 1997

4064   White pearl embroidered alencon slip gown with tulip skirt

$1700

4065   White short sleeved bodice in alencon lace with shadow striped yoke, full tulle skirt with matching deep alencon border and sweep train.

$2500

Advertised in Brides magazine Feb/Mar 1997 "By Invitation Only" Exclusive

GALINA

| 4066 | White delicately floral embroidered short sleeved bodice with scalloped waistline over full silk satin faced organza skirt. | **$2500** |

Advertised in Brides magazine Feb/Mar 1997 "Images"

| 4067 | White silk faced satin princess line, halter neckline with sage banding at arm and hem. | **$1700** |

| 4068 | White silk faced satin gown with pleated bodice released into full skirt, square strapped neckline with tailored bows. | **$1600** |

| 4072 | Ivory silk petal satin, dropped waist bodice with white lattice venise over banded ivory short sleeve and full skirt. | **$1950** |

Advertised in Bride's magazine Feb/Mar 1997 "Point of View Exclusive"

| 4073 | White venise lace sheath with silk satin faced organza yoke and detachable appliquéed train. | **$1700** |

Advertised in Modern Bride magazine Feb/Mar 1997

| 4081 | White silk faced satin sleeveless bodice, v-back, over sage satin midriff with multi-colored floral accent and full flared skirt. | **$1600** |

Advertised in Modern Bride magazine Feb/Mar 1997

| 4088 | White silk faced satin dropped waist bodice with sculpted bateau collar and v-back over satin banded tulle skirt. | **$1300** |

| 4089 | White silk satin faced dropped waist bodice with venise yoke over full skirt with venise hem line. | **$1700** |

| 4090 | White silk petal satin, scoop neckline, short sleeved bodice with embroidered alencon midriff over pleated full skirt. | **$1500** |

Advertised in Modern Bride magazine Feb/Mar 1997

❖ **Galina Informal Bridal Gowns** ....

| 1591 | White pique sleeveless dress, daisy lattice venise trimmed midriff and slip. | **$350** |

| 1592 | White silk satin faced organza gown, slip style bodice over three tiered flared skirt with sweep train. | **$600** |

| 1593 | White silk shantung over pink lining dress, v-neck bodice belted waist, pleated bell shaped skirt. | **$350** |

| 1594 | White alencon lace slip dress with sheer neckline. | **$590** |

⇥ JANELL BERTE ⇤

Contact info. Janell Berté, 248 E. Liberty St., Lancaster, PA 17602. For a dealer near you, call (717) 291-9894.

Internet. This designer does not have an official web site yet. Our web site (www.bridalgown.com) will have updates on this designer.

Background/Our view. If money is no object, you need to check out Janell Berté. Yes, this Lancaster, PA-designer is pricey, but few other designers provide as much value and styling as Janell Berté.

Berté offers some of the most unusual fabrics in the bridal market today. How unusual? Try a silk jacquard, silk gauze, or a silk organza with metallic threads. The latter has an unusual shimmery feel that is among the most unique fabrics we've seen.

And the fabrics are the just the beginning. The accents are equally stunning, with golden embroidered Chantilly lace and fabric flowers like camellias. One hand-painted floral silk organza dress featured a tartan plaid sash. You get the idea.

Janell Berté's informal dresses (no trains) range from $1380 to $1950, while her regular bridal gowns are $1470 to $2650. There are also a few couture dresses (not listed below) which top $3000 and $4000. On the upper-end, one dress for $4340 featured a crystal-studded bodice with (count 'em) 1500 crystals. Catch the sunlight just right in this gown and you could power up a small town for a year.

We love the style of the gowns, with a-line and sheath silhouettes as well as a few unusual styles (a bridal pantsuit, anyone?). Fabric combinations with contrasting textures (like chiffon over a crepe skirt) are a signature look.

In business since 1981, Berté's gowns are in 75 stores nationwide and the designer does many trunk shows a year. During these events, you can check out the entire line. Call the designer for their latest travel schedule. **Rating: A**

Delivery. About 12 weeks. Rush cuts (eight week delivery) are available for $80. "Panic" rush cuts (four week or less delivery) are $150.

SIZING CHART

Sizing Chart

	2	4	6	8	10	12	14	16	18	20
Bust	32.5	33.5	34.5	35.5	36.5	38	39.5	41	43	45
Waist	23	24	25	26	27	28.5	30	31.5	33.5	35.5
Hips	35	36	37	38	39	41.5	43	44.5	46.5	48.5

Sizing notes:
• *Standard gown length (as measured from hollow of the neck to the desired dress hem) is 56.5" for a size 6. The length is adjusted (up or down) by one-eighth of an inch for each size above or below size 6.*

• *Petite cuts are available (the bodice is one inch shorter in the waist and the skirt is three inches shorter) for $50 additional.*

Extra changes for options/changes:

1. Custom changes are available. The minimum charge for any change (even if features are removed from a dress) is $20.

2. Custom cuts (made to your measurements) are available for an additional $100.

3. For longer skirt length (up to three inches), add $60 to the gown price. For four to six inches of extra length, add $90 to the gown price.

4. For sizes 18 and 20, add 5% to the gown price.

5. For sizes larger than 20, add 10% to the gown price.

NEW BRIDAL GOWNS FOR SPRING 1997

❖ **Regular Bridal Gowns** ....

STYLE #	DESCRIPTION	SUGGESTED RETAIL
7100	Princess line gown features scoop neckline, V-back, short set-in sleeves and scattered beading on bodice and sleeves. Sweep length train features full-length buttons and loops ending at a small bow at base of train. *Double Faced Silk Satin.*	$1820
7105	Princess line dress with off-the-shoulder neckline has floral interest on bandeau sleeves. Back of gown has large scalloped cut-outs adorned with pressed camellia flowers and has a tulle underskirt with scattered petals. *Silk jacquard with Tulle*	$1950
7110	Bodice of silk matelasse' has scooped neckline and short straight sleeves. Box pleated skirt falls from dropped waistline. Rolled roses adorn small of back at waistline. Sweep train. *Silk Matelasse with Silk Satin Taffeta*	$2050
7115	Fitted Venice lace bodice with sabrina neckline and short sleeves. Dropped waistline has fully gathered skirt Rolled roses decorate small of back at waistline. *Venice Lace with Silk Faced Satin*	$2140
7120	Fitted bodice with small Sabrina neckline and dropped scooped waistline. Box pleated skirt features self banding which rises to an arch at center of sweep with bow at point. *Silk Faced Satin*	$2250
7125	Sleeveless, straight sheath Venice lace gown with fishtail has silk chiffon bandeau shirring. Detachable silk chiffon sweep train flows from deep V-back.	

J A N E L L   B E R T E

Venice Lace with Silk Charmeuse
Detachable Silk Chiffon Train **$2170**

7130   Strapless pantsuit with maxi coat features long straight
        sleeves with French cuffs. Heavy Venice lace covers the
        bustier and bodice of jacket. Jacket and cuffs are closed
        with decorative buttons.
        Silk Crepe with Venice Lace **$2490**

7135   Empire A-line gown has bodice of beaded golden
        embroidered Chantilly lace with poet sleeves and sweet-
        heart neckline. Small bow with long streamers at back.
        Sweep length train.
        Silk Crepe with Gold Chantilly Lace **$1950**

7140   Beaded Alencon lace Empire bodice features square
        neckline and short sleeves. A-line chiffon overskirt has
        graduated cut-away hem line into sweep train.
        Silk Chiffon, Silk Crepe with Beaded
        Alencon Lace **$2070**

7145   Empire maxi overcoat with poet sleeves and scooped
        neckline covers strapless Venice lace sheath bridal dress
        with fishtail.
        Silk Chiffon, Silk Suiting with Venice
        Lace Sheath **$2650**

7150   Hand-painted, floral silk organza embroidered dress
        features Sabrina neckline and circular skirt. Tartan sash
        at waistline forms constructed bow in back with flowers
        tucked in folds. Streamers flow into sweep train.
        Floral Silk Organza with Tartan Dupioni **$1470**

❖ JASMINE ❖

Contact info. Jasmine, 2401 W. Hassell Rd., Suite 1525, Hoffman Estates, IL 60195. For a dealer near you, call (847) 519-7778.

Also known as. Ashley Love.

Internet. http://bridalsearch.com/jasminecollection/ is a site where you can view Jasmine's catalog on-line. In addition, our web site (www.bridalgown.com) will have updates on this designer.

Background. Jasmine owner Kyle Yin fell into the bridal business by accident. His sister, Jade, had started Jasmine in 1985 as a costume-maker. Kyle, meanwhile, was happily employed in the computer business in Taiwan. All that changed in 1987, when Jade passed away after a long battle with cancer. Kyle took over his sister's company and began its transformation into a bridal manufacturer.

The bridal business apparently runs in the Yin family. Kyle's sister Carole Hai owns Moonlight. In fact, Jasmine and Moonlight used to share production facilities in Taiwan before Jasmine moved their production to China in 1992.

The biggest news at Jasmine for Spring 1997 is their new line of all-silk bridesmaids dresses. Jasmine raised eyebrows recently when they announced the line would be made in China; most other bridesmaids manufacturers make dresses domestically for quicker deliveries. Industry observers will watching this venture closely; if it's a success, it may prompt other bridesmaids makers to consider Chinese production.

Our view. Jasmine is one of those bridal manufacturers with something for everyone. Clean, simple dresses contrast with over-the-top designs like all-over lace sheaths and dresses with big puff sleeves.

Jasmine divides its dresses into two groups: the Collection features a couple dozen designs in the $460 to $800 price range. Most of these dresses are in matte satin, although a few silk gowns are value stand-outs for under $800.

The Haute Couture collection features more luxurious fabrics such as silk shantung and Italian satin. Most of these dresses run $850 to $1200.

We were most impressed with the quality and flexibility that Jasmine offers. Every dress can be made into a sheath style silhouette for $150 extra. You can swap the fabric, request a longer train, make the sleeves shorter and so on. While other designers offer such custom changes, it's rare at this price point.

If there is anything to criticize about Jasmine, it would have to be their deliveries and customer service. The company hit a few bumps recently as it switched its production to a new facility in China. In a telephone interview with owner Kyle Yin, the company promised to do a better job as it irons out the kinks in China and opens a new distribution facility outside Chicago. **Rating: B+**

J A S M I N E

Delivery. 12 to 14 weeks. Rush cuts (about 8 to 10 weeks) are available.

Tags. Jasmine identifies its gowns with a hang tag and a sewn-in label.

SIZING CHART

Type: Jasmine uses a GARMENT measurement size chart. For information on this subject, refer to the introduction of the designer review section of this book.

	4	6	8	10	12	14	16	18	20
Bust	33"	34	35	36	37.5	39	40.5	42.5	44.5
Waist	23	24	25	26	27.5	29	30.5	32.5	34.5
Hips	35	36	37	38	39.5	41	42.5	44.5	46.5
Length*	59	59	59.5	59.5	60	60	60	61	61

	38	40	42	44
Bust	47	49	51	53
Waist	38	40	42	44
Hips	49	51	53	55
Length*	61	61	61.5	61.5

Sizing notes:
• **Length is measured from the hollow of the neck to the natural waistline, and then the natural waistline to the dress hem.*
• *Sleeve length is 18 inches.*
• *For sheath style gowns, Jasmine recommends using the bride's body measurement for the hips. A custom cut may be necessary if this measurement does not correspond to an existing size (see below for price information).*

Extra charges for options/changes:
1. For sizes 38 to 44, add $60 to the gown price of Jasmine Collection dresses and $100 to the gown price of Jasmine Haute Couture dresses.
2. For gown length changes, add $60 to the gown price.
3. For sleeve length changes, add $40 to the gown price.
4. All styles are available in sheath silhouettes for an additional $150.
5. For a shorter train length, add $60 to the gown price for Jasmine Collection dresses and $100 to the gown price of Jasmine Haute Couture dresses.
6. For a longer train length, add $70 to $90 per foot for Jasmine Collection dresses (this varies by the type of fabric). Add $200 per foot for longer train lengths on Jasmine Haute Couture gowns. Note: all gowns are NOT available with extra train length; consult a local retailer for more information.
7. Custom cuts (made to your measurements) are available. For sizes 4 to 20, add $80 to the gown price. In sizes 38 to 44, add $140 to the gown price.
8. Sleeve changes are available. To change a sleeve from long to

short (or short to long), add $100 to $150 for Jasmine Collection gowns. (This varies depending on the fabric type.) For Jasmine Haute Couture gowns, add $200 for sleeve changes as described above. Note: all gowns are NOT available to be made with long sleeves; consult a local retailer for more information.

9. Fabric changes are available on all Jasmine gowns. For example, to change the fabric on a Jasmine Collection gown to silk, add $150. A myriad of other fabric options are also available for $60 to $200, depending on fabric.

NEW BRIDAL GOWNS FOR SPRING 1997

Note: Most of these gowns are featured in Jasmine's Spring/Summer 1997 catalog. The following page numbers refer to this catalog.

❖ **Haute Couture Gowns** ....

STYLE #	DESCRIPTION	SUGGESTED RETAIL

830   Silk Shantung/Chiffon. Scoop neckline, extended cap sleeves, and rounded waist are trimmed with delicate piping. Guipure appliqués shape the slimming bodice. The full ball skirt of softly gathered chiffon is embellished with a pearled embroidery along the hem line. The detachable chiffon train flows from the flowers at the back waist. *Catalog page 10.*

$850

832   Italian Satin. Clusters of pearls highlight the floral pattern in the unique Venise lace. The portrait bodice caresses the neckline. The full skirt and cathedral train are embellished with bouquets of floral appliqués above the hem line lace. A double bow on the back waist is detailed with appliqués on the streamers. *Catalog page 7.*

$1090

833   Organza. Open sweetheart neckline is finished with delicate embroidered organza. Piping defines the V of the basque waist. The embroidered floral pattern grows along the full skirt. An airy bow with embroidered streamers brings the full detachable train together with the ball gown. *Catalog page 3.*

$898

834   Silk Shantung. Sophisticated portrait neckline with a shirred upper torso. A pearled circular lace fills the corselete bodice. The round waistline influences the unadorned full silhouette. Shirred V back is enhanced with scattered pearls. Venise roses decorate the double butterfly bow on the back waist. *Catalog page 4.*

$798

835   Venise Lace/Italian Satin. Pearled Venise lace designs the
       fitted sheath. The V neckline complements the short set
       in sleeves. The daring plunge of the V-back leads to a
       dramatic cluster of roses on the exaggerated bow.
       The detachable train is unadorned. *Catalog page 5.*
                                                        $1050

836   Italian Satin. Alencon lace complements the fitted sweet-
       heart bodice and dropped waist. Long sheer appliquéed
       sleeves end with a bridal point. Appliqués extend the hem
       lace on the fitted skirt. A looped bow rests on the waist-
       line below the V back. Alencon appliqués are placed along
       the detachable train. This style is beaded with 80,000
       pearls and sequins. *Catalog page 6.*
                                                        $858

837   Italian Satin. Piping defines the scoop neckline and cuffs
       of the long set in sleeves. Re-embroidered fabric appliqués
       detailed with silver baguettes and pearls accent the fitted
       bodice. The plunging scoop back leads to a grand bow at
       the waist. The detachable train is adorned with three sets
       of detailed streamers that attach under the bow.
       Catalog page 11. $970

838   Italian Satin/Organza. Sweetheart open bodice with halter
       straps. Three dimensional Venise lace details the slimming
       bodice and gauntlets. Soft petals of appliqués cascade the
       front skirt below the basque waist. The cathedral train
       releases tendrils of floral appliqués.
       Catalog page 8. $998

839   Italian Satin. Pearled scalloped lace shapes the sweetheart
       neckline and on the shoulder short sleeves. The empire
       bodice is filled with pearled appliqués. The princess line
       slims the waist. Appliqués highlight the skirt and train.
       Three tiered bow with a floral center and ribbon stream-
       ers cascades down the train from the back waist.
       Catalog page 14. $1030

840   Silk Shantung. The square neckline contours the bodice.
       Appliquéed illusion long sleeves caress the shoulder.
       Appliqués flow from the basque waist. Illusion back has
       button closures. Appliqués spill along the train from the
       simple bow on the waist. *Catalog page 13*
                                                        $830

841   Silk Shantung. Elegant sweetheart neckline with short set
       in lace sleeves. Delicate pearls scroll the patterned lace
       around the basque waist. Silk buttons close the bodice at
       the side seam. Silk lattice defines the back bodice. Cotton
       lace woven in a swirl design completes the hem on this
       ball gown. *Catalog page 2.* $798

842   Silk Shantung. Delicate pleating defines this neo-classic
        scoop neck tank top. Slim empire sheath with a back slit
        has a modified watteau train A hint of color is added to
        the back bow by a soft shell pink silk satin.
        Catalog page 16.   **$690**

843   Silk Satin/Organza. Bows with a pearl center rest on the
        shoulders of this scoop neckline tank. The rounded waist
        is trimmed with a silk satin ribbon. Ribbon bows are
        placed along the zipper on the back bodice. The full ball
        skirt is soutache embroidered organza.
        Catalog page 15.   **$950**

783   Silk Shantung. Elegant V neckline and dramatic V back.
        Appliqués cascade down the sides of the front skirt and
        throughout the train. Bouquets of silk rosettes sit along
        the back waist of the cathedral train.
        Catalog page 9.   **$990**

❖ **Jasmine Collection Gowns** ....

811   Matte Satin. Illusion dropped sabrina neckline with
        sweetheart underlay and soft cap sleeves with lace edge.
        Slimming lace application along the basque waist.
        Appliqué bouquets bloom along the cathedral train
        creating a dramatic bustle under the triple looped bow.
        Catalog page 22.   **$610**

812   Matte Satin. Traditional scalloped sweetheart neckline
        and fully appliquéed torso. Piped basque waist leads to
        full silhouette draped with appliqués. Elegant V back
        features butterfly bow centered with rolled rosettes.
        Catalog page 19.   **$650**

813   Matte Satin. Wedding band collar contours the neck. Leaf
        appliqués shape the sheer V neckline and long illusion
        sleeves. Appliqués cascade down the front skirt from the
        waistline. Mystical V back leads to a detailed double bow
        with folded streamers. Cathedral train is accented with
        alencon lace appliqués. *Catalog page 18.*
                                                              $690

814   Matte Satin. Open sweetheart neckline with alencon lace
        bodice, short tapered sleeves, and flattering basque waist.
        Patterns of appliqués centered with a single rosette drape
        along the skirt and train. A looped bow with four stream-
        ers edged with appliqués finishes the back waist.
        Catalog page 20.   **$590**

815   Matte Satin. The scalloped portrait neckline hugs the
        shoulder. Beaded appliqués enhance the long illusion
        sleeves. The placement of detail on the fitted bodice slims

the torso. Buttons cover the zipper-up back. Rolled rosettes with petals and ribbon loops round the back waist. Pearls outline the delicate hem line lace.
Catalog page 29.   **$550**

816 Matte Satin. This princess silhouette features a tank inspired neckline. Basket weave trellis trimmed with floral shaped Venise appliqués defines the raised torso and hem line of the ball gown. Streamers with a floral basket weaved edge decorate the modified watteau train, attached by gathered roses at the empire waist.
Catalog page 34.   **$630**

817 Alencon Lace/Tulle. Alencon lace pencil sheath with a modified Queen Anne neckline. Long fitted sleeves end with a soft point at the wrist. Delicate buttons close the sheer lace back. Rolled roses with ribbon loops center the butterfly bow. Alencon lace borders the hem line of the floating detachable train.
Catalog page 26.   **$730**

818 Matte Satin. Portrait collar with V neckline, front and back. Pleating defines the bust line on the lace appliquéed bodice. Lace pyramid adorns the fitted skirt. Delicate looped bows sit along the back waist. Appliqués spill down the hipline detachable train.
Catalog page 25.   **$590**

819 Matte Satin. Rounded portrait neckline with sweetheart underlay and long sleeves. Appliquéed torso complements the A-line silhouette. Appliqués placed on the sweep train give elegance to the gown and bustle.
Catalog page 24.   **$470**

823 Matte Satin/Organza. Beaded appliqués outline the dropped jewel neck. Illusion fills the neckline above the sweetheart bodice. Organza roses open the short sleeves. The gentle basque waistline flows into the full organza skirt. Organza roses center the six loop bow at the back waist. A collage of appliqués flow along the train. Matching lace borders the hem.
Catalog page 28.   **$610**

824 Matte Satin. Scooped sweetheart neckline with cap sleeves. Alencon lace appliqués accent the basque waist. The back neckline is an exaggerated V. A looped flower sits in the center of the bow at the back waistline. The hem line is completed with a rich lace.
Catalog page 21.   **$618**

825 Matte Satin/Organza. Piping shapes the scoop neckline and cap sleeves. Venise appliqués design the upper bodice.

Rounded dropped waist releases the full silhouette. A wide band of matte satin trims the ball gown and detachable train. Matte satin edges the streamers and loops of the double bow along the back waistline.
Catalog page 23. **$470**

826 Silk Shantung. Daisies stencil the rounded portrait neckline. The smooth fitted bodice and full silhouette are embellished with variegated daisy appliqués. The soft V back leads to bows along the waist.
Catalog page 27. **$750**

827 Matte Satin/Tulle. Venise appliqués shape an illusion heart in the center of the haltered bodice. Bare shoulders lead to the appliquéed gauntlets. Covered buttons close the diamond shaped illusion back. Clusters of rosettes are placed at the back waist. The cathedral train is trimmed with beaded lace.
Catalog page 30. **$770**

828 Matte Satin/Chiffon. The illusion overlay is highlighted with alencon lace appliqués on the high neckline, long sleeves and empire bodice. The strapless underlay is a fitted pencil sheath. The detachable chiffon train wraps around to the front skirt and attaches under the empire bodice.
Catalog page 32. **$590**

829 Taffeta. Off the shoulder sweetheart neckline and appliquéed fitted bodice with a basque waist. Inverted box pleats accent the full skirt. The back bow is rich with detail. Appliqués cascade down the cathedral train.
Catalog page 31. **$550**

→JESSICA McCLINTOCK←

Contact info. Jessica McClintock, 1400 16th St., San Francisco, CA 94103. For a dealer near you, call (800) 333-5301 or (415) 495-3030. For a catalog, send a check for $4 to the above address.

Also known as. Gunne Sax, Scott McClintock.

Internet. This designer does not have an official web site yet. Our web site (www.bridal-gown.com) will have updates on this designer.

Background/Our view. Jessica McClintock is one of the few ready-to-wear designers to make it big-time in the world of bridal.

You've probably seen the McClintock name in dress department stores nationwide, but you may not realize the company offers an extensive and popular bridal line (wedding dresses, bridesmaids gowns, flower girls and more). One reason for that popularity: the prices are hard to beat. Bridal gowns start at $150 (no, that's not a typo). Heck, even McClintock's most expensive gowns run only $500.

Want an even better deal? Check out one of Jessica McClintock's six outlets nationwide, where the sale prices on gowns are hard to believe (see below for more information). You can even find McClintock's gowns at David's, the off-the-rack retailer reviewed in the money-saving tips chapter of this book.

McClintock got her start in the fashion world in 1970 in San Francisco. She purchased Gunne Sax, a small dress manufacturer, that specialized in "granny-style" dresses that were the rage at the time. Back then, it was one-woman operation. Jessica cut the fabric, sewed the gowns and delivered them to department stores.

Today Jessica McClintock employs a staff of 500 and offers a wide range of bridal gowns, from informal designs with no trains to traditional gowns with lace and beading. The designs (all made in the U.S.) are feminine and innovative; several stand-outs include sheaths and strapless gowns. A few of the dresses even have matching flower girl dresses. As you might expect to see in this price range, most of the fabrics are polyester in a variety of finishes (organza, satin, crepe).

Delivery is much faster than typical bridal designers, averaging just two to six weeks (now, *that's* speedy). Unlike other manufacturers who limit their distribution, Jessica McClintock seems to have a "more is better" philosophy about their gowns. Besides the aforementioned outlets, you'll see McClintock gowns in regular bridal shops and even department stores. If that isn't enough, the designer also has 23 "Jessica McClintock Company Stores" (and plans for five more in 1997). There you can order a gown without ever having to step foot in a regular bridal shop. **Rating: A**

Outlet Stores. Jessica McClintock has not one but SIX outlets for her popular line of bridal apparel. The flagship outlet store is the Gunne Sax outlet in San Francisco (415) 495-3326, which not only has 20,000 dresses discounted 20% to 70%, but includes a fabric outlet too. Also in California, the company has "Jessica McClintock Company Stores" in South San Francisco (415) 737-2525, Mont Clair (909) 982-1866 and Huntington Beach (714) 841-7124. If you live in the East, check out the Jessica McClintock outlets in Reading, PA (610) 478-0810 or Central Valley, NY in Woodbury Commons (914) 928-7474. All outlet stores carry past-season styles of bridal gowns, bridesmaids dresses and all kinds of accessories.

We recently visited the Gunne Sax outlet in San Francisco and were impressed. This is a factory outlet in the original sense of the term—on the third floor of an old warehouse in a downtown business district. Outside, there's little parking (search for a space on the side streets). Inside, you'll find concrete floors, open dressing rooms and rack after rack of gowns.

We saw over 1000 bridal gowns (priced from $225 to $500), plus bridesmaids dresses, flower girls, party dresses and more. Most of the bridal gowns were discounted 10% to 25%, but we're told periodic sales offer even better deals. We've heard of brides who found $5 formal bridal gowns (no, we're not making this up). While the deals weren't that fantastic when we were there, we did notice a large rack of informal gowns on sale for just $80. You can then buy a separate train ($20 each) or walk over to the fabric outlet on the other side of the store. There you can find bridal fabrics and laces at incredible prices to help make a train or alteration. Top off this bargain with a pair of white shoes with lace trim, on clearance while we visited for just $5 a pair. Wow.

Most gowns we saw at the Gunne Sax outlet were sizes 8-14, although a few 4-6's and 16-20's were floating around. Surprisingly, the dresses were in pretty good shape—most were in protective bags and had very little damage or wear. Watch for those end-of season clearances for the best deals (you can put your name on their mailing list to get notices).

Delivery. About two to six weeks. No rush cuts, but certain in-stock styles may be available for quicker delivery.

Tags. Jessica McClintock identifies its gowns with a hang tag and a sewn-in label.

SIZING CHARTS

Type: Jessica McClintock uses a BODY measurement size chart. For information on this subject, refer to the introduction of the designer review section of this book.

Jessica McClintock has two size charts: average sizes and womens sizes.

Average Sizes

	4	6	8	10	12	14	16
Bust	33"	34	35	36.5	38	39.5	41.5
Waist	25	26	27	28.5	30	31.5	33.5
Hips	36	37	38	39.5	41	42.5	44.5
Sleeve	22.75	23	23.25	23.5	23.75	24	24.25

Sizing notes:
• *Sleeve length is measured from armpit to wrist.*
• *For floor length designs, gown length (as measured from the hollow of the neck to the desired dress hem) is 57.5" to 62", depending on the size ordered. Consult with a local retailer for more information.*

Womens Sizes

	14w	16w	18w	20w	22w	24w
Bust	44"	46	48	50	52	54
Waist	34	36	38	40	42	44
Hips	45	47	49	51	53	55
Sleeve	23.75	23.88	24	24.13	24.25	24.38

Sizing notes:
• *Only a selected number of styles are available in womens sizes. There is an extra charge for these sizes; consult a local retailer for more information.*
• *Sleeve length is measured from armpit to wrist.*
• *For floor length designs, gown length (as measured from the hollow of the neck to the desired dress hem) is 57.5" to 60.75", depending on the size ordered. Consult with a local retailer for more information.*

NEW BRIDAL GOWNS FOR SPRING 1997

Note: All bridal gowns are available in white or ivory, unless otherwise noted. In addition, all gowns are available in sizes 4 to 16 unless otherwise noted.

CATALOG PAGE #	NAME	STYLE #	FABRIC	SUGGESTED RETAIL
2	Diana	21161	Satin	$448
3	Natalie	21165	Satin	$400
4	Drew	21158	Tulle	$300
	• Veil included.			
5	Valentina	21109	Embroidered Organza	$600
6	Chloe	21099	Crepe	$330
7	Brigitta	21162	Satin	$400
8	Helena	21155	Satin	$280
9	Ryann	21172	Organza/Satin	$340
10	Jade	21111	Satin	$350
11	Mia	21106	Satin	$300
12	Quincy	21174	Brocade	$340
	• Veil included.			
	• Also available in rose.			
	• Also available in large sizes 14W to 24W as style #27174			$360
13	Frederica	21092	"Rosalind" Silk brocade	$640
	• Veil included.			
	• Only available in ivory.			

JESSICA McCLINTOCK

CATALOG PAGE #	NAME	STYLE #	FABRIC	SUGGESTED RETAIL
14	Emma	21160	Satin/Illusion	**$240**
	• Also available in large sizes 14W to 24W as			
	style #27160			**$280**
15	Gwendalyn	21137	Satin	**$330**
16	Claire	21154	Satin	**$292**
	• Veil included.			
17	Bushawn	21144	Satin	**$360**
	• Also available in large sizes 14W to 24W as			
	style #27144			**$400**
18	Bonnie	21087	Metallic Brocade	**$360**
	• Only available in gold.			
19	India	21163	Satin	**$440**
20	Laura	21156	Organza	**$400**
21	Sloane	21128	Organza	**$500**
22	Same as page 12 "Quincy"			
23	Chynna	21143	Brocade	**$320**
24	Hope	21148	Satin	**$400**
25	Opal	21130	Satin	**$400**
26	Adriana	21153	Crepe	**$268**
27	Devlyn	21086	Brocade	**$320**
	• Veil included.			
28	Rosemary	21159	Chantique	**$360**
29	Daisy	21147	Lace	**$350**
30	Kimber	24176	Satin	**$130**
	• Informal gown also available in seven colors.			
31	Paige	21169	Satin/Organza	**$240**
	• Also available in blue or rose.			
32	Marcela	22076	Crepe	**$300**
33	Tyra	21151	Satin	**$460**
34	Prelude	22103	Lace	**$280**
35	Melody	22080	Crepe/Chiffon	**$298**
36	Gabby	22094	Crepe	**$220**
37	Joella	22075	Crepe/Lace	**$296**
	• Also available in sizes 14W to 24W as			
	style # 27075			**$336**
38	Luisa	22067	Crepe/Lace	**$270**
39	Margot	22088	Crepe/Chiffon	**$240**
40	Grace	21179	Silk Dupioni	**$480**
	• Only available in ivory.			
41	Jordan	22077	Satin	**$296**
42	Tia	21157	Crepe/Lace	**$240**
	• Also available in sizes 14W to 24W as			
	style #27157			**$280**
42	Alice	22107	Lace/Chiffon	**$280**
43	Janelle	22105	Satin	**$250**
44	Georgene	22108	Pebble Georgette	**$330**
45	Flora	22106	Crepe	**$240**
46	Paris	24154	Pebble Georgette	**$172**
	• Also available in four other colors.			

J E S S I C A   M c C L I N T O C K

CATALOG PAGE #	NAME	STYLE #	FABRIC	SUGGESTED RETAIL
46	Sage	22061	Georgette	$360
47	Felicia	22084	Crepe/Lace	$270
	• Also available in sizes 14W to 24W as style #27084			$310
48	Vera	22104	Lace	$280
49	Angelique	22101	Pebble Georgette	$300
50	Mailyn	22092	Crepe/Illusion	$200
51	Lorna	22083	Georgette/Lace	$200
	• Also available in peach.			
	• Also available in sizes 14W to 24W as style #27083			$220

⟶ J I M   H J E L M ⟵

Contact info. Jim Hjelm's Private Collection, Ltd., 501 7th Ave., 10th Fl., New York, NY 10018. For a dealer near you or a free catalog, call (212) 764-6960.

Also known as. JH By Jim Hjelm, Lazaro, Jim Hjelm Couture, Private Collections, Visions, Pure Romance.

Internet. This designer does not have an official web site yet. Our web site (www.bridalgown.com) will have updates on this designer.

Background. Jim Hjelm's Private Collection is unique among other bridal designers—it's the only publicly-traded manufacturer of bridal apparel in the U.S. or Canada. As a result, we know more about this company than other designers because much of its history and financial information is public.

Designer Jim Hjelm did stints at other top designer houses before founding the company that bears his name in 1987. Hjelm's bridal gowns have always been high style and are often copied by lower-price manufacturers.

The company hit a rough spot during the early 1990's and began losing money as brides opted for lower-price gowns. It took Hjelm four years to turn around this situation and the company is now back in the black. How did they do it? Joseph L. Murphy, president and CEO, said in a statement in 1996 that "the company continues to benefit from its strategy of differentiating its lines by styling niche and price point, which it began to implement two years ago. All our lines have a strong fashion direction. I think that's what the consumer is reacting so favorably to," said Murphy.

In 1996, Hjelm's restructuring paid off. While many other bridal designers reported flat or down sales, Hjelm posted a sales increase of 63% for the first nine months of their fiscal year. Profits are up 251% over the same period last year. In 1995, Hjelm sold about $8 million of bridal gowns and bridesmaids dresses. Using their average price point, we estimate Hjelm sells about 10,000 bridal gowns a year.

Our view. Jim Hjelm divides their gowns into four collections. The lowest price point is the "Visions" group, which is an all-satin line for $730 to $1150. The "Couture" line features dresses in the $1590 to $2390 range. As you'd expect in this more expensive line, the fabrics are more luxurious (silk satin, charmeuse, crepe, taffeta) and the gowns feature hand-embroidery. At the upper-end, the Jim Hjelm "Private Collection" features dresses that go up to $2700.

Besides the Hjelm gowns, the company also produces the separate "Lazaro" collection, designed by Lazaro Perez. These gowns are still high-style, but more feminine that some of Hjelm's gowns. Instead of a plain illusion neck or sleeves, for example, you're more likely to see illusion overlaid with delicate lace embroidery on a Lazaro gown.

Although used sparingly, exquisite beading and lace detailing are the hallmark of Hjelm's dresses. The big ball gown is a typical silhouette in this line, although that's the only thing that is "big" about these dresses. Most feature clean lines with little or no flourishes.

While none of these dresses is an incredible bargain, you do get a top-quality dress for your money. And the unique fashions may make it worth the investment. One plus: unlike other expensive designers who ignore the large size market, Hjelm offers all its dresses in sizes up to 24. **Rating: B+**

Delivery. 10 to 12 weeks for Hjelm dresses, 14 weeks for Lazaro. Rush cuts are available for an additional charge.

Tags. Jim Hjelm identifies its gowns only with a style number on the inside of the gown.

SIZING CHART

Type: Jim Hjelm uses a BODY measurement size chart. For information on this subject, refer to the introduction of the designer review section of this book.

	2	4	6	8	10	12	14	16	18
Bust	32.5"	33.5	34.5	35.5	36.5	38	39.5	41	42.5
Wais	22.5	23.5	24.5	25.5	26.5	28	29.5	31	32.5
Hips	33	34	35	36	37	38.5	40	41.5	43
Length	57.25	57.5	57.75	58	58.25	58.5	58.75	60	60.25

	20	22	24
Bust	44	46	48
Wais	34	36	38
Hips	44.5	46.5	48.5
Length	60.5	60.75	61

Sizing notes:
• *Gown length is measured from the hollow of the neck to the desired dress hem.*
• *Standard sleeve length is 18".*
• *Custom changes are available on certain gowns; consult with a local retailer for more information.*

Extra charges for changes/options:
1. For size 2, add $150 to the gown price.
2. For sizes 18 and 20, add $150 to the gown price.
3. For sizes 22 and 24, add $200 to the gown price.

NEW BRIDAL GOWNS FOR SPRING 1997

❖ Jim Hjelm Couture Collection ....

Note: The following gowns are "confined," which means their distribution is limited. Not all Jim Hjelm dealers will carry these dresses.

J I M   H J E L M

STYLE #	DESCRIPTION	SUGGESTED RETAIL

1560 White silk organza sleeveless princess gown.
Hand embroidered and beaded bodice on a plain
organza skirt, chapel train.   **$1990**
Advertised in Bride's magazine Feb/Mar 1997

1561 White duchess silk satin sheath off the shoulder scoop
neckline adorned with hand beaded pearls, drop waist,
plain satin skirt. Back bow with a detachable satin chapel
length train.   **$1950**
Advertised in Bride's magazine Feb/Mar 1997

1562 White satin, strapless princess gown with pale pink trim.
Back is adorned with pale pink back bow and floor length
streamers, chapel train.

                                                         $1590

Advertised in Bride's magazine Feb/Mar 1997
Featured in an editorial in Bridal Guide magazine
Jan/Feb 1997

1563 White silk matte lasse sleeveless sheath, sabrina neckline,
back rosettes with detachable taffeta chapel train.
                                                         $1750

Advertised in Modern Bride magazine Feb/Mar 1997

1564 White duchess satin sleeveless gown, scooped neckline,
drop waist. Satin organza skirt adorned with satin bands
and bow at hem. Chapel train.   **$1790**
Advertised in Bride's magazine Feb/Mar 1997

1565 White duchess satin sleeveless sheath, illusion neckline
drop waist with front satin bows. Attached Swiss dot tulle
train. Chapel train.   **$1590**

Advertised in and featured in an editorial in Bride's
magazine Feb/Mar 1997

1566 White peau d' soie taffeta sleeveless gown, scalloped neckline, hand embroidered beaded bodice, dropped waist,
full taffeta skirt, chapel train.   **$2190**
Advertised in Bride's magazine Feb/Mar 1997

1567 White tulle gown, sleeveless duchess satin halter like neckline. dropped waist, full tulle skirt with scattered silk flowers
and pearls, silk flowers at back waist, chapel length train.
                                                         $1650

Advertised in Bride's magazine Feb/Mar 1997

1568 White Swiss dotted tulle dress, tip of the shoulder duchess
satin bodice, adorned with front bow at neckline, sweep train.
                                                         $1590

J I M   H J E L M

Advertised in Bride's magazine Feb/Mar 1997
Featured in an editorial in Modern Bride magazine
Feb/Mar 1997

❖ **A Private Collection Gowns** ....

STYLE #	DESCRIPTION	SUGGESTED RETAIL

6024   Ivory silk shantung, bateau neckline, sleeveless bodice, floral pastel embroidered organza overlay, basque waist, chapel train, attached bows down back   **$2300**
Advertised in Bride's magazine Feb/Mar 1997
"Inner Circle"

6025   White satin bodice with organza skirt, bateau neckline, beaded sleeve with bow detail, low back with cascading bows, sweep train.
$1990
Advertised in Modern Bride magazine Feb/Mar 1997

6026   White Italian satin off-the-shoulder short sleeve, beaded alencon lace bodice with pearl clusters down center, full skirt with inverted pleats and lace appliqués, cathedral train with deep border of lace- and scattered appliqués.
$1250
Advertised in Modern Bride magazine Feb/Mar 1997

6027   White silk shantung, scalloped "V" neckline with long sheer lace- sleeve, beaded alencon bodice with low illusion back, full skirt with scattered appliqués, cathedral train with double-border of lace on hem.   **$1350**
Advertised in Modern Bride magazine Feb/Mar 1997

❖ **Visions Bridal Gowns** ....

Note: All of these gowns are advertised in Modern Bride magazine Feb/Mar 1997.

STYLE #	DESCRIPTION	SUGGESTED RETAIL

720   White Italian Satin sleeveless bodice. Pearl clustered neckline. dropped waist with covered buttons at back. Full skirt. Chapel length train.   **$900**

721   White Italian satin sheath. Pearl beaded empire waist square neckline. short sleeve with beaded trim. Bow detail at back, detachable chapel length train   **$990**

722   White Italian satin gown. Illusion satin trim neckline. short sleeve with rosette detail. corded dropped waist with covered buttons at back. Full gathered skirt, chapel length train.   **$990**

J I M   H J E L M

723   White Italian satin princess gown. Short sleeve. pearled
       and sequined beaded empire bodice with dimensional
       organza rosettes. Covered buttons at back, chapel
       length train.   **$1090**

724   White Italian satin gown. Short sleeve, square neckline
       with center bow detail. Full box pleated skirt, chapel
       length train.   **$990**

725   White satin princess gown. off the shoulder neckline
       adorned with silk flowers. Bow detail and rosettes.
       Covered buttons at back, chapel length train.   **$1050**

726   White silk shantung princess gown. Halter neckline with
       corded empire bodice. skirt adorned with venise lace
       streamers front and back. Covered buttons at back,
       chapel length train.   **$950**

727   White silk shantung princess gown. Sleeveless. scooped
       neckline, watteau bow with streamers. Covered buttons
       at back, chapel length train.   **$1050**

728   White satin sleeveless sheath. bateau neckline. low V back.
       Godet train with bow accent.   **$790**

❖ **Lazaro Bridal Gowns** ....

*Note: Lazaro bridal gowns are manufactured by Jim Hjelm but
marketed under the name "Lazaro."*

STYLE #	DESCRIPTION	SUGGESTED RETAIL

2000   Mint English net ball gown, sleeveless silk satin organza
       bodice with bateau neckline and horizontal waist.
       Full gathered skirt of floral embroidered English net
       sweep train.   **$1850**
       • *Also available in white.*

2001   Ice blue English net ball gown, sleeveless silk satin organ-
       za bodice, 'V' neckline, basque torso, full gathered skirt of
       floral embroidered English net, sweep train.   **$1850**
       • *Also available in white.*

2002   White silk organdy princess line gown, off -the- shoulder
       neckline with hand made flowers at shoulder flounce hem
       line adorned with silk flowers, chapel train.   **$3650**

2003   White silk organdy with pleated tulle, sculptured sweet-
       heart neckline, basque torso, full gathered organdy skirt
       drawn up at waist with hand made corsage over pleated
       tulle underskirt, chapel train   **$2350**

2004	Buttercup tulle ball gown, silk satin organza halter bodice, basque torso, full gathered tulle skirt with flower bustle at back, sweep train adorned with cascading petals. **$1750** • *Also available in white.*

2005	White organza ball gown, sleeveless scoop neckline, horizontal waist, full gathered skirt with embroidered ribbon hem, train. **$1590**

2006	White silk crepe sheath with crystal encrusted scoop neckline, oval sweep train. **$1790**

2007	White Belgium lace, off-the-shoulder neckline with long sheer sleeve, curved torso, full gathered tulle skirt, sweep train. **$1950**

2008	White silk shantung princess line gown, sculptured sweetheart neckline, short tulip sleeve, skirt encircled with venise lace appliqué, chapel train. **$1990**

2009	White silk shantung princess line gown, beaded venise lace appliqué at torso, chapel train. **$1990**

2010	White silk shantung sleeveless bateau neckline, horizontal waist, full gathered skirt with wide border of appliquéed alencon lace, chapel train. **$2300**

2011	Celedon silk satin striped organza ball gown, scoop neckline, horizontal waist and back corset, full gathered floor length skirt. **$1990**

2012	White silk satin striped organza ball gown, off-the-shoulder neckline adorned with handmade silk flowers, horizontal waist, full gathered floor length skirt. **$2590**

2013	White silk satin ball gown, off-the-shoulder neckline with narrow banded sleeve, princess silhouette with side gathered skirt adorned with beaded venise lace appliqué, chapel train. **$2850**

2014	White silk satin organza gown, hand embroidered jeweled bodice, "V" neckline and short sleeve, basque torso, full gathered skirt with sweep train. **$2300**

2015	White silk crepe sheath, empire bodice hand embroidered with floral motif sleeveless "V" neckline, oval sweep train. **$1900**

2016	White silk satin princess line gown, elaborately embroidered empire bodice, beaded straps, chapel train. **$2250**

J   I   M   H J E   L   M

2017   Ivory pleated tulle ball gown, hand embroidered beaded
        bodice, "V" neckline, short sleeve, basque torso, full
        gathered pleated tulle skirt, sweep train.   **$2250**

2018   White silk satin strapless ball gown with crumb catcher
        bodice, horizontal waistline, full gathered skirt with
        sweep train.   **$2650**

2019   Black and gold threaded English net ball gown, strapless
        bustier bodice with corset, curved waistline, full gathered
        skirt, sweep train.
        Price not available at press time
        • *Also available in white.*

⇒ LILA BROUDÉ ⇐

Contact info. Lila Broudé, 1375 Broadway, 4th Fl., New York, NY 10018. For a dealer near you, call (212) 921-8081 or (212) 921-8084.

Internet. This designer does not have an official web site yet. Our web site (www.bridalgown.com) will have updates on this designer.

Background/Our view. Designer Lila Broudé had 40 years of bridal experience before she started her own company in 1989. All that experience shows—Lila Broudé produces some of the most unique-ly styled bridal gowns in the couture market today.

The small line (about 40 dresses) features unusual fabrics, such as silk twill (which has an rich, finely ribbed texture). You'll find designs with silver embroidery, watteau trains and crystal and pearl detailing. Guipure lace accented a sweater-like bodice in one standout design.

Most of Lila Broudé's gowns are variations on the ball gown sil-houette. The skirt is usually unadorned and a few bodices have lace appliqués, but they're the exception.

As with many couture designers, perhaps the biggest drawback to this line is the price: gowns start at $1030 and go to $2350. Most are about $2000. The quality is excellent, however. **Rating: B+**

Delivery. 12 weeks. Rush cuts (2 to 6 weeks) are available for $200.

SIZING CHART

Type: Lila Broudé uses a BODY measurment size chart. For infor-mation on this subject, refer to the introduction of the designer review section of this book.

	2	4	6	8	10	12	14	16	18	20
Bust	32"	33	34	35	36	37.5	39	40.5	42	44
Waist	23	24	25	26	27	28.5	30	31.5	33	35
Hips	33	34	35	36	37	38.5	40	41.5	43	45

Sizing notes:
• Gown length (as measured from the hollow of the neck to the desired dress hem) is 58". Sleeve length is 18".

Extra charges for changes/options:
1. For sizes 18 and 20, add 10% to the gown price.
2. For longer gown length (five inches), add $100 to the gown price.
3. For shorter gown length, add $100 to the gown price.
4. For extra sleeve length, add $50 to the gown price.
5. For shorter sleeve length, add $40 to the gown price.
6. For buttons over zipper, add $50 to the gown price.
7. For buttons and loops (no zipper), add $70 to the gown price.
8. For dresses in ivory with Venise lace, add $130 to the gown price.
9. Some dresses are available in a less expensive fabric. See the gown descriptions below for more information.

L I L A   B R O U D E

NEW BRIDAL GOWNS FOR SPRING 1997

Note: The following are new styles for Spring/Summer 1997.
Lila Broude also has "carryover styles," dresses from previous seasons
that are not listed here.

STYLE #	DESCRIPTION	SUGGESTED RETAIL

500   Self fabric mini rolled roses define the décolletage on a silk shantung bustier gown. A matching bouquet enhances the pleated details of the ballroom skirt.

$1450

Featured in an editorial in Wedding Dresses magazine Winter 1997

501   Princess darts and pleats shape a double silk taffeta floor length gown with a sweetheart halter neckline. A tailored bow and streamers accent the circular back skirt.

$1350

Advertised in Martha Stewart Weddings early 1997

502   Venise appliqués cover the off-the-shoulder bodice and short sleeves on the Lila Broude signature silhouette. Wedding bells and daisies drift along the silk shantung skirt.

$1670

Advertised in Modern Bride magazine Feb/Mar, Apr/May 1997 "Creme de la Creme"

503   French knots accent random venise appliqués on a tank top, A-line silk shantung floor length gown with a removable train.   **$1630**

Advertised in Elegant Bride magazine Feb/Mar/Apr 1997

504   A dolman sleeved midriff jacket compliments a strapless silk shantung ball gown with a voluminous floor length skirt. Twisted bias details define the waistline and midriff.

$1490

Featured in an editorial in Bride's magazine Feb/Mar 1997

505   An embroidery of silver bullion, ice blue thread work, satin bugles, Ceylon beads and Austrian crystals embellishes the shoulders of a silk satin organza gown with basque waistline and gathered skirt. Accents of embroidery highlight the back bow and piping.   **$1890**

506   A perfect marriage of silk organza and silk Duchesse satin on a floor length gown with bold venise lace skirt appliqués. The scoop neck empire bodice, hem line and removable Watteau train are of satin.   **$1740**

Featured in an editorial in Elegant Bride Magazine Feb/Mar/Apr 1997

507   Pearl beaded venise appliqués mold the bodice of a gown
       with sweetheart neckline and cap sleeves. A combination
       of princess darts and pleats combine to shape this silk
       shantung gown with lace scalloped hem line.   **$1630**

508   Our "Emma" dress of silk taffeta boasts a tiny empire
       bodice embroidered with Ceylon beads, gimp, Austrian
       crystals and pearl braid. The Watteau train is removable.
                                                            $1990

       Featured in an editorial in Bridal Guide magazine
       Mar/Apr 1997

509   French darts covered with padded floral venise appliqués
       shape this A-line silk shantung gown with scoop neckline
       and short sleeves. Available white silk over pink or all white.
                                                            $1670

       Advertised in Modern Bride magazine Feb/Mar 1997

510   Guipure lace encircles the midriff and borders the hem
       line on a sophisticated silk shantung sheath gown with
       halter neckline and a removable circular train.   **$1400**

       Advertised in Bridal Guide magazine Mar/Apr 1997

511   A halter bodice of three dimensional venise lace joins a
       silk organza circular skirt covered with a profusion of
       floral and daisy appliqués.   **$1770**

       Advertised in Bride's magazine Feb/Mar 1997

512   Alencon lace embroidered with venise flowers and beads
       covers the off-the-shoulder bodice on a silk organza gown
       and drifts asymmetrically down the circular skirt.
       Matching Alencon borders the floor length hem line.

                                                            $1740

513   Venise vines and floral appliqués outline the off-the
       shoulder basque bodice and decorate the hem line on an
       Irish Linen gown with a turn of the century silhouette.
                                                            $1750

       Featured in an editorial in Martha Stewart Weddings
       magazine early 1997

514   Guipure lace lilacs embellish the bodice of a silk shantung
       princess gown with sweetheart necklace and short sleeves.
       The lilac appliqués drift aimlessly toward the lace edged
       hem line.

                                                            $1780

       Advertised in Bride's magazine Feb/Mar 1997

515   The tank top takes a new turn in a basque waisted venise
       lace gown with a swing skirt and a long sleeved bolero.
                                                            $1980

✧ L I L I ✧

Contact info. Lili, 1245 Johnson Dr., City of Industry, CA 91745. For a dealer near you, call (818) 369-2488.

Also known as. Rumours by Lili.

Internet. In a recent interview, a spokesperson for Lili told us they plan to have a web site up and running soon. Meanwhile, you can get updates on this designer by checking out our web site (www.bridal-gown.com).

Background. Lili got its start in the retail end of the business. Owner Ivor Hodis, a native of England, built a chain of California bridal shops under the name "Hacienda Brides International" before he branched out into manufacturing. The company traces its roots back to 1974 and now has five retail stores (including a recent addition in San Jose) that sell just Lili gowns. Of course, you don't have to live in California to buy a Lili dress; the company has dealers nationwide.

Our view. Lili's specialty is knocking-off other designers' looks at a lower price.

You'll find gowns in silks and polyester satins, plus a variety of lace like battenburg and venise in this line. The prices are certainly affordable: $415 to $790. Lili told us they plan to debut a new line of dresses in 1997 that will feature luxurious fabrics in the under $800 price range.

While the value is definitely there, Lili could learn a thing or two about customer service and deliveries. The company's rapid growth caught up to it in recent years, when import quota problems prompted it to discontinue several styles. The company continues to plug along, despite being ranked at the bottom of one industry survey for deliveries and reliability. The quality of the gowns, however, is about average. The gowns are hand-beaded and the company touts their hand-crafted rosettes. **Rating: C+**

Outlet stores. While not technically called "outlets," Lili does operate five company-owned stores in California that sell nothing but Lili gowns. The stores (which go under the name "Hacienda Brides International") are located in Huntington Beach, Beverly Hills, San Gabriel, San Diego and San Jose.

Delivery. 14 to 16 weeks. Some styles are in stock for quicker delivery.

SIZING CHART

Type: Lili uses a GARMENT measurement size chart. For information on this subject, refer to the introduction of the designer review section of this book.

L I L I

	4	6	8	10	12	14	16	18	20
Bust	34"	35	36	37	38.5	40	42	44	46
Waist	25	26	27	28	29.5	31	33	35	37

	22	24	26	28
Bust	48	50	52	54
Waist	39	41	43	45

Sizing notes:
• *Gown length (as measured from hollow of the neck to the desired dress hem) is 60". No extra length is available.*
• *For sizes 22 to 28, add $70 to the gown price.*

NEW BRIDAL GOWNS FOR SPRING 1997

STYLE #	DESCRIPTION	SUGGESTED RETAIL

3713   Off the shoulder; long sleeve, semi-cathedral train. Full gown detailed with cut-out hand embroidered satin with pearls and sequins. **$752**

3714   Off the shoulder long sleeve, semi-cathedral detachable train. Sheath gown detailed with cut-out hand embroidered satin with pearls and sequins. **$728**

3715   Off the shoulder, long sleeve, semi-cathedral train. Bodice detailed with cut-out hand embroidered satin. Full satin skirt detailed with hand cut-out design. **$704**

3716   Scoop neckline, long sleeve, bodice detailed with clustered bead work. Semi-cathedral satin train with matching hem lace. **$520**

3717   Scoop neckline, short sleeve, bodice detailed with clustered bead work. Semi-cathedral detachable satin train with matching hem lace. **$510**

3718   Stretch illusion long sleeve, high neck sheath gown. Embellished with venise lace throughout bodice and detachable satin train. **$550**

3720   Long sleeve, V-neck, mermaid, permanent chapel train. Detachable cathedral train with matching hem lace and appliqués. **$550**

3721   High neck, long sleeve, illusion sweetheart neckline. Heavily beaded re-embroidered lace with semi-cathedral beaded train. **$592**

3722   European scoop neckline with long sleeves. Sheath gown with detachable cathedral train detailed with cut-out Italian work. **$510**

L I L I

3723	Elegant halter neckline with a full tulle skirt. Bodice softly detailed with lightly beaded venise lace.	**$504**

3724	Off the shoulder, short sleeve enhanced with pearl trim. Re-embroidered lace bodice with pearls and sequins. Full satin semi-cathedral skirt with appliqués.	**$464**
	• Large sizes	**$538**

3725	A-line gown with a sabrina neckline and long illusion sleeves, re-embroidered lace throughout bodice. Semi-cathedral train with matching hem lace. V-cut back.	
		$494

3726	High neckline trimmed in pearls, long sleeve, re-embroidered lace bodice with pearls and sequins. Cathedral train enhanced with matching high hem lace.	**$550**

3727	Modified V-neck, long sleeve, appliqués on skirt, semi-cathedral train, hem lace, sequins and pearls.	**$520**
	• Large sizes	**$596**

3728	Semi-off the shoulder V-neckline. Venise lace throughout bodice and long sleeves. Lightly beaded. Semi-cathedral satin train.	**$532**

3729	Traditional illusion high neck, long sleeve, cathedral train, battenburg lace with sequins and pearls.	**$538**

3730	A-line with square neckline with cut out lace, sequins and pearls, long sleeve.	**$510**

3731	Sleeveless A-line scoop neck satin gown with removable short sleeve venise lace, beaded jacket.	**$466**

3732	Long sleeve, sweetheart neckline, re-embroidered lace on bodice train and hem line, sequins and pearls.	**$538**
	• Large sizes	**$614**

3733	Continental venise lace sheath gown, detachable train, matching hem lace, long sleeve, modified V-neck.	**$586**

789	Off the shoulder, semi-scoop neckline, silk gown with scalloped cathedral train, hand crafted rosettes with pearls.	
		$664
	• Large sizes	**$740**

3502	Hand beaded, pearls and sequins, cut out lace throughout, extended cathedral train.	**$606**

3520	Stretch illusion long sleeve, high neck, tulle gown, embellished with venise lace throughout bodice and appliqués on full skirt.	**$568**

L I L I

3522	Semi off the shoulder V-neck, long sleeve, cathedral train. Cut out Italian lace.	$572

3633	Informal sheath gown with a halter neckline and matching bolero jacket.	$372

3634	Informal strapless sheath with front slit and sweep train. Removable bolero jacket.	$418

3635	Informal A-line gown with modified sweetheart neckline. Short sleeves with re-embroidered lace bodice and V-back.	$386

3636	Informal sheath gown with front slit, sweep train, scoop neck and long satin sleeves.	$430

3637	Informal sleeveless floor length gown. Bodice embellished with venise lace and enhanced with buttons. Matching lace shawl.	$492

✦ M A R I S A ✦

Contact info. Marisa Collection, 1385 Broadway, Suite 1703, New York, NY 10018. For a dealer near you, call (212) 944-0022.

Internet. This designer does not have an official web site yet. Our web site (www.bridalgown.com) will have updates on this designer.

Background. Marisa's founders Lee Fein and Ron Colnick envision their company as a "bridge line." Veterans of the bridal business, Fein and Colnick spotted a void in the bridal market in the late 80's: there were plenty of cheap (and cheaply made) dresses under $1000 and plenty of high-quality couture designs with price tags over $2000. In 1988, the team started Marisa with the mission to create high-quality gowns sewn in the U.S. that are priced between the low and high end ($1000 to $2000). The company owns its own factory and uses modernized production techniques to keep costs down.

Marisa's young designer, Tamara Kristen, already had experience at Galina and Carmi Couture before recently joining the company. A graduate of the Pratt Institute, Tamara's goal is "understated elegance," with an emphasis on body shaping instead of overdone detail.

Our view. Marisa is our pick as one of the best bridal manufacturers in the market today. "Romantic" is the best word to describe Marisa's original designs. While the skirts are often left unadorned, the bodices of these gowns feature subtle detailing and, occasionally, delicate appliqués.

Marisa is a small line that debuts about a dozen new dresses each season. While the prices are not cheap (most gowns run $1050 to $1500), you do get value for the dollar. All the gowns have a built-in petticoat and feature excellent craftsmanship. The fabrics (silk shantung, silk-faced satin, organza) are top-notch. Another note: Marisa offers matching headpieces and gloves for most styles.

If you want to splurge, this designer is an excellent choice. **Rating: A**

Delivery. 12 to 16 weeks. Rush cuts are available.

Tags. Marisa sometimes uses a sewn-in label to identify their gowns.

SIZING CHART

Type: Marisa uses a BODY measurement size chart. For information on this subject, refer to the introduction of the designer review section of this book.

	4	6	8	10	12	14	16	18	20
Bust	32"	33	34	35	36	37.5	39	40.5	42
Waist	23	24	25	26	27	28.5	30	31.5	33.5
Hips	33	34	35	36	37	38.5	40	41.5	43

Sizing notes:
• *Gown length as measured from the hollow of the neck to the desired*

dress hem is about 57". This varies somewhat by size; consult a local retailer for more information.

• *Sleeve length as measured from the armpit to the wrist is 18".*

Extra charges for changes/options:

1. For sizes 18 and 20, add $100 to the gown price.
2. For extra length (five inches only), add 10% to the gown price.
3. For buttons over zipper, add $80 to the gown price.
4. For buttons and loops, add $100 to the gown price.

NEW BRIDAL GOWNS FOR SPRING 1997

STYLE #	DESCRIPTION	SUGGESTED RETAIL
262	Beaded alencon lace/tulle. A heavily beaded all-over lace halter bodice with a basque waist. The back torso features lace adorned straps graduated in shape. The circular multi-tulle skirt has a ribbon hem on its chapel train.	$1190
264	Silk face satin/embroidered tulle. A sheath silhouette which is defined by a fitted basque waist and halter top. The matching embroidered back bodice features buttons and loops. The detachable sweep train is of embroidered tulle.	$1050
265	Organza guipure lace. This all over guipure lace sheath features a slip top and detachable train of organza. *Advertised in Modern Bride Feb/Mar, Apr/May '97*	$1190
266	Silk face satin/embroidered tulle. A halter bodice of silk face satin has a sweetheart neckline and basque waist. The circular skirt of embroidered tulle features a sweep train. *Advertised in Modern Bride Feb/Mar, Apr/May '97*	$1190
267	Silk face satin organza multi-beaded detail. A sleeveless silk satin organza tank with a fitted elongated waistline and full circular skirt. A multitude of varying sized pearls and crystals frame the neckline and plunging back. *Advertised in Modern Bride Feb/Mar, Apr/May '97*	$1450
269	Silk shantung guipure lace. The all over lace bodice has a sweetheart neckline which is in symmetry with the fitted basque waistline. The draped shantung flows over the lace sleeve which become streamers accenting the circular skirt.	$1250
270	Silk shantung beaded guipure lace. Pearls and crystals are hand embroidered on this guipure tank bodice. The circular skirt is defined with silk flowers at the waist.	$1390

274   Silk satin crystal beaded alencon lace/tulle skirt. This contemporary sleeveless features fitted elongated torso with a crystal galloon of alencon lace. The circular tulle skirt of multi-layers has a ribbon trim.   **$990**

275   Silk shantung beaded alencon lace. A princess silhouette of silk shantung with a tear drop neckline and long lace sleeves. Beaded lace in a descending halo accents the flow of the a-line skirt.   **$1450**

276   Silk shantung venise lace. An on-shoulder princess of silk shantung with a petite pearled daisy bodice and long lace sleeves. Full size beaded daisies add texture too the overall look as they cascade down the back.   **$1300**
       Advertised in Modern Bride Feb/Mar, Apr/May '97

277   Silk face satin organza beaded venise. The jewel neckline on shoulder t-shirt style features beaded venise motifs flowing over the bust too the basque waist. The shaped open back is defined by lace adorned streamers.   **$1300**
       Advertised in Modern Bride Feb/Mar, Apr/May '97

❖ **"Marisa Too" Gowns** ....

800   Imported satin beaded lace & organza. A sleeveless halter sheath featuring a fitted basque waist and back skirt slit. The detachable organza train has a bias satin hem line. The waist line is defined by a multi-beaded lace trim.   **$790**
       Advertised in Modern Bride Feb/Mar, Apr/May '97

801   Silk shantung beaded alencon lace. A tank top of beaded and sequined lace with elongated torso and full circular skirt. The key-hole back is complimented by satin roses at the waist.   **$990**
       Advertised in Modern Bride Feb/Mar, Apr/May '97

802   Imported satin beaded lace tulle. An on shoulder t-shirt of satin with a raglan sleeve and elongated torso. Beaded lace encircles the neckline and waist. The multi-tulle skirts are fully circular.   **$700**
       Advertised in Modern Bride Feb/Mar, Apr/May '97

803   Silk shantung vermicelli beading. The on shoulder short shaped sleeve, basque waist make this the perfect dress for every figure. The bodice and sleeves are embroidered with pearls and bugle beads in an original design for "Marisa too."   **$850**

804   Silk face satin organza/ imported satin. A youthful sleeveless gown features an open neckline and fitted shaped waist. The waistline is adorned with a contrasting satin sash which streams down the train.   **$900**
       Advertised in Modern Bride Feb/Mar, Apr/May '97

✦ M A R Y ' S ✦

Contact info. PC Mary's Inc., 10520 Kinghurst Dr., Houston, TX 77099. For a dealer near you, call (713) 933-9678.

Internet. This designer does not have an official web site yet. Our web site (www.bridalgown.com) will have updates on this designer.

Background/Our view. Texas-based importer Mary's produces basic bridal gowns that are in the middle-of-the-road when it comes to quality and fashion.

The company has a good selection of both formal gowns (with trains) for $400 to $1060 and informal dresses (without trains) for $318 to $460. Most formal designs average $600 to $700.

While the prices are about average, the fashion seems somewhat behind the times. In business since 1986, Mary's still turns out styles with trumpet skirts and gowns that can only be charitably described as "ruffle explosions." This look was hip in the late 1980's, but seems passé now. Other styles are just your basic traditional wedding dress—ball gowns with basque waists and Queen Anne necklines, topped off with beaded and sequined alencon lace bodices and sleeves.

The fabrics aren't that impressive, either. Despite prices that approach $1000, Mary's uses polyester satin instead of silk for most of their designs. And the satin is the shiny variety, instead of the more common matte satins in vogue today. Overall, the quality of Mary's gowns is just average.

On the upside, Mary's does offer large sizes (to a size 30) with a very small up-charge ($30 to $50 depending on the style). **Rating: C**

Delivery. 10 to 12 weeks. Rush service is available for $50.

Tags. Mary's identifies its gowns with hang tags and sewn-in labels.

SIZING CHART

Type: Mary's uses a GARMENT size chart. For information on this subject, refer to the introduction of the designer review section of this book.

	4	6	8	10	12	14	16	18	20
Bust	32"	33	34	35	36.5	38	39.5	41.5	43.5
Waist	22	23	24	25	26.5	28	29.5	31.5	33.5
Hips	33	34	35	36	37.5	39	40.5	42.5	44.5

	22	24	26	28	30
Bust	45	47	49	51	55
Waist	35	37	39	41	45
Hips	46	48	50	52	56

Sizing notes:
• *Standard gown length (as measured from the hollow of the neck to the desired dress hem) is 58" to 59", depending on the size.*

• *Mary's also offers "custom cuts" made to your measurements; see below for specific options and charges.*

Extra charges for options/changes:

1. For extra gown length, add $100 to the gown price.
2. For extra sleeve length, add $100 to the gown price.
3. For a longer train, add $100 (for 120") or $200 (for 140") to the gown price.
4. For sizes 18 to 22, add $30 to the gown price.
5. For sizes 24 to 30, add $50 to the gown price.

NEW BRIDAL GOWNS FOR SPRING 1997

Note: All gowns are available in white or ivory unless otherwise noted.

❖ **Formal Bridal Gowns** ....

STYLE #	RETAIL	DESCRIPTION
3701	$558	Duchess satin, A-line tank style, V-front/back, beaded long sleeve bolero jacket, cathedral train.
3702	$518	Illusion yoke, long sleeves, satin edging on round neckline & hem, Venice lace, tulle cathedral train.
3703	$558	Duchess satin, A-line, Venice laced short sleeves, bow back, cathedral train.
3704	$478	Satin, scalloped V- neck, long sleeves, floral bustle, scalloped cathedral train.
3705	$598	Sweetheart neckline, heavy beaded bodice, long sleeves, gorgeous cascade of appliqués on cathedral train.
3706	$558	Satin sheath, Queen Anne neck, long sleeves, soutache lace appliqués, detachable. Cathedral train.
3707	$558	Chiffon halter top with beading design, gauntlet:, rosettes accent back, chiffon cathedral train.
3708	$458	Satin A-line tank with double straps, heading design, short sleeves bolero jacket, cathedral train.
3709	$518	Duchess satin A-line, sweetheart neck, intricate bead designs, pleated bodice, gauntlets, cathedral train.
3720	$498	Duchess satin, sweetheart neckline, choker heavy beaded design on short sleeves and hem line, cathedral train.

M A R Y ' S

3721	$538	Duchess satin, scalloped V-neck, long sleeves, princess cut 7-pieces bodice. Beautiful double bow, cathedral train.
3723	$598	Satin/diamond organza ruffles, V-neck, short puff sleeves with gauntlets, keyhole back, detachable royal ruffle train with hidden Velcro that converts into floor length.
3724	$438	Satin sheath, tank top style, Venice lace, detachable cathedral train.
3725	$558	Duchess satin/diamond organza ruffle, sweetheart neck, short, puff sleeves, gauntlets, ruffle cathedral train.
3726	$458	Satin/tulle tank top with two beaded straps, crisscross back, box bow, tulle cathedral train.
3727	$598	Duchess satin sheath, European lace appliqués, long sleeves, V-front/back, beautiful cut-outs on detachable cathedral train.
3728	$558	Duchess satin tank style, overlace bodice. Beautiful bow with rosette center, cathedral train.
3729	$538	Duchess satin A-line, sweetheart neck, short sleeves, gorgeous lace arrangement, detachable cathedral train.
3751	$698	Duchess satin, round neck, long sleeves, V-back, rosette accents back; scalloped cathedral train, rosette anchors.
3752	$478	Chiffon halter top, sheer long sleeves, French cuffs; all-over pearl bodice, chiffon cathedral train.
3753	$438	Duchess satin, on/off shoulder, short sleeves, gauntlets, 3-D floral accents on bodice, beautiful bow, cathedral train.
3754	$678	All-over lace strapless mini, overcoat with front pearl closures, pleated front skirt, cathedral train.
3756	$598	Satin bodice, high crown neck, illusion long sleeves, cascading lace from waist, scattered lace on cathedral train.
3757	$658	All-over Alencon lace sheath, cap sleeves, jeweled round neck, chiffon detachable cathedral train.

M A R Y ' S

3758	$558	Duchess satin, V-neck, short sleeves, re-embroidered lace, cascading lace appliqués on royal train.
3761	$738	All-over Venice lace sheath, tank style, jeweled neckline, Duchess satin detachable train.
3762	$698	Satin, high crown neck, long sleeves, European lace appliqués, splendid bow, cascading lace on cathedral train.
9701	$498	Satin brocade in delicate floral pattern A-line tank style, pearl trimmed yokes. Double bow, cathedral train.
9702	$658	Couture fabric with hint of golden highlights, halter top, bare back. Floor length-skirt with detachable cathedral train and bustle. *Available in ivory only.*
9703	$558	Tank top style, bugle beaded straps, exquisitely beaded bodice; chiffon floor length skirt, detachable. cathedral train.
9704	$498	Duchess satin, clean bodice design of Venice floral lace, stretch illusion yoke, short cuffed sleeves. Inset hem lace, butterfly bow.
9705	$538	Over-lace tank top style, A-line with empire waistline, organza skirt with over-lace long sleeve bolero jacket, buttons and organza cathedral train.

→ MON CHERI ←

Contact info. Mon Cheri Bridals Inc., 1018 Whitehead Road Extension., Trenton, NJ 08638. For a dealer near you, call (609) 530-1900.

Internet. This designer does not have an official web site yet. Our web site (www.bridalgown.com) will have updates on this designer.

Background. Bridal industry veteran Steve Lang knew an opportunity when he saw it. In 1991, the bridal market was saturated with look-alike gowns that suffered from two problems: cheap quality and no style. Lang saw a niche to produce high-quality gowns, but without the corresponding high price tag. Mon Cheri was founded with just that mission.

Lang teamed with Taiwanese designer Amy Yen to start the company. Yen had 17 years of experience in bridal; she helped put Private Label by G on the map and even worked for Demetrios.

Until recently, it was hard to even get a look at Mon Cheri gowns; the company rarely advertised. That's changed somewhat, with the company taking out a limited number of ads in bridal magazines. The marketing strategy is intentional; Lang told us Mon Cheri would rather invest in the quality of its dresses (all sewn in China) than glossy advertisements. (In order to see their gowns, call the above number to find a store near you that carries Mon Cheri).

Our view. Mon Cheri has achieved a rare feat in the bridal business: it produces gowns that are high-style at prices that are very down to earth. Of course, many other designers talk about doing just this, but they often just put out gowns that have a thin veneer of couture styling. Underneath the hood, it's still a cheap dress.

How good is Mon Cheri's quality? First, every dress is fully lined, so you won't see any loose seams or cheap finish work inside the gown. The hems of Mon Cheri gowns are finished with horse hair stitching and each dress has a full two-inch seam allowance (which makes alterations easier).

The fabrics are top-quality as well. You'll see silk, Italian satin and French tulle in the designs. Mon Cheri uses only high thread-count fabrics; while other designers rely on starches and resins to give their fabrics body, Mon Cheri resists this shortcut. Moreover, the company doesn't use any nylon in its piece goods (such as tulle netting).

So, how much is all this quality going to cost you? $1000? $2000? Nope, most of Mon Cheri gowns are far under $1000.

The designer divides its dresses into several collections. The regular Mon Cheri gowns are just $400 to $800 and feature satin, polyester shantung and matte satin fabrics. If you want an informal gown, Mon Cheri offers several styles without trains for $300 to $400.

Want even better value? Check out Mon Cheri's "Pure Silks" gowns. These 18, all-silk styles retail for only $600 to $850, yet feature top-notch styling and detailing. If that wasn't enough, the designer also has several "Traditional Value Styles" for about $675 that are a great deal: "Royal Satin" fabric, built-in crinolines, cathedral trains and more.

Despite its young age, Mon Cheri offers a quite extensive line, with over 100 active styles. The fashion is very current and you can find everything from traditional silhouettes to more avante garde styling. We especially liked the two-tone styles, which combined white and rum pink accents on some gowns. The designer even offers a silk "couture" collection ($760 to $1000) that offers hand-embroidery and head-beading in styles that echo couture designers like Scaasi.

If that weren't enough, Mon Cheri also offers matching headpieces/veils and flower girl dresses at very affordable prices. The sizing is also reality-based, with large sizes up to 44 available for a very small up-charge ($20 to $60).

With all these advantages, it's not surprising they ranked as the number one bridal manufacturer (out of a field of 35) in a recent survey of bridal retail shops. The quality, value, delivery and service are all excellent. **Rating: A**

Delivery. 12 weeks. No rush cuts, but some dresses are in stock for quicker delivery.

Tags. Mon Cheri identifies its gowns with a sewn-in label.

SIZING CHARTS

Type: Mon Cheri uses a GARMENT size chart. For information on this subject, refer to the introduction of the designer review section of this book.

Average Sizes

	4	6	8	10	12	14	16	18	20
Bust	32.5"	33.5	34.5	35.5	36.5	37.5	39	41	43
Waist	23	24	25	26	27	28	29	31	33
Hips	34	35	36	37	38	39.5	41	43	45
Length	57.5	57.75	58	58.25	58.5	58.75	59	59.25	59.5

Large Sizes

	38	40	42	44
Bust	45"	47	49	51
Waist	35	37	39	41
Hips	47	49	51	53
Length	59.5	59.75	60	60

Sizing notes:
• *Sleeve length (as measured from armpit to wrist) is 18".*
• *For Spring 1997, Mon Cheri is introducing a "Custom Plus" sizing program for large sizes on selected styles. This program allows for a better fit with fewer alterations. Consult a local retailer for more information.*

M O N   C H E R I

Extra charges for changes/options:

1. For sizes 18 and 20, add $20 to the gown price (except for silk dresses, add $40 total).

2. For sizes 38 to 44, add $40 to the gown price (except for silk dresses, add $60 total).

3. For sleeve length changes, add $60 to the gown price.

4. Custom gown lengths are available; add $100 to the gown price. This option adds two weeks to Mon Cheri's average delivery.

5. Dresses with detachable trains are available with no train at all.

NEW BRIDAL GOWNS FOR SPRING 1997

Note: Many Mon Cheri gowns are available in white, ivory or in a combination of ivory and "rum pink" or "cafe" (a darker ivory color). A gown that is available in colors "white-ivory-ivory/rum pink" means you can order it white, ivory or a combination of ivory and rum pink.

❖ Traditional Value Bridal Gowns ....

STYLE	PRICE	COLORS
TV9	**$678**	White-Ivory-Rum Pink *Available in Large Sizes 38-44*
TV10	**$678**	White or Ivory *Available in Large Sizes 38-44*
TV11	**$678**	White or Ivory *Available in Large Sizes 38-44*

❖ Regular Bridal Gowns ....

STYLE	PRICE	COLORS
800	**$518**	White-Ivory-Ivory/Rum Pink *Available in Large Sizes 38-44*
801	**$518**	White-Ivory-Ivory/Rum Pink *Available in Large Sizes 38-44.* *Matches Flower Girl Style 443*
802	**$558**	White-Ivory-Ivory/Rum Pink
803	**$598**	White or Ivory
804	**$598**	White-Ivory-Ivory/Rum Similar Style is 821 in Pure Silk Shantung *Available in Petite Sizes 3-11 as 804P*
805	**$618**	White-Ivory-Ivory/Rum *Available in Custom Plus Sizes 38-44 as 805CP*

M O N   C H E R I

STYLE	PRICE	COLORS
806	**$618**	White or French Vanilla *New Fabric: Glazed Satin*
807	**$638**	White or Ivory
808	**$658**	White-Ivory-Ivory/Rum *Available in Petite Sizes 3-11 as 808P.* *Matches Informal Bridal Style 134 and* *Flower Girl Style 445*
809	**$678**	White or Natural
810	**$678**	White or Ivory *Two Piece Gown*
811	**$698**	White or French Vanilla *New Fabric: Glazed Satin* *Available in Custom Plus Sizes 38-44 as 811CP*
812	**$718**	White-Ivory-Ivory/Rum *Matches Flower Girl 443*
814	**$718**	White or Ivory *Matches Informal Bridal Style 136*
815	**$738**	White or Ivory
816	**$738**	White or Ivory
817	**$778**	White-Ivory-Ivory/Cafe *Matches Informal Bridal 130*
818	**$698**	Natural Only
819	**$698**	Natural Only
820	**$778**	White or Ivory
821	**$798**	Natural or Natural/Rum *Similar to style 804 in Italian Silky Satin*

✦ M O N I Q U E ✦

Contact info. Monique Bridal, 10511 Valley Blvd., Suite 388, El Monte, CA 91731. For a dealer near you, call (818) 401-9910.

Also known as: Monique Bridals, Monique Couture, Monique Collections

Internet. This designer does not have an official web site yet. Our web site (www.bridalgown.com) will have updates on this designer.

Background/Our view. You've got to give it to Monique for at least trying something different. One of their styles is reminiscent of pre-French revolution fashion, with three-quarter Renaissance sleeves, trimmed in ribbon. You just don't see many Marie Anntoinette-type gowns gracing the runways of bridal designers these days.

Of course, that's just one style in a collection that is all over the board, fashion-wise. Most gowns feature rather plain skirts, wedded to incredibly beaded or laced bodices. Monique's signature appears to be patterned beading and embroidery—another style that caught our eye featured metallic gold thread embroidery that echoed Scaasi's designs, but went one step further. Whether you like or don't like this effect, you've got to give Monique bonus points for effort.

This young manufacturer (in business since 1993) still has to learn a few tricks about advertising. Most of its ads don't do justice to the gowns, but the company has pledged to do better.

The majority of Monique's bridal gowns are in the $800 range, although prices start at $520 and can rise to about $1200. Typical fabrics include silk-faced satins, organza and either silk or polyester shantungs. The quality is above average and the sizing is generous, with selected styles in sizes up to a 28. **Rating B.**

Delivery. 10 to 12 weeks. No rush cuts, but some styles are in stock for quicker delivery.

SIZING CHARTS

Type: Monique uses a BODY size chart. For information on this subject, refer to the introduction of the designer review section of this book.

	2	4	6	8	10	12	14	16	18	20
Bust	33.5"	34.5	35.5	36.5	37.5	39	40.5	42	44	46
Waist	23.5	24.5	25.5	26.5	27.5	29	30.5	32	34	36
Hips	35.5	36.5	37.5	38.5	39.5	41	42.5	44	46	48

	22*	24*	26*	28*
Bust	48	50.25	52.5	54.75
Waist	38	40.25	52.5	44.75
Hips	50	52.25	54.5	56.75

M O N I Q U E

Sizing notes:
• *Gown length (as measured from the hollow of the neck to the desired dress hem) is 59.5"*
• *Sleeve length (as measured from armpit to wrist) is 25."*

Extra charges for changes/options:

1. For sizes 18 to 20, add $80 to the gown price.
2. Only selected styles are available in sizes 22 to 28. This option adds $160 to $250 to the gown price, depending on the style.
3. To lengthen or shorten sleeves, add $50 to the gown price.
4. To change the gown length, add $60 to the gown price.
5. Some short sleeve gowns are available in long sleeves; add $100 to the gown price for this option. Ask a local retailer for more information.

NEW BRIDAL GOWNS FOR SPRING 199

❖ **Formal Bridal Gowns** ....

Note: All gowns are available in white or ivory unless otherwise noted.

STYLE #	DESCRIPTION	SUGGESTED RETAIL
6671	Duchess Satin/French tulle. Sheer illusion yoke with sweet heart neckline, pearl-studded bodice atop floating French tulle bell-shaped sweep skirt, side zipper opening.	**$778**
	• *Featured on the front cover of Monique's catalog.*	
121	Crepe Chiffon/Cotton Stretch Lace. Long sleeve, cotton stretch lace bodice with scoop neck line, piping trim; crepe chiffon full skirt with built-in crinoline; floral bow back; sweep train.	**$498**
110	Duchess Satin. Short sleeve, off the shoulder, Princess silhouette, Duchess satin, with all-over floral accent embroidery, box pleat skirt with 15" embroidered hem; cathedral train. Built-in crinoline	**$738**
	• *Available in "cafe on ivory" color only.*	
113	Silky Organza over Italian Silky Satin. Sleeveless, square neck ball gown silhouette; natural piped waist; embroidered lace border with sweep train, built-in crinoline.	**$738**
	• Option: organza shawl	**$118**
134	Italian Silky Satin. Sleeveless halter with illusion bodice; pleated waist, full gathered skirt with built-in crinoline; cathedral train.	**$458**
	Also available in "rum pink with ivory"	
119	Silky Organza/Embroidered Schiffli Lace. Long sleeve,	

pearl accent embroidered schiffli lace on silky organza;
illusion bodice with satin piping; basque waist, full skirt
with built-in crinoline; embroidered bow, wide bordered
lace trim; cathedral train. **$258**

102   Italian Silky Satin. Short sleeve, Princess silhouette with
"daisy" Venice lace bodice; "V" back; Italian silky satin;
rosebud chapel train accent back. **$552**

128   Italian Silky Satin. Long sleeve, "A" line silhouette, embroidered Venice lace bodice with "V" neck and back; skirt
with bow trim down the back; chapel train. **$538**

137   Silky Chiffon. Sleeveless, silky Princess silhouette in "Iris"
embroidered silky chiffon; sweetheart neckline; basque
waist; rosette back accent with streamers; built-in
crinoline; sweep train. **$538**
• Option: chiffon shawl **$98**

105   Silky Organza with Soutache Embroidery. Long sleeve,
silky organza with soutache embroidery, sweetheart satin
neckline under organza; basque waist; double butterfly
organza bow back; built-in crinoline, semi-cathedral train.
$638

103   Duchess Satin. Short sleeve, off the shoulder, basque
waist; "daisy" Venice lace bodice; "V" back with bow;
sweep train, built-in crinoline. **$596**

126   Italian Matte Satin. Short sleeve, off the shoulder, pearl
encrusted bodice; natural piped waist; full, Italian matte
satin, box pleat skirt with built-in crinoline; chapel train.
$596

132   Italian Silky Organza. Short sleeve, traditional silhouette
with sweetheart neckline, basque waist; pearl accent
Venice lace bodice; full, silky satin skirt with built-in
crinoline; cathedral train. **$658**

104   All over Brussels Lace. Sleeveless, all over "Brussels " lace
ball gown; basque waist, sweetheart neckline; "V" back
with covered button zipper; full skirt with scalloped hem;
floral bow back, built-in crinoline, chapel train. **$598**
• Option: short sleeves **$70**

116   Duchess Satin. Short Sleeve, scoop neck bodice in organza
over satin; beaded French alencon lace trim on bodice;
basque waist; full skirt in Duchess satin with built-in
crinoline, box pleat detail, plain hem; covered button
back; chapel train. **$498**

125   Duchess Satin. Short sleeve, embroidered "cut out" bodice

with pearl accent trim; sweetheart neckline, closed back; full, duchess satin skirt with built-in crinoline; embroidered "cut-out" bow with streamers; cathedral train. **$798**

136 French Alencon Lace. Short sleeve; French alencon lace bodice with "corset seaming"; full, triple layered French tulle skirt with beaded re-embroidered lace hem; "V" neckline, basque waist; embroidered bow, lace trim; chapel train.   **$918**

123 Silky Organza/Venice Lace. Short cap sleeve; illusion bodice with floral, Venice lace, piped scoop neckline; full, double layered silky organza skirt with butterfly bow back, sweep train.   **$498**

101 All over Embroidered Silky Organza. Long sleeve, "A" line silhouette with illusion bodice; embroidered silky organza over satin; detachable chapel train with floral bow back, built-in crinoline.   **$678**

106 Italian Silky Satin/French Tulle. Sleeveless ball gown silhouette with pearl encrusted bodice; "V" neckline; triple layered French tulle skirt, built-in crinoline; sweep train.
                                                                   $698
• Option: tulle shawl   **$98**

1335 Pure Silk Shantung. Sleeveless, ball gown silhouette in pure silk shantung, all over beaded French alencon lace; basque waist; full, gathered skirt with built-in crinoline, cathedral train.   **$798**
• *Available in "natural" color only*
• Option: long sleeves   **$98**

138 Silky Organza. Long sleeve, scoop neck bodice in silky organza over satin: hand beaded floral embroidered bodice with embroidered sheer sleeves; scoop back; natural waist, full gathered double layered silky organza skirt with built in crinoline. Chapel train.   **$638**

6665 Duchess Satin. Hand rolled roses accenting all around opened sweet heart neckline, piped basque waist line, multi-layers of French tulle skirt scattered with tiny hand rolled roses, semi-chapel train accented with rosettes.
                                                                   $718
• *Long tapped sleeves also available.*

6662 French Alencon/French Tulle. Halter neckline with beaded French alencon lace bodice; basque waist; triple layered French tulle skirt with ribbon edging hem; sweep train. **$738**
• *Available in white with silver beading or ivory with rum pink beading.*
• Option: tulle shawl   **$98**

6629   Italian Silky Satin. Off the shoulder, short sleeve, illusion
        neck line; hand rolled rosette trim; Princess silhouette
        with rosette trim at the waist. Cathedral Train.   **$658**
        • *Also available in "champagne" color*

6638   Italian Silky Satin. Off the shoulder sleeve with scoop
        neckline; Italian silky satin; natural waist; heavy
        re-embroidered alencon lace appliqués all around
        cathedral train.   **$738**

6648   Italian Silky Satin. Hand embroidered floral design, off-
        the-shoulder neckline, long fitted sleeves, basque waist,
        semi-cathedral train with wide embroidered hem and
        floral cut-outs.   **$798**

117   Crepe Chiffon. Off the shoulder, crepe chiffon; chiffon
        floral trimmed neckline with pearl cluster centers; floral
        accented back with streamers; detachable sweep train.
                                                            $538

6664   Duchess Satin. Off-the-shoulder scoop neckline, silhou-
        ette princess line cut out waist falls to skirt, hand embroi-
        dered metallic lace made by antique gold thread creates
        an arabesque all over floral design descending through
        the edge of semi-cathederal train.   **$1250**
        • *Available in white/ivory with silver or antique gold
        metallic lace.*
        • *Also available in "full figure" sizes.*

6672   Italian Silky Satin. Sleeveless, pearl accented "cut out",
        embroidered bodice, scoop neckline, "V" back; full,
        gathered Duchess satin skirt with built in crinoline;
        "cut out" embroidered butterfly bow back with streamers;
        chapel train.   **$798**

✦ M O N T I Q U E ✦

Contact info. Montique Creations Inc., 2580 Corporate Pl., Suite F105, Monterey Park, CA 91754. For dealer near you or a free catalog, call (800) 510-3232 or (213) 266-3232.

Internet. This designer does not have an official web site yet. Our web site (www.bridalgown.com) will have updates on this designer.

Background/Our view. Montique is a small gown manufacturer with about 40 gowns in a wide variety of styles. The "Silk Ensemble" is probably this designer's stand-out as far as value goes; these dresses in silk dupioni and silk satin run $560 to $860.

If you'd prefer satin, the "Romantic Satin" collection offers several styles in the $500 to $700 price range. Montique even has a "Budget Plus Size" series of dresses that are available in large sizes up to 30 for $360 to $400.

It's hard to pin down Montique's fashion. The dresses range from ultra-plain looks to gowns completely encrusted with beads and sequins. While we thought some of the styles were quite elegant, Montique went overboard with others—too much beading, lace or both. A little more fashion focus would help clarify the designer's direction.

Montique doesn't advertise much, so you may want to take up their offer for a free catalog (see above for details). While we like the affordable silk designs, the finish on many of these gowns (silk dupioni) isn't one of our favorites, as we mentioned earlier in this book.
Rating: B-

Delivery. 6 to 14 weeks. Rush cuts (eight week delivery) are available.

SIZING CHART

Type: Montique uses a BODY size chart. For information on this subject, refer to the introduction of the designer review section of this book.

Standard Sizes

	4	6	8	10	12	14	16	18	20	22
Bust	34"	35	36	37	38	39.5	41	43	45	48
Waist	24.5	25.5	26.5	27.5	28.5	30	31.5	33.5	35.5	38
Hips	37	38	39	40	41	42.5	44	46	48	50
Length	58	58.13	58.25	58.5	58.75	59	59.25	59.5	59.75	60

Extra Large Sizes

	26	28	30
Bust	52.5	54.75	57
Waist	42.5	44.75	47
Hips	54.5	56.75	59
Length	60.35	60.5	60.5

M O N T I Q U E

Sizing notes:
• *Length is defined as the measurement from the hollow of the neck to the desired dress hem.*

Extra charges for options/changes:

1. For sizes 20 to 22, add $50 to the gown price.
2. For sizes 26 to 30, add $200 to the gown price.
3. Custom cuts (made to your measurements) are available; add $200 to the gown price for this service.
4. Shorter or longer gown length (up to six inches) is available for an additional $100.

NEW BRIDAL GOWNS FOR SPRING 1997

Note: All bridal gowns are available in white or ivory unless otherwise noted.

❖ Couture Elegance by Montique ....

Note: The following styles can be ordered without a train. The price for each gown would then be $458.

STYLE #	FABRIC/DESCRIPTION	SUGGESTED RETAIL
9027	Duchess Satin with detachable train	$518
9028	Duchess Satin with detachable train	$518
9029	Duchess Satin with detachable train	$518
9031	Duchess Satin with detachable train	$518

❖ Informals by Montique ....

STYLE #	FABRIC/DESCRIPTION	SUGGESTED RETAIL
9025	Organza full skirt in two tier	$378
9026	Italian Satin with tulle skirt	$378

❖ Montique Classiques ....

STYLE #	FABRIC/DESCRIPTION	SUGGESTED RETAIL
1063	Italian satin Princess line, 130" train	$718
1080	Italian satin square neckline with 120" train	$658
1081	Satin high neckline with 120" train	$658

❖ Montique Silk Collection ....

Note: Montique Silk Collection gowns are available in white only

STYLE #	FABRIC/DESCRIPTION	SUGGESTED RETAIL
2019	Silk with pleated waistline	$698
2023	Silk with tan top full skirt	$698

M O N T I Q U E

❖ **Montique Plus Sizes Collection** ....

Style #	Fabric/Description	Suggested Retail
5007	Satin with bows appliqués on train.	**$398**
	• *Also available in sizes 26-30*	**$518**

❖ **Montique Couture Collection** ....

Style #	Fabric/Description	Suggested Retail
2202	Italian satin with rum pink trimming	**$598**
2205	Chiffon with Venise lace	**$598**
2201	Tan top with pink lace in tulle	**$658**

→MOONLIGHT←

Contact info. Moonlight, 50 E. Commerce, Suite G, Schamburg, IL 60173. For a free catalog or to find a dealer near you, call (847) 884-7199.

Also known as. Carole Hai (she's the designer).

Internet. This designer does not have an official web site yet. Our web site (www.bridalgown.com) will have updates on this designer.

Background/Our View. Designer Carole Hai cites fairy tales as the inspiration for her dress designs. And it doesn't take too much imagination to envision Cinderella or Sleeping Beauty decked out in a Moonlight gown—most of Carole's designs feature big ball gown silhouettes and big tulle skirts that echo animated Disney fashion.

As mentioned earlier in this book, Carole Hai is the sister of Kyle Yin, the owner of Jasmine. At one time, the two manufacturers used to share production facilities, but since 1992 they've gone their separate ways. While Jasmine has focused on innovative styling, Moonlight has chosen a more traditional path.

Moonlight's gowns are somewhat pricey, considering the fabrics are typically polyester satins (not silks). The Moonlight Collection weights in at $530 to $796. At the upper-end, the Moonlight Couture line ($950 to $1690) features lots of alencon lace but, once again, little silk fabric. Instead, you'll find detailing such as silver bugle beads or illusion fitted sleeves.

Moonlight redeems itself on the value side with the "Moonlight Silks" collection. These silk shantung gowns range from $635 to $1590, although half are under $600. Another quality note: Moonlight gowns feature built-in crinolines.

You won't find much cutting-edge fashion in this line. Instead of halter tops or tank top looks, you'll find traditional ball gowns with high necklines covered in illusion. Other dresses use that other standard bridal neckline: the sweetheart.

Like Jasmine, Moonlight gets better marks on quality than it does for delivery reliability or customer service, which are merely average. We'd be more excited about this line if their prices were more in line with the competition. Especially disappointing were the upper-end gowns: we expected fancier detailing and silk fabrics, not the same old traditional styling and polyester satin. On the upside, at least Moonlight offers all its dresses in large sizes (up to size 44).
Rating: B

Delivery. 12 to 14 weeks. Rush cuts (nine week delivery) are available for $50 extra.

Tags. Moonlight identifies their gowns with hang tags and sewn-in labels.

M O O N L I G H T

SIZING CHARTS

Type: Moonlight uses a BODY size chart. For information on this subject, refer to the introduction of the designer review section of this book.

Standard Sizes

	4	6	8	10	12	14	16	18	20
Bust	33"	34	35	36	37.5	39	40.5	42.5	44.5
Waist	23	24	25	26	27.5	29	30.5	32.5	34.5
Hips	35.5	36.5	37.5	38.5	40	41.5	43	45	47
Length	58	58	59	59	59	60	60	60	60

Full Figure Sizes

	38	40	42	44
Bust	47"	49	51	53
Waist	38	40	42	44
Hips	49.5	51.5	53.5	55.5
Length	60	60	60	60

Sizing notes:
• Length is defined as the measurement from the hollow of the neck to the desired dress hem.
• Sleeve length (armpit to wrist) is 18."

Extra charges for options/changes:

1. For sizes 38 to 44, add $80 to $120 to the gown price (this varies depending on the style).
2. Sleeve changes (longer or shorter) are $50 extra.
3. Custom gown lengths are also available for an additional $60.
4. For a longer train (36" extra only), add $200 to the gown price for dresses made of "Regal Satin" and $300 to the gown price for dresses made of Italian satin or silk shantung.

NEW FOR SPRING 1997

Note: The following dresses are Moonlight's new dresses for spring 1997. Not included here are Moonlight's carryovers (dresses from previous seasons). We hope to have carryover information for many designers on our web page (www.windsorpeak.com).

❖ **Moonlight Couture Gowns** ....
Note: All dresses are available in white or ivory.

STYLE #	DESCRIPTION	SUGGESTED RETAIL
H8555	Open off-shoulder, basque waist, illusion fitted sleeves, Italian satin, alencon lace, monarch train. Beading: silver bugle/pearl/sequin.	**$1500**

M O O N L I G H T

| H554 | Open off-shoulder, basque waist, illusion fitted sleeves, satin/organza, alencon lace, detachable cathedral train. Beading: pearl/sequin. | **$1300** |

| H8553 | Scoop neck, basque waist, illusion fitted sleeves, satin/tulle, alencon lace, detachable satin monarch train. Beading: silver bugle/pearl/sequin. | **$1300** |
| | *Advertised in Modern Bride Magazine Feb/Mar 1997 "Ingenue"* | |

| H8552 | Square neck sheath, basque waist, satin illusion sleeves, Italian satin, alencon lace, detachable cathedral train. Beading: pearl/ sequin. | **$1300** |

| H8551 | Sweetheart neckline, pricness A-line, basque waist, short capped sleeves, Italian satin, Venise lace, chapel train. Beading: pearl/sequin. | **$1190** |

| H8540 | High neck, basque waist, ilussion fitted sleeves, Italian satin, alencon lace, monarch train. Beading: pearl/sequin. | **$1190** |

❖ **Moonlight Silk Gowns** ....
Note: All dresses in this collection are available in white only. The fabric for all these dresses is 100% silk shantung.

STYLE #	DESCRIPTION	SUGGESTED RETAIL
S6158	Queen anne neckline, basque waist, illusion fitted sleeves, alencon lace, monarch train. Beading: pearl/sequin/silver bugle.	**$1598**
S6156	Halter sweetheart neckline, basque waist, sleeveless, alencon lace, monarch train. Beading: pearl/sequin. *Advertised in Modern Bride magazing Feb/Mar 1997 "Creme de la Creme"*	**$1500**
S6152	Open off-shoulder, basque waist, short fitted sleeves, Venise lace, chapel train. Beading: pearl/sequin/silver bugle.	**$750**
S6150	Queen Anne neckline, basque waist, silk fitted sleeeves, alencon lace, chapel train. Beading: pearl/sequin.	**$598**
S6149	V-neckline, basque waist, sleeveless, alencon lace, cathedral train. Beading: pearl/sequin.	**$650**
S6148	Open off-shoulder, basque waist, ilussion fitted sleeves, alencon lace, chapel train. Beading: pearl/sequin.	**$598**
S6147	Sweetheart neckline, basque waist, short fitted sleeves, alencon lace, chapel train. Beading: pearl/sequin.	**$598**

❖ **Moonlight Collection Gowns** ....

Note: All dresses in this colleciton are available in white or ivory. The fabric for all these dresses is "Regal Satin," and all are beaded with pearls and sequins. All these dresses also feature alencon lace.

Style #	Description	Suggested Retail
B8530	Open off shoulder, basque waist, short fitted sleeves, monarch train.	$790
B8515	High neckline, basque waist, ilussion fitted sleeves, monarch train.	$690
B8513	Scoop neckline, basque waist, short fitted sleeves, chapel train.	$598
B8512	Square neckline, basque waist, ilusion fitted sleeves, chapel train.	$590
B8511	Sheath dress, V-neckline, basque waist, ilussion fitted sleeves, detachable chapel train.	$580
B8504	V-neckline, basque waist, satin fitted sleeves, chapel train.	$580
B8503	Open off-shoulder, basque waist, short fitted sleeves, chapel train.	$570
B8501	Sheath, open off-shoulder, basque waist, short fitted sleeves, detachable chapel train.	$550

❖ M O R I L E E ❖

Contact info. Mori Lee Associates, 498 7th Ave., 15th Floor, New York, NY 10018. For a dealer near you, call (212) 947-3490.

Also known as. Regency by Madeline Gardner.

Internet. This designer does not have an official web site yet. Our web site (www.bridalgown.com) will have updates on this designer.

Background. Here's an interesting story about how this designer got his name. When the founding families of this designer (the Udells and the Leibowitzs) were brainstorming names for their young company in 1945, they decided to name the company after one of the founder's wives Sarah. Unfortunately, they discovered the name—Sara Lee—was already taken. So instead they abbreviated the name of founder Morris Leibowitz into "Mori Lee," thus saving many brides the embarrassment of wearing wedding gown with the same name as a pound cake.

But, seriously . . . designer Madeline Gardner has been with Mori Lee since 1984. Straight out of the Fashion Institute of Technology at the time, Madeline's fresh and innovative looks gave Mori Lee a big shot in the arm. By the 1990's, Mori Lee had established itself as one of the bridal industry's powerhouses.

Our view. Why is Mori Lee arguably the country's hottest bridal designer? We'll give you three reasons: price, price, price.

Combine designer Madeline Gardner's current fashion looks with rock-bottom pricing and you'll quickly realize why these gowns are selling like hot cakes.

With over 100 styles, you can find both traditional and contemporary looks in the Mori Lee line. With prices ranging from $400 to $710, Mori Lee's formal wedding gowns are a very good buy indeed.

If you want a silk gown, consider the Regency by Madeline Gardner line, also made by Mori Lee. (Interestingly enough, Regency's ads don't mention its connection to Mori Lee, even though Gardner designs all the dresses.) These looks, mostly in silk shantung, run $500 to $890. Mori Lee doesn't forget brides who want an informal look, either. Their collection of informals is surprisingly large (about a dozen options) in prices that range from $330 to $550.

Mori Lee's main success has been translating expensive couture looks (like watteau trains, halter necklines, tank tops) into gowns priced for the mainstream. And, best of all, the designer doesn't compromise on the fabrics, offering silk shantungs, matte satins and other stylish options.

If we had to fault Mori Lee on anything, it would have to their quality. These dresses are merely average when it comes to construction and finish. The company could also stand to improve its deliveries and customer service, which get just average marks from retailers.

Another negative: Mori Lee tends to nickel and dime you to death: if you want an ivory (instead of white) gown, that's an extra

$10. If you need extra skirt length, you're out of luck—the designer doesn't offer this option. The sizing is also very limited (just 4 to 20), although a few styles are available in a size 42.

Despite these criticisms, it's hard not to like a manufacturer like Mori Lee. As the industry's price leader, they're often the designer to watch. **Rating: B+**

Delivery. 10 to 12 weeks. No rush cuts are available.

Tags. Mori Lee only identifies its gowns with hang tags (no sewn-in labels).

SIZING CHART

Type: Mori Lee uses a BODY size chart. For information on this subject, refer to the introduction of the designer review section of this book.

	4	6	8	10	12	14	16	18	20	42*
Bust	32.5"	33.5	34.5	36	37	38.5	40	42	43.5	47
Waist	23.5	24.5	25	26.5	27.5	29	30.5	32.5	33.5	37
Hips	34	35	36	37	38.5	39.5	41.5	43	44.5	47

Sizing notes:
• *Gown length is 59.5" to 60", depending on the size.*
No extra length is available.

Extra charges for changes/options:
1. For sizes 18 and 20, add $20 to the gown price.
2. *Only selected styles are available in size 42. For this size, add $80 to the gown price.
3. Dresses ordered in ivory are an additional $10.

NEW BRIDAL GOWNS FOR SPRING 1997

❖ **Mori Lee Gowns** ....

STYLE #	DESCRIPTION	SUGGESTED RETAIL

2341   Satin and Battenburg lace dress with halter neckline has sheer yoke inset on a basque waist bodice. Full skirt is embellished with beaded Battenburg lace cut-outs. Battenburg lace peplum is accented with a rose. Scalloped train is also has Battenburg lace. Detachable gauntlets. *White and Ivory.*   **$730**

2342   Dull satin with re-embroidered lace has sweetheart neckline covered with re-embroidered, beaded lace. Long sleeves of English net and full, floor length skirt is edged with re-embroidered lace. Deep scalloped back treatment accented with covered buttons. English net court train is detachable. *White only.* Available size 42.   **$690**

M O R I   L E E

2343 Dull satin with pearl and crystal trim. Bodice has scooped neck, edged with pearls and crystals. Set-in cap sleeves are also edged with trim. Slightly dropped waist with a wide trim, falls to box-pleated full skirt. Deep V back, full chapel sweep trail accented with bow at back waist.
White and Ivory.   **$390**

2344 Satin gown is trimmed with schiffli lace. Modified sabrina neckline is beaded and has sheer insert. Illusion sleeves are appliquéed. Full skirt has three pyramid lace inserts, hem is edges in lace. Back has four strands of pearls leading to a beaded back bow accenting V back.
White and Ivory. Available in size 42.   **$490**

2345 Tank top style venise lace sheath is beaded and sequined. Illusion back. Tulle skirt is detachable with venise appliqués.
White only.   **$750**

2346 This square, scalloped neckline has pouf cap sleeve. The entire satin bodice and train with Battenburg lace. Plunging back leads to English net, set-in train lace appliqués. Back bow with streamers completes look.
White only. Available in size 42.   **$790**

2347 Dull satin and venise lace. Scalloped V-neck with an elongated venise lace bodice flowing into an A-line skirt with short, illusion, venise trimmed sleeves. V-back is detailed with roses and streamers attached to back waist.
White and Ivory. Available in size 42.   **$550**

2348 Dull satin and schiffli lace. A notched open neckline features long, hug-the-shoulder English net sleeves, trimmed with re-embroidered schiffli. The basque waisted, full skirt has cut-out schiffli medallions with scroll work of pearls. Scalloped carriage back treatment and chapel train.
White and Ivory. Available in size 42.   **$660**

2349 Dull satin and battenburg lace. The sweetheart neckline is covered with battenburg lace accenting the sheer sleeves, also covered with medallions. The skirt is a full empire, princess line. Detachable court train is concealed underneath the back bow and is fully appliquéed with battenburg cut-out trim.
White and Ivory. Available in size 42.   **$598**

2350 Satin combined with battenburg lace. The sweetheart neckline is accented with large pearls, and the entire bodice is overlaid with battenburg lace. The short sleeve has an insert of satin with a double banding of pearls. The basque waisted full skirt has sheer pyramid, pointed cut-out medallions flowing into a full cathedral trimmed train.
White and Ivory. Available in size 42.   **$650**

MORI LEE

2351   Tulle and venise lace. A beautiful halter neckline, with venise lace, has long medallions flowing onto the natural-waisted tulle skirt. Detachable train features lace appliquéed. Detachable gauntlets.
        White only.   **$670**

2352   Lace combined with dull satin. Square neck features short sleeves. Modified empire, princess silhouette is overlaid with lace and edged with satin banding. Detachable satin train features a wide panel of lace.
        White and Ivory.   **$470**

2353   Satin and schiffli lace. Fitted, scalloped, scooped neckline is trimmed with schiffli, and has sheer, short sleeves. Gown has basque waistline and skirt is edged in beaded schiffli lace. The back has roses at the waistline and a three-layered, detachable court train.
        White and Ivory. Available in size 42.   **$598**

2354   Dull satin with tulle and venise lace trim. The sleeveless, jeweled neckline has a venise lace bodice. Appliquéed lace medallions flow onto the sheath skirt. Squared back is trimmed with three roses and there is a detachable, venise appliquéed train.
        White only.   **$590**

2355   Satin and re-embroidered lace. Traditional V-neckline with sheer long sleeves. Basque waisted full skirt and cathedral train is edged with re-embroidered lace. Cut-out back is accented with self roses at the waist. Medallion cut-outs decorate the train.
        White and Ivory. Available in size 42.   **$650**

2356   Dull satin and venise lace. The wide, scalloped, scooped neckline features a venise lace bodice, and banded caplet sleeves. The empire, princess-line features a detachable dull satin skirt with an inserted panel of lace.
        White and Ivory.   **$500**

2357   Dull satin with re-embroidered lace. Square, scalloped, notched neckline has sheer, long sleeves with re-embroidered lace appliqués. The empire skirt features a redingot lace edged overskirt, and appliquéed chapel train. Square back has self bow. Available in three lengths, standard, 60"/61", add $25.00 for cut to length 58", and 56", hollow to hem.
        White only.   **$670**

2358   Satin and organza trimmed with schiffli lace. Heavily beaded, scalloped, notched neckline with short pouf sleeve. The basque waist features a full skirt, with pyramids of lace on multi-layer hem. The back flows into an extra long chapel train with cut-out appliqués and multi-ruffled back.
        White only. Available in size 42.   **$580**

M O R I   L E E

2359   Dull satin and battenburg lace. Modified sabrina neckline
       flows into a short sleeve. Battenburg lace covers the
       bodice to the basque waist. Box pleated skirt has a full
       chapel train. The sculptured cut-out back is trimmed
       with beaded lace and the large bow at the waist features
       extremely long English net streamers trimmed with lace.
       White and Ivory.   **$420**

2360   Chiffon and venise lace. Venise lace halter neckline is deli-
       cately trimmed with sea pearls and sequins. Basque waist
       flows into a multi-layered chapel train. The back features
       a keyhole, and a cluster of roses streamers at the waist.
       White only.   **$598**

2361   Tulle and re-embroidered lace. Sweetheart neckline is cov-
       ered in alencon lace. Cap sleeves have scalloped edged. Dress
       has basque waist and alencon lace edged hem. Open sculp-
       tured back features roses and ribbons flowing onto train.
       White only. Available in size 42.   **$698**

2362   Dull satin and re-embroidered lace. All lace sabrina neck-
       line has short cap sleeves. The empire, princess silhouette
       features cut out medallions on skirt and is edged with a
       detachable band of pearls at the hem. Square back has
       alternating panels of lace and satin.
       White and Ivory. Available in size 42.   **$650**

2363   Satin and schiffli lace. High neckline with sheer long
       sleeves. Dress has basque waisted bodice trimmed with
       embroidered schiffli lace. The full skirt decorated with
       cut-out pyramids of lace. The back features a re-embroi-
       dered schiffli peplum.
       White and Ivory. Available in size 42.   **$690**

2364   Dull satin and venise lace. Venise lace scooped neckline
       with tight fitted short sleeves, slightly dropped waist and
       box-pleated skirt. Detachable train is edged with venise
       lace, and includes pleated bow at the waist.
       White and Ivory.   **$598**

❖ **Regency Bridal Gowns** ....

STYLE #   DESCRIPTION   SUGGESTED RETAIL

R-231   Harmony silk with re-embroidered alencon lace.
        Sleeveless, sabrina neckline tops bodice with re-embroi-
        dered alencon lace. Slightly dropped waist has a full
        length skirt. The bare back features silk roses with long
        streamers and self buttons.
        White only.   **$550**

M O R I   L E E

R-232   Harmony silk and venise lace. Silk halter neckline accent-
        ed by venise lace. The slight basque waist leads to plain
        full skirt with chapel train. Bare back has covered buttons
        and self roses on a ribbon layered bow at waist.
        Natural only.   **$620**

R-233   Silk shantung and venise lace. The scooped tank top is
        trimmed with pearls at the neckline and arm. The princess
        line skirt has venise lace appliqués. The back features cov-
        ered buttons extending to the edge of the chapel train.
        Natural only.   **$670**

R-234   Harmony silk and venise lace. Empire waist features set-in
        padded shoulders. Bodice is covered with venise lace.
        Scooped back has rose edging. Back skirt has pleated back
        paneling trimmed with roses.
        Natural only.   **$750**

R-235   Venise lace and Harmony silk. Beautiful tank top, venise
        lace, godet sheath over silk. The double strapped back has a
        silk bow which flows into a detachable, watteau silk train.
        Natural only.   **$850**

R-236   Harmony silk and venise lace. Halter neckline is banded
        with venise lace at the neck and illusion yoke is accented
        with a band at the edge. Bodice is covered in venise lace.
        The back features an illusion key-hole with silk buttons,
        and the pearl streamed bow. Detachable train.
        Natural only.   **$650**

R-237   Italian satin and silk yarned embroidered English net.
        Tight fitting bodice with slightly dropped waist, banded
        with pearls and crystals. The ball gown skirt is heavily
        embroidered English net. Self buttoned back ends in
        detachable silk chapel length train.
        White only.   **$750**

R-238   Harmony silk and venise lace. Squared neckline with
        scalloped edge has short cap sleeves. The slightly dropped
        waist is overlaid with venise lace. The flat circle skirt has a
        detachable train.
        White only.   **$690**

R-239   Re-embroidered alencon lace over silk. A wide banded
        halter neckline with a deep U-plunge. Basque waist meets
        an A-line skirt. Alencon lace covers the dress and the back
        features cut-away paneling with self covered buttons.
        Detachable all silk train has bands of alencon lace.
        White and Ivory.   **$890**

M O R I   L E E

❖ **Informal Bridal Gowns** ....

STYLE #	DESCRIPTION	SUGGESTED RETAIL

2381   Dull satin and re-embroidered lace. Double strapped halter neckline with fully beaded lace bodice and back. Bow with long streamers at top of detachable train completes this princess-line gown.
White and Ivory. **$350**

2382   Dull satin with re-embroidered lace. Fitted shoulders with empire bodice overlaid with re-embroidered lace skirt is paneled princess line with brush train. The back has large self roses, with streamers on the double bow.
White and Ivory. Available in size 42. **$290**

2383   Dull satin and re-embroidered lace. Modified sweetheart neckline covered with re-embroidered lace. Cap sleeves feature a triple-fold cuff of satin on lace. Basque waist with pleated skirt and brush train. The back waist has pleated bow with long streamers.
White and Ivory. Available in size 42. **$310**

2384   Dull satin and re-embroidered lace. Halter-style neckline is overlaid with beaded re-embroidered lace. The empire waist is banded with three pleated rows edged with pearls. Princess panel skirt has sweep train. The back features long streamered bow edged with pearls.
White and Ivory. **$298**

2385   Shantung with crystals and beads. Reverse fabric details a "sailor-boy" collar decorated with pearls and crystals matching the cuff on the short sleeves. The princess A-line skirt with reverse banding at the hem also has sweep train. Low square cut back is accented with self-covered buttons to the edge of the train.
White and Ivory. Available in size 42. **$290**

2386   Dull satin with beaded trim. Sleeveless sabrina neckline has pearl edging. The empire waist is accented with a band of pearls and crystals. The princess, A-line skirt ends in a brush train. The back features a deep V cut-out, and beaded bow.
White and Ivory. **$278**

2387   Sparkle organza with schiffli lace. The halter neck top is banded at neckline and arm with rows of beading. Heavily embroidered bodice features a basque waist falling to a, ruffled, floor-length skirt. An illusion cut-out back has a satin bow.
White only. **$350**

M O R I   L E E

2388   Dull satin and re-embroidered lace. Square neckline has
       banding and re-embroidered lace all over the dull satin.
       A-line silhouette. The back has criss-cross straps of
       re-embroidered lace, and detachable train.
       White and Ivory.   **$350**

2389   Dull satin and venise lace. The sabrina neckline features a
       fully overlaid panel of wide venise lace. Princess line skirt
       also overlaid in lace as is the back waist. Detachable
       chapel length train.
       White and Ivory.   **$330**

2390   Lace with satin trim. An all lace princess-line halter, with
       the neckline and arm detailed with satin banding.
       Princess skirt with sweep train.
       White and Ivory.   **$330**

✦ N A N C Y   I S S L E R ✦

Contact info. Nancy Issler "A Bride's Collection," 4446 Route 27, Box 582, Kingston, NJ 08528. For a dealer near you, call (609) 921-0002.

Internet. This designer does not have an official web site yet. Our web site (www.bridalgown.com) will have updates on this designer.

Background/Our view. Nancy Issler's "A Bride's Collection" wins our award for the best little-known bridal designer in the market today. The name might not ring a bell, but the dresses are incredible silk creations that have very reasonable prices.

Designer Nancy Issler designed sportswear in New York City before getting into bridal in the mid '80's. For eight years, she custom crafted bridal gowns in her Princeton, New Jersey shop and then began nationwide distrubution in 1994.

The dresses are amazing—silk fabrics, expert tailoring and quality construction are the hallmarks of Issler's gowns. Inspired by the clean lines of Carolina Herrera and Bill Blass dresses, Issler only uses a minimal amount of lace and detailing. Contrasting fabrics (silk organza with a satin band hemline) help add interest to the styles. All the gowns are lined with cotton and hems have horsehair stitching.

The prices range $650 to $1600, with most about $1000—that's pretty amazing considering every gown is custom cut to each bride's measurments. Issler requests seven meaurments to make sure each dress is an exact fit. We thought the dress quality and construction was excellent, as are the unique fabrics. Besides silk, you'll also discover linen bridal gowns (a rarity in the market) and a new embriodered pique cotton. **Rating: A**

Delivery. 8-12 weeks. Rush cuts (six week or less delivery) are available for an additional $100.

SIZING CHART

Sizing Chart

	4	6	8	10	12	14	16	18	20
Bust	32.5	33.5	34.5	35.5	36.5	37.5	39	41	43
Waist	23	24	25	26	27	28	29	31	33
Hips I	34	35	36	37	38	39.5	41	43	45
Hips II	36	37	38	39	40	41.5	43	45	47
Length	57	57.5	58	59	60	61	61	61	61

Sizing notes:
* *Hips I is the measurment of the hips three inches below the waist.*
* *Hips II is the measurment of the hips nine inches below the waist.*
* *Other required measurements include sleeve length and bicep circumference.*

Extra charges for options/changes:

1. Custom changes are avialble.

N A N C Y   I S S L E R

New Bridal Gowns for Spring 1997

Style #	Description	Suggested Retail
702	Cotton sateen piped bodice, embroidered skirt.	**$950**
703	Silk satin pin-tucked bodice with sheer sleeve, full satin organza skirt.	**$990**
	• *Option (703X): with train*	**$1190**
704	Pique with cotton sateen trim, squared armholes, sweep train, porcelain buttons and flowers.	**$1050**
705	Shantung A-line, embroidered bodice, skirt inserts.	**$1100**
	• *Option (705X): with train*	**$1300**
706	Embroidered satin A-line.	**$1190**
	• *Option (706X): with sweep attached organza train*	**$1390**
707	Embroidered silk charmeuse bodice with plain skirt.	**$1100**
	• *Option (707X): with embriodered tails*	**$1300**
708	Embroidered bodice/hem cuff, organza over satin.	**$1190**
	• *Option (708X): with train*	**$1500**
709	Embroidered satin bodice with silk organza skirt.	**$990**
	• *Option (709X): with train*	**$1190**
710	Satin organza over silk satin bodice and skirt, sheer shoulders.	**$990**
	• *Option (710X): with train*	**$1190**
711	Silk satin, veed off-the-shoulder neckline, unusual back center detail.	**$1050**
	• *Option (711X): with train.*	**$1300**
712	Linen with vertical Venise lace bands.	**$990**
	• *Option (712X): with train*	**$1200**
609-07	Silk-satin bodice and hem cuff, organza skirt.	**$900**
	• *Option (609-07X): with train*	**$1150**
713S	Pique sheath with Venise lace cut-out inserts.	**$650**
714S	Silk charmeuse sheath, key-hole back, rolled collar.	**$700**
715S	Embroidered silk satin sheath.	**$900**
716S	Linen off-the-shoulder sheath, guipure lace detail.	**$790**
717	Linen A-line with detachable train.	**$1050**

❖ PRISCILLA ❖

Contact info. Priscilla, 40 Cambridge St., Charlestown, MA 02129. For a dealer near you, call (617) 242-2677.

Internet. This designer does not have an official web site yet. Our web site (www.bridalgown.com) will have updates on this designer.

Background. Priscilla will celebrate its 50th anniversary in 1997, a feat few other manufacturers can match. Founded by designer Priscilla Kidder, the company is still best known for the presidential weddings it did in the late 60's and early 70's. Those dresses earned Priscilla national attention and established the Boston manufacturer as one of the country's most renowned bridal designers.

Unfortunately, the company went into decline in the 1980's. The designer's distribution base (department stores) abandoned bridal and hot new couture designers such as Diamond stole the attention of upper-end customers. Worst of all, Priscilla began to look stale; year in and year out, the line simply didn't change much. By the time Kidder retired in 1994, the company was on the verge of becoming a bridal dinosaur.

Enter Patricia Kaneb, a recent Boston University MBA graduate. Kaneb bought the company in 1993 and began the process of a turn-around. First, she sought to beef up Priscilla's distribution, adding new dealers and even opening Priscilla-owned boutiques in several cities. More importantly, Kaneb reinvigorated the line's fashion and style, adding a couture line and updating the look of the gowns.

Yet, Priscilla isn't out of the woods yet. Competing with manu-facturers who import from China isn't easy; this is a company that still sews all its gowns by hand in Charlestown, MA. Priscilla hopes its quality advantage will enable it to thrive in a crowded marketplace.

Our view. Priscilla's trademark is their beautiful fabrics. Where else can you find bridal gowns made of Irish linen or Swiss silk?

Of course, you can find plenty of satin and silk in the Priscilla line, but it's these special touches that set the Boston designer apart. Lace is used sparingly in these gowns—don't expect dangling beads or flashy sequins.

Priscilla divides its gowns into four collections. The rarely advertised informal gowns in the Vineyard collection run $850 to $1180. Although the designer describes these dresses as "informal," many of these gowns have short trains.

Next in price are the regular Priscilla gowns, with pricing rang-ing from $900 to $3200. "Silk cloud satin" is a common fabrication, as is silk shantung, tulle and the aforementioned Swiss silk. A couple of cotton dresses also make an appearance.

At the couture (read: really expensive) end, Priscilla even has a couple of dresses that run $4000 to $6300.

Petite-sized brides have never been ignored by Priscilla and the designer continues to showcase a "Petite Collection" especially designed for this market. Once again, prices are $980 to $2200 with fabrics that are similar to the regular Priscilla gowns.

P R I S C I L L A

Overall, the designer's 67 gowns feature "classic" styling, including such hip silhouettes as A-lines and ball gowns. A sheath or two is thrown in for variety.

So, are the gowns worth it? Well, the quality is impeccable. First, just about any sort of change is available. Brides can customize any gown with a series of alterations, major or minor. All the gowns are hand-stitched; Priscilla doesn't use any "piecework," the separately assembled gown parts favored by lower-price manufacturers for their cost savings.

On the other hand, the price points of Priscilla's gowns are so expensive (most recent designs come in at $1800 to $2000), this designer's handiwork is probably beyond the reach of most brides. Yet, we have to give Priscilla's new owner bonus points for trying. Her fresh outlook has given this old designer new life. **Rating: A-**

Outlet. Priscilla doesn't have an outlet, but their annual factory sale is worth a visit if you're in the Boston area. Usually held in the spring (May or June), the sale features sample sizes 8 and 10, plus petite size 5 dresses. (This year there was even a few size 14 and 16 gowns.) How good are the deals? How about a dress for $99? Other styles range up to $700—slightly under wholesale prices. The sale attracts a big crowd, so plan ahead. (In 1996, Priscilla actually held the sale twice—once in May and again in September. It remains to be seen if the fall sale will continue in future years). For the latest sale dates, call the designer at the above contact number.

Delivery. 8 to 12 weeks, although certain styles are available for quicker delivery (about four weeks). Rush cuts are available for $100 extra.

Tags. Priscilla identifies its gowns with a hang tab and a sewn-in label.

SIZING CHARTS

Type: Priscilla uses a BODY size chart. For information on this subject, refer to the introduction of the designer review section of this book.

Priscilla has both a regular and a petite size chart. Unlike other designers, Priscilla also asks for two hip measurements (see below for more information).

Standard Sizes

	2	4	6	8	10	12	14	16	18	20
Bust	32.5"	33.5	34.5	35.5	36.5	38	39.5	41	42.5	44.5
Waist	24	25	26	27	28	29.5	31	32.5	34	36
Hips I*	33	34	35	36	37	38.5	40	41.5	43	45
Hips II**	35.5	36.5	37.5	38.5	39.5	41	42.5	44	45.5	47.5

P R I S C I L L A

Petites

	1	3	5	7	9	11	13	15
Bust	31.5"	32.5	33.5	34.5	35.5	36.5	37.5	39
Waist	21	22	23	24	25	26	27	28.5
Hips I*	31	32	33	34	35	36	37	38.5
Hips II*	34	35	36	37	38	39	40	41.5

Sizing notes:
• **Hips I is the hip measurement 3.5" below the natural waist.*
• ***Hips II is the hip measurement 9" below the natural waist.*
• *Standard gown length is 44" as measured from natural waist to hem for regular gowns, 42" for petites.*

Extra charges for changes/options:

1. For regular sizes 18 and 20, add $100 to the gown price.
2. For petite sizes 13 and 15, add $100 to the gown price.
3. Extra gown length and custom cuts are available for an extra charge.

New Bridal Gowns for Spring 1997

Note: Most gowns have a matching headpiece and veil, referred to below as a "headpiece."

❖ Vineyard Gowns ....

STYLE #	DESCRIPTION	SUGGESTED RETAIL

1750   Poly-peau satin empire sheath with two bands at join line that form a bow at back.
        Available in white or ivory **$900**
        • Matching headpiece (7750) **$170**
        Advertised in Modern Bride magazine Feb/Mar 1997

1751   Off-the-shoulder poly-organdy gown with border of diamond shaped Venise lace. Corded basque waistline. Full gathered dirt diamond shaped border five inches above hem.
        Available in white only **$1100**
        • Matching headpiece **$170**

1753   100% silk shantung A-line, short sleeves, square neckline adorned with Venise lace. Corded basque waistline and full skirt.
        Available in white only **$1180**
        • Matching headpiece (7753) **$240**
        Advertised in Modern Bride magazine Dec/Jan 1997

1754   Off-the-shoulder sleeveless poly-organdy gown. Scooped neckline, arms, and basque waistline adorned with pearl beading.

P R I S C I L L A

Available in white only.   **$980**
• Matching headpiece (7754)   **$190**
Advertised in Modern Bride magazine Dec/Jan 1997

1755   Off-the-shoulder sheath gown of 100% silk shantung.
        V-neckline, bodice trimmed with alencon lace re-embroi-
        dered lace appliqués. Deep V back neckline.
        Available in white or ivory   **$1100**
        • Matching headpiece   **$180**

1757   A-line 100% silk shantung gown. Sweetheart illusion
        front neckline and deep V back. Short sleeves, bodice of
        alencon lace. Lace extends from bodice to skirt.
        Available in white or ivory   **$1050**
        • Matching headpiece   **$240**

❖ **Priscilla Bridal Gowns** ....

STYLE #	DESCRIPTION	SUGGESTED RETAIL

1617   Silk cloud satin, bateau neckline, V-back, cummerbund
        waistline, silk cloud streamers and silk flowers on back
        waistline, full skirt.
        Available in white or ivory   **$1780**
        • Matching headpiece   **$220**
        Advertised in Bride's magazine Feb/Mar 1997

1417   Satin organdy, sleeveless gown, beaded bodice, bateau
        front neckline, V-back, basque waist trimmed in pearl
        and sequin beading. Full skirt.
        Available in white only   **$1780**
        • Matching headpiece   **$340**
        Advertised in Bride's magazine Aug/Sept 1997

1331   Sleeveless A-line gown of silk cloud satin. Scooped front
        neckline and deep scooped back neckline beaded with
        pearls and crystals.
        Available in white or ivory   **$2400**
        • Matching headpiece (7768)   **$350**
        Advertised in Bride's magazine Dec/Jan 1997
        and Elegant Bride magazine Feb/Mar/Apr 1997
        and Wedding Dress magazine

1327   Silk cloud satin and tulle skirt. Open neckline, sleeveless
        bodice beaded with rosettes, pearls and crystal iris. Tulle
        skirt has scattered rosettes and pearls.
        Available in white only.   **$1750**
        • Matching headpiece (7727)   **$250**
        Advertised in Bride's magazine Apr/Mar 1997

1702   Irish linen, off-the-shoulder short sleeve gown. The
        bodice, sleeves and skirt are inset with white organdy and

point d' esprit and adorned with Venise lace garlands.
Available in white only **$1980**
• Matching headpiece **$270**
Featured in an editorial in Bride's magazine

1703 A-line gown of silk cloud satin. Short sleeves. Band across
bodice has self-pleated satin. Re-embroidered alencon lace
on bodice with square neckline and basque waistline.
Available in white or ivory **$1580**
• Matching headpiece **$300**

1704 Silk shantung halter style gown with basque waistline and
full gathered skirt. Low scooped front neckline and deep
V back. Pearl chain beading on upper bodice.
Available in white or ivory **$1380**
• Matching headpiece **$250**

1705 Silk shantung, scoop neckline and set-in short sleeves
trimmed with pearl and crystal beading. Crescent of pearl
and crystals adorns the mid-bodice. Pearl beading accents
the basque waistline. Full shirred skirt.
Available in white or ivory **$2400**
• Matching headpiece (7705) **$350**
Advertised in Bride's magazine Feb/Mar 1997

1706 Silk shantung sheath dress. Short sleeves and sweetheart
neckline adorned with beaded alencon lace. Sheath skirt
has a 12" cut-out inset of beaded alencon lace.
Available in white or ivory **$1980**
• Matching headpiece **$250**

1707 Silk shantung off the shoulder short sleeve gown. White
venise lace appliqué adorns the sleeves and bodice. Front
of skirt has trail of Venise lace appliqué, as does the full
skirt and train.
Available in white or ivory **$1980**
• Matching headpiece (9707) **$280**
Advertised in Wedding Dress Magazine Feb/Mar 1997
and Bride's magazine Apr/May 1997.

1708 Capped sleeve, dropped shoulder satin back shantung
A-line gown. Scooped front and V back neckline.
Basque waistline has four inch beaded band of satin-
faced shantung.
Available in white or ivory **$2600**
• Matching headpiece **$270**
Advertised in Bride's magazine Apr/May 1997

1709 Dropped waistline, silk cloud satin and taffeta gown. Pearl
beaded silk satin bodice is form fitting with sleeveless
dropped shoulders and wide scoop neckline. Pearl beaded
gathered waistline, full taffeta skirt.

Available in white only **$1700**
• Matching headpiece (7709) **$370**
Advertised in Bride's magazine Feb/Mar 1997

1710   On-the-shoulder short sleeve gown of Irish linen and
venise lace. V front neckline falls into basque waist.
A-line skirt with three tiers of venise lace appliqués.
Available in white only **$1700**
• Matching headpiece (7710) **$190**
Advertised in Elegant Bride Nov/Dec/Jan 1997
Featured in an editorial in Elegant Bride

1711   Off the shoulder short sleeve Princess gown of satin
backed silk shantung. Corded sweetheart neckline and
scooped back neckline. Bodice adorned with shirred silk
shantung criss cross under bust to back join line, meeting
in a full bow.
Available in white or ivory **$1500**
• Matching headpiece **$250**

1713   Silk organdy gown. Low scooped front neckline and
V backline have silk organdy flowers with hint of pink.
Corded basque waistline, full skirt. Organdy flowers
adorn back join line and streamers cascade down the
back of skirt.
Available in white only **$1500**
• Matching headpiece **$170**
Featured in an editorial in Modern Bride magazine

1714   Silk cloud satin princess line gown. Extended shoulder
sleeves and square front neckline have scallop detail.
Basque waist and sweep skirt.
Available in white or ivory **$1780**
• Matching headpiece **$300**

1715   Peau de satin sleeveless bodice with cut-in shoulders and
scooped front neckline. Venise lace appliqués and curved
satin bands at the hip. Floor length tulle skirt with venise
lace appliqués.
Available in white only **$2400**
• Matching headpiece **$120**

1716   On-the-shoulder short sleeve Irish linen gown. Low
scooped front neckline and basque waistline adorned
with Venise lace appliqué in shape of hydrangeas.
Full skirt is scattered with Venise lace. Full train is
edged with Venise lace.
Available in white only **$1900**
• Matching headpiece (7716) **$260**
Advertised in Bride's magazine Feb/Mar 1997

P R I S C I L L A

1717   Off-the-shoulder sleeveless bodice of Venise lace
appliqués. A-line skirt of 100% silk shantung.
Available in white or ivory   **$1580**
• Matching headpiece   **$300**
Advertised in Bride's magazine Feb/Mar 1997

1720   Off-the-shoulder short sleeve bodice of Venise lace
appliqués. A-line skirt of 100% silk shantung.
Available in white or ivory   **$1580**
• Matching headpiece (7720)   **$300**
Advertised in Bride's magazine Feb/Mar 1997

1721   Off-the-shoulder sleeveless A-line gown. Satin-faced
organdy fabric detailed with silk organdy flowers.
Available in white only.   **$1700**
• Matching headpiece (7721)   **$350**
Advertised in Bride's magazine Dec/Jan 1997

1722   Off-the-shoulder short sleeve princess gown of silk cloud
satin. V-front and back neckline of pleated satin.
Available in white or ivory.   **$1700**
• Matching headpiece   **$220**

1723   Off-the-shoulder short sleeve sheath gown of silk shantung.
Sweetheart neckline with alencon lace and rose buds.
Available in white or ivory.   **$1780**
• Matching headpiece   **$250**

1725   Silk shantung A-line. Bodice and short sleeves trimmed
in Venise lace.
Available in white or ivory.   **$1580**
• Matching headpiece   **$250**
Advertised in Bride's magazine Dec/Jan 1997

1727   Short sleeve A-line gown of silk shantung. Sleeves of alen-
con lace, scoop front neckline and scoop illusion back.
Basque waist. A-line skirt has alencon lace border.
Available in white only.   **$1900**
• Matching headpiece   **$250**

1728   All-over alencon lace bodice, iridescent tulle skirt edged
in alencon lace. Sleeveless bodice with scalloped waistline.
Available in white only.   **$1580**
• Matching headpiece   **$250**

1729   Off-the-shoulder sleeveless gown of silk cloud satin.
Scattered beading on bodice, scalloped neckline and
pleated skirt.
Available in white and ivory.   **$1980**
• Matching headpiece   **$180**

1731   English cotton net gown with beaded alencon lace. Short
        sleeves of beaded alencon lace. Scoop neckline, scalloped
        waistline, full gathered skirt with alencon lace appliqué
        and border.
        Available in white or ivory   **$2900**
        • Matching headpiece   **$300**

1732   Off-the-shoulder sleeveless gown of silk shantung.
        Neckline, bodice and skirt have Venise lace appliqués.
        Sheath skirt and detachable tube train.
        Available in white or ivory   **$1580**
        • Matching headpiece   **$460**

1733   Silk shantung. Dropped shoulder edged in caviar embroi-
        dery. Sabrina neckline, basque waistline and sweep skirt.
        Available in white or ivory   **$1780**
        • Matching headpiece   **$500**

1734   Satin-backed shantung off-the-shoulder gown, front
        panel flows straight from neckline to hem. Side skirt in
        back falls in gathers from join line to full train. Cording
        edges the neckline and sleeves. Single flowers adorns back.
        Available in white or ivory   **$1780**
        • Matching headpiece   **$190**

1735   Silk georgette empire gown. Set-in short sleeves with
        banded embroidery. Crystal highlights on bottom of
        sleeves and bustline. Horseshoe front neckline and
        deep V back, princess skirt.
        Available in white or ivory   **$1780**
        • Matching headpiece   **$220**

❖ **Petite Gowns** ....

Style # Description   Suggested retail

700   Irish linen gown with Venise appliqué on scoop neckline,
        sleeves and basque waist. Criss-cross linen detail on
        sleeves and hem. Venise lace appliqués.
        Available in white only.   **$1780**
        • Matching headpiece   **$210**

702   Sleeveless sweetheart neckline gown of silk shantung.
        Venise lace bodice with basque waist. Deep V back, full
        gathered skirt with Venise lace border.
        Available in white or ivory   **$1780**
        • Matching headpiece   **$300**

705   Silk shantung dress with scoop neckline and short sleeves
        trimmed with pearl and crystal beads. Crescent of pearl
        and crystal beading adorns the mid bodice. Pearl beading
        accents basque waistline. Full shirred skirt.

P R I S C I L L A

Available in white or ivory **$2400**
• Matching headpiece **$350**
Advertised in Bride's magazine Feb/Mar 1997

706   Silk shantung sheath with rounded hem on both sides
      edged in Alencon lace. Off-the-shoulder cap sleeves of
      Alencon lace. Bodice and basque waist adorned with
      Alencon lace.
      Available in white or ivory **$1900**
      • Matching headpiece **$270**

707   Sleeveless silk cloud satin bodice with full skirt of silk
      organdy. Neckline, basque waistline and hem are banded
      in border of silk satin.
      Available in white or ivory **$1580**
      • Matching headpiece **$190**
      Advertised in Bride's magazine Feb/Mar 1997

708   Short sleeve silk shantung gown. V-neckline embellished
      with Alencon lace. Basque waistline and hem accented
      with Alencon lace.
      Available in white or ivory **$2400**
      • Matching headpiece **$370**

709   Short sleeve scoop neckline bodice of Alencon lace.
      Full pleated silk shantung skirt.
      Available in white or ivory **$1500**
      • Matching headpiece **$210**

711   Off-the-shoulder short sleeve princess gown of satin-
      backed silk shantung. Corded sweetheart neckline, bodice
      adorned with shirred silk shantung criss-cross under bust.
      Flowing bow at back.
      Available in white or ivory **$1500**
      • Matching headpiece **$250**

*Priscilla also offers a "Retrospective Couture Collection." Dress
descriptions and prices for these gowns are posted on our web page
(www.bridalgown.com).*

⇥ P R I V A T E   L A B E L   B Y   G ⇤

Contact info. Private Label by G, 6015 Obispo Ave., Long Beach, CA 90805. For a dealer near you, call (800) 858-3338 or (310) 531-1116.

Also known as. Ginza Collection.

Internet. This designer does not have an official web site yet. Our web site (www.bridalgown.com) will have updates on this designer.

Background/Our view. Private Label by G (also known as Ginza) was one of a new wave of Taiwanese knock-off manufacturers that took the bridal market by storm in the late 1980's. Private Label's strategy was simple: using cheap foreign labor, they offered a stylish bridal gown for much less than domestic designers. Quality was Private Label's trump card: the gowns featured sewn-on (not glued) beading and detailing—a rarity for gowns that retailed for under $500.

In short order, Private Label by G became one of the industry's fastest-rising stars. Brides flocked to stores and requested their gowns. Yet, in many ways, Private Label became a victim of its own success. Its triumph prompted a flood of competitors who knocked off Private Label's knock-offs. Worse yet, the company failed to innovate—many of their designs today look decidedly dated.

For example, Private Label is still pumping out styles dripping with beads and lace-cut outs on the trains. Meanwhile, the rest of the market has toned down this noise, opting for matte satins instead of Private Label's shiny fabric, for example. The big sleeves, encrusted bodices and large back bows still on their gowns were hip . . . when Reagan was president.

Yet, Private Label still plugs along, relying on its price advantage. And, yes, these gowns still represent a good value. Basic Private Label by G gowns run $590 to $800, mostly in man-made fabrics like polyester satin and organza. Why Private Label markets a separate collection under the name "Ginza" is a mystery to us; the gowns have almost the same prices, fabrics and styling as the main line.

On the upside, we liked the company's "Signature Collection" for its use of silk fabrics and venise lace. These gowns ($530 to $850) represented an outstanding value. The designer even has an informal line (dresses with no trains) in the reasonable price range of $320 to $450.

Despite our criticism's of Private Label's fashion, we still like these guys. The quality of the dresses is above average, with the aforementioned sewn-on beading still a major advantage. The deliveries and customer service also rank among the industry's better performers. We also like the fact that large sizes (up to a 42) are available for a very small up-charge.

Now, if Private Label could just give their fashion a jump-start, they'd be among our top recommendations. **Rating: B+**

Delivery. 10 to 12 weeks. Rush cuts (8 weeks) are available for $50 extra and some styles are in stock for quicker delivery.

P R I V A T E   L A B E L   B Y   G

Tags. Private Label By G identifies its gowns with hang tags and sewn-in labels.

Type: Private Label by G uses a GARMENT size chart. For information on this subject, refer to the introduction of the designer review section of this book.

Standard Sizes

	4	6	8	10	12	14	16	18	20
Bust	32"	33	34	35	36.5	38	39.5	41.5	43.5
Waist	22	23	24	25	26.5	28	29.5	31.5	33.5
Hips	34	35	36	37	38.5	40	41.5	43.5	45.5

Extra Sizes

	38	40	42
Bust	44.5"	46.5	48.5
Waist	34.5	36.5	38.5
Hips	47.5	49	51

Sizing notes:
• *Gown length (as measured from the hollow of the neck to the desired dress hem) is 58".*
• *Sleeve length is about 17", although this varies somewhat by style.*

Extra charges for changes/options:

1. For sizes 38 to 42, add $100 to the gown price.
2. To change the sleeve length, add $60 to the gown price.
3. To change the gown length, add $60 to the gown price.
4. Custom cuts (made to your measurements) are available; add $100 to the gown price for this options.

❖ Private Label by G Gowns ....

STYLE #	DESCRIPTION	SUGGESTED RETAIL

584   An organza over satin gown with an open neckline, and short pouf sleeves. Schiffli lace, and mini rosettes add elegance to the sleeves, bodice, skirt, and cathedral train.
$690

585   An Italian satin gown with a V neckline, and long tapered cut out sleeves. Pearls in a criss cross pattern accent the heavily beaded alencon lace featured throughout this style.
$890

586   An organza over satin gown with a low jewel illusion
      neckline, and long tapered cut out sleeves. Schiffli lace
      is featured on the heavily beaded bodice, skirt, and
      cathedral train.   **$770**

587   An Italian satin gown with a V neckline, and short tulip
      sleeves. Beaded schiffli lace cut outs highlight the skirt,
      and train. A heart shaped cut out back with hanging
      pearl strands, and an elegant bow accented with beaded
      appliqués add romance to this style.   **$760**

588   An Italian satin gown with an open neckline, bare shoul-
      ders, and long tapered cut out sleeves. Heavily beaded
      alencon lace enhances the bodice, cut out skirt, and
      cathedral train.   **$770**

589   An Italian satin gown with open neckline, and short
      layered satin sleeves. The scalloped Italian satin skirt is
      accented with a tulle insert. Schiffli lace tastefully flows
      through this elegant style.   **$750**

590   An Italian satin sheath gown with long tapered cut out
      sleeves. An open neckline tried with three layers of Italian
      satin enhance the heavily beaded alencon lace on the
      bodice. Detachable train.   **$760**

591   An Italian satin Victorian style gown with open neckline.
      The cut out elbow length sleeves, and bodice are high-
      lighted with alencon lace. A delicate bow at the back
      waistline is enhanced by layers of scalloped Italian satin,
      and alencon lace.   **$760**
      • *Available in ivory with rum pink or all ivory or all white.*

592   An Italian satin princess gown with V neckline. The short
      sleeves are accented with schiffli lace roses. Schiffli lace
      enhances the bodice, and cut out skirt.   **$650**

593   An Italian satin gown with open neckline, and short cap
      sleeves. Heavily beaded schiffli lace enhances the bodice.
      Schiffli lace highlights the skirt, and detachable train. **$670**

❖ **Ginza Collection** ....

STYLE #   DESCRIPTION   SUGGESTED RETAIL

86271   An Italian satin gown with an open neckline. Short pouf
        sleeves are highlighted with roses, and an overlay of
        schiffli lace. Beaded schiffli lace adds elegance to the
        bodice, cut out skirt, and cathedral train.   **$650**
        • *Available in gold with ivory or all ivory or all white.*

P R I V A T E   L A B E L   B Y   G

86272   An Italian satin gown with V neckline, and long tapered cut out sleeves. Beaded cotton lace highlights the bodice, cut out skirt, and cathedral train. $790

86273   An organza over satin gown with an open neckline, and long tapered cut out sleeves. Cotton lace daises with pearls centers tastefully flow through this romantic style. $760

86274   An Italian satin gown with a pearl trimmed V neckline, and long tapered cut out sleeves. Beaded alencon lace enhances the bodice, and detachable train. $770

86275   A chiffon gown with sweetheart shaped Queen Anne neckline trimmed with beaded schiffli lace. Long lycra sleeves are accented with beaded schiffli lace bracelets. High lycra back neckline, and a small beaded bow are featured above the cathedral train. $690

86276   An Italian satin gown with a V neckline, and short cut out sleeves. Beaded satin lace tastefully flows through the bodice, cut out skirt, and cathedral train. $730

86277   An all over alencon lace sheath gown with a high jewel neckline, and no sleeves. A detachable organza train, and shawl accent this elegant style. $780

86278   An Italian satin V neckline gown. The short sleeves are highlighted with a delicate bow. The bodice is adorned with pearls formed to give it a corset look. Schiffli lace gracefully flows through this style. $598

86279   An organza over satin A-line gown with V neckline, and long tapered cut out sleeves. Beaded schiffli lace adds elegance to this style. $650

86280   An Italian satin gown enhanced with beaded cotton lace. Rows of cotton lace daises outline the V neckline, short sleeves, and skirt. $630

❖ **Signature Collection** ....

STYLE #   DESCRIPTION   SUGGESTED RETAIL

134   A silk gown with a sweetheart shaped Queen Anne neckline, and short sleeves. Cotton lace is featured on the bodice adding elegance to the plain skirt. $750

135   An Italian satin gown with an all over cotton lace bodice, V neckline, and short sleeves. Cotton lace daises highlight the skirt, and cathedral train. $770

PRIVATE   LABEL   BY   G

136   An Italian satin princess gown with an open neckline,
         and satin layered cap sleeves. A simple beaded bow on the
         bodice enhances the satin lace featured on this style.
                                                            $598
         • *Available in ivory with rum pink or all ivory or all white.*

137   An Italian satin gown with low jewel neckline, and long
         tapered sleeves. An all over cotton lace bodice, and
         spectacular bow accent this elegant style.   **$760**

138   An Italian satin bodice features cotton lace, with an open
         neckline, and short sleeves. Cotton lace bows, and small
         daises highlight the sleeves, and organza skirt.   **$670**

139   An Italian satin gown with short cap sleeves. Italian satin
         roses outline the V neckline, and basque waistline. A sin-
         gle rose, and layered satin highlight the cathedral train.
                                                            $590
         • *Available in ivory with rum pink or all ivory or all white.*

140   A silk gown with high scoop neckline. Silk roses lined
         with pearls highlight the short sleeves. Alencon lace, and
         a spectacular bow above the train add beauty to this
         romantic style.   **$770**

141   An all over alencon lace bodice with a high neckline, and
         no sleeves. An organza skirt is highlighted with beaded
         alencon hem lace.   **$750**

142   An open neckline gown with long tapered sleeves high-
         lighted partially with cotton over-lace. An all over cotton
         lace bodice is featured above a plain silk skirt.   **$750**

143   Beaded spaghetti straps add elegance to this all over
         cotton lace sheath gown. An Italian satin detachable
         train accents this style.   **$770**

144   An all over criss cross cotton lace bodice with V neckline,
         and short sleeves. A plain silk skirt, and watteau train
         accented with three silk roses add beauty to this
         romantic style.   **$750**

145   An Italian satin princess gown with an open neckline,
         and short sleeves. An empire waistline is featured with
         an all over alencon lace bodice.   **$590**

✦SCAASI BRIDE *for* EVA FORSYTH✦

Contact info. Forsyth Enterprises, PO Box 7139, Charlottesville, VA 22906. For a dealer near you, call (804) 971-3853.

Also known as. The parent company, Forsyth Enterprises, markets gowns under both the names "Scaasi Bride" and "Eva Forsyth."

Internet. This designer does not have an official web site yet. Our web site (www.bridalgown.com) will have updates on this designer.

Background/Our view. Got money to burn? Then if you want serious bang for your big bucks, check out Scaasi. He's the designer superstar whose spectacular dresses for celebrities and politicians (including Barbara Bush's inauguration ball gown in 1988) have made his name world renown.

Mainly available through tony salons and upper-end department stores, Scaasi's line starts at $1800 and goes up to a whopping $4100. For that kind of money, you'll see silk fabrics like organza and satin. But Scaasi is best know for his incredible embroidery, lace and detailing. With a collection of over 90 styles, you can find a little of everything—stunning looks with knock-out pearls, beading and embroidery to more understated looks with Lyon lace. Scaasi's signature, of course, is the gold embroidery look but since it's been copied by everyone else, the designer seems to have moved on to new ideas like pattern lace and dotted swiss.

Along with Scaasi's collection, Eva Forsyth offers her own designs (over 80 of them) ranging in price from $1600 to $3600. While she may not have the fancy name, Eva sill churns out dresses that can rival Scaasi's for drama. A ballerina-inspired style with big tulle skirt and sequined bustier bodice was one look. Eva's design tastes are slightly more traditional than Scaasi, although she will surprise you with a few styles that are over the top. **Rating: B+**

Delivery. 12 weeks (or about 90 days). Rush cuts are available for an additional 10% charge.

SIZING CHART

Sizing Chart

	4	6	8	10	12	14	16	18*
Bust	33"	34	35	36	38	39	40	41.5
Waist	24	25	26	27	27.5	29	30	32
Hips	34	35	36	37	38.5	40	41	42.5

Sizing notes:
• Gown length (as measured from the hollow of the neck to the desired dress hem) is 58".

Extra charges for options/changes:

1. No changes in color, fabric or style may be made to dresses under $2000 retail. Changes are allowed for dresses that retail for over $2000.
2. To length or shorten a dress, add 10% to the gown price.
3. *For size 18, add 15% to the gown price. No sizes larger than an 18 are available.

NEW BRIDAL GOWNS FOR SPRING 1997

❖ Scaasi Bridal Gowns ....

STYLE #	NAME/DESCRIPTION	SUGGESTED RETAIL
2198	*Kitty.* Imperial satin princess bodice with cut-in shoulder, stand up collar and trapunto stitching.	**$1800**
2199	*Jean.* Imperial satin off the shoulder layered bodice with a full skirt.	**$1800**
2200	*Tina.* Imperial satin criss cross halter with a fitted sheath. Full over skirt with train.	**$1800**
2201	*Ellen.* Imperial satin pure simplicity tank top with an athletic accent. Refined workmanship. Full skirt.	**$1800**
2202	*Cindy.* Imperial satin fitted bodice deeply scooped neckline. Accentuated with bias bands. Stylish netting covers the bare back. Full skirt with chapel train.	**$1800**
2203	*Maggie.* Imperial satin sleeveless fitted slim sheath with detachable train. Delicate trim on the midriff with the same accent on the neckline and arm.	**$1800**
2204	*Liz.* Imperial satin empire halter accentuated with beaded bands. Flowing skirt with chapel train.	**$1900**
2205	*Beth.* Imperial satin off the shoulder fitted sheath with double bands beaded with pearls and crystals.	**$2200**
2206	*Giselle.* Imperial satin fluid princess. Slightly off the shoulder with short cap sleeves with beading.	**$1900**
2207	*Seductive.* Re-embroidered gold lace combined with gold chantilly slip top, full trumpet skirt with flowing train.	**$3000**
2208	*Jennifer.* Imperial satin tank top, gold beading.	**$3000**
2209	*Palma.* Ivory tulle bustier bodice over very full ballerina skirt, gold beaded bolero jacket.	**$3300**

2210   *Becky.* Tapestry beaded tank top over very full ballerina tulle skirt. Featured on the cover of the spring issue of *Elegant Bride* magazine.   **$2700**

2211   *Coco.* Imperial satin fitted glamorous sheath with beaded French lace trimming.   **$2400**

2212   *Vanity.* Duchess silk satin. Very sophisticated halter neck line. Bare back. Very full skirt. Cathedral train.   **$2400**

2213   *Kay.* Duchess silk satin. Halter neckline accentuated with embroidered bands over Scaasi signature wrap-around skirt. Cathedral train.   **$2500**

2214   *Daniella.* Duchess silk satin ball gown. Slightly off the shoulder. Tiny cap sleeves. Very full skirt with asymmetrical bias bands.   **$3200**

2215   *Frosty.* White lace embroidered with satin ribbons and sequins. In a horizontal design. High neck sleeveless bodice. Very full ballerina skirt. Detachable train on request.   **$2500**

❖ Eva Forsyth Bridal Gowns ....

STYLE #	NAME/DESCRIPTION	SUGGESTED RETAIL

8847   *Debbie.* Glamorous halter accentuated with beaded criss cross. Bands and pleated bustline. Fitted sheath with mermaid bottom. Detachable train with beaded band edging.   **$2400**

8848   *Olivia.* Classic princess slightly off the shoulder decorated with delicate beaded lace.   **$1900**

8849   *Donna.* Elegant princess scooped neckline with tiny sleeves covered with tapestry beading. Chapel train.   **$2100**

8850   *Lory.* Imperial satin fitted on the shoulder, scooped neck line, trumpet skirt with beaded lace godet.   **$1900**

8851   *Edith.* Duchess silk satin sheath with beaded lace.   **$1900**

8852   *Sherry.* Silk satin bustier bodice. Full skirt with beaded chantilly lace over duchess silk satin.   **$2500**

8853   *Lisa.* Classic conservative bodice. Full skirt with re-embroidered French lace edging.   **$2700**

8854   *Grace.* Princess gown of satin covered with tulle. Elaborate embroidery on the skirt.   **$2400**

8855   *Judy.* Beaded re-embroidered lace mermaid silhouette with trailing trainette.   **$2400**

8856   *Michelle.* All over beaded Rachel lace, square neckline, short sleeve, satin midriff with scalloped bolero effect.   **$3000**

8857   *Corinne.* Beaded French chantilly lace. High jewel neckline, long sleeves, elongated bodice. Ribbon ruffles ornament the skirt.   **$3200**

8858   *Veronique.* Duchess silk satin bodice over English tulle skirt elegantly ornamented with lace of Lyon.   **$2700**

8859   *Beatrice.* Lace of Lyon bodice with very full skirt. English net yoke And see through back, high jewel neckline and buttoned down back treatment.   **$3300**

8860   *Ann.* Duchess silk satin with exquisite tapestry embroidery on off shoulder bodice with short sleeves. Detachable Cathedral train.   **$1450**

8861   *Karina.* Off the shoulder neckline with long sleeves. A very full skirt made of lace of Lyon combined with most delicate embroidery make this gown a masterpiece.   **$3300**

8862   *Christina.* Fitted sheath. Geometrically placed square motif over beaded re-embroidered lace. Same design borders the bottom of the skirt. Very full detachable train with lace border.   **$3300**

8863   *Josephine.* Duchess silk satin with a Renaissance bodice of re-embroidered beaded lace. Very full skirt. Cathedral train.   **$3200**

8864   *Melanie.* White crystals and pearl embroidery in a paisley design on candlelight organza. Elongated fitted bodice. High neckline. Long sleeves. Jewel neck, cuffs and waistline accentuated with a beaded border. Very full ballerina skirt of tulle.   **$2400**

8865   *Valerie.* Very fine hand embroidery on pale ivory silk organza. Fitted bodice, v-neckline. Little caplet sleeves. Embroidered border edging over very full tulle skirt.   **$2100**

8866   *Gaby.* Beaded bodice with scooped neckline. Tiny caplet sleeves. All white beading with tiny pearls and tiny crystals over Floor length full skirt made of imperial satin. Detachable train by request.   **$1600**

8867   *Tammy.* Off shoulder beaded bodice of imperial satin with a full ballerina tulle skirt.   **$1600**

⇢ ST. PUCCHI ⇠

Contact info. St. Pucchi Inc., 2277 Monitor, Dallas, TX 75207. For a dealer near you, call (214) 631-8738 or (214) 631-4039.

Also known as. Avine Perucci, St. Pucchi Signature.

Internet. This designer does not have an official web site yet. Our web site (www.bridalgown.com) will have updates on this designer.

Background/Our view. We've always had a soft spot for the impossibly over-the-top bridal gowns from St. Pucchi. Perhaps this is because one of this book's authors grew up in Dallas, Texas, which is also St. Pucchi's home base. For those of you who've never been to Dallas, it's a city that doesn't like to do anything in a small way. Folks down there got big hair, big cars . . . and big dresses.

Which brings us to St. Pucchi. "Volume" is an understatement for these gowns, which have been known to swallow small children on occasion. One of our current St. Pucchi faves features a tank-style neckline, cummerbund bodice and a ball gown covered in pearls. And when we say covered, we really mean *obliterated*—it's hard to see the fabric on the waistline for all the pearls on this dress.

The scaled-back 1990's must have come as somewhat of a let-down for St. Pucchi's designer, Rani. To her credit, she's tried to tone-down some of her designs (no more gowns with jewels scattered across the bodice. Darn.) We see less lace on her most recent creations and the cut-work on the trains has been reduced. Some of Pucchi's current designs even feature plain skirts. What is the world coming to?

As you might expect, your oil well may still have to hit a gusher to afford these dresses. Regular St. Pucchi gowns will set you back a cool $1790 to $2790. Not expensive, enough? Try the St. Pucchi Signature collection, with dresses that might equal a mortgage payment for a home in the Dallas suburb of Highland Park (translation: $2790 to $5000).

In case your Daddy doesn't have box seats at Texas Stadium, St. Pucchi does make a more affordable line of gowns, advertised under the name "Avine Perucci." These more traditional silhouettes go light on the beading and decoration and cost $850 to $1300.

The quality of these gowns is above average, although deliveries are painfully slow (you'll have to cool your heels for four months before your dress arrives). On the upside, the designer does have a "wholesale outlet" in Dallas where you can find discounted samples and discontinued styles (see below for more info). **Rating: B**

Outlet store. St. Pucchi's "wholesale warehouse" near downtown Dallas (2277 Monitor, phone: (214) 631-8738) sells samples and overstock at below wholesale prices.

Delivery. Four months (16 weeks) is the standard delivery time. For Avine Perucci gowns, rush orders are processed in 45 days for an extra $200. For St. Pucchi gowns, rush orders are processed in two months for extra $600. In a real hurry? You can get a St. Pucchi on a "super rush" in just four to six weeks for a mere $800 extra.

SIZING CHARTS								
4	**6**	**8**	**10**	**12**	**14**	**16**	**18**	**20**
Bust 33"	34	35	36	37.5	39	40.5	42.5	44.5
Waist 23	24	25	26	27.5	29	30.5	32.5	34.5
Hips 34.5	35.5	36.5	37.5	38.5	40	41.5	43.5	45.5

Sizing notes:
• *Standard gown length (measured from the hollow of the neck to the desired dress hem) is 58" to 58.5".*

Extra charges for changes/options:

For Avine Perucci gowns:
1. For a gown length change (up to three inches), add $100 the gown price.
2. For sizes 18 and 20, add $160 to the gown price.
3. For sizes over 20 (custom cuts made to your measurements), add 25% to the gown price.

For St. Pucchi gowns:
1. For gown length changes, add 10% to the gown price.
2. For sizes 18 and 20, add 20% to the gown price.
3. For sizes over 20 (custom cuts made to your measurements), add 35% to the gown price.
4. To shorten or length the bodice, add $160 to the gown price.
5. To raise or lower the neckline, add $160 to the gown price.
6. Fabrics are available by the yard. Silk fabrics are $116 per yard. Lining is $76 per yard. Extra buttons are $4 each.

Dress descriptions and prices for both Avine Perucci and St. Pucchi gowns are posted on our web page (www.bridalgown.com).

⇢ S W E E T H E A R T ⇠

Contact info. Sweetheart, 1375 Broadway, 6th Floor, New York, NY 10018. For a dealer near you, call (800) 223-6061 or (212) 947-7171.

Internet. This designer does not have an official web site yet. Our web site (www.bridalgown.com) will have updates on this designer.

Background/Our view. To their credit, middle-of-the road bridal manufacturer Sweetheart has kept pace with the market. Unlike other importers who are still doing encrusted gowns with big puff sleeves, Sweetheart has toned-down the look of their gowns to reflect current fashion.

The variety of fabrics is good for this price range, with choices ranging from polyester shantung and chiffon, to matte satin and taffeta. Unfortunately, the line offers very few silk gowns. This was disappointing, considering the price on some gowns approaches $800.

Overall, prices started at $240 and averaged about $600. The traditional ballgown silhouette is a common Sweetheart look; a lace-covered bodice is usually fitted with a basque waist. A plain skirt sometimes features a hem-lace border.

Delivery is a story with two endings. Sweetheart keeps in stock most styles (and some designs are available in plus sizes up to a 44). As a result, you may be able to get very quick delivery. On the other hand, any gown order with a custom change (shorter sleeves? extra train length?) takes a whopping 22 weeks (yes, that's nearly six months). Sweetheart blames its overseas production for slow delivery on such orders, but we think they could do better. The quality of the gowns is about average. **Rating: B-**

Delivery. 10 weeks. However, most styles are in stock (even in plus sizes) for quicker delivery. (For a gown with a special request such as longer length or a sleeve change, delivery takes 22 weeks.)

Tags. Sweetheart uses a hang tabs to identify its gowns. The style number is also noted inside the dress.

SIZING CHART

Type: Sweetheart uses a GARMENT size chart. For information on this subject, refer to the introduction of the designer review section of this book.

Standard Sizes

	4	6	8	10	12	14	16	18	20
Bust	33"	34	35	36	37.5	39	40.5	42.5	44.5
Waist	25	26	27	28	29.5	31	32.5	34.5	36.5
Hips	37	38	39	40	41	42.5	44	46	48

Plus Sizes

	38	40	42	44
Bust	45.5"	47.5	49.5	51.5
Waist	36	38	40	42
Hips	48	50	52	54

Sizing notes:
• *Gown length, as measured from hollow to hem, is 59".*
• *Sleeve length, as measured from armpit to wrist, is 18".*

Extra charges for changes/options:

1. For sizes 18 to 20, add $40 to the gown price.
2. Only a selected number of styles are available in sizes 38 to 44. Add $50 to the gown price for these sizes.
3. For gowns larger than sizes 44, custom cuts (made to your measurements) are available for an additional 25% of the gown price.
4. To lengthen or shorten a gown, add $70 to the gown price.
5. Extra sleeve length is $50.
6. Buttons on zipper (or with loops) adds $50 to the gown price.
7. Buttons added to sleeves is an additional $30.
8. Long sleeves can be ordered for a short sleeve gown; add $150 for this option.
9. Extra train length (one half yard) is available for an additional $100.
10. On some styles, extra train length of one yard is available as well. Add $200 to the gown price for this option.
11. To change the sequins on a gown, add $100 to the gown price.

NEW BRIDAL GOWNS FOR SPRING 1997

(Note: All gowns are available in white and ivory unless otherwise noted).

STYLE	FABRIC	SUGGESTED RETAIL
2220	Silk Backed Satin	$418
2247	Peau Satin and Cotton Tulle	$558
2188	Peau Satin and Tulle	$518
2207	Silk Backed Satin	$278
2187	Peau Satin	$558
	• *Also available in "mist"*	
2203	Peau Satin	$258
	• *Also available in "mist"*	
2218	Peau Satin	$378
	• *Also available in "mist"*	
2243	Peau Satin	$498
2194	Peau Satin and beaded lace	$598
2222	Peau Satin	$550
2189	Peau Satin	$478
2229	Peau Satin	$598
2193	Silk Backed Satin	$370
2224	Peau Satin	$598
2190	Peau Satin	$338

S   W   E   E   T   H   E   A   R   T

2180	Silk Backed Satin	**$518**
2183	Peau Satin	**$550**
2185	Peau Satin and Venise lace	**$550**
2227	Peau Satin and organza	**$498**
2238	Peau Satin	**$450**
2219	Peau Satin	**$378**
2212	Peau Satin	**$338**
	• *Also available in oyster/ivory, all white or all ivory*	
2242	Peau Satin	**$378**
	• *Also available in oyster*	
2039	Peau Satin	**$418**
2092	Peau Satin	**$458**
4801	Peau Satin	**$450**
2201	Silk-backed satin	**$258**
2210	Peau Satin	**$238**
2208	Satin	**$258**
2202	Lace	**$258**
2206	Beaded lace and chiffon	**$270**
2214	Chiffon	**$398**
2259	Satin and Organza	**$240**
	• *Also available in pink*	
2257	Satin and Organza	**$238**
	• *Also available in pink*	
2260	Satin and organza	**$250**
	• *Also available in pink*	
2227	Peau Satin and organza	**$498**
2187	Peau Satin	**$558**
	• *Also available in "mist"*	
2242	Peau Satin	**$378**
	• *Also available in oyster*	
2218	Peau Satin	**$378**
	• *Also available in "mist"*	

⇢ TATIANA OF BOSTON ⇠

Contact info. Tatiana Fashions, 73 Newbury St., Boston, MA 02116. For a dealer near you, call (617) 262-4914.

Internet. This designer does not have an official web site yet. Our web site (www.bridalgown.com) will have updates on this designer.

Background. Now here's a double major for you. Russian-born bridal designer Tatiana holds college degrees in both costume design *and* mechanical engineering. So, if this bridal gig doesn't work out, we suppose Tatiana might be able to go to work designing automobiles or diesel engines. Given the designer's most recent gown designs, however, it looks like that second career option won't be necessary. Tatiana of Boston creates some of the most stunning bridal gowns available on the market today. Before Tatiana went into bridal, she worked for designer Bill Blass. After noticing the bridal market was flooded with a sea of look-alike gowns, Tatiana struck out on her own in 1982. In her own words, she attempts to design "sleek silhouettes and styles" that are "innocent, romantic, sensual or sophisticated."

Our view. Fresh and innovative, Tatiana is one of a new group of couture bridal designers that is continuing the Boston bridal tradition started by Bianchi and Priscilla.

What most impressed us about this designer's work was her use of fabrics. One design features "cut velvet," while others feature delicate silk in a variety of finishes (peau de soie, organza, moires and brocades). For added flexibility, Tatiana offers some gowns both in silk or polyester fabric versions (that latter is less expensive, as you might expect). Since the dresses are often unadorned, the quality of the fabric is key.

The fashions are on the vanguard of the market. Tatiana uses contemporary silhouettes set off with special touches, such as hand-rolled fabric roses or flowers with a slight tint of blue. Coats, jackets and capes seem to be her trademark. One simple dress features an organza jacket trimmed in satin and rhinestone buttons. Another featured a short cape trimmed with satin and pearl buttons. Instead of giant ball gowns, you're more likely to see A-lines, sheaths and empire waist silhouettes.

As with other couture designers, all this fashion and fabric doesn't come cheap. Prices for Tatiana's dresses run $1100 to $3900. While that isn't inexpensive, the aforementioned fabric swaps can make some styles more affordable. Overall, most styles are in the $2200 to $2400. Matching headpieces are available for most gowns.

In the research for this book, we saw a lot of expensive dresses from designers who claimed they were doing "couture quality." Yet Tatiana of Boston is of the few couture designers who are worth their hefty price tags. These are *quality* dresses, not pretenders. **Rating: A**

Retail Store. Tatiana of Boston has a boutique in Boston (see above for the address). Her gowns are also available at a limited number of bridal retailers nationwide.

T A T I A N A   O F   B O S T O N

Delivery. Two months (on regular sizes 4-16). Rush orders are available; add 10% to the gown price for this option.

Sizing Chart

Type: Tatiana of Boston uses a BODY size chart. For information on this subject, refer to the introduction of the designer review section of this book.

	4	6	8	10	12	14	16	18	20
Bust	33.5"	34	35	36	37.5	38.5	40	42	44
Waist	24.5	25.5	26	27	28	29.5	31	33	35
Hips	37	38	39	40	41	42.5	44	46	48

Extra charges for changes/options:
1. For sizes 18 and 20, add 10% to the gown price.
2. To add length to a sleeve, add 5% to the gown price for unbeaded sleeves or 7% to the gown price for beaded sleeves.
3. To add train length, add 10% to the gown price.
4. Extra gown (skirt) length is available.
5. Additional buttons as well as fabric and lace are available by the yard; Consult a local retailer for more information.

New Bridal Gowns for Spring 1997

Style Name	Description	Suggested Retail
Alexandra	Short organza jacket with bows and rhinestone or covered buttons over strapless dress of peau de soie bodice with full organza skirt. *Style #: 1001/J*	**$2200**
Irina	Organza cape over strapless fitted sheath. Kick pleated train. *Style #: 1003.*	**$2200**
Victoria	Peau de soie sheath with chapel train (can be detachable on request). Hand woven flower garland. *Style #: 1004*	**$3400**
Vanda	Organza and peau de soie dress, A-line off the shoulder sheath with chapel train. *Style #: 1007.*	**$2200**
Violetta	Peau de soie bodice with fill skirt and chapel train, long sleeves. Hand woven flower garland. *Style #: 1009*	**$3400**
Ella	Peau de soie bodice with portrait collar trimmed with bows, full organza. skirt with peau de soie border. *Style #: 5002.*	**$2300**

TATIANA   OF   BOSTON

Grace	Peau de soie sheath gown rolled collar into plunging back with detachable square organza train. *Style #: 5003.*	**$2200**
Audrey Two	Silk shantung A-line gown decorated with hand rolled roses around neck line and bustle, short sleeves and chapel train. *Style #: 5004.*	**$1950**
Alyssium	Sheath gown rolled collar into plunging back with detachable floral train. *Style #: 5011.*	**$2200**
Ava	Peau de soie A-line gown with piping and satin organza train. *Style #: 5101.*	**$3900**
Ostara	Peau de soie A-line gown with open back and satin organza train. *Style #: 5102.*	**$3200**
Windsor	Halter style shantung bodice with stripe shantung and organza skirt. *Style #: 5103.*	**$2400**
Adriana	Silk shantung gown with bouffant skirt and garland of softly colored roses pearls. (Garland available in all one color as gown). *Style #: 5104.*	**$3000**
Scarlette	Brocade gown with corseted bodice, bustled skirt and lace petticoat. Features laced bodice and colored pansy trim or white roses. Also available in Ivory Peau de soie and metallic organza. *Style #: 5105.*	**$3200**
Jacquie-O	Empire bodice with bow trim, gored organza skirt. *Style #: 5106.*	**$1800**
Bella	Peau de soie gown with A-line silhouette, long sleeves and a rolled collar with corsage. *Style #: 5107.*	**$1900**
Maria	Peau de soie bodice, off shoulder, with belt and rose pattern organza skirt. *Style #: 3001.*	**$2200**
Natasha	Peau de soie sheath, empire waist, square neckline, long sleeve, with organza apron and train. *Style #: 3002.*	**$2400**
Yvonne	Peau de soie sheath, empire waist, scoop neckline, sleeveless with floral organza apron and train. *Style #: 3003.*	**$2400**

T A T I A N A   O F   B O S T O N

Cape	Hooded, chapel length train, available in metallic organza or satin organza. *Style #: 3004.* **$960**
CiCi	Satin dupioni short dress, off shoulder with belt, and built in petticoat. *Style #: 3005.* **$1400**
Dion	Peau de soie sheath, halter top with buttons in back, kick train. *Style #: 3006.* **$1200**

⊹ V E N U S ⊹

Contact info. Venus Bridal Gowns/Lotus Orient, PO Box 280, San Gabriel, CA 91778. For a dealer near you, call (800) 648-3687 or (818) 285-5796.

Also known as. Pallas Athena.

Internet. This designer does not have an official web site yet. Our web site (www.bridalgown.com) will have updates on this designer.

Background/Our view. With 150 to 175 styles, Venus is probably one of the largest import bridal manufacturers in the country. With dealers in both the U.S. and Canada, Venus splits its voluminous line into four groups: regular Venus, Venus Silk, informals and a separate collection called Pallas Athena.

The regular Venus dresses have a wide price range ($450 to $1800), although most are in the $800 to $900 ballpark. Matte satin is a common fabric in this group, but there are a few styles in chiffon and shiny polyester satin. In a nod to an increasingly tight-fisted bridal market, Venus recently introduced more lower-price designs in this group (around $600).

The fashion for regular Venus gowns seemed a little dated to us. Huge puff sleeves and bead-encrusted bodices were common themes on gowns that are anything but subtle. One mermaid-style gown featured an all-over beaded bodice that was high on candlepower. If the light in the church caught this gown just right, you might have to have a medical crew on hand to revive guests blinded by the bride.

In contrast, the Venus Silks line has a more toned-down look. More contemporary silhouettes (princess lines, empire waists) and elegant fabrics (silk shantung, crepes, velvets) made these dresses seem more stylish than Venus' other offerings. Prices for these gowns are $600 to $1600, with an average of about $900.

If that weren't enough choice, Venus also offers the Pallas Athena line, a lower-priced and even less ornate collection of gowns. Prices for these dresses average $500 (although a few styles touch the $1000 mark). The fashion of these gowns was also quite pleasing. Stylish, contemporary silhouettes like A-lines are complimented by minimal amounts of lace and beading. It's a toned-down, sweeter look.

In business since 1985, Venus gets better marks for quality than other, similar importers. We also like that the manufacturer offers all gowns in petite sizes, a rarity these days. If the company beefed up its value with more silk gowns in lower price points (under $800), they'd definitely earn a higher rating. **Rating: B+**

Delivery. 12 to 14 weeks. Rush orders are available for $40 to $80 extra, depending on how quickly delivery is needed.

Tags. Venus identifies its gowns with hang tags and sewn-in labels.

SIZING CHARTS

Type: Venus uses a GARMENT size chart. For information on this subject, refer to the introduction of the designer review section of this book.

Standard Sizes

	4	6	8	10	12	14	16	18	20
Bust	33"	34	35	36	37	38.5	40	42	44
Waist	24	25	26	27	28	29.5	31	33	35
Hips	35.5	36.5	37.5	38.5	39.5	41	42.5	44.5	46.5

	22	24	26
Bust	46	48	51
Waist	38	41	44
Hips	51	54	57

Sizing notes:
• *Standard gown length (as measured from hollow of the neck to the desired dress hem) is 59".*
• *Standard sleeve length is 18".*

Petite Sizes*

	3	5	7	9	11	13	15
Bust	32"	33	34	35	36	37	38.5
Waist	23	24	25	26	27	28	29.5
Hips	34.5	35.5	36.5	37.5	38.5	39.5	41

Sizing notes:
• *Petite sizes gown length (as measured from hollow of the neck to the desired dress hem) is 55".*
• *Petite sizes sleeve length is 17".*

Extra charges for options/changes:
1. For sizes 18 and 20, add $40 to the gown price.
2. The extra charge for sizes 22 to 26 varies depending on the gown price. For size 22, add $70 to $150 to the gown price. For size 24, add $110 to $200. For size 26, add $150 to $300. (Consult a local retailer for more information.)
3. *For petite sizes 3-15, add $40 to the gown price.
4. To change sleeve length, add $40 to the gown price.
5. To change the gown length (five inches longer or shorter), add $40 to the gown price.
6. For a custom-measured gown length (made to your measurements), add $80. For this option, Venus requires three measurements: from the hollow of the neck to the natural waist, from the natural waist to hem and the total hollow to hem measurement.
7. For a custom-measured bodice length (one inch shorter or longer) add $40 to the gown price. For this option, measure from the hollow of the neck to the natural waist.

NEW BRIDAL GOWNS FOR SPRING 1997

❖ **Venus Collection** ....

STYLE #	DESCRIPTION	SUGGESTED RETAIL
7328	Off shoulder, scalloped sweetheart, short sleeve. Heavily beaded bodice. Layers of tulle over satin. Scattered appliqués throughout skirt and train. Semi cathedral train.	**$698**
7329	Scalloped V neckline with short sleeves. Elaborate beadwork on entire gown. Extended chapel train.	**$598**
7331	Modified sweetheart neckline with long fitted illusion sleeves. Princess line. V back. Heavily beaded hem lace with rays of beaded appliqués on skirt. Extended cathedral train.	**$850**
7333	Squared sweetheart neckline with short illusion cap sleeves. Beautifully beaded front panel with trails of lace coming up from bottom of skirt and train. Squared sweetheart back. Back bow has center rosette. Cathedral train.	**$698**
7339	V-neck, short sleeve sheath, with pearl scalloped edge trim along neckline and sleeve. Beaded appliqués adorn bust, sleeve and front of skirt. V back with bow. Detachable semi cathedral train.	**$550**
7341	Scoop neckline with short cap sleeves. Satin trim outlines the neckline and sleeves. Beaded appliqués enhance bodice. Beaded basque waist trim Scoop back. Almost cathedral train.	**$450**
7344	Sweetheart neckline with beaded appliqués. Long fitted illusion sleeve. Deep scoop back. Tulle peplum accents back of waist. Fine tulle skirt. Cathedral train.	**$550**
8943	V-neckline with exposed lace edge on rounded short sleeves. Partial illusion v back. Layer of organza over satin skirt. Double satin ribbon trim Extended cathedral train.	**$798**
8944	Modified Queen Anne, diamond cut sweetheart neckline with short cap sleeve. Beautiful beaded appliqués featured on bodice and sleeves. Oval keyhole illusion button back. Heavily beaded lace accent on skirt hem Almost cathedral train.	**$798**
8946	Jewel neck, point d esprit beaded illusion with sweetheart neckline. Deep inset cut, sleeveless top. Beautiful beaded	

lace on bodice and trims waist. High beaded illusion button back. Crystal beaded point d esprit tulle skirt. Floor length.   **$650**

8947   Jewel neck, Venice pearled lace top sheath with empire silhouette. Deep cut inset shoulder, sleeveless. Silk charmeuse skirt slightly flares at the knee and extends to a cathedral train.   **$750**

8948   Satin piped V neckline with heavily beaded lace bodice, sleeveless. Layers of tulle over satin skirt. Pearl and sequins scattered throughout skirt. Almost cathedral train.   **$550**

8949   Scoop neckline point d'esprit illusion sweetheart with heavily beaded corded lace on bodice and sleeve. Short illusion sleeve. Neckline has beaded trim. Point d' esprit illusion back. Princess silhouette. Extended cathedral train.   **$1098**

8950   Jewel neckline, sleeveless sheath with illusion sweetheart front. Beaded lace decorates the bodice. Illusion keyhole back. Detachable semi cathedral length train.   **$750**

8951   Deep scoop neck adorned with braided pearl cluster trim Long illusion fitted sleeve. Heavily beaded appliqués over entire gown. Scattered window appliqués throughout skirt and train. Beautiful lace detail on train. Extended cathedral train.   **$1298**

8952   Short bell sleeves with cutouts on waist and down center of train. Basque waist. Lace appliqué adorns bodice. Hem lace has cutouts also. Detachable extended cathedral train.   **$898**

8953   Similar to 8952 but skirt is made of tulle.   **$798**

8954   Sweetheart neckline, sheath. Long fitted illusion sleeves. Heavily beaded motif. Detachable train has beautiful windowed appliqués. Cathedral train.   **$798**

8955   Modified Queen Anne. Long fitted illusion sleeve with pearled Venice lace. Front of bodice has two trails of Venice lace which beautifully accents gown. High illusion back with buttons. A line skirt. Detachable train with double tiered bow accented with satin rosettes. Cathedral train.   **$998**

8956   Jewel neckline illusion, sleeveless, with satin piping detail around the neckline and shoulder. Beaded lace motif decorates bodice in simulated strapless pattern. High illusion button back. Detachable cathedral train.   **$998**

V E N U S

8957   Sleeveless v neckline. Organza diamond lace adorns empire silhouette. Pearl scrolls along edge of neckline. Small bow accents bust. Satin ribbon detail enhances empire waist. V back with back bow accented with satin rosette and diamond organza lace. Extended streamers down length of train Wide hem lace with diamond organza lace coupled with same pearl scrolls as on neckline. Almost cathedral train.   **$898**

8958   Wrap around neckline with satin piping along neckline, sleeve and waist. Waist adorned with corded lace with beading. Wide lace motif circling front skirt and train. Semi-cathedral train.   **$650**

8959   Bateau neckline, long fitted illusion sleeve, basque waist. Corded lace adorns bodice. Partial illusion V-back with buttons over zipper. Extended cathedral train.   **$598**

8960   Illusion sabrina neckline. Beautifully beaded bodice. V back. Detachable train has double tiered bow. Windowed lace extending from back bow down to hem line. Scattered window lace throughout train. Extended cathedral train.   **$898**

8962   V-neckline with pearl trim fitted illusion long sleeve. Bodice covered with beaded appliqués. Hanging pearl beads adorn the front of waist. V back. Satin overlay frames tulle skirt. Beaded appliqués scattered on detachable train. Extended cathedral train.   **$998**

8963   Scoop neck, cap sleeve corded lace empire silhouette. Top of gown detailed with satin, pearls and satin rosettes along sleeve and waistline. Illusion back. Detachable train with satin rosettes and corded lace bow attached to train. Semi cathedral train.   **$598**

8964   Jewel illusion neckline, sweetheart. Pearl edged beaded organza bodice with diamond pattern made of pearled bugle beads, pearls and floral crystals. Beautiful detail on this gown make it extravagant! Layers of tulle over satin skirt. Almost cathedral train.   **$898**

❖ **Venus Couture Gowns** ....

Style #   Description   Suggested Retail

1012   Strapless sheath in ivory silk satin with wrap around train. Removable jacket made of corded French lace with re-embroidered ribbon and pearls. Queen Anne neck. Beaded lace and rosettes adorn front of gown in asymmetrical pattern. Lace is repeated on front panel of gown and bottom of wrap around train. Jacket has button

back closure. Skirt has back box pleat detail. Extended
chapel train. $2200

1015 Portrait collar with intricate thread and ribbon passementerie work, accented with small pearls and crystals.
Small silk satin rosettes along each side of neckline.
Champagne silk satin bodice. Full tulle skirt with same
intricate passementerie work along trim of hem Rosettes
accent back. $1990

1016 Scoop neck, short sleeve in silk satin adorned with pearl
and beaded woven patches of silk satin n1) bon on sleeve
trimmed in pearl. Beautiful beaded woven silk satin waist
also trimmed with pearl. Tulle layered over satin skirt
with scattered silk satin woven ribbon patches throughout. Jewel back. Buttons over zipper. Chapel train.

$2400

1019 Asymmetrical wrap bodice, sleeveless in silk with front
keyhole detail. Skirt has tulip patterned lace with embroidered satin rosettes embellished with pearls. Chapel train.
$1990

1021 Jewel neck, sleeveless Italian silk satin floral jacquard
with deep inset cut shoulder with crystal and pearl detail
along neckline, sleeve and basque waist. Keyhole back.
Cathedral train. $1898

1022 Jewel neck point d' esprit illusion. Sleeveless bodice with
corded French lace embellished $795 with pearl and satin
ribbon embroidery. Satin edging trim armholes and neckline. Point d' esprit tulle skirt. High illusion button back.
Floor length. Gown comes in White only.

$1590

1023 Scalloped jewel neck illusion sheath in re-embroidered
French lace. Short scalloped edged sleeves. Silk satin
pleated waist with obi-style side draped panel with lace
which extends to train. Gown comes in White lace/Rum
pink, all white or all ivory. $3190

1025 V-neckline sleeveless, re-embroidered French lace over
nude lining. Lace scalloped waistline. Deep v back with
center flower detail. Floor length tulle skirt. Tulle skirt in
two colors: White/White and White/Nude.

$1390

1027 Scoop neck. long sleeve with beautiful ribbon basket weave
trim along cuff of sleeve with button accent. Neckline
and cuff of sleeve trimmed with silk satin edging. A line.
Buttons trail down entire back side of gown. Gown in
Italian silk satin. Almost cathedral train. $1990

V E N U S

1028	Scoop neck stretch illusion top with soft cotton and silk embossed jacquard fabric along neckline and throughout bodice and skirt. Small flowers edge shoulders. Dropped torso shapes lower from front to back. Self piping at waist. Floral detail at back of gown. Cathedral train. Gown comes in Ivory only.	**$1350**
1029	Square neck with v inset. Silk satin bodice with silk satin piping down all the seams Short silk gazar sleeves and skirt. Square back with buttons and floral detail. Chapel train.	**$1790**
1030	Scoop neck, sleeveless silk passementerie jacquard bodice with pearl and crystals along neckline, sleeve and waist. Solid silk satin organza bottom Silk passementerie jacquard back bow enhanced with pearls. Cathedral train. Gown comes in White only.	**$1990**
1031	V neck, sleeveless in silk satin with satin piping along neckline, sleeve and waist. Pleated skirt off basque waist. V back with buttons and back bow. Beautiful silk flowers create bustled effect down back of train. Cathedral train. *Gown comes in Rum Pink, White, and Ivory.*	**$2390**
1032	Scoop neck French lace illusion embellished with pink pearl, overlays sweetheart neckline gown in silk satin. A line. V back. Back bow accent. Almost cathedral train. *Gown comes in White/Pink, White/white.*	**$2390**
1034	Square neck short sleeve with piping along neckline, sleeve and waist. Gown in Italian Silk dotted jacquard. Inverted pleats below waist are embellished with bow and flowers. Narrowed deep square back. Floral back bow. Extended chapel train. *Gown comes white with ivory dot only.*	**$2390**
1035	Swan lake inspired bodice of feathers dyed natural, beige and pale pink over Italian silk satin. Satin ribbon straps criss-cross back. Tulle skirt has alternating ivory and white layers. Skirt is embellished with crystal and aurora stones. Gown comes in Ivory only. Floor length.	**$1190**

❖ Pallas Athena Collection ....

STYLE #	DESCRIPTION	SUGGESTED RETAIL
9444	V neckline with illusion cap sleeve modified square back with double tiered peplum bow. Chiffon layer over satin. Semi cathedral train.	**$498**

9445   Halter high neck illusion with Venice all over pearled
detail with layer of tulle over satin. Illusion back.
Ball gown skirt with cathedral train.   **$598**

9446   Scoop neckline, sleeveless with back bow accented with
appliquéed streamers. Venice lace hem line. Princess
silhouette in satin. Extended chapel train.   **$750**

9447   Jewel illusion neckline with Venice lace. Satin ribbon
accent under bustline. A line silhouette. Gown in
matte satin with detachable extended chapel train
with hem lace.   **$598**

9448   Strapless sweetheart neckline, with Venice lace detailing.
Removable short Venice lace jacket. Layers of tulle over
satin skirt. Detachable cathedral train.   **$650**

9449   Halter top enhanced with beaded Venice lace. Layers of
tulle over satin. Back bow treatment. Beautiful beaded
Venice lace hem. Floor length.   **$598**

9451   Square neckline sheath, with Venice lace detailing. Long
sheer fitted sleeves. Simulated empire waist. Deep V back.
Detachable train with back bow. Cathedral train.
      $498

9452   Sweetheart neckline, sleeveless A line. Beautifully detailed
with corded alencon lace. Square back. Cathedral train.
Gown in satin.   **$498**

9453   Sweetheart neckline with pearled illusion cap sleeves.
Satin ribbon trim along neckline and sleeves. Princess
silhouette. Modified V back. Cathedral train.   **$550**

9454   Sleeveless jewel neckline features beaded illusion lace
empire waist. Satin piping trims the neckline, sleeve, and
under bustline. Beaded illusion back with bow accent.
Bow enhanced with satin cord. Almost cathedral train
with extravagant border.   **$550**

9455   Point d esprit scoop illusion neckline, short cap sleeve,
full skirt with layers of tulle over satin. Wide satin ribbon
trim outlines the neckline, sleeve and hem. Floor length.
      $598

9456   Modified Queen Anne neckline with continuous tea cup
sleeves. High neck illusion button back. Pearled Venice
lace detailing on bodice, sleeve, waist and hem.   **$560**

9457   Sleeveless scoop neckline accented with Venice lace.
Square back. Full skirt with layers of tulle over satin.
Almost cathedral train.   **$498**

VENUS

| 9458 | High neck illusion with exposed shoulder. Venice lace trims short cap sleeve and enhances bodice. High illusion V-back. Cathedral train. | **$598** |

9458   High neck illusion with exposed shoulder. Venice lace trims short cap sleeve and enhances bodice. High illusion V-back. Cathedral train.   **$598**

9459   Jewel neck with Venice lace (illusion). Satin ribbon along neckline, sleeve and empire waist. V back with bow and streamers. Princess silhouette with cathedral train.

                                                                                   $398

9460   V neckline, princess, with short cap sleeve. Bodice features Venice lace throughout. V back with bow accent. Chapel train. Gown in satin.   **$598**

9461   High neck illusion with padded illusion cap sleeve. Heavily beaded bodice. Keyhole back. Cathedral train. Gown in satin.   **$498**

9462   Beautiful satin gown. Scoop neckline, cap sleeve princess with a peek-a-boo lace center. Sweep train.   **$450**

9544   Similar to 9444, but done in tulle. No back bow.   **$498**

⇥ V O W & V O G U E ⇤

Contact info. Vow & Vogue International Inc., 20265 Valley Blvd. Unit B-C, Walnut, CA 91789. For a dealer near you, call (909) 598-6569.

Internet. This designer does not have an official web site yet. Our web site (www.bridalgown.com) will have updates on this designer.

Background/Our view. Vow & Vogue burst onto the scene in 1993, offering exceptional values and good styling. For a while, it looked as if the designer might become one of the industry's fast-rising stars; however, subsequent delivery snafus have sent them back into the pack of average import manufacturers (more on this later).

Vow & Vogue offers two collections, their regular line and the "signature" group. There really isn't much difference between the two, however. Most are about $600, although prices range from a low of $300 to a high of nearly $1000.

The designer's silk gowns are stand-outs as far as value goes. These dresses, mostly in silk shantung, average $600 to $700, which is a good deal indeed. Watch the tag closely with this designer, however. Vow & Vogue likes to use a lot of polyester fabrics with names like "silk-like satin" and "silk-like shantung." Translation: they're man-made versions of the real thing.

The fashion is very traditional. Most of the gowns feature ball-gown silhouettes, although a few sheaths and princess lines dot the collection. Occasional touches like fabric roses on the sleeves or ribbon lace accents set the gowns apart from the competition. With 70+ styles overall, you can find everything from the big tulle skirt look to a more understated style with a bateau neckline.

While the quality and value is average or above average, deliveries are another story. Vow & Vogue promises to deliver gowns in 12 weeks, but retailers we interviewed laughed at that assertion. While the designer promises a three month turnaround, it's more like four or five months before the dress shows up. Part of the problem stems from a lack of stock—Vow & Vogue keeps very few gowns on hand, even with their hot-selling silk styles. So, if you want a Vow & Vogue gown, make sure you leave plenty of time before your wedding when ordering. **Rating: C+**

Delivery. Allegedly 12 weeks. 16 to 20 weeks may be closer to reality. Rush orders are sometimes available for an extra free.

Tags. Vows & Vogue identifies their gowns with only hang tags.

SIZING CHART

Type: Vow & Vogue uses a GARMENT size chart. For information on this subject, refer to the introduction of the designer review section of this book.

V O W   &   V O G U E

	4	6	8	10	12	14	16	18	20
Bust	34"	35	36	37	38	39.5	41	43	45
Waist	24.5	25.5	26.5	27.5	28.5	30	31.5	33.5	35.5
Hips	37	38	39	40	41	42.5	44	46	48

	22	24	26
Bust	48	50.25	52.5
Waist	38	40.25	42.5
Hips	50	52.25	54.5

Sizing notes:
• Gown length as measured from the hollow of the neck to the desired dress hem is 58".
• Sleeve length as measured from armpit to wrist is 23".

Extra changes for changes/options:

1. For sizes 18, 20 and 22, add $20 to the gown price.
2. For sizes 24 and 26, add $50 to the gown price.
3. For extra sleeve length, add $10 to the gown price.
4. For extra gown length (five inches only), add $40 to the gown price.

New Bridal Gowns for Spring 1997

Note: All gowns are available in white or ivory unless otherwise noted.

❖ Formal Bridal Gowns ....

Style #	Description	Suggested Retail
7102	Bridal Satin, featuring sweetheart neckline, long fitted sleeves, Basque waist, Royal Cathedral train, accented with Schiffli lace, sequins and pearls.	$578
7103	Organza, featuring scoop neckline, long fitted sleeves, drop waist, Cathedral with Venise lace.	$598
7105	Delustered Satin and Organza, featuring square neckline, short fitted sleeves, Empire waist, A-line Princess silhouette, detachable Court train, accented with Alencon lace, sequins and pearls.	$538
7106	Royal Satin, featuring square neckline, short fitted sleeves, Basque waist, Royal train, accented with Madeira and Alencon lace, sequins and pearls.	$598
7107	Modern Bride - Feb/Mar '97 - Alencon lace, sequin and pearled sheath accents the sleeveless, V-neckline, featuring a detachable Delustered Satin Semi-Cathedral train. $550 *Advertised in Modern Bride magazine Feb/Mar 1997*	
7108S	100% Silk Shantung, featuring a scoop neckline, short fitted sleeves, Basque waist, Cathedral train, accented	

with Alencon lace, rosebuds and pearls. $660
• Available in natural white only
Advertised in Modern Bride magazine Feb/Mar 1997

7109   Royal Satin sheath features an off-the-shoulder neckline,
long fitted sleeves, Basque waist, detachable Royal train,
accented with Alencon lace, sequins and pearls. $578

7111   Organza, featuring high illusion neckline, long fitted
sleeves, Basque waist, Semi-Cathedral train, accented
with Alencon lace, sequins and pearls. $450

7113   Royal Satin, featuring scoop neckline, sleeveless bodice,
Empire waist, A-line Princess silhouette, detachable
Chapel train, accented with Alencon lace, sequins
and pearls. $370

7132   Delustered Satin, featuring V-neckline, sleeveless bodice,
Basque waist, Chapel train, accented with Venise lace
and pearl clusters. $598

7136   Organza Ball gown, featuring sweetheart neckline,
cap sleeves, Basque waist, detachable Cathedral train,
accented with Alencon lace, sequins and pearls. $698
Advertised in Modern Bride magazine Feb/Mar 1997

7137   Royal Satin, featuring high illusion neckline, long fitted
sleeves, Basque waist, Cathedral train, accented with
Venise lace. $598

7139   Royal Satin, featuring modified Queen Anne neckline,
long fitted sleeves. Empire waist, Princess seams,
Cathedral train, accented with bows, Alencon lace,
sequins and pearls. $698
Advertised in Modern Bride magazine Feb/Mar 1997

7140   Matte Satin, featuring a V-sweetheart neckline, short
fitted sleeves, Basque waist, Royal train, accented with
Madeira lace, flowers and pearls. $598

7144   Matte Satin and Embroidered English Net Ball gown,
featuring Court neckline, sleeveless bodice, drop waist,
sweep train, accented with Venise lace. $498

7144F   Same as 7144, but floor length $498

7150   Matte Satin, featuring scoop neckline, short fitted sleeves,
Basque waist, Cathedral train, accented with Alencon lace,
sequins and pearls. $650

7153   Matte Satin, featuring scoop neckline, short fitted sleeves,
Basque waist, Cathedral train, accented with Venise lace. $798

7154   Royal Satin, featuring scoop neckline, sleeveless bodice, Basque waist, Cathedral train, accented with Embroidered Soutache lace.   **$550**
        Advertised in Modern Bride magazine Feb/Mar 1997

7156   Royal Satin, featuring off the shoulder neckline, short fitted sleeves, Basque waist, Cathedral train, accented with Alencon lace.   **$498**
        Advertised in Modern Bride magazine Feb/Mar 1997

7157   Matte Satin, featuring off-the-shoulder neckline, short fitted sleeves, Basque waist, Cathedral train, accented with Embroidered Scroll, bugle beads, pearls and silk flowers.
                                                              $850

7161   Matte Satin, featuring wide scoop neckline, cap sleeves, Basque waist, detachable Cathedral train, accented with embroidered pearls.   **$538**

7169   Matte Satin, featuring scoop neckline, short fitted sleeves, Basque waist, Semi-Cathedral train, accented with bugle beads, sequins and pearls.   **$598**
        Advertised in Bridal Guide magazine Jan/Feb 1997

7181   Bridal Satin, featuring sweetheart neckline, short fitted sleeves, Basque waist, Royal train, accented with lavish, fine embroidered lace and pearls.   **$798**
        Advertised in Modern Bride magazine Feb/Mar 1997

7182S   Embroidered 100% Silk Shantung, featuring a Sabrina neckline, sleeveless bodice, A-line Princess silhouette, sweep train, accented with sequins and pearls.   **$650**
        • Available in Natural White only
        Advertised in Bridal Guide magazine Jan/Feb 1997
        and Bride's magazine Feb/Mar 1997

7184   Bridal Satin, featuring scoop neckline, short fitted sleeves, Empire bodice, Princess A-line skirt, Cathedral train, accented with embroidered bugle beads, sequins and pearls.
                                                              $550
        Advertised in Modern Bride magazine Feb/Mar 1997

✦ W A L L E N T I N ✦

Contact info. Wallentin, 2030 Century Center Blvd., Suite 15, Irving, TX 75062. For a dealer near you, call (800) 925-5954 or (214) 721-7048 or (214) 721-7049.

Also known as. Camelot Collection, Crown Collection.

Internet. www.bridalsearch.com/wallentin. Wallentin's web site features pictures of their gowns and style numbers (but no prices). Our web site (www.bridalgown.com) will have updates on this designer.

Background/Our view. Wallentin is another example of a bridal retailer who branched out into gown manufacturing. The retailer in this case was Mii's Bridal of Dallas, Texas. Owned by Thai natives Mii and Tony Boosmongkol, Wallentin got its start after Texas brides continued to request Mii's exquisite custom-made gowns.

Sewn in Thailand, Wallentin points out that its fabric is higher quality than other competitors; the designer only uses 100% "Grade A" Thai silk. Mii and Tony take great care of their silk worms back in Thailand, making sure they eat just the right mulberry leaves to produce the special silk.

Wallentin's gowns feature intricate beading and exquisite lace cut-outs. While the styling is quite traditional (basque waists, sweetheart necklines, cap sleeves), the gowns feature special touches. You'll see lattice embroidery, rolled silk roses, mushroom pleating and other features. Wallentin's signature design feature appears to be skirts with pyramid-shaped lace cut-outs.

In order to pay for all those mulberry leaves, Wallentin charges a hefty premium for its dresses. Prices range from $790 to a whopping $4000. The average is about $1100. (The least expensive gowns are marketed under the name "Camelot Collection" by Wallentin.)

The quality gowns are above average. Each has a completely lined bodice, attached bra cups and full petticoats. All the beading and embroidery is done by hand.

While these dresses are spectacular, the designer's ads just don't do justice to them. And that's if you can see any ads at all—Wallentin rarely advertises in the bridal magazines. On the upside, at least the company has a web site, which provides front and back views of all their dresses (see above for the address). **Rating: B**

Tags. Wallentin identifies their gowns with hang tags and sewn-in labels.

Delivery. 12 weeks. For gowns with a custom change, delivery is 16 weeks. Rush cuts on regular gowns are available in 10 weeks for an extra $200 (or 8 weeks for $240). Rush cuts on gowns with custom changes are available in 12 weeks for $240 (or 10 weeks for $300 or 8 weeks for $360).

SIZING CHART

Type: Wallentin uses a BODY size chart. For information on this subject, refer to the introduction of the designer review section of this book.

	4	6	8	10	12	14	16	18	20
Bust	33.5"	34.5	35.5	36.5	37.5	39	40.5	42.5	44
Waist	23.5	24.5	25.5	26.5	27.5	29	30.5	32.5	34
Hips	34.5	35.5	36.5	37.5	38.5	40	41.5	43.5	45

	22	24	26	28
Bust	46.5	48.5	50.5	52.5
Waist	36.5	38.5	40.5	42.5
Hips	48.5	50.5	52.5	54.4

Sizing notes:
• *Gown length as measured from the hollow of the neck to the desired dress hem is 58".*
• *For Wallentin gowns, sleeve length as measured from the armpit to wrist is 19".*
• *For Camelot Collection gowns, sleeve length as measured from the armpit to wrist is 20".*

Extra charges for changes/options:

For Wallentin gowns:
1. For sizes 18 and 20, add $100 to the gown price.
2. For sizes 22 and 24, add $120 to the gown price.
3. For sizes 26 and 28, add $140 to the gown price.
4. Custom sizes over sizes 28 are available; add $160 to the gown price for this option.

For Camelot Collection gowns:
1. For sizes 18 and 20, add $60 to the gown price.
2. For sizes 22 and 24, add $90 to the gown price.
3. For sizes 26 and 28, add $120 to the gown price.
4. Custom sizes over sizes 28 are available; add $140 to the gown price for this option.

❧ THE BEST *of* THE REST ❧

Quick reviews of other bridal gown designers of note

Here are several more bridal designers who didn't make the cut to be included in our "Top 40" best bridal designers list. Note that the following companies are not rated. We didn't assign these designers letter grades because we didn't have enough information about their gowns to issue a rating. Nonetheless, in most cases, we have seen the gowns first-hand and wanted to pass along our general impression of their styling, prices and delivery. If you think any of these companies deserve a full review (or if you have comments on the dresses), feel free to contact the authors (see the back of this book for our contact information).

❖ *Aaron Hornsby To find a dealer near you, call (800) 240-9098 or (770) 736-1188. Internet: www.aaronhornsby-bridal.com* With 17 years of experience in running bridal retail stores in Georgia, Aaron Hornsby probably has their target market down to a science—the Southern bride. The three dozen or so styles that Hornsby turns out from their Atlanta headquarters are very traditional, with ball gown silhouettes and alencon lace. While the styling isn't something Scarlet O'Hara would recognize, it is more flashy than other designers (big puff sleeves, large butt bows). The prices are moderate ($550 to $900) and the value is just average (most of the fabrics are man-made satins and taffeta, although a few silk dresses dot the line). Delivery is 12 weeks, with rush cuts available. Sizing is 4 to 28, with an extra charge for sizes 18 to 28. If you live in Atlanta, you can visit Aaron Hornsby's retail store, which goes under the name Bridal and Formal Direct.

❖ *Alfred Sung* See the Canada section of this book for a full review of this designer.

❖ *Antonio Fermin To find a dealer near you, call 913-967-6779.* Kansas City-based designer Antonio Fermin designs bridal gowns for the Midwestern bride. Unlike his competitors on the east coast who charge high prices for plain gowns, Fermin at least gives you some bang for the buck. Most of the dresses (which are hand-sewn in the Orient) feature ornate bodices and trains and the prices ($558 to $1098) represent a good value. We liked the fabrics, including a "frosted European satin" and a high-quality silk shantung. In business since 1990, Fermin does quite a few trunk shows where you can meet the designer and see the entire collection.

❖ *Birnbaum & Bullock To find a dealer near you, call 212-242-2914.* Has this ever happened to you? You go bridal gown shopping and find a top with one dress you like, but not the skirt? Designers Birnbaum & Bullock have a solution: component gowns. The New York-based bridal manufacturer separately offers 10 tops and nine skirts—mix and match to your heart's content. The tops are hand-embroidered with looks that are more whimsical than other designers (one features bumble bees), while the skirts are made of such interesting fabrics as metallic crinkle silk organza, tissue taffeta and silk pique. While the prices are high ($1600 to $3100 for a complete gown), you've got to give these guys bonus points for originality.

❖ *Carmela Sutera* To find a dealer near you, call 212-921-4808. Carmela Sutera is a minor player in the couture bridal market whose overpriced creations are both dull and uninspired. A Sutera gown will set you back $1200 to $3100, not a small chunk of change. The emphasis is less on decoration and more on the fabric, although you can find such options as Duchess satin and silk shantung for less elsewhere. Sizes 4 to 20 are available (with a whopping $200 extra charge for sizes 18 and 20) and delivery takes 10 to 12 weeks. Sutera's sparse look does have some fans, but don't count us among them.

❖ *Carolina Herrera* To find a dealer near you, call (212) 575-0557. Carolina Herrera made a name for herself in bridal when she did a big Kennedy wedding in the 1980's. Back then, her simple but elegant gowns were cutting edge. Today, the rest of the bridal fashion market has caught up to her, cranking out similarly "elegant" gowns with less beading and decoration. As a result, Herrera's gowns now seem less innovative . . . and just plain expensive. How expensive? Try $1500 to $3900. While we liked the fabrications (all silk, with finishes like shantung, crepe, gazar and the like), we kind of got the feeling Herrera phoned in her latest bridal designs. Call us crazy, but we expect more innovation from Herrera (or any designer that charges these prices). Instead, she seems to be coasting on the same looks she did ten years ago.

❖ *Cupid Bridal Gowns* To find a dealer near you, call (314) 726-0416. Cupid is the latest Taiwanese bridal manufacturer to invade the U.S. market. After selling gowns in Europe and Australia earlier in the decade, Cupid came to the U.S. in 1995 with a collection that is somewhat schizophrenic in its styling. It seems the folks at Cupid have decided to make a little of everything (ball gowns, empire waists, princess lines, halter-style necklines) and hope something sticks. Despite the scattershot approach to styling, the fashion is pleasing, with a restrained use of lace accents and beading. We wish there were more natural fabrics, though; most were man-made satins and organzas. Cupid's gowns retail for $460 to $720, available in sizes 2 to 26 (extra gown length is available). Delivery is 10 to 12 weeks and rush cuts are available.

❖ *Designer Collection* For a dealer near you, call 203-746-8221. This Connecticut-based importer has rounded up some of the best affordable British designers to debut in the U.S. market. Included under the Designer Collection label are designers Elizabeth Emanuel ($780 to $1580), Rebecca Harte ($670 to $1320), Andrea Wilkin ($640 to $1700) and Rena Koh ($580 to $1190). While each designer obviously has her slightly different look, there is a common thread among British bridal manufacturers—simple looks and an emphasis on fabrics. You'll find Italian satin, French tulle and Thai silk among these gowns, which ranged from size 6 to 22. The only aspect of these designs that breaks the "European look" is the use of color: quite a few gowns featured gold lace, piping and silk roses as accents. Another gown featured an aqua blue bodice with contrasting toffee-colored silk skirt. While that dress probably won't play in Peoria, we applaud the Designer Collection for bringing affordable British bridal design to America.

❖ *Fiorito* For a dealer near you, call (800) 266-9716 or (602) 705-9184. Most bridal designers in the United Kingdom take their fashion marching orders from Paris. And the current rage in Europe is the clean (read: plain) look. Well, someone forgot to tell this to Fiorito, the Nottingham, England designer of bridal gowns that can only be described as "over-the-top." We visited with Fiorito's designer at a recent trade show and viewed the gowns, which she described as "adventuresome." How adventuresome? How about plunging neck-lines with giant cabbage roses (in contrasting colors like deep red) adorning the bodice? Color is another unique part of Fiorito's look, with dresses in pink, gold, peach and antique ivory. Of course, there are some simple looks in this collection, but it was the impossibly cheeky Renaissance-style gowns with full skirts and dripping lace that caught our eye. Importing to the U.S. since 1986, Fiorito's dresses range from $460 to $3310. All the gowns are made of silk and many styles have matching headpieces. Fiorito has an Arizona-based dis-tributor, so delivery and customer service is more prompt than other British designers who sell in the U.S. and Canada.

❖ *Illustra* For a dealer near you, call (800) 362-7170 or (316) 681-0952. Wichita, Kansas-based Illustra offers middle-of-the-road styling and pricing for its collection of 90 bridal styles. Priced from $450 to $918, most Illustra gowns are made of synthetic fabrics like "shantique" and polyester satin. While other Midwestern bridal designers can go over-board with dress styles that tend toward the hokey, we found Illustra's dresses to be more restrained and tasteful. The silhouettes are still quite traditional, but the lace and beading compliments instead of overpowers the dresses. As a side note, Illustra also has an extensive flower girl dress collection.

❖ *Jacquelin Bridals* For a dealer near you, call (941) 277-7099. Jacqueline Bridals features more contemporary fashion than other mid-priced designers who import gowns from overseas. A typical offering from Jacquelin is an A-line tank neckline with detachable Venise lace cropped, short-sleeve jacket. Not bad for $600. In fact, the entire line is quite affordable, ranging from $278 to $650 for formal bridal gowns, $200 to $340 for informals. You will find a little of everything in their collection of 70 styles, from fashion-forward looks to dresses that are covered in ruffles (a la the 1980's). Most of the fabrics are man-made, with a smattering of matte satin, chiffon and crepe. Our reports from brides say the quality is above average and the sizing is generous (sizes 4 to 42). Delivery is 10 to 12 weeks with rush cuts available. The company even offers custom cuts (made to your measurements), style changes and fabric swaps. Based in Fort Meyers, Florida, Jacqueline Bridals' dealers seem concentrated in the southeast, but this may be one bridal designer to watch.

❖ *Justine (Bridals By) For a dealer near you, call (800) 866-4696 or (818) 305-1338.* Justine (also known as Bridals by Justine) is our pick as one of the best buys in the market today. The company focuses on high-quality, yet affordable bridal gowns. How affordable? Try $430 to $690. And we're not just talking man-made fabrics here. There are several silk gowns in their collection of 75 dresses, as well as satin, chiffon and organza fabrications. Justine basically clones the looks of upper-end designers, with contemporary silhouettes and lace and beading that isn't overdone. What most impressed us, however, was the quality of construction and finish. Delivery is 12 to 14 weeks; sizes 4 to 20 (and large sizes 36 to 42 for an extra charge) are available. In business since 1986, Justine also has a large selection of informal gowns ($298 to $460) and matching flower girl dresses too.

❖ *L'Amour Bridals For a dealer near you, call (800) 664-5683 or (714) 838-5683.* L'Amour is one of the most affordable bridal manufacturers available today, with dresses that sell from $318 to $558. The import designer based in Tustin, CA offers 60 styles with lots of custom options—you can change the sleeves, skirt length and other details. We also liked the long gown length (60.75" to 62"), which would be a plus for tall brides. The only downside is the fashion: L'Amour offers only very basic silhouettes that are simply not fashion forward. With a collection that's this large, there are bound to be some winners and losers. Yet a few of the styles (like the all-over ruffle dress or gowns with lace portrait necklines) seemed obviously dated. Adding insult to injury, L'Amour's ads don't show the dresses off well either. Yet, if you can find a style that works for you, the prices certainly can't be beat. Delivery is 12 to 14 weeks.

❖ *Paula Varsalona To find a dealer near you, call (212) 221-5600.* Varsalona is an upper-end bridal designer whose star has faded since its peak in the 1980's. One big reason: while the dresses are stylish, the prices can be eye-popping ($2000, $3000). Well, apparently the folks at Varsalona have woken up to the fact that most brides can't spend that kind of cash. In a belated attempt to appeal to a mass market, Varsalona has rolled out the "Bow-tique" collection, which despite it's goofy name, has some good points. The gowns here range from $570 to $1390, while Varsalona's regular dresses (under the names In Vogue and Couture) are still $1000 to $3000. We liked the Bow-tique gowns, which featured satin and chiffon fabrics in a variety of sheath and empire-waisted styles. As you might expect, the silk fabrics and most fashion-forward looks are still in the Couture (read: expensive) line. Paula Varsalona's bridal gowns used to be known for their ornate detailing and embroidery. She's changed with the times, though and most of the skirts today are plain and the bodices feature just a touch of beading. Despite the new lower-price collection, Varsalona's prices still seem high in our opinion. Whether the "Bow-tique" gowns will catch on or be a case of "too little, too late" is an open question. Delivery is 8 to 12 weeks and rush cuts are available. Sizing is limited

(4 to 20, with an extra charge for sizes 18 and 20). We should also note that Varsalona has a rather large bridesmaids dress collection with some attractive styles.

❖ *Richard Glasgow* For a dealer near you, call (212) 683-1379. Glasgow has two bridal collections: the expensive and the super-expensive. The "lower-priced" line is the Ricardo line (which used to be called Riccio), but we'd be hard-pressed to call these dress prices "low." Ricardo gowns *start* at $1790 and then go up to $2550. Want to spend more? How about a regular Richard Glasgow dress for $2550 to $4550. So, what does $4550 buy you? Well, we have to admit this is a pretty amazing gown. The dress, in silk-faced satin, featured beaded Guipure lace on the scoop neckline and cap sleeves. The lace forms a pyramid on the front of the skirt. Whether or not it's worth four grand is debatable, but the gown is rather spectacular. We wish we could say the same thing about Glasgow's other gowns. The "low-price" Ricardo line is a disappointment. While the styling is very current, we were amazed that most of these dresses are not made of silk. Instead, you pay $1500 to $2000 for "Italian acetate satin." Hello? If you want a man-made fabric, you can find that for a fraction of the price elsewhere.

❖ *Tomasina* For a dealer near you, call (412) 563-7788 or (212) 719-5721. Sometimes you find an amazing bridal designer in a place you wouldn't expect it. Like Pittsburgh, PA. While this town isn't home to many bridal designers, we were pleasantly surprised to find Tomasina there, creating some of the most interesting bridal gowns in America. What makes Tomasina special? Check out the embroidery on these gowns. There are styles with delicate hummingbirds or musical notes, and others with intricate woven ribbons. Okay, that sounds cheesy, but trust us, it isn't. While the prices aren't inexpensive ($1850 to $3800), you'd be hard pressed to find these looks anywhere else. This is a small line (about 20 dresses) and the sizing is limited (4-22). Delivery takes 12 to 16 weeks and some gowns have matching headpiece.

❖ *Vera Wang* For a dealer near you, call (800) VEW-VERA or (212) 575-6400. In the bridal market there are pricey gowns that are worth it. And then there are those that are made by Vera Wang—exorbitantly priced gowns that are definitely *not* worth your hard earned money. For those of you who didn't watch the Winter Olympics of 1994, Wang came to prominence in the fashion market after she designed a white outfit for Nancy Kerrigan. After conquering the skating outfit market, Wang rolled out bridal gowns and, shortly thereafter, bridesmaids (reviewed separately later in this book). After looking at these dresses, we came away with the following impression: what's the big deal? At prices that approach a down payment for a nice house (a $6000 bridal dress, anyone?), you'd expect the gowns to be made from some precious metals and trimmed with 14K gold beading. No such luck. The fabrics are merely average and, worst of all, the fashion is "been there, done that." And why spend a fortune on a Wang dress when you can get it at a discount? That's right—Wang quietly does "trunk show" sales in New York (call the above number for the latest schedule). According to an article in the *Los Angeles Times*, one bride picked up a $3000 gown for just $400 at this sale. "The only downside," the bride told the reporter, "was I had to stand in line for two hours with 1500 other bitchy brides." Now, $400 is a more realistic price for a Wang bridal gown. If you don't live near New York City and can't get to this sale, we suggest forgetting about this designer . . . and buying that home instead.

❖ *Victoria's For a dealer near you, call (714) 847-2550.* Victoria's designer Shu Ling Chen's most unusual gown is reminiscent of "Romeo & Juliet." The design, with sleeves bearing the name of the Shakespearean heroine, is a stand-out in a line that is fairly traditional overall. In business since 1990, Victoria's is part of the import wave that has swept the bridal market in recent years. Prices for most of their dresses are $550 to $850, with $600 as an average price point. If we had to criticize anything about this line, it would have to their fabrics. Almost every gown is made of polyester (typically satin or organza). For the same price, you can often find silk gowns from other designers. On the other hand, the quality of their gowns is above average, as is their deliveries and reliability. Another plus: Victoria's offers a surprisingly large selection of styles and options. The collection has over 120 designs, with a wide variety of silhouettes and the sizing is equally generous (both petites and large sizes up to a 44). You can add train length, change short sleeves into long sleeves, request extra skirt length and more—an impressive list of customization for a lower-priced designer.

PART THREE

How to Buy a Brides- maids Dress

THE BRIDESMAID DRESS

Tips, tricks and advice on picking the dresses for your attendants

What are the two schools of thought when it comes to bridesmaids dresses? What are the common problems (and solutions) with this process? You'll learn this, plus five more do's and don't's when it comes to bridesmaids dress shopping. Next, we'll discuss how to pick the right size and seven money-saving tips. Finally, we'll reveal the biggest rip-offs with bridesmaids dresses, from "sight unseen colors" to surprisingly big fees for large sizes.

IS THERE A GARMENT MORE DESPISED than the lowly bridesmaid's dress? Next to shopping for a bathing suit, most woman rank having a root canal slightly higher than wearing these gowns.

Now that you've just completed the long journey of picking a gown for yourself, it's on to the next gut-wrenching fashion dilemma: what will the bridesmaids wear? And what can they afford?

Since bridesmaids usually pay for all or part of the dress (plus alterations and any accessories like shoes, gloves, etc.), that last question is not a moot point. Bridesmaid dresses have earned that special place as a permanent exhibit in the Bridal Fashion Hall of Shame—they're both ugly *and* expensive! This is truly a feat of modern engineering. Scientists have labored for years to combine just the right amount of polyester taffeta molecules with a dash of puff sleeves and giant "butt bows."

And the dress is just half the problem with bridesmaids. Let's not forget the bridesmaids themselves. Shopping for this dress is complicated by the following three situations:

1 **Bridesmaids who are nuts.** Sure, they have been your friend since third grade, but suddenly they've taken leave of their fashion sense. Yes, it's the bridesmaid who INSISTS that you should select the gown that looks like the Prom Dress from Hell. *Reality Check:* Yes, it is *your* wedding, but that doesn't give you any rights under international law to torture your bridesmaids. Of course, there is a solution if you find a bridesmaid who's lost her marbles: don't ask her to be a bridesmaid. She'll probably be relieved to be demoted to simple "guest" status and you can pick other bridesmaids who have more mental stability.

2 **Bridesmaids who can't agree on anything to save their souls.** You know who they are—ask three of these folks and you'll get four opinions. There are 4000 bridesmaids styles out there and, no, you don't have to try each one on to make a decision. *Reality Check:* As a bride, you have to take control of this process to keep it from turning into a bureaucratic nightmare. Later in this chapter, we'll give you some specific tips.

3 **Bridesmaids who are dirt poor.** Let's be honest: being a bridesmaid may be an honor, but it doesn't come cheap. As you'll notice in our designer reviews, some *bridesmaids* dresses can top $300 and $400. Add in any travel expenses, hotel stays and gifts to the bride and groom, and you've got one expensive "honor." *Reality Check:* Don't burden bridesmaids who are "financially challenged" with a dress that will sink an entire paycheck. Asking a college student or struggling actress to pay big money on a dress they'll never wear again isn't quite fair. Of course, you have two basic courses of action: don't ask these folks to be bridesmaids or pick up the cost of the dress (and alterations, and accessories, and . . .).

The Two Schools of Bridesmaids Dresses

Sensitive diplomatic negotiations aside, once you actually start looking at bridesmaids dresses you'll realize that these gowns have been divided into two distinct categories: The Prom Dress and The Evening Gown. Let's take a quick look at how each evolved:

1. *The Prom Dress.* Quick! Think of an image of a bridesmaid dress. Yards of taffeta in colors with such prosaic names as "bubble gum pink" and "buttercup yellow." Giant puff sleeves that flash the words BRIDESMAID! BRIDESMAID! A giant bow at the back of the dress to accent your, well, you know. Don't forget the satin pumps that are carefully died to match that aforementioned dress.

All of this gives the look not only of a circus act but also . . . a prom gown! And wouldn't you know it—that bridal shop also has the words "and prom dresses" on their business card. Hmmm. Could these shops be selling the exact same dresses, just

putting them on different racks with the labels "PROM" and
"BRIDESMAIDS"?

Perhaps what is so disgusting about these "traditional" bridesmaids gowns is how cheaply they're made. The low-end dresses seem
more like a Halloween costume than a real garment: unfinished
seams, flimsy fabric, glued-on detailing and worse. No wonder the
industry refers to these bridesmaids gowns as "disposable dresses."

2. *The Evening Gown.* At some point during the 1980's, a few
bridesmaid dress designers wondered aloud "what if we made
bridesmaids dresses for grown-ups?" The "evening gown" as
bridesmaids dress was born.

The first sophisticated bridesmaids gowns echoed the power
suit of the 1980's: severe two-piece ensembles with a short
peplum jacket and maybe a touch of lace. The career look soon
faded (some bridesmaids were confused as to whether they were
attending a wedding or going for a job interview) and more
"feminine-looking" dresses took the stage.

The fabrics were a big part of this renaissance: instead of
noisy taffeta and shiny satin, designers rolled out flowing crepes
and chiffons. Silk has become such a common bridesmaids fabric, you can find it many price ranges (not just $300+ gowns).

"Pared down" and "understated" are the buzzwords for style,
as bridesmaids designers actually decided to look at real dresses
for inspiration. As a result, some bridesmaids dresses today look
like something you'd wear out for an evening at the ballet or theater. And that's great news: as you'll read later in the chapter, a
great money-saving tip is to avoid the bridal shop altogether
when selecting a dress like this.

To create today's bridesmaids dress styles, designers have
stolen from the just about every time period of fashion history.
"Audrey Hepburn" is a name you'll hear invoked constantly. The
ball gown has also made a return, yet with more simple lines and
no giant "butt bow." You can probably dismiss some of the 60's
trends like empire waists and halter style tops as fads, but the
trend toward more grown-up styling is probably here to stay.

At this point, you may be saying "Great! With all these choices, how the heck will I ever be able to make a decision?" Don't
worry—most bridal shops carry dresses from both fashion
epochs. The traditional bridesmaids dress (read: prom gown)
isn't going anywhere. After all, this is an industry that still refers
to brides and bridesmaids as "girls."

The Do's and Don'ts of Picking a Bridesmaids Dress.

As we mentioned earlier in this chapter, selecting a bridesmaids
gown is often like negotiating a complicated nuclear test ban

treaty. You need to be both diplomatic and decisive. Here are some tips:

1. Don't go shopping with more than one bridesmaid. Let's be honest—you can't make this decision by committee. Of course that doesn't mean you don't get input from the other bridesmaids. Use catalogs, web site addresses and bridal magazine pictures to gauge their reaction to certain colors, styles and skirt lengths. Just do the actual shopping with only one trusted bridesmaid.

2. Do get swatches and catalog pictures. While many bridal shop owners would rather be boiled in hot oil than give brides catalogs of bridal gowns, bridesmaids are another matter—suddenly, catalogs are quite available, thank you.

3. Don't pick a dress that's too expensive. Yes, that $375 silk designer gown would go perfectly with your bridal dress. But . . . remember it's $375. Plus another $20 to $40 in alterations. And accessories like shoes, slip, jewelry and so on.

4. Do take into account not only what would look good on them, but also what fits with the wedding. Let's be honest: everyone doesn't have a body like a super-model. Choosing a silhouette that works on all sizes (like a dress with an A-line silhouette) is smart. Make sure the dress also fits the *style* of wedding: a garden wedding at 2 pm requires a different look than a formal 7 pm wedding with sit-down dinner.

5. Don't use the bridesmaids dresses as a way to improve the bride's image. Let's be honest: some brides intentionally pick hideous bridesmaids dresses to make sure the bride is the prettiest girl at the ball. That's cruel and unusual punishment.

One Size Does Not Fit All

Life is rarely perfect. Neither are bridesmaids. Here are some dilemmas and solutions to common bridesmaid challenges:

1 *The Pregnant Bridesmaid.* Let us give you a piece of advice on this one: don't ask a pregnant friend to be a bridesmaid. *You* try to be seven months pregnant and stand up for an hour or so as a maid of honor. If you have your heart set on doing this, however, here are a few ideas:

❦ Order extra bridesmaids fabric and have a maternity dress custom-made. Most bridesmaid designers offer their fabrics by the yard. Have a seamstress copy the basic dress pattern in a maternity size for your expectant friend.

❦ Depending on how pregnant the bridesmaid is, some regular dress styles might work. For example, gowns with an empire waist (see glossary) may be able accommodate a moderately-pregnant body.

❦ The designer Dessy (phone: 800-52-DESSY, 212-354-5808, internet: www.dessy.com) has a couple of maternity bridesmaids styles. See our review of this manufacturer later in the book.

2 *The big and the small.* If you have bridesmaids with vastly different body types, make sure to pick a style that can work in both size 4 and 24. Good picks include A-lines, princess lines or empire-waist dresses.

3 *I'm late for an important date.* As you'll read next, the average bridesmaid dress can take three to four months to get in. But you don't have that much time? Several designers have "quick ship" programs—a limited number of styles in a wide variety of sizes available for "immediate delivery." Another option is to check out the money saving tips later in this chapter. Many of these ideas can quickly unite you with a bridesmaids dress.

4 *The Out of Town Bridesmaid.* How do you coordinate far-flung bridesmaids? Well, one good idea is to deal with a mail-order service like Discount Bridal Service (DBS) or a catalog like Talbot's. We'll discuss both ideas shortly. These companies can directly ship your bridesmaids a dress (and at a great price, as an added bonus).

How long does this take?

It takes about 12 to 16 weeks to order a bridesmaid's dress, regardless of the type of dress you buy. A cheap, taffeta design takes as long to order as a more expensive silk gown from a fancy designer. Yes, a few designers offer rush service or have a limited number of styles available for "immediate" (read: four to six week) delivery. But . . . you might be hit with a rush charge ($30-$40 *per dress*) or have to choose among a very small number of "quick service" styles. And then don't forget the time needed for alterations: even a little nip and tuck can take a week or two.

The bottom line: plan in advance. Order those bridesmaid dresses at least five months before the wedding (six or more months is even better).

Money-saving Secrets

1 **Three words of advice: Discount Bridal Service (DBS).** As you read in our money-saving tips chapter, this company offers savings of up to 40% on bridesmaids dresses. See the review of DBS earlier in this book (Step #4) for more details.

2 **Sew your own.** What's a bridesmaid dress, anyway? A basic dress pattern with little detailing or fuss? And can't you just

buy typical bridesmaid fabrics like taffeta or crepe at a fabric store? We've heard from several brides who had their favorite aunt sew their bridesmaids dresses. While not a solution for everyone, this concept has its merits.

3 Avoid rush cuts. Bridesmaids dresses are expensive enough when ordered at full retail. Add in that extra "rush" fee and you'll see the price rise another 20%. Don't delay making this decision as you plan the rest of your wedding.

4 Pick a color, any color. Instead of forcing all the bridesmaids to wear the same dress, just give them a color (a swatch is best) and then have them buy separate dresses. Sure, they won't exactly match in style, but who cares? Let the bridesmaids hit the department stores and find a style that they can wear again. Obviously, you can't be a control freak to follow this tip, but it might be worth a shot.

5 Package discounts. Order your bridal gown and bridesmaids dresses from the same shop and they might offer a package discount. This typically is 10% to 20% off retail. Some shops have stated discount policies, while others quietly offer deals to their "best" customers. The bottom line: always ask about any package discounts.

6 Rent. Yes, a few stores actually rent bridesmaids dresses. **Formals Etc.** has six stores in Louisiana and two in Houston, Texas that rent bridesmaids gowns for as little as $65 (call 318-640-3766 for a store near you). **An Alternative** in Kansas City (800) 995-2338 rents bridesmaids at half their retail cost. (Check out Step #4 earlier in this book for more sources on shops that rent gowns.)

7 Consignment shops. Yes, some second-hand shops carry bridesmaids dresses. And the prices are usually a fraction of retail. Check in the phone book under "Bridal Shops" or "Clothing-Resale" for local sources.

8 Mail-order catalogs. A few catalogs sell elegant dresses that could easily pass as a contemporary bridesmaid dress. One of our favorites is Talbot's, which is both a mail-order catalog and retail chain (call 800-882-5268 for a catalog or to find a store near you). See the box below for an e-mail from a bride who had a happy experience with this mail-order option.

E-MAIL FROM THE REAL WORLD
Bridesmaids Bargains by Mail

Gosh, we just love mail order. Who needs all the hassle of special ordering a gown from a retail store anyway? Check out this story from a bride in New Hampshire who told us Talbot's solved her bridesmaids dress problem:

"Talbot's is a wonderful option for bridesmaids dresses. I ordered three dresses and then, two months later, needed another dress. Plus, I had to exchange one of the earlier dresses. I ordered through the catalog, but I was able to return the other dress to their local store (which is very convenient). They also have a bridal consultant who confirmed that the colors were from the same dye lot and helped expedite the purchase. They even sent a follow-up letter from the president's office thanking me for my business. Now *that* is good old customer service at its absolute best!

"Also, when we added and changed the two dresses later, they were on sale. As a result I was able to save my bridesmaids $30 each! This brought the cost per gown down to $150. I opened a Talbot's charge and ordered the dresses at the same time. This allowed my bridesmaids to reimburse me immediately or in installments. It was wonderful to have that flexibility. (I paid the interest charges.) Best of all, my bridesmaids have beautiful dresses of the highest quality that can be worn again (and I'm not just saying that!)."

Author's note: we should point out that you can find a bridesmaids-type dress at Talbot for much less than $150. We've seen several wonderful designs (some in silk) that are about $125 or less—that's half the cost of a similar dress in a bridal shop. Another bride wrote to us to say she found several beautiful dresses at a winter sale at Talbot's for 75% off.

As you read above, one of the best advantages of going this route is the customer service. Dresses from catalogs tend to run in "real-world sizes." Not only can your bridesmaids see the dress pictured in a catalog, but then they can get sizing advice over the phone. And what if the dress comes in and simply doesn't fit? Just send it back. Catalogs like Talbot's have no-hassle return policies—you send back the dress, they'll send you a different size or you get a refund. What a concept! Just try that at a bridal shop. ✍

Scams to Avoid

 ❖ SIGHT UNSEEN COLORS.
"I ordered $300 bridesmaids dresses in 'blue onyx' from a local bridal shop. The only problem? I didn't see the color chart or a swatch before ordering. The shop had samples in green and burgundy, but only a catalog picture of the blue. When the dresses came in, I was shocked. The color looked nothing like the picture and was terrible!"

Since bridal shops carry a limited amount of inventory, you may be tempted to order a bridesmaids dress in a color you can't see. You may want a velvet dress in "cranberry," but the shop only carries the same style in a "hunter green" taffeta. And even the same color can look different in certain fabrics (velvets versus chiffons, etc.).

The best protection is to insist on seeing a color swatch or color chart to make sure that it's what you want. Catalog pictures can be notoriously unreliable—funky lighting in the photo or simple variations in printing can make a "deep plum" dress seem more like bright purple.

Another related problem to this rip-off: designers who use combo fabrics. To spice up their collections, some designers will combine a velvet bodice with organza sleeves. The only problem? The colors in different fabrics might not match as you think they should.

The above story is an actual letter we received from a New Jersey bride. Unfortunately, she was stuck with dresses she described as "god-awful ugly." (Actually, she used more colorful language than that, but you get the idea.) The bridal shop asked the manufacturer to fix the problem and guess what? The manufacturer refused, saying "that's what 'blue onyx' is supposed to look like."

We expect to see more complaints like this in the future. Bridesmaids' dress designers are rolling out more "sophisticated" gowns, with fancy fabrics, two-tone colors and other doo-dads. The sheer variety of choices is overwhelming some retail stores, who don't have samples or swatches that show the myriad of options. As a result, brides are gambling on a color or fabric choice, sometimes with less-than-great results.

The bottom line: make sure you see the color(s) in the fabric(s) you want before committing to a special-order bridesmaids dress.

❖ IN FIVE SECONDS, THIS DRESS WILL SELF-DESTRUCT.
"My bridesmaids called their dresses 'mission impossible' gowns. At any moment they seemed like they might self-destruct. While my maid of honor was up at the altar next to me, we could actually hear her dress popping apart!"

All the stories we get about lousy bridesmaids dresses would be funny if it weren't for one fact: these dresses aren't free. If we gave you $150, $175 or $200 and told you to go buy a nice dress at a department store, would you choose one with threads hanging from every seam? With buttons that fall off when you try it on? Or with lace detailing that is sewn on crooked?

Each day dresses like that are shipped to innocent bridesmaids. You've got to ask yourself, where are the fashion police? Yet since a bridesmaids dress purchase is a one-shot deal (you're not going to go back next week to the bridal shop and say, "Order me some more of those taffeta gowns!"), it's no surprise that some manufacturers think they can get away with this.

The best advice we can give you is to order early. That way you'll have time to have the mistakes fixed. Or forget ordering a "bridesmaids dress" and instead use one of the alternate methods we described above. Department stores, regular dress shops and mail-order catalogs can get you a beautiful dress that's made much better than a traditional bridesmaid's gown. And you'll get the last laugh at the bridal industry since the dress will probably cost less too!

❖ CLASHING COLOR MOTIFS.
"I was a bridesmaid in a wedding recently. The bride picked out lovely peach bridesmaids' gowns. Unfortunately, the church was decorated in bright red—all her pictures looked like 'Night of the Clashing Circus Clowns!' It wasn't pretty."

Be careful when you select bridesmaids' gowns to take into account the decor of your ceremony site. Many of your wedding pictures will have the site as a backdrop. Try to pick a color that not only pleases you but also doesn't clash with the decor of your ceremony location.

❖ LARGE SIZE FEES.
"A couple of my bridesmaids need large sizes. The bridal shop told us they'd have to pay an additional fee of $40 per dress! What a rip-off!"

Even if they offer large sizes, bridesmaids designers usually ask a premium for this option. Anything above a size 16 typically incurs a surcharge. For example, Bill Levkoff charges an $8 fee for sizes 18 and 20, and $20 for sizes 38, 40 and 42. And those are the *wholesale* prices Levkoff charges retailers, who then turn around and double the charge to the consumer. The result is a fee that can run as high as $40 extra—that's an additional 15% to 25% on top of the dress price.

And the difference between a size 20 and a size 38 can be small. According to Levkoff's size chart, a size 18 fits a 43.5" bust.

If your bridesmaid's bust line is bigger than that figure, you're into the large sizes of 38, 40 or 42. (By the way, a size 38 has a 45.5" bust line measurement).

❖ DUPED BY DUPIONI

"My bridesmaids ordered five dresses made of dupioni silk.
What a disaster! The dresses looked like the girls had slept in them
and we couldn't iron those wrinkles out!"

Dupioni silk is one of those hip fabrics for bridesmaids dresses that doesn't always live up to its billing. While the sample dress you first try on may look fine, the actual dresses may have flaws like slubs, dark threads, wrinkles and more. Designers say these "flaws add to the character of the fabric and are part of its natural beauty." Nice try. We think the designers are trying to pass off low-quality silks on an unsuspecting public. You shouldn't pay that much money for dresses that look like they've been slept in. Our best advice is to ask the shop to see a recently arrived order of dresses from that manufacturer—that way you can see what you'll be getting. Or just avoid dupioni silk dresses altogether.

Picking the right size

The process of picking a bridesmaids dress size is similar to bridal gowns: the shop will take your bridesmaids' bust, waist and hip measurements, consult the sizing chart and then pick a size. There are a few quirks to bridesmaids dresses, however. Here's an overview of some things to look out for:

❦ *"Low hip measurements."* The return of slim styles has prompted some designers to ask for "low hip" measurements for bridesmaids. Alfred Angelo, for example, defines this measurement as seven inches below the waist.

❦ *Range sizing.* A few designers offer a range of measurements for each size. For example, Watters and Watters says their size 8 fits waist sizes 27.5" to 29.25". According to their size chart, the lowest number in a range allows for ease and comfort. The highest number in a range only allows a .25" ease, which most people find to be very uncomfortable. As always, seek out the advice of an experienced shop before making a sizing decision.

❦ *Fabric give.* In picking a size, don't forget that some fabrics don't give or allow free movement. Examples of these restricting fabrics include velvet and such silks as shantung and dupioni. Hence, if you are at the top of a size range and are using one of those fabrics, you may want to go with the next larger size.

❦ *High fashion can also restrict movement.* The use of such stylish features as fitted jackets and molded shoulders in bridesmaids dresses is quite hip, but remember these can restrict movement. Don't forget to factor this in when you pick sizes. Off-the-shoulder styles can also be tricky to size.

❦ *Skirt lengths may vary.* Each bridesmaids designer seems to have a different approach when it comes to the issue of skirt length. For example, ballerina-style dresses usually come in just one length. But floor length gowns may be available in extra length (usually 3" to 5") for taller bridesmaids.

Some designers show short lengths in their catalogs, but allow you to order the same style in a floor-length skirt (for an extra charge, of course). Other manufacturers will even offer extra length for tea-length skirts.

And to totally confuse you, the designer Dessy offers four different lengths for their gowns: short (38" from back of neck to hem), tea length (51"), full length (58.5") and even ankle length (54").

❦ *Garment versus body size charts.* As with bridal gown designers, bridesmaids manufacturers use either a "garment" or "body" size chart. A designer who uses a body measurement sizing chart makes gowns to correspond to the actual physical measurements of the bride. On the other hand, a *garment* sizing chart is just that—a measurement of the outside of the dress. We gave an example of how this works earlier in this book (in the introduction to the bridal gown designer reviews). As always, be sure to ask the bridal shop to clarify any sizing questions before the order is placed.

Reality Check

 Dye lots may vary. When you order three "plum" bridesmaids dresses, you probably don't want them to arrive in three different shades of purple. Yet, this apparently is a challenge with bridesmaids designers, who warn ominously that unless the orders are all placed at the same time, "dye lots may vary." Hence, you'll have to have all the bridesmaids deposits lined up at one time to avoid this problem. (And, as always, put those deposits on a credit card.)

Notes on the designer reviews

In the next section of this book, we'll review and rate the country's top bridesmaids designers. We divide these companies into three categories: primary, secondary and the "best of the rest." Primary designers are companies that solely produce bridesmaids dresses (such as Bill Levkoff, Dessy, and Watters & Watters).

Endangered species?
Bridesmaids designers are furiously working on their own demise

Are bridesmaids' dress manufacturers going the way of the typewriter and buggy whip? Ask real-life brides and bridesmaids their opinions about the styles, prices and quality of the dresses these companies churn out and you'll quickly realize why these companies may soon be pictured at a post office near you.

Sure, they're a joke and a permanent resident of the back of many closets, but the bridesmaids dress has more problems than just a lack of style. When we researched this section of our book, we were shocked at more than just a stunning lack of fashion sense among the country's top bridesmaids designers. Ridiculously high prices, cheap fabrics and flimsy construction haunt the industry. The upshot: many brides are abandoning the bridal shop and shopping department stores, catalogs and other "alternative" sources for the bridesmaids dress.

But don't shed a tear for the big bridesmaid manufacturers. In many ways, the companies have only themselves to blame for this mess. They steadily raised prices during the 1980's, in part to feed the ever-hungry advertising monster they themselves created. Meanwhile, "bridesmaids fashion" quickly became an oxymoron. With the exception of a few innovators in Dallas and Boston, the designers have been content to turn out a sea of look-alike gowns with shiny taffeta puff sleeves and huge butt bows.

Worst of all is the quality. We constantly hear stories of "special-order" dresses arriving in stores with mis-matched lace, zippers that don't work and seams that look like failed junior high sewing experiments. And those are the dresses that are in good shape.

Meanwhile, the prices for these works of art continue to skyrocket. Bridesmaids are now expected to shell out a minimum of $150 for a flimsy dress made from polyester. Many designs are now $200 and even $300 or more. You can't blame consumers for noticing the same amount of money will buy you a damn nice dress in a department store.

The bridal retail shops are often caught in the middle of this mess. It's the retailer that's often left to fix a dress with an unfinished sleeve or missing buttons. Customer service (from the manufacturer to the retailer) ranges from mediocre to abysmal. Many bridesmaids manufacturers not only ship defective merchandise but then steadfastly refuse to fix the problem when retailers complain. No wonder so many bridal retailers burn out after a few short years of dealing with the boys in New York.

When you read the reviews of bridesmaids manufacturers, you'll note that very few earned A's. Most were in the low B to high C range. And we graded on a curve for this exam. When we say a bridesmaids designer's dress quality was "average," you can bet we're using that word very loosely.

Can this industry be saved? Can bridesmaids manufacturers actually turn out a quality gown at a reasonable price? Stay tuned.

Secondary designers are regular bridal gown manufacturers who also have a bridesmaids line (such as Alfred Angelo, Bianchi and Mori Lee). You'll note that most of these reviews don't contain sizing charts. That's because most of the designers use the same chart for bridal gowns as bridesmaids dresses; refer to the designer's review earlier in the book for sizing information. (There are two exceptions: Galina and Jim Hjelm use different sizing charts, which are noted separately after their review.)

Finally, we have the "best of the rest," other designers who do bridesmaids that merit mention.

We rated the bridesmaids designers based on quality, delivery, value, fashion and sizing. And of course, when we use the word "quality" in the same sentence as the words "bridesmaid's dress," we are being quite generous.

PART FOUR

BRIDES-MAIDS DESIGNER REVIEWS

→ A L Y C E ←

Contact info. Alyce Designs, 7901 N. Caldwell, Morton Grove, IL 60053. For a dealer near you, call (847) 966-9200.

Internet. *http://www.alycedesigns.com/* is Alyce's official web site, although there is not much on-line yet. We did see a listing of authorized stores, but there's no on-line catalog. Other parts of the site (placing an order, checking available inventory) are apparently intended for retailers. Meanwhile, you can always check our web site (http://www.bridalgown.com) for updates on this designer.

Background/ Our view. Alyce offers your basic, bread-and-butter bridesmaids look. Based in the Midwest, this manufacturer churns out a very large collection of styles, with a plethora of empire waists, fitted and A-line silhouettes. While the overall fashion is good, the more updated styles contrasted with a few dresses with lace accents that looked just plain dated. The fabrics are mostly crepes, although a few silks, chiffons and velvets (for fall) were also in evidence.

While the quality of the gowns is average, Alyce gets better marks for its deliveries and reliability. The customer service is also very good.

What's Alyce's biggest downside? The prices are not a bargain. Alyce's gowns start at $110 and go up to $470 for a silk design. The average is about $200 and many of their silk dresses hover around $300, a bit pricey for the quality of construction, in our opinion.

We also didn't like the scatter-shot sizing that Alyce uses. While most dresses are available in sizes 2 to 24, quite a few styles are only made in more limited sizes. There seems to be no rhyme or reason as to why one style is available in sizes 2 to 24, another in just 4 to 16 and still a third in 6 to 24.

Since Alyce has many of those combo fabric styles (chiffon sleeves with a crepe bodice), make sure you see the dress you want in the desired color before ordering. **Rating: B**

Delivery. 14 to 16 weeks. Rush cuts are available for an extra $30 fee; some styles are available in stock for quicker delivery.

Tags. Alyce identifies its gowns with hang tags. Sometimes a label is also sewn inside the dress as well.

SIZING CHART

Type: Alyce uses a GARMENT measurement size chart. For more information on this subject, refer to the introduction of this section.

Sizes

	2	4	6	8	10	12	14	16	18	20	22	24
Bust	31"	32	33	34	35	36	37.5	39	41	43	45	47
Waist	23	24	25	26	27	28	29.5	31	33	35	37	39
Hips	35	36	37	38	39	40	41.5	43	45	47	49	51

Extra charges for changes/options:

1. For sizes 18 to 24 in styles without sequins, add $20 to the gown price.
2. For sizes 18 to 24 in styles with sequins, add $50 to the gown price.
3. For extra skirt length (three inches without sequins), add $20 to the gown price.
4. For extra skirt length (three inches with sequins), add $40 to the gown price.
5. For extra skirt length (more than three inches with sequins), add $50 the gown price.
6. No extra length is available on high-low hemlines styles.
7. For extra sleeve length (three inches extra without sequins), add $10 to the gown price.
8. For extra sleeve length (three inches extra with sequins), add $20 to the gown price.

✦ BARI JAY ✦

Contact info. Bari Jay, 1400 Broadway, 30th Floor, New York, NY 10018. For a dealer near you, call (212) 391-1555 or (212) 921-1551. Although Bari Jay doesn't offer a catalog for consumers, the designer typically takes out multi-page ads in *Modern Bride* magazine that show all their styles.

Internet. *http://sgi.computek.net/apparel/bridal/webpages/bari-jay/* is Bari Jay's official web site. It has an on-line catalog and store locator. Our web site (http://www.bridalgown.com) will also have updates on this designer.

Background/Our view. Bari Jay is a good example of what's wrong with the bridesmaids market today. Like many manufacturers in this category, the company churns out average dresses with average styling . . . at above average prices.

Don't expect to find anything overly innovative in this line, which has about 40 styles. The only slightly different feature is Bari Jay's skirts, which are somewhat fuller than other designers. Other than that, it's the same empire waist silhouettes in fabrics such as chiffon, satin and crepes that you'll see elsewhere. "Espresso" is among the better colors the designer offers.

The prices? Are you sitting down? Bari Jay's dresses range from $160 to $250; most gowns are about $200. And the quality? Bari Jay only gets fair ratings from bridal retailers.

While the company does offer dresses in sizes 4 to 20, only a selected number of styles are available in large sizes 38 to 42. Another note: there are no seam allowances in many of Bari Jay's dresses, which means you should choose the size very carefully. **Rating: C**

Delivery. 12 to 14 weeks. Some styles are in stock for quicker delivery.

Tags. Bari Jay uses hang tags to identify its gowns. Sometimes, a label is also sewn inside the dress.

Type: Bari Jay uses a GARMENT measurement size chart. For information on this subject, refer to the introduction of this section.

Standard Sizes

	3/4	5/6	7/8	9/10	11/12	13/14	15/16	17/18	19/20
Bust	33"	34	35	36	37	38.5	40	42	44
Waist	24	25	26	27	28	29.5	31	33	35
Hips	35	36	37	38	39	40.5	42	44	46

Large Sizes*

	38	40	42
Bust	44"	46	48
Waist	37	39	41
Hips	48	50	52

Sizing notes:
• *Large sizes 38 to 42 automatically have five inches of extra gown length. These dresses cannot be special-ordered without extra length.*

Extra charges for changes/options:
1. For sizes 18 and 20 in all fabrics except chiffon, add $16 to the gown price.
2. For sizes 18 and 20 in chiffon fabric, add $24 to the gown price.
3. *Only selected styles are available in large sizes 38 to 42.
4. For sizes 38 to 42 in all fabrics except chiffon, add $40 to the gown price.
5. For sizes 38 to 42 in chiffon fabric, add $60 to the gown price.
6. Extra length (five inches only) is available for an additional $16 for all fabrics except chiffon ($24 for dresses in chiffon).

✦BILL LEVKOFF✦

Contact info. Bill Levkoff, 1385 Broadway, 5th Floor, New York, NY 10018. For a dealer near you, call (800) LEVKOFF or (800) 538-5633 or (212) 221-0085. Bill Levkoff dresses are also available in Canada; call (514) 384-2451 for a dealer near you. Most of Bill Levkoff's dresses are featured in *For the Bride by Demetrios* and *Elegant Bride* magazines, available on newsstands nationwide.

Internet. *http://www.ramnetsys.com/apparel/bridal/webpages/lev-koff/index.html* is Levkoff's web site, comlete with an on-line catalog and store locator. Our web site (http://www.bridalgown.com) will also have updates on this designer.

Background/Our view. Bill Levkoff is certainly the "big fish" of bridesmaids manufacturers. Besides offering his own voluminous line, Levkoff owns (or has a significant ownership interest) in three other bridesmaids designers—Champagne, New Image, Watters & Watters. (Since each of these other lines operates more or less independently, we'll review each separately in this section.)

Levkoff is the market's style leader, splashing his gowns over numerous pages of ads in most major bridal magazines. With over 100 styles, you'll see lots of combo-fabric styles in this line . . . velvet and crepe, velvet and satin, etc. We were impressed with the wide variety of fabrications, from chiffon to brocades, velvets to tulle—everything, that is, except silk.

And it's the lack of silk fabric that makes the prices ($120 to $270) somewhat hard to swallow. Typical of Levkoff's offerings was a style that graced the cover of one of his catalogs last year: the three-piece cotton velvet tuxedo with floor length skirt featured a long-sleeve jacket and satin vest and label. The price: $264. Ouch.

While the style and fabrications are certainly market leaders, the quality of the dresses is another story. On this subject, Levkoff dresses garner merely fair ratings. While Levkoff's *samples* are beautifully tailored, the actual dresses shipped to bridesmaids can be all over the board. We've even heard of problems that occurred within an individual order, where one dress is fine, a second has unfinished seams and a third has a mismatched zipper. To be fair, these consistency problems plague many bridesmaids manufacturers, but we expect more from a market leader like Levkoff. If you plan to order one of these gowns, make sure you leave plenty of time to deal with any "surprises." **Rating: C+**

Delivery. 12 to 14 weeks. Rush cuts are available and certain styles are in stock for quicker delivery.

Tags. Bill Levkoff identifies its gowns only with a style number, noted inside and outside the dress.

SIZING CHART

Type: Levkoff uses a GARMENT measurement size chart. For information on this subject, refer to the introduction of this section.

	4	6	8	10	12	14	16	18	20
Bust	33"	34	35	36	37	38.5	40	41.5	43.5
Waist	24	25	26	27	28	29.5	31	32.5	34.5
Hips	36	37	38	39	40	41.5	43	44.5	46.5

	38	40	42
Bust	45.5	47.5	49.5
Waist	36.5	38.5	40.5
Hips	48.5	50.5	52.5

Extra charges for options/changes:

1. For sizes 18 and 20, add $16 to the gown price.
2. For sizes 38 to 42, add $40 to the gown price.
3. For extra gown length (5" for floor length or 3" for tea length) with sizes 4 to 20, add $16 to the gown price.
4. For extra gown length with sizes 38 to 42, add $20 to the gown price.

✦ C H A M P A G N E ✦

Contact info. Champagne Formals, 1385 Broadway, 5th Floor, New York, NY 10018. For a dealer near you, call (212) 302-9162.

Internet. *http://www.ramnetsys.com/apparel/bridal/webpages/champagne/index.html* features a Champange catalog and store locator. Our web site (http://www.bridalgown.com) will also have updates on this designer.

Background/Our view. Champagne is sort of like "Levkoff-lite:" same designs, less aftertaste. This division of Bill Levkoff offers many similar styles as their parent company, but at lower prices. A Champagne bridesmaids gown is likely to cost $120 to $165.

While Levkoff is a style leader, Champagne's fashion is all over the board. You've got your "traditional" bridesmaids look with high-low hem line, puff sleeves and shiny taffeta. You've also got some more contemporary looks like crepe designs with empire waists, halter-style tops and satin detailing.

On the other hand, there are some real losers in the Champagne line as well. When you see dresses in a fabric named "Glo-Brite" taffeta, well, you get the idea.

The quality of Champagne's gowns is slightly better than it's parent, Levkoff, although that isn't saying much. **Rating: B-**

Delivery. 14 to 18 weeks, although Champagne stocks a significant number of their styles for quicker delivery. Rush cuts are available for $40 extra, although rush cut availability varies depending on the time of the year.

Tags. Champagne identifies its gowns only with a style number, noted inside and outside the dress.

SIZING CHART

Type: Champagne uses a GARMENT measurement size chart. For information on this subject, refer to the introduction of this section.

	4	6	8	10	12	14	16	18	20
Bust	33"	34	35	36	37	38.5	40	41.5	43.5
Waist	24	25	26	27	28	29.5	31	32.5	34.5
Hips	36	37	38	39	40	41.5	43	44.5	46.5

	38	40	42
Bust	45.5	47.5	49.5
Waist	36.5	38.5	40.5
Hips	48.5	50.5	52.5

Extra charges for options/changes:

1. For sizes 18 and 20, add $16 to the gown price.
2. For sizes 38 to 42, add $40 to the gown price.
3. For extra gown length (5" for floor length or 3" for tea length) with sizes 4 to 20, add $16 to the gown price.
4. For extra gown length with sizes 38 to 42, add $20 to the gown price.

→ D E S S Y ←

Contact info. Dessy Creations, 1385 Broadway, 17th Floor, New York, NY 10018. For a free catalog, call (212) 354-5808. Call (800) 52-DESSY to be connected to a local dealer.

Internet. *http://www.dessy.com/* is Dessy's official web site. You can view some gowns on-line, check out wedding-related links and order a catalog to be mailed to you. As always, our web site (http://www.bridal-gown.com) will also have updates on this designer.

Background/Our view. You don't often hear the word "stylish" in the same sentence as "bridesmaid's designer," but this company is definitely the exception. Dessy has taken the best "ready-to-wear" looks to create some of the best styled bridesmaid's gowns on the market today.

"Glamorous" is how we'd describe many of these dresses; you'll see looks reminiscent of Audry Hepburn and others straight from the Oscars. Over 150 styles are available and Dessy's smart tailoring makes nearly every dress a winner.

The fabrics are unusual too. Besides standards like chiffon, satin and taffeta, you'll also see special fabrications like "crepe boucle," a soft fabric with a nubby texture. Color is another reason Dessy rises above the competition—metallic shades such as copper, slate and silver were standouts, plus several hips hues like pale green and "mocha."

Unfortunately, all this glamour doesn't come cheap. Dessy gowns start at $150 and can soar to $400. Most are about $200 to $250, a big chunk of change to ask any bridesmaid to spend.

And what about the quality? Well, while Dessy is well above average, it's still a notch or two below industry leaders Bianchi and Watters & Watters. Hence, you're paying big bucks for a good (but not great) gown.

On the upside, Dessy's delivery and reliability are excellent. We also like the fact that Dessy has a few "maternity styles" for pregnant bridesmaids, a first in the industry. Unfortunately, sizes are limited for everyone else (only 4 to 20, with no large sizes). **Rating: B+**

Delivery. 14 to 16 weeks. Rush cuts are available for $10 to $30 per dress, depending on the style and number of gowns ordered.

Tags. Dessy identifies its dresses with a sewn-in label.

SIZING CHART

Type: Dessy uses a BODY measurement size chart. For information on this subject, refer to the introduction of this section.

	4	6	8	10	12	14	16	18	20
Bust	34"	35	36	37	38.5	40	41.5	43.5	45.5
Waist	25	26	27	28	29.5	31	32.5	34.5	36.5
Hips*	36	37	38	39	40.5	42	43.5	45.5	47.5

Sizing notes:
• **The measurement for hips should be taken 8" below the natural waist.*
• *Gown length (as measured from the back of the neck to the dress hem) is 58.5" for full-length dresses, 54" for ankle-length dresses, 51" for tea-length dresses or 38" for short-length dresses.*
• *Maternity styles are available in XS (4/6), S (8/10), M (12/14), and L (16/18); consult a local dealer for more sizing information on these styles.*

Extra charges for options/changes:
1. For dresses in sizes 18 to 20, add $30 to the gown price.
2. For separates in sizes 18 to 20, add $20 to the gown price.
3. Extra gown length (five inches) is available only on floor-length dresses; add $20 for this option.

⇢ J O R D A N ⇠

Contact info. Jordan Fashions, 1385 Broadway, 20th Floor, New York, NY 10018. For a dealer near you, call (212) 921-5560.

Internet. This designer does not have an official web site. Our web site (http://www.bridalgown.com) will have updates on this designer.

Background/Our view. Jordan consistently ranks at the top of industry surveys that track top-selling bridesmaids. While it doesn't have the numerous divisions and sub-lines like its competitor Levkoff, Jordan offers a huge collection of gowns. In one season alone last year, the company rolled out nearly 40 new designs. All together, Jordan offers bridesmaids about 100 different styles.

"Conservative" is how we'd describe Jordan's fashion. While the company has tried to update its styling, the majority of the line still consists of the "traditional" bridesmaids dress (tea length, puff sleeves, shiny taffeta fabric, etc.). New this year is a faux silk fabric called "sylk" (isn't that creative?), although most of the dresses are in the old stand-bys of satin, crepe, velvet and polyester shantung.

Price is Jordan's strong point. Dresses range from $128 to $282, although most are in the $180 to $200 range. While that doesn't rank as an incredible bargain, the dresses aren't overpriced either.

The quality of Jordan's dresses is also in the middle of the pack. While not as bad some of the industry's laggards, Jordan's dresses can't compare with the gowns from the market's top designers. But, then again, Jordan isn't charging top-dollar prices either.

On the upside, Jordan's customer service and deliveries get above average marks from bridal retailers. The company offers "jet service" (quick delivery) on a half dozen styles for an extra charge.

Rating: B

Delivery. 10 to 12 weeks. Jordan offers "jet service," a selected number of styles in stock for quicker delivery.

Tags. Jordan identifies its gowns with hang tags and sewn-in labels.

SIZING CHART

Type: Jordan uses a GARMENT measurement size chart. For information on this subject, refer to the introduction of the designer review section of this book.

	3/4	5/6	7/8	9/10	11/12	13/14	15/16	18	20
Bust	33"	34	35	36	37	38.5	40	41.5	43.5
Waist	24	25	26	27	28	29.5	31	32.5	34.5
Hips*	36	37	38	39	40	41.5	43	44.5	46.5
LWB**	15.75	16	16.25	16.5	16.75	17	17.25	17.5	17.75

	38	40	42
Bust	46.5	48.5	50.5
Waist	37.5	39.5	41.5
Hips*	49.5	51.5	53.5
LWB**	18	18.25	18.5

Sizing notes:
• **Hip measurement is defined as 9" below the natural waist.*
• ***LWB (long waist back) is measured from the back of the neck to the natural waist.*
• *Gown length as measured from hollow of the neck to the desired dress hem is 50" for tea length or 59" for floor length.*

Extra charges for options/changes:
1. For sizes 18 and 20, add $16 to the gown price.
2. For sizes 38, 40 and 42, add $40 to the gown price.
These sizes are cut with extra length; consult a local retailer for more information.
3. Extra gown length (five inches) is available for $16 extra.
A tea length dress can be lengthened to floor length for $16 extra.

⇢ LORALIE ⇠

Contact info. Loralie Originals, 4350 Caterpillar Rd., Redding, CA 96003. For a dealer near you, call (800) 468-7464 or (916) 244-2351.

Internet. *http://www.loralie.com/index.html* is Loralie's web site, but there isn't much to look at yet. You can request a free catalog, though. Our web site (http://www.bridalgown.com) will also have updates on this designer.

Background/Our view. With 150+ styles, Loralie has one of the largest selections of bridesmaids gowns on the market today. Unfortunately, the company is still in the Dark Ages as far as its styling goes. Loralie offers an abundance of high-low hemlines, big puffy sleeves and shiny taffeta. Other accents are overdone, with too much lace here or too much beading there.

Of course, with a collection as large as Loralie's, there are some winners too. We liked the a-lines and tank-style necklines and a few empire waists are sprinkled in for variety. The designer is big on pastel colors as well as evergreens and plum hues. One unusual option: Loralie is one of the few bridesmaids designers left who offers floral prints. This Laura Ashley-type look might be a good choice for an outdoor/garden wedding ceremony.

It's hard to beat Loralie's prices, which start at $96 and average about $150. This is about what we'd expect for man-made fabrics like polyester taffeta, crepe and brocades. On the upper end, Loralie's "Social Occasions" line features more sophisticated styles that echo cocktail fashions (more beading and lace). These gowns run $200 to $350. Another interesting point: the company also offers quite a few informal bridal gowns (styles without trains) for $300 to $360, a pretty good deal.

Loralie gets average to above average marks on quality, in our opinion. The designer's delivery and reliability are excellent. Loralie offers quite a few "Quick Maid" styles that ship in just two weeks. **Rating: B**

Delivery. 8 weeks is the average, but Loralie offers 30+ "Quick Maids" styles that can be shipped in two weeks for no additional charge. Rush cuts are also available on other styles (for an extra fee).

Tags. Loralie identifies its dresses with hang tags. The style number is also noted inside the gown.

SIZING CHART

Type: Loralie uses a GARMENT measurement size chart. For information on this subject, refer to the introduction of the designer review section of this book.

	4	6	8	10	12	14	16	18	20
Bust	33"	34	35	36	38	40	42	44	46
Waist	25	26	27	28	30	32	34	36	38
Hips	36	37	38	39	41	43	45	47	49

	22	24	26
Bust	49	52	55
Waist	41	44	47
Hips	52	55	58

Sizing notes:
• *Gown length (as measured from waist to desired dress hem) is 44"
for floor-length styles, 36" to 40" for tea-length styles, 22" to 24" for
short-length styles. The gown length for "Social Occasions" dresses
is 25" for short-length styles or 44" for floor-length styles.*

Extra charges for options/changes:
1. For sizes 18 to 26, add $30 to the gown price.
2. For extra length, add $30 to the gown price.

✦ NEW IMAGE ✦

Contact info. New Image, 1385 Broadway, 5th Floor, New York, NY
10018. For a dealer near you, call (800) 421-IMAGE or (212) 764-
0477. New Image dresses are also available in Canada; call (514) 384-
2451 for a dealer near you.

Internet. New Image's web site *http://www.ramnetsys.com/apparel/
bridal/webpages/newimage/index.html* includes an on-line catalog and
store locator. As always, our web site (http://www.bridalgown.com)
will also have updates on this designer.

Background/Our view. New Image is another one of those Bill
Levkoff-owned bridesmaids lines that offers stylish designs at prices that
aren't much of a bargain. We saw many styles in this catalog that were
similar to Levkoff's offerings: a-lines and empire waists, many with simple accents like lycra netting on the sleeves or a small bow treatment.
   In a way, New Image is an edited version of Levkoff's line, with
about 50 styles to choose from. Available fabric choices range from
crepes to cottons, velvets to satins.
   If the fashion and fabrics are similar to Levkoff, what makes
New Image different? Quality, for one. For some reason, the construction and finish of these dresses is a couple of notches above
Levkoff (perhaps they have different contractors).
   And it's a good thing the quality is better, because (like Levkoff)
a gown from New Image isn't cheap. Prices for New Image dresses
range from $170 to $250, still quite pricey in our opinion. **Rating: B-**

Delivery. 12 to 14 weeks. Rush cuts are available (for $40 extra) and
certain styles are in stock for quicker delivery.

Tags. New Image identifies its gowns only with a style number, noted inside and outside the dress.

SIZING CHART

Type: New Image uses a GARMENT measurement size chart. For information on this subject, refer to the introduction of this section.

	4	6	8	10	12	14	16	18	20
Bust	33"	34	35	36	37	38.5	40	41.5	43.5
Waist	24	25	26	27	28	29.5	31	32.5	34.5
Hips	36	37	38	39	40	41.5	43	44.5	46.5

	38	40	42
Bust	45.5	47.5	49.5
Waist	36.5	38.5	40.5
Hips	48.5	50.5	52.5

Extra charges for options/changes:
1. For sizes 18 and 20, add $16 to the gown price.
2. For sizes 38 to 42, add $30 to the gown price.
3. For extra gown length with sizes 4 to 20, add $16 to the gown price.
4. For extra gown length with sizes 38 to 42, add $30 to the gown price.

→WATTERS & WATTERS←

Contact info. Watters & Watters Inc., 4320 Spring Valley, Dallas, TX 75244. For a dealer near you or a free catalog, call (972) 991-6994.

Internet. You can view their gowns on-line, check out the location of local dealers and read about the background of this designer on their web page *http://www.rammetsys.com/apparel/bridal/webpages/watters/index.html.* Of course, our web site (http://www.bridalgown.com) will also have updates on this designer.

Background/Our view. It took two sisters from Thailand, Archariya and Batana Watters to turn the bridesmaids market on its ear in the 1980's. This Dallas-based duo had a radical concept back in 1986—hey, why not make a bridesmaids dress that looks like a real gown? Their company, Watters & Watters (WW), chucked the giant puff sleeves and shiny taffeta so prevalent in the bridesmaids market for elegant designs in luxurious fabrics.

The results were a smash hit and soon WW became one of the hottest-selling bridesmaids designers. This didn't escape notice from the big boys in New York, who quickly adopted an "if you can't beat 'em, join 'em" approach to the upstart. Many other designers copied WW's two-piece looks and one designer (Bill Levkoff) even invested in the company. Although Levkoff owns a partial interest in WW, the company is still run as a semi-autonomous division in Texas. Levkoff has helped the company expand its distribution; over 1500 shops in the U.S., Canada and Europe now carry WW designs.

While the rest of the bridesmaids market has slowly caught up to them in terms of fashion, WW is still a style leader. The company's innovative use of color and fabrics sets the tone for other designers in this category. An example? Try an ivory, beaded silk-chiffon jacket with long sleeves and silk chiffon pants. Don't like the pantsuit look? The same style is also available with a silk chiffon skirt.

It's flexibility like this that explains WW's popularity. Many styles are available in separates that let you mix and match certain styles (jackets, blouses, pants and skirts). You can also swap the fabric on certain styles.

The designer's current fashion ranges from a ball gown that looks like something Grace Kelly wore, to empire waistlines with velvet bodices and satin skirts. Subtle touches like small bows or cummerbunds accent, but never overpower, the dresses. We also liked the colors from WW. You'll see beautiful pastels like "latte" and "sea foam" (a pale mint green), along with more innovate hues like "passion" (a rosey red) and "rum pink" (a creamy pink). Bright colors like cobalt blue are also stand-outs.

Silk is a common fabric and you'll find it in several finishes, including dupioni, chiffon and more. WW also has iridescent organzas, velvets and satins.

What's the catch, you say? Well, unfortunately, all this high-style and quality fabrics comes at a high price. While WW's dresses start at $126, most average between $200 and $250. A few styles can even cost $500. On the other hand, you are actually getting a high-quality garment for your money. A dress from WW is a real gown, not some flimsy costume.

Besides price, another drawback with this line is sizing. The designers only offers sizes up to a 24. And while the company deserves an A for style and quality, we'd have to give their customer service a failing grade. Sure, mistakes can (and do) happen with many dress manufacturers, but we're concerned about the reports we hear about WW's customer service. Industry observers say the company fails to fix problems (albeit rare in occurrence) promptly, often hassling the bridal shop in the process.

As a result, we recommend leaving extra time when ordering a WW dress. Even though the company quotes a standard eight week turnaround time, we'd recommend ordering these dresses 12 to 16 weeks in advance—that way, if a problem develops, there is enough time to deal with any unforeseen delays. **Rating: A-**

Delivery. 8 weeks. Rush cuts are available (for an extra $40 fee) and a few styles are in stock for quicker delivery.

Tags. Watters & Watters identifies their gowns with hang tags.

SIZING CHART

Type: Watters & Watters uses a BODY measurement size chart. For information on this subject, refer to the introduction of this section.

The following sizing chart uses a range of measurements for each size. According to Watters & Watters size information, the lowest number in the range allows for ease and comfort. The highest number in the range only allows a .25" ease, which most people find to be very uncomfortable.

You should consider the type of fabric and dress style when making a final sizing decision. Most Watters & Watters fabrics, especially dupioni silk, shantung and velvet do not give or allow for free movement. Many dresses with jackets, molded shoulders, off-the-necklines also restrict movement. Consult a local retailer for more advice on sizing decisions.

	2	4	6	8
Bust	32.5-33.75"	34-35.25	35-36.25	36-37.25
Waist	24-25.75	25.5-27.25	26.5-28.25	27.5-29.25
Hips	34.5-35.75	36-37.25	37-38.25	38-39.25

	10	12	14	16
Bust	37-38.25	38.5-39.75	40-41.25	41.5-43.75
Waist	28.5-30.25	30-31.75	31.5-33.25	33-35.75
Hips	39-40.25	40.5-41.75	42-43.25	43.5-44.75

	18	20	22	24
Bust	43.5-45.75	45.5-47.75	47.5-49.75	49.5-51.75
Waist	35-37.75	37-39.75	39-41.75	41-43.75
Hips	45.5-46.75	47.5-48.75	49.5-50.75	51.5-52.75

Sizing notes:
• Gown length (as measured from waist to desired dress hem) is 42" for floor-length skirts. For ballerina-length skirts, the gown length is 37".

Extra charges options/changes:
1. For sizes 18 and 20, add $20 to the gown price.
2. For sizes 22 and 24, add $50 to the gown price.
3. Extra skirt length (five inches) is $14 extra.

✦MORE BRIDESMAIDS REVIEWS✦

Manufacturers who make both bridal and bridesmaids lines

The following designers manufacture both brides and bridesmaids dresses. Except where noted, the designers use the same sizing chart for both types of gowns. For contact info and other details, refer to the designer's main review in the bridal gown section of this book.

❖ **Alfred Angelo** Like their bridal gowns, Alfred Angelo's bridesmaids dresses have never been on the cutting-edge of fashion. Yet, we have to give them bonus points for trying—many of the new fashions reflect an updated look with empire waists and A-line silhouettes. The value of the dresses, on the other hand, could use some work. Prices start at $86 and most gowns average $150 to $200. Hard to believe, but a few Alfred Angelo bridesmaids even top $300. And what about the quality? Well, a couple of years ago Alfred Angelo required its dealers to sign agreements saying they wouldn't rent their dresses. Why? They said the bridesmaids dresses aren't designed for more than one wearing. We couldn't have said it better ourselves.
Rating: C+

Sizing notes: Only selected styles are available in large sizes. For sizes 18 and 20, add $10. For sizes 38 to 44, add $30. Extra skirt length (on sizes 4 to 20 only) is $16.

❖ **Bianchi** Finally, a designer who makes stylish bridesmaids gowns that don't cost $300 or $400. Boston-based Bianchi sets the style for other designers with their fitted silhouettes, A-lines and other current fashions. We loved the pearl button accents, two-tone designs, and delicate fabric roses. About 50 styles are available, with prices ranging from $154 to $278. Okay, that isn't cheap, but the quality of these gowns is excellent, as is Bianchi's delivery and reliability. **Rating: A**

❖ **Bridal Originals** Yes, the fashion is bland, but the prices are easier to swallow. Basically, what you get from Bridal Originals is an Alfred Angelo-like dress for less money. The designers 50+ styles range from $100 to $200, although most are about $150. You'll see many of the old standbys of bridesmaids fashion (high-low hemlines, shiny taffeta). The colors are nothing special, but at least the designer offers a wide variety of hues. If you're in a hurry, Bridal Originals has several "express" styles available for quick delivery. The quality, customer service and reliability of this designer are only average. **Rating: C+**

Sizing notes: Most styles are available in sizes 4 to 30. Sizes 18 and 20 are $10 extra. Sizes 22 to 30 are $30 extra. Additional skirt length is $20 extra.

❖ **Eve of Milady** Eve's bridesmaids (which go under the name Cryselle) are rarely advertised, but you're not missing much. Despite the designer's reputation for innovative styling in bridal gowns, the bridesmaids look like an afterthought. A typical dress featured a sleeveless bodice, sweetheart neckline, fitted skirt. Other styles in chiffon featured more flowing skirts and shirred bodices accented with fabric roses. The quality and customer service from this designer is merely average. The prices are $180 to $240. **Rating: C**

Sizing notes: For sizes 18 and 20, add $20. Extra length (5" only) is $30 additional.

❖ *Galina* This designer has recently re-introduced its bridesmaids line after a several year hiatus. The very limited collection (about two dozen choices) range from $170 to $220. We liked the selection of colors, which included a silvery "platinum" among other hues. The styling is definitely current, with a mix of sleeveless sheaths and empire waist silhouettes. What about the quality? Well, the line is too new to get an accurate reading, but given Galina's good reputation for construction and finish, we assume they are a safe bet. Delivery is little slow, taking 12 weeks on average. Rush cuts are offered "upon availability" for $50 extra. **Rating: B**

SIZING CHART

(Galina Bridesmaids only)

Type: Galina uses a BODY measurement size chart. For information on this subject, refer to the introduction of the designer review section of this book.

	2	4	6	8	10	12	14	16
Bust	32"	33	34	35	36	37.5	39	40.5
Waist	22	23	24	25	26	27.5	29	30.5
Hips	35	36	37	38	39	40.5	42	43.5

	18xs	20xs	22xs	24xs
Bust	42	44	46	48
Waist	32	34	36	38
Hips	45	47	49	51

Sizing notes:
• *Gown length is 58" as measured from the hollow of the neck to the desired dress hem.*

Extra charges for changes/options:
1. For sizes 18 and 20, add $30 to the gown price.
2. For sizes 22 and 24, add $40 to the gown price.
3. For extra gown length (5" only), add $20 to the gown price.

❖ *Jasmine "Belsoie".* The splashiest and most talked about new entrant in the bridesmaids sweepstakes is Jasmine, which debuted its all-silk "Belsoie" line of bridesmaids dresses in 1997. What makes the line unique is its emphasis on "separates"—each style starts with a basic bodice. Then you can choose from one of three or four skirt styles in various fabrics or, in some cases, silhouettes (slim versus full skirt). The result is an amazing array of options that allows you to customize your bridesmaids look without paying the custom price. In addition to separates, the line also has complete dresses. Belsoie's 24 basic dress styles range from $178 to $296—that's not bad for an all-silk line. The detailing (lattice work beading on one bodice, alencon lace and a bolero jacket on another) is quite impressive too. The looks are similar to Watters and Watters but at a price that's 20% to 40% less. So, how's the quality? Well, since the line is brand new, we don't have any quality reports yet. However, Jasmine has an above average reputation for its bridal gowns and we assume the company won't drop the ball on its bridesmaids. The biggest question for Jasmine's Belsoie bridesmaids is their production and delivery—this is the first major bridesmaids line to be made in China. Most other companies do bridesmaids production domestically to ensure quicker delivery. Whether Jasmine is able to pull off Chinese production of an all-silk bridesmaids line and get the orders to the stores on time is an open question. Stay tuned. **Rating: A-**

❖ *Jessica McClintock* Yes, McClintock's bridesmaids dresses are traditional, but at least they aren't as cheesy-looking as others on the market today. San Francisco-based McClintock produces more tea length dresses than many other designers, although you'll see plenty of floor-length ball gowns and sheaths too. One stand-out was a teal design in dupioni silk, although we thought the many black velvet options were quite chic as well. The prices ($100 to $240, with an average of $160) are a little high compared to the competition, although at least the delivery is quick. Jessica McClintock's bridesmaids have above-average quality, although the company's customer service could stand some improvement. "It sucks," said one retailer of McClintock's customer service, while another bride complained to us that her botched bridesmaids dress order took far too long to remedy. So, it's a mixed review for McClintock—nice styling, decent prices, above-average quality but not-so-great customer service. **Rating: B-**

❖ *Jim Hjelm* Occasions is the name for Jim Hjelm's bridesmaids line and style-wise, it's a definite winner. We loved the colors (mocha, cognac, ice blue are the better hues) and the combo-fabric looks are spectacular. One standout was a floor-length, velvet halter-style sheath with removable satin overskirt. Yowsa! Hjelm's other designs have little jackets and tuxedo vests; heck, there's even one with a matching stole. So, how much is this going to cost you? Prices are $180 to $250; no bargain but not an outrageous overcharge either. While we loved the styling and think the prices are at least in the ballpark, the quality and deliveries of Hjelm's bridesmaids is another story. Quite frankly, the designer has struggled with timely deliveries of its bridesmaids line. While the quality is OK, we've heard of late-arriving dresses and other production problems. Hjelm quotes a 10 to 12 week "average" delivery time for bridesmaids, but we'd suggest padding that by a few weeks if you decide to order. Since the designer has a good reputation for bridal gowns, we can only hope they can work out the kinks in the bridesmaids operation. **Rating: B-**

SIZING CHART

(for Jim Hjelm's Occasions bridesmaids line only)

Type: Jim Hjelm uses a BODY measurement size chart. For information on this subject, refer to the introduction of the designer review section of this book.

The following sizing chart uses a range of measurements for each size. The lower number will provide the maximum level of comfort, while the higher number will only provide a minimum amount of ease.

	2	4	6	8	10	12
Bust	32-33.5	33-34.5	34-35.5	35-36.5	36-37.5	37.5-39
Waist	23-24.5	24-25.5	25-26.5	26-27.5	27-28.5	28.5-30
Hips	34-35.5	35-36.5	36-37.5	37-38.5	38-39.5	39.5-41
Length	57.25	57.5	57.75	58	58.25	58.5

	14	16	18	20	22	24
Bust	39-40.5	40.5-42	42-43.5	44-45.5	46-47.5	48-49.5
Waist	30-31.5	31.5-33	33-34.5	35-36.5	37-38.5	39-40.5
Hips	41-42.5	42.5-44	44-45.5	46-47.5	48-49.5	50-51.5
Length	58.75	60	60.25	60.5	60.75	61

Sizing notes:
• *"Length" is measured from the hollow of the neck to the desired dress hem.*
• *Standard sleeve length is 18".*

Extra charges for options/changes:
1. For sizes 18 and 20, add $30 to the gown price.
2. For sizes 22 and 24, add $40 to the gown price.
3. For extra skirt length, add $20 to the gown price.

❖ *Mori Lee* Like their bridal gowns, Mori Lee's bridesmaids dresses are known more for their low prices than innovative styling. Basically, Mori Lee just copies the best-selling designs from other manufacturers. The silhouettes, fabrics and colors are what you'll see elsewhere. The prices, on the other hand, are an innovation—most sell for just $100 to $150. That's 20% to 40% less than what competitors charge. And Mori Lee doesn't sacrifice quality in its drive for lower prices: most of these gowns are actually above average in construction and finish. In an earlier book, we complained about Mori Lee's slow deliveries for these dresses. Well, we're happy to report the designer has fixed this problem. Mori Lee changed production facilities for its bridesmaids and now we hear deliveries and customer service is excellent. **Rating: A-**

Sizing notes: All styles are available in sizes 6 to 42 (sorry, no size 4's.) For sizes 18 and 20, add $10 to the dress price. Size 42 is an extra $24.

❖ *Vera Wang* Who takes the award for the most overpriced bridesmaids dresses available today? Why it's Vera Wang, the ice skating-outfit-designer-turned-bridal-mogul. Her bridesmaids look similar to those offered from designers, but wait! Check out those price tags—a Wang bridesmaid will cost you $278 to $410! Boy, won't your bridesmaid be happy to know you've picked out a gown that costs three times more than it should? And what do you get for those big bucks? Satin, tulle, crepe—just like every other dress on the market. The styles are nothing special either: some are big skirts and satin tank tops, while others are slim, fitted silhouettes. Most dresses are in "lollipop" colors like lilac, mint, coral or ivory with black accents, but it's hard to tell that from Vera Wang's ads. For some reason only known to her, the ads are done in black and white. And we hope your bridesmaids don't wear any size larger than a 14—Wang piles on an extra charge of $40 to $80 for sizes 16 to 20. Please. **Rating: C-**

SIZING CHART

(for Vera Wang's bridesmaids only)

	4	6	8	10	12	14	16	18	20
Bust	33	34	35	36	37.5	39	40.5	42	44
Waist	24	25	26	27	28.5	30	31.5	33	35
Hips	36	37	38	39	40.5	42	43.5	45	47

Sizing notes:
Gown length (hollow to hem) is 59".

Extra charges for options/changes:
• Size 16 is $40 extra.
• Size 18 is $60 extra.
• Size 20 is $80 extra.
• Extra length $30.
• Extra fabric is $44 a yard.

→THE BEST *of* THE REST←

Quick reviews of other bridesmaid dress designers of note

❖ **Currie Bonner** *Call (800) 409-9997 or (404) 231-5441 for more information.* With three retail stores (in Atlanta, Charlotte, and Dallas), Currie Bonner is a custom-manufacturer of bridesmaids' dresses. A wide assortment of fabrics are available, from the ordinary (taffeta and satin) to the exotic (linen, velvet and shantung). Styles are quite impressive, including some drop-waisted designs, several dresses with ruffles and others with full skirts and fitted bodices. What if you don't live near those cities listed above? Well, you can order from their mail-order catalog (call 1-800-409-9997 for a copy) which features a sampling of their bridesmaids dresses. Prices, which vary depending on the fabric and style chosen, range from $135 for the simplest plain taffeta design to $300 for a silk gown. **Rating: B**

❖ **Jim Holmes** *For a dealer near you, call 213-653-4124.* Who's the hottest new bridesmaid designer in 1997? The answer is Jim Holmes, a Los Angeles-based dress maker who's designs had the bridal market buzzing last year. As a designer, Holmes certainly has a strong resume: 12 years in ready-to-wear dress design and stints as an assistant to Arnold Scaasi, Carole Little and legendary bridal designer Frank Masandrea. In 1992, Holmes joined Lanz, a dress manufacturer famous for their floral print dress line (and nightgowns). Holmes was the creative force for Lanz's brief foray into bridesmaids gowns, which were popular with brides but a money-loser for the company. After Lanz decided to abandon the bridal business in 1994, Holmes struck out on his own with bridesmaids dresses, which he describes as "classic, yet unusual with personality and a touch of whimsy." The colors are fantastic: mixed pastels and plaids as well as vibrant corals and buttercups. Some of the gowns echo the English garden-style that Laura Ashley made famous. Most of the 25 styles are what you'd call "party dresses," and definitely don't look like standard bridesmaids gowns. So, how much do they cost? Well, they aren't cheap. At prices ranging from $240 to $460, you might have to revive your bridesmaids when they ask about the price. Yet, these are real dresses—fully lined, made from silk and other luxury fabrics (crepe, chiffon, linen). And, yes, you can really wear these styles again. Delivery is 12 weeks and only sizes 4 to 16 are available. As a side note, Holmes told us he plans to open his own retail store in Los Angeles near the Beverly Center in 1997. **Rating: A**

❖ **Liz Claiborne's Liz Night** *To find a dealer near you, call (212) 626-1804.* After tip-toeing into the bridesmaid dress market in 1995, Liz Claiborne seems more committed to making an impact this year. First, the company lowered prices—instead of gowns that sell for $200, most Liz Night dresses sell for about $140 (with a range from $136 to $218). When it comes to styling, Claiborne's "wear again" sensibility is a breath of fresh air. Most gowns are fitted and floor-length, although a couple of styles featured short or tea-length skirts.

The colors were pleasant (blueberry, raisin, corn silk and kiwi) and a few designs were two-tone (black and ecru, or black and rose). Liz Night's fabrics include chiffon, satin-backed crepes and duchess satin for spring, velvet with crepe and chiffon for fall. While there's a buzz among brides about this line, bridal retail shops may be hesitant to take on Claiborne until they straighten out customer service issues. At a recent bridal market, a company representative acknowledged production and delivery glitches last year and vowed to fix them for 1997. We'll wait and see. **Rating: B+**

❖ *Marlene* *For a dealer near you, call (800) 826-2563 or (412) 243-7560.* One of our favorite moments in the bridal business is when a manufacturer from Nowhere, USA shows up the big boys in New York City. Such is the case with Marlene, a bridesmaids gown maker based in the tiny burg of Charlotte, Michigan. Why is Marlene, in business since 1991, so successful? Well, first, check out the prices. Most dresses are $120 to $200. That's not bad, especially when you consider that Marlene offers impressive customization options. You can swap fabrics (12 choices), choose from different trims (bows, roses, rhinestones or nothing) and then select from various bodices and skirt styles. The result is a custom look at a price that won't break the bank. And how long does this take? Would you believe just two to four weeks? No kidding—Marlene does all this custom work in half the time that those New York designers take to turn out one of those taffeta nightmares that isn't customized. The quality is also high, according to a survey of bridal shops. The only downside is that Marlene's distribution is somewhat limited to shops in the Midwest and Mid-Atlantic part of the U.S. If you can find them, we'd recommend giving Marlene a try. **Rating: A**

❖ *Victor Costa* *For a dealer near you, call (800) 646-2840 or (212) 302-2540.* Victor Costa is the Dallas designer who was famous in the 1980's for his lavish copies of couture designer dresses. His bridesmaids collection (manufactured by Nahdree) isn't cheap ($250 to $400), but you've got to admit the style is definitely, well, unique. While the rest of the bridesmaids market is doing simple looks with A-line bodices, Victor is way out in left field. An example: a satin lilac dress with butterfly back and cascading tulle. It's a sumptuous look that you'll either love or hate. Another stand-out was a dress on the cover of their recent catalog: a "shocking pink" (their words, not ours), tight-fitting, off-the-shoulder bustier look with giant pouf tulle skirt where you could hide several small children. Most Victor Costa bridesmaids dresses feature accents like bows with giant buckles, stoles and bolero jackets. Sizes 4 to 20 are available. **Rating: B+**

❖ *Zilka* *For a dealer near you, call (518) 583-0889.* Saratoga, New York-based designer Carla Zilka creates dresses for the "upscale" bridesmaids market. The sophisticated gowns are made from a variety of fabrics, including crepe-backed satin, cotton velvet, silk, chiffon and charmeuse. Zilka's is one of the few bridesmaids designers doing short skirt lengths and also offers a line of matching hats and gloves for a complete look. Retail prices range from $100 to $290 and Zilka even has a few informal bridal gowns for $350 to $400. The quality of construction is good, even though delivery can be a little long (12 weeks is the official quote). Sizes 2 to 20 are available and there's an extra charge for sizes 18 and 20. Zilka's dresses are advertised in *Martha Stewert's Wedding* magazine. **Rating: B**

PART FIVE

CANADA'S TOP BRIDAL DESIGNERS

Gown Buying Advice for Canadian Brides

It has come to our attention that the Canadian bridal market is controlled by woman who wear no clothes.

We came to this conclusion after noticing that one of Canada's largest bridal gown manufacturers is a company named, "Gordon." This, of course, is also the name of the first CD from those wacky Canucks, the Barenaked Ladies. Coincidence? We think not. It's obvious. that the Barenaked Ladies, in addition to being the best rock band in the universe, must secretly control the entire Canadian bridal market. Alert Yoko Ono.

But, perhaps we're mistaken.

Seriously, folks, here's a quick overview to buying a wedding gown in Canada

What does the average Canadian bride spend on a wedding dress?

The average bridal gown in Canada sells for $700 to $1000 Canadian. When you factor in the exchange rate, that works out to about $500 to $700 U.S. That's about the same as (or a little less than) brides spend in the U.S., give or take a $100.

How does that compare to total wedding expenses? In Canada, the average wedding is about $10,500, so the bridal gown is about 10% of total expenses. That's somewhat higher than the U.S., where the dress accounts for about 5% of marriage expenses. What's the difference? According to surveys we've read, the average Canadian couple invites about 125 guests to the wedding—that's much less than the 175 guests invited to U.S. weddings. We must conclude that this means Canadians have much fewer friends than U.S. brides and we strongly suggest a change in bathing habits may be in order.

Just kidding! Actually, this disparity probably indicates that Canadian brides and grooms are much more sane than their U.S. counterparts. Instead of inviting fourth cousins and all their co-workers from work, Canadian brides probably invite people they actually like and this cuts down on that guest list dramatically.

In other ways, the Canadian bridal market is similar to the U.S. The average engagement is 10.7 months (about the same as the U.S.) and over half of the couples are paying for their wedding themselves. The average age of Canadian brides and grooms could have something to do with that statistic: the bride is typically 29, the groom 30.

Of course, there are important differences. The number of weddings in Canada each year is about 159,000. That contrasts to the U.S., where 2.4 million weddings occur annually. As a result, Canadian's bridal "industry" is not as developed as the U.S.—and that's both good and bad news. On the upside, the less-lucrative nature of the Canadian market means scam artists are more likely to concentrate their efforts in the U.S., not Canada. On the other hand, the smaller number of brides translates into a smaller number of bridal dress shops. And less competition usually means higher prices and less selection.

 ### Money-saving tips
Yes, the average bridal gown in Canada costs a cool $1000. Is that too much money? Here are five tips to save money:

1 **Go mail order.** Discount Bridal Service, the mail-order discounter we mentioned earlier in this book, services Canada. While the company doesn't have reps on-site in Canada, you can order a dress by calling their Arizona office at (800) 874-8794 or (602) 998-6953.

How much can you save? Well, Discount Bridal Service sells all those name-brand designer bridal gowns, bridesmaids dresses and accessories you see in the bridal magazines. The discount is typically 20% to 40% off the retail price. The only downside? You have to pay shipping, duties and GST, which might make some of the savings disappear. On the other hand, DBS sells many designers that are not even distributed in Canada. Hence, if you see a dress during a shopping excursion to the U.S. and you can't live without that gown, DBS may be the answer.

2 **Check out the Sposabella outlet.** The U.S. designer Demetrios (see review earlier in this book) has quietly opened a "sale outlet" in Quebec City (418) 622-3262. That store sells gowns at discounts up to 70% (only sizes 10 to 20 are available). Elsewhere in Canada, Demetrios has full-price stores (which go under the name "Sposabella") in Toronto, Montreal, and Edmonton. These stores do not regularly discount dresses. For a location, call the Sposabella headquarters in Canada at (514) 385-5777.

Shop in the U.S. and Save?
Duties and taxes can dampen cross-border bargains

Okay, this isn't the most patriotic subject, but shopping across the border in the U.S. can be a money-saver for many Canadian brides. Even with the exchange rate, many of the more affordable bridal gowns available in the U.S. are less than the $1000 Canadian average for a wedding dress. So, with all this North American Free Trade Agreement (NAFTA) stuff, does that mean you can save a bundle by going south for a bridal gown?

Well, yes and no. While NAFTA is definitely lowering trade barriers, a series of duties and taxes still await cross-border shoppers. The bad news? There are three main fees: duties, GST and provincial sales taxes. The good news? Depending on how long you're absent from Canada, you can claim a personal exemption. Here are the details:

❧ **Personal exemptions.** Personal exemptions allow you to bring goods of a certain value into Canada without paying duties or Goods and Services Tax (or GST). You still have to pay provincial or territorial sales tax, though (see below). Unfortunately, the exemption amounts are quite small, despite a recent increase in the figures. For example, if you're absent from Canada for less than 24 hours, you can claim an exemption for goods that total less than $50 Canadian, which will hardly buy a wedding dress. For a 48-hour absence, the exemption is $200. Even if you are gone for seven days or more, the total exemption is just $500 Canadian. That works out to $360 U.S. The good news: even though you have to pay duty on any dress that's over $500 Canadian, you still get to apply the exemption to the first $500 (if you're gone more than seven days).

❧ **Duties.** Thanks to NAFTA, Canada now has a two-tier duty structure. Goods made in the U.S. or Canada qualify for a lower duty rate. In 1997, this rate (combined with the GST) is about 8%. The good news is that in 1998, the duty will be phased out completely—you'll only owe the GST, which is about 7%.

The bad news? Well, 95% of the wedding dresses sold in the U.S. are made overseas—hence, they won't qualify for this tax break. As a result, you have to pay the duty rate for "goods not eligible under NAFTA." When combined with the GST, this works out to about 15%. So, let's have a real-life example. You take a week long vacation to the U.S. and buy a wedding dress made overseas worth $1000 Canadian. On the first $500, you'd owe no duty. On the balance ($500), you'd owe the 15% duty and GST, or roughly $75. What if the wedding dress was made in the U.S. or Canada? You'd owe about $40.

❧ **Provincial and territorial sales taxes.** In addition to the above duties, you also must pay any provincial and territorial sales tax on the goods you bring back to Canada. In some cases this is a double whammy—you'll not only have to pay U.S. sales taxes, but the Canadian amount too. One way to avoid the U.S. sales tax is to have the dress shipped back to your home in Canada (see below).

❧ **Mail order dresses.** If you buy a gown in the U.S. and have it shipped to your home in Canada, you can still use the $500 personal exemption. When you arrive back home, you must ask the customs officials for a Form E24, "Returning Persons Declaration." You will need your copy of the form to claim your goods when they arrive. Otherwise, you may have to pay the regular duties on them.

When you have goods that arrive in Canada after you do, you have 40 days to clear them with customs by producing your copy of Form E24 mentioned above. When the goods arrive, the carrier who delivers them will ask you to pay the duties that apply along with a processing fee. You then have two options:

1. *You can accept delivery by paying the full amount of the assessment and then file a claim for a refund with Revenue Canada.*
2. *Or you can refuse to accept delivery.*

If you refuse delivery, the carrier will return the package to customs and ask you for a telephone number where customs can reach you to discuss the assessment. The carrier will give you a copy of the assessment notice for your reference. Once the government has determined that the goods are eligible for free importation as declared on your Form E24, they will release them for delivery to you without an assessment.

Confusing, eh? Well, you can always contact a local Revenue Canada or Customs office to ask a specific question. Look in the phone book in the government listings for an office near you. (Or check the Internet—Revenue Canada's web sit at http://www.revcan.ca/) Here are the regional offices of Revenue Canada that can also answer questions:

Regional Customs Offices

• *Atlantic*—Halifax (902) 426-2911
• *Québec*—Montreal (514) 283-9900 or (418) 648-4445
• *Northern Ontario*—Ottawa (613) 993-0534 or (613) 998-3326 *(after 4:30 p.m. and weekends)*
• *Southern Ontario*—Toronto (416) 973-8022 or
(416) 676-3643 *(weekends and holidays)*
Hamilton (905) 308-8715 and 1-800-361-5603
Windsor (519) 257-6400
• *Prairies*—Winnipeg (204) 983-6004
Calgary (403) 292-8750 and (403) 292-4660
• *Pacific*—Vancouver (604) 666-0545

384 BRIDAL GOWN GUIDE

3 **Watch out for "designer dumps."** What happens when bridal designers have too many gowns and not enough customers? It's sale time! Yet, these designers don't want to sully their fancy, full-price image in the United States. So, they load up the truck and head north. The designers rent a hotel ballroom, take out ads that scream "MONSTER BRIDAL DRESS SALE! ONE DAY ONLY" and let the bargains rip. While there is no schedule to these sales, you might want to keep an eye on the papers to see if one comes to your town.

4 **Check out David's.** As we mentioned earlier in this book, David's is an off-the-rack operation that has more than three dozen outlets in the U.S. One is in Buffalo, New York (716) 834-6100, which told us they see quite a few brides who make the short trip from Toronto. David's periodically has $99 gown sales, but even their regular dresses ($300 to $600) are a pretty good deals. (Since David's is growing rapidly, you may be able to find a store closer to you by calling 800-399-2743 or 610-896-2111). Of course, cross-border shopping has its own drawbacks—see the following box on the subject for more details.

5 **Go for one of our "best buy" designers.** Earlier in this book we identified several designers who offer extraordinarily good value. And there's more good news: many of these designers are also available in Canada. For example, Mori Lee has extensive distribution in Canada (contact their Canadian distributor, the Richman Group (416) 789-9911 for a store near you).

6 **Dicker the price.** Off the record, Canadian bridal manufacturers tell us it's a buyer's market for wedding dresses in Canada. The plain fact: there are too many gowns chasing too few brides. As a result, shops are hungry for business and may cut a deal for you. While that doesn't mean they'll knock 40% off that dream dress, you might be able to negotiate a small discount . . . it can't hurt to ask!

Internet source for bridal shop locations

Where are the best bridal shops in Canada? Whose designer lines do they carry? The answers are on the Internet, specifically, WeddingBells Magazine web site at (www.weddingbells.com). Their excellent database lets you search by province/town for gown shops, custom designers, fabric shops and other wedding merchants.

Gown preservation

As you read earlier, there are lot of scam artists in the business of bridal gown "cleaning and preservation." Fortunately, we did find one honest person who does this in Canada—Forever Yours Bridal Gown Preservation in Toronto (800) 683-4696 or (416) 703-4696. Owner Jerry Shiner's family has been cleaning delicate garments since 1933 and his company now specializes in bridal gown cleaning and preservation. Forever Yours charges a base price of $200 to $300, with a more specific price quote offered depending on the type of gown, detailing and so on. The process takes about six to eight weeks and the company offers pick-up and delivery across Canada. Jerry's knowledge of bridal cleaning and preservation can't be matched in Canada; while the service is pricey, you're getting museum-quality preservation and tremendous care that insures beads and lace isn't damaged in the cleaning process.

⧫CANADIAN BRIDAL DESIGNERS⧫

As a Canadian bride, you basically have two choices when it comes to selecting a bridal gown: imported or domestic. Many U.S. designers have Canadian distribution (most notably Mori Lee and Demetrios/Sposabella). Therefore you can use the U.S. designer reviews earlier in this book to gauge various style and price options (although Canadian duties on dresses made in Asia may add slightly to the retail prices you see in Canada).

Of course, you can go domestic. Canada has a dozen or so manufacturers of bridal gowns and their reputation for quality is earning fans on both sides of the border. Unlike their U.S. counterparts, most Canadian bridal designers actually make their gowns in Canada. On the upside, the workmanship and construction quality is generally excellent, especially compared to the imports. On the downside, the price is usually higher (as you'll read below in more detail).

As a side note, many Canadian bridal manufacturers are attempting to expand their distribution in the U.S. In 1997, several Canadian designers debuted in the U.S. and, while their distribution may be spotty at this point, expect to see more Canadian bridal gowns in the lower 48. Why? Well, NAFTA is one reason— the trade agreement recently lowered tariffs and duties on goods made in Canada that are imported into the U.S. (and vice versa). A weak Canadian dollar has also spurred exports. Of course, another explanation is obvious: many Canadian designers are simply looking for new markets. Since the U.S. has 15 times more weddings than Canada, the designers look to the U.S. market as one of their few growth opportunities. They're hoping their quality gowns and clean styling will appeal to U.S. brides, despite prices that can be high at times.

What follows is an overview of the best Canadian bridal designers. Note that the following prices are in Canadian dollars. At the time of this writing, prices for these dresses in the United States were quite similar to the Canadian prices.

❖ *Alfred Sung.* Alfred Sung is sort of like the Calvin Klein of Canada. Pop into any department store in the Great White North and you'll see Sung's name plastered on everything from luggage to perfume. Sung even designed the Canadian Girl Guide uniforms (the Girl Guides are similar to the Girl Scouts in the U.S.). Since the Sung name has such cachet, Jai International licensed the moniker for use with bridal apparel. Introduced in 1993 in Canada, Jai both designs and manufactures the Alfred Sung Bridal Collection. The gowns debuted in the U.S. in 1995.

Jai's strategy has apparently worked—the Alfred Sung Bridal Collection is probably the most successful Canadian bridal import in the U.S., with a large number of dealers on both sides of the border.

"Clean, modern and timeless" is how Jai describes the Alfred Sung Bridal Collection and we have to agree. These gowns are definitely not dirty, old and dated. (Just kidding.)

Seriously, the dresses are very simple and we like the look. Little or no beading lets the rich fabrics (chiffons, matte satins and organzas) shine through. Our only complaint: a few of the sleeve treatments could use some work. The voluminous sleeve designs on some dresses overpowered the simple lines of the gowns. On the other hand, we liked the hem detailing. Instead of lace and beading, one Sung gown featured an elegant satin band on the hem. Clean, indeed.

As for value, Alfred Sung gowns are no bargain. The dozen or so gowns in the collection average just under $1200, with some topping $1500. Prices start at $890. Is that out of line with the competition? Probably not. For a silk gown with similar styling, Alfred Sung's bridal gowns are about average in price.
For a dealer near you or a free catalog, call (800) 981-5496 or (416) 597-0767.

❖ *Amici* Toronto designers Renella De Fina and Claudia Stante have been turning out lavish couture bridal gowns since 1992. The dresses are made of 100% silk and "custom cut" (made to your measurements). One dress that caught our eye was a "six panel gathered skirt with halter bodice and beaded silk ribbon embroidered band." How much? About $2000. In fact, most of Amici's gowns were in the $2000 to $4000 range. Many dresses feature elaborate beading, pearls and crystals, as well as built-in crinolines. Fabric swaps and large sizes are available (above a size 20, add 20% to the gown price).
Call (905) 264-1466 to find a dealer near you.

❖ *Paloma Blanca* Paloma Blanca's manufacturer (Bluebird) has been turning out bridal gowns in Canada for 60 years. The looks are stylish without the big style price tag—most dresses retail for $900 to $1850. We saw the gowns at a recent trade show and were impressed. All dresses are completely lined and feature elegant detailing. As a side note, the company also markets dresses under the name BB Couture.
Call (416) 504-4550 to find a dealer near you.

❖ *Gordon* According to a late breaking bulletin received here at the home office, we'd like to announce that the Barenaked Ladies have absolutely nothing to do with Gordon. Actually, Gordon (the bridal

gown manufacturer) has been in business since the 1970's and turns out dresses in the $800 to $1000 range. The looks are "simple and elegant," according to a representative we spoke to. A typical Gordon dress features a plain skirt and train and just a touch of beading or lace on the tight-fitting bodice. Fabrics include silk and duchess satin. Sizing starts at a 4 and Gordon does offer large size dresses. Delivery takes four to six weeks, which makes Gordon one of the more speedy Canadian bridal manufacturers.
Call (416) 593-0688 for a dealer near you.

❖ *Guzzo* Looking for something daring? Check out some of the gowns from couture bridal dressmaker Guzzo. Designer Frances Guzzo has been turned out bustier-style gowns since 1982 from her downtown Toronto retail "studio." And these gowns leave little to the imagination. An example? Try a strapless silk satin hand-beaded bustier bodice with a silk organza skirt for $3000. The gowns (which have been featured in *Wedding Dresses* and *Modern Bride* magazines) start at $1100, but most are in the $2000 to $3000 range. Most of the dresses are made of silk and all are custom cut (made to your measurements).
Call (416) 585-9820 to find a dealer near you.

❖ *Ines Di Santo* If we were to give an award for Canada's most flamboyant bridal designer, Ines Di Santo would win hands down. This Argentina-born Italian designer has a flair for the dramatic, accenting her dresses with tiny porcelain roses, Austrian crystals and intricate metallic embroidery. As you might expect, all this extravagance doesn't come cheap—most Ines Di Santo bridal gowns start at $2000 and range up to a whopping $4600. Yet you are getting value for the dollar; we saw the dresses at a recent fashion show and found the looks to be extravagant. All the fabrics are silk and each gown's price includes a matching headpiece (hey, it's the least they could do). In business since 1976, Ines has her own shop called Chez Moi in Woodbridge, Ontario (just outside Toronto). Sizes 4 to 20 and a few petite sizes are also available.
Call (905) 856-9115 to find a dealer near you.

❖ *Justina McCaffrey* Justina McCaffrey is our pick as the best bridal designer in Ottawa. Okay, she's probably the only bridal designer in Ottawa, but don't hold that against her. McCaffrey designed a women's evening wear collection for Creed's of Toronto before launching her own company in 1989. McCaffrey's all-silk bridal gowns feature slick European styling (that is, plain skirts and only minimal detailing on the bodices). Typical of the looks is "Cecelia," an elegant silk peau de soie gown with six rosebuds on strings trailing the detachable train. The emphasis here is on the fabric (including silk brocade and dupioni), not extravagant beading and lace. The dresses sell for $1500 to $2000 in Canada, about $1700 to $2500 in the U.S. You can visit Justina McCaffrey's retail store in Ottawa or check out another bridal shop that carries her dresses (about dozen or so in the U.S.).
Call toll-free (888) 874-GOWN or (613) 789-4336 to find a dealer near you.

❖ *Madison Collection* The best buy among Canada bridal designers has to be the Madison Collection, a Toronto-based company that turns out beautiful dresses at affordable prices. With gowns that start at $600, you can find "European styling" and natural fabrics in a variety of fashion-forward looks. A good example is style 8815, a sleeveless silk bodice with deep square back edged with pearls. A wide venise lace band with pearls accents the waist and the dress features a "knife-pleated" silk skirt. The price? $598, a great deal on a silk dress. Other dresses range from $700 to $1100 and feature guipure lace and chiffon or tulle skirts. Sizing is somewhat limited (sizes 6 to 20), but the quality is top-notch.
Call The Richman Group at (416) 789-9911 for a dealer near you.

❖ *Rivini* Toronto-based Rivini's signature look is hand-crafted roses and delicate hand-beaded bodices. The company divides its gowns into six fabric groups and offers such options as Austrian crepe, silk peau de soie, silk satin-faced organza, and silk duchess satin. We saw the gowns at a recent trade show and were impressed with the clean, fashion-forward looks. One stand-out was an empire gown with beaded tank-style neckline, bias skirt and chiffon train for $1750. Other dresses ranged from $1250 to $3000. Sizes range from 4 to 16.
Call (416) 977-1793 to find a dealer near you.

❖ *William S* In business since 1981, William S is a Toronto-based manufacturer that makes mother-of-the-bride gowns, bridesmaids dresses and, yes, bridal gowns. The latter range from $500 to $900 and typically feature man-made fabrics (satin, organza) and traditional styling. William S offers custom changes such as fabric swaps, sleeve changes, and train extensions. We saw the dresses at a recent bridal market and were pleased—while William S probably won't win any fashion awards, the dresses' clean and simple lines hit the mark.
Call (416) 504-7278 to find a dealer near you.

Do you have any bargain tips for bridal dress shopping in Canada? Other questions or comments? Contact the authors of this book by phone, fax or e-mail—check out the page at the back of this book for more information.

❖ G L O S S A R Y ❖

Fabric, Finishes and Laces

❖ *Fabric Content* . . . .
Here's a look at common bridal fabrics:

Silk. This is the premiere wedding fabric for softness, luster and beauty. Silk is made from silkworm cocoons, discovered by the Chinese in 2600 B.C. France became the most famous producer of finished silk fabric, hence the use of so many French names such as *dupioni* and *peau de soie* (later in this chapter, we'll define fabric finishes).

Until recently, silk has always been an expensive fabric and silk bridal gowns have been equally pricey—most used to cost over $1000. In the last five years, however, more affordable silk fabrics (and silk blends) have dropped that price considerably. Today, there are even designers who are churning out all silk gowns for just $600.

Despite increasing competition in silk production, China still makes 70% to 85% of the world's silk. Other countries like Thailand turn out great silk fabric as well; the designer Wallentin brags that it only uses 100% Thai silk in their gowns.

Cotton. Used as thread and fabric as long ago as 600 B.C., cotton is made from the fibers of its namesake plant. Cotton's popularity in everyday clothes has probably contributed to its absence as a bridal fabric—there's little cachet to a cotton bridal gown. While a few designers use the fabric (woven in sheer or embroidered varieties), it's still rare to see cotton on the bridal dress racks.

Linen. Made from flax fibers, this fabric was first utilized for clothing by the ancient Egyptians. Linen is often combined with cotton or other fabrics; by itself it wrinkles badly. As a result, you're more likely to see linen as a fabric in suits and other informal bridal dresses.

Rayon. Invented during World War II when silk was rationed for use in parachutes, rayon is made from plant fibers. An affordable fabric, rayon often shows up in blends of various bridal fabrics.

Man-made fabrics. Nylon, acetate and polyester are those affordable man-made wonders that became unavoidable in 70's fashion. In the bridal world, manufacturers could weave these fabrics into shiny or glossy finishes, giving a special look at a lower price. Most affordably priced gowns (under $600) are made of man-made fabrics. While most brides don't think "Hey, I want a polyester bridal gown," most popular bridal fabric finishes such as "satin" and "taffeta" are made of just that.

❖ *Fabric Finishes* . . . .
It's easy to confuse fabrics with fabric *finishes*. The finish is what the cloth feels and looks like after it's woven. Most bridal fabrics (both natural and man-made) can be woven into the wide variety of finishes described below:

Charmeuse. (SHAR-moose) A tasty, low fat, non-dairy dessert. Just kidding! Actually, charmeuse is a lightweight version of satin with a softer and more clingy look. Charmeuse is a common finish with silk or rayon and has less body than traditional silk finishes.

Chiffon. (SHI-fon) A transparent lightweight fabric finish, chiffon may be made from just about any fabric. It is often layered and has an unusual luster.

Damask. (DAM-ask) The hallmark of this finish are threads woven into a pattern that create a white-on-white or ivory-on-ivory appearance. Often woven in a floral pattern, this fabric finish doesn't need any additional beading or lace.

Duchess (Duchesse) satin. Also referred to as silk-faced satin, this finish weighs less than traditional silk finishes and is usually less expensive as well. Most Duchess satins are a blend of silk and rayon woven into a satin finish.

Dupioni. (doo-pee-OH-nee) Similar to shantung (see below) but with thicker, coarser fibers woven into a taffeta-like fabric, dupioni has shown up quite frequently in recent bridesmaids designs.

Faille. (rhymes with "pail") Faille is a ribbed fabric finish with structure and body. This finish is also seen in bridesmaids styles today. Most faille finishes are woven from silk, cotton, rayon or polyester fabrics.

Net, illusion, or tulle (pronounced "tool"). This mesh-like fabric is most often woven from synthetic fibers. A recent fad saw several designers adding tulle skirts to their gown designs. Varying weaves can increase or decrease the weight of this finish.

Organdy. A crisp transparent fabric finish made from cotton.

Organza. Similar to chiffon (see above), but heavier and with more body.

Peau de soie (skin of silk). (po-day-swa) A heavy, smooth satin with very fine ribbing. This finish is actually somewhat dull in sheen compared to traditional silk finishes.

Satin. A tightly woven effect that creates a fabric with a beautiful sheen on one side. Typically made in man-made fabrics like polyester, satin is probably the most common bridal gown fabric finish. While satin is most often associated with a high gloss look, it is also available in a matte finish with a toned down glow.

Shantung. Originally known as wild (or natural) silk, this finish has a rougher, nubby appearance. Once associated exclusively with silk fabrics, shantung is now seen as a finish for man-made fabrics as well.

Taffeta. This crisp finish is often woven from man-made fabrics. A close second to satin, taffeta finishes are not only common in bridal gowns but bridesmaids dresses too. In the latter, you might find taffeta fabrics with woven moiré patterns.

Velvet. Most folks are familiar with this finish, which has a thick nap. Once associated with silks, velvets can be a finish on cotton or rayon blends today as well. A variation of this finish, crushed velvet is made with a high and low nap to give a shimmering effect.

❖ *Laces* ....

   Boy, if you thought fabric finishes had funny sounding names, just wait to you check out the laces bridal designers use. Here's a wrap-up of the names you'll encounter:

Alencon. (al-ON-son) Probably the most popular of wedding laces, alencon lace has a background of flowers and swags which are re-embroidered along the edges with cording. This lace may be pre-beaded or beaded after it is sewn on the dress.

Battenburg. This type of lace is made by stitching a strip of linen fabric into a pattern of loops, then connecting them with thread. Besides bridal gowns, battenburg is often found on table and bed linens.

Chantilly. (Shan-TILL-ee)Flowers and ribbons on a plain net background define chantilly lace. These details are usually edged with fine cording. Feel free to sing the song now.

Dotted Swiss. Small circles of flocked fabric over a background of netting typify this lace, which is often used on necklines or layered over skirts.

Eyelet. This lace is usually made of cotton, which has perforated holes embroidered around the edges.

Guipure. (gwi-PURE) This lace has a seen a resurgence in recent years—it seems to be the hip lace of the moment. Guipure features a large series of motifs connected by a few threads. Common guipure patterns may be roses, daises or other geometric designs like ovals. The result is often a retro 70's look.

Ribbon. A random pattern of ribbon that is sewn over a net background.

Schiffli. (SHIF-lee) A light weight lace with an all-over embroidered design on a net background.

Venise. (ven-EES) This type of lace is a needlepoint-type design. An example connects small flowers with irregularly placed threads.

Dress Components and Styles

Fabric and lace is just the beginning when it comes to strange bridal terms. Next up is a list of bridal silhouettes, skirt widths plus a handy pocket translator for all those "lines:" waistlines, hemlines, necklines and more. Then we'll go over terms for back treatments, sleeves, and trains.

❖ *Silhouettes* ....

Silhouettes are basically the outline of the dress including the type of skirt, bodice and waistline. Note that a silhouette is the overall look of the dress; we'll go over the individual terms for sleeves, necklines and detailing later. Here are the basics of silhouettes:

1. Ball gown. This is probably the most traditional of all bridal gown silhouettes. The ball gown look is typified by a fitted bodice and waistline that leads to a very full skirt. In recent years, this look as been quite fashionable, as designers try to echo the golden age of Hollywood.

2. Empire. A high waistline (right under the bust) which falls to a slimmer skirt width is the hallmark of an empire style gown. This look was hip in the 60's, all but disappeared in the 70's and 80's, only to return with a vengeance in the 90's.

3. A-Line or Princess. This style has vertical seams flowing from the shoulders down to a flared skirt. Unlike the ball gown, the waistline in an A-line/Princess style is not as defined. Because of its versatility, this style is quite popular as a silhouette that fits many different body types.

4. Sheath. As you might guess, the slim skirt is a key attribute of a sheath silhouette, probably one of the more contemporary bridal gown looks. It goes without saying that the body-hugging sheath style isn't for everyone. A variation of the sheath is the mermaid-style gown, which is also form-fitting but flares below the knees.

❖ *Skirt Widths* . . . .

Whether you want a floor length gown or a shorter skirt, the *width* of the skirt also influences the style of a bridal gown. Here's a look at the options:

Bouffant. (BOO-font) This is the fullest skirt available, with yards and yards of fabric falling from a gathered waist. A good example: Glenda the Good Witch in the Wizard of Oz.

Circular. The skirt forms a circle at the hemline with a smooth (as opposed to a gathered) waistline.

Flared. The gown gradually widens from waist to floor.

Full. This skirt is gathered at the waist and has more volume than a circular skirt, but less than a bouffant.

Slim. A rarely-seen skirt width style, a slim skirt is only slightly tapered from waistline to floor. Unlike the sheath silhouette, it is not a body-hugging style.

Sheath. A straight skirt with no flair, most sheaths are designed to hung the body. Note: you may not be able to kneel during the ceremony in this style skirt.

Three-tiered. A tiered skirt of different fabrics and/or textures.

Trumpet/Mermaid. Fitted to the hips, this design flares out below the knees. Like the sheath skirt width, this style may also be difficult to kneel in during the ceremony.

Ballerina. An extra full skirt falling just above the ankle, this looks especially pretty in layers of tulle.

❖ *Waistlines* . . . .

Most waistlines are defined in relation to your "natural waist," which is the smallest part of your torso.

A-Line. An A-line (or princess) waistline is fitted at the bodice and then flares out to the skirt. This is one of the few waistlines that compliments virtually any body type.

Antebellum. This V-shaped waistline falls 2 to 2.5 inches below the natural waist. It is similar to the basque waist (see below).

Asymmetrical. *(not pictured)* This unique look drops down on one side. This waistline is more common with bridesmaids dresses than bridal gowns.

Basque. (pronounced "bask") Usually a fitted, V-shaped waist treatment that starts two to three inches below natural waist. This is one of the most common bridal gown waistlines.

Drop waist. Settling around your hips, this waistline is usually 3 to 5 inches below natural waist. A dress with a drop waist may help elongate the torso, giving the illusion of extra height.

Empire. This waistline flows from the bustline. An empire waist is another style that looks good on a variety of body types.

Raised. This style is made to fall one inch *above* the natural waist.

❖ *Hemlines* . . . .

Ballerina. This is an extra full skirt that falls just above the ankle.

Floor Length. A floor-length gown should allow the toes of your shoes to show, although some brides may prefer a slightly shorter length.

Handkerchief. This is a tea-length skirt designed with panels that end in points. The effect looks like a series of handkerchiefs sewn together.

Midi/intermission. This skirt falls between the knee and mid-calf.

Mini. As you might guess, the mini skirt hemline is more often seen on the runaway than on real brides. Some designers offer a detachable overskirt that a bride can wear during the ceremony.

Street. This length falls just below the knee.

Tea length. A popular length for bridesmaids, tea length ends at mid-calf.

Details

This category includes necklines, backs, trains, sleeves and head-pieces/veils as well as any special detailing like bows, florets, gathers and pleats.

❖ *Necklines* ....

Bateau (boat). (BAT-toe) This neckline extends straight across the shoulder with a slight curve at the front.

Portrait. Similar in shape to the bateau, this style stands away from the bride's face and shoulders.

Sabrina. Also like a bateau neckline, the sabrina is different in one way: it starts two inches in from each shoulder. As a result, it has a narrower neck opening.

Bertha collar. A decorative panel (about nine to 18 inches in length) attached around the neckline.

Décolletage. (day-COAL-e-taj) For the adventurous types, this is a deep, plunging neckline.

Elizabethan. An Elizabethan style neckline has a high neckline at the nape of the neck.

Halter. This neckline echoes the 70's with a scoop or v-neck in front and fabric band wrapping around the neck. It's a great look with sleeveless designs.

Illusion. An illusion neckline can be any style (V, scoop, heart, etc.) that is covered with transparent netting.

Jewel. A high, yet rounded neckline.

Keyhole. This teardrop-shaped opening starts two inches in from the shoulders and looks like an old-fashioned keyhole.

Queen Anne. A heart-shaped opening in front, combined with high neckline in back.

Scoop. A curved neckline that may be low in front.

Square. This style forms a half-square.

Sweetheart. One of the most common neckline styles in bridal today, this neckline is heart-shaped. Many variations can be seen with strapless and illusion-covered designs.

Wedding-band collar. A high circle of fabric is fitted around the middle of the neck. For a traditional Victorian look, designers often use this style/

❖ *Back Treatments* ....

Remember that you will spend a large part of your ceremony with your back to your guests. Here are some treatments that add some interest to the back of your gown.

Bustle. Victorian women were famous for their ornate bustles, made of fabric panels that are gathered and draped with floral details. Even if your dress doesn't have a bustle detail, you will want to "bustle" your train (which we explained in Step 6 earlier in this book) to keep it from dragging on the floor at your reception.

Butterfly. This detail may be shaped like a big bow or could just be a gathering of fabric flowers at the base of the back (some brides derisively refer to them as "butt bows").

Buttons. A long row of fabric-covered buttons is a common back treatment.

Keyhole. A cut-out in the shape of a key-hole that exposes the back or is covered in illusion.

Ruffles. Many gowns are designed with tiers of ruffles that cascade down from the waistline.

Scoop/Square. A curved or boxy backline that sometimes plunges down the back.

❖ *Sleeves* ....

Bishop. A sleeve that is somewhat full and gathered all the way to the wrist.

Cap. One of the shortest of sleeves, a cap just barely covers the top of the shoulder and may incorporate flower details or pleats. (With off-the-shoulder styles, cap sleeves may extend somewhat down the arm).

Dolman. A style we don't see as much lately, a dolman is full at the top where the fabric meets the bodice. A dolman sleeves tapers to the forearm, where it is fitted.

Fitted. In various lengths, these sleeves that are tailored closely to the arm. Juliet fitted sleeves are long sleeves with a small pouf at the shoulder. Three-quarter fitted sleeves end just below the elbow.

Gibson. This sleeve is puffed at the top and full to the wrist.

Leg o' mutton/gigot. Full at the shoulder, this sleeve is combined with a fitted forearm.

Poet. Very full sleeves with pleats at the shoulder. Picture Bill Shakespeare.

Pointed/gauntlet. *(not pictured)* These long, fitted sleeves end in a point at the wrist.

Puff. As the name implies, the puff sleeve features gathered fabric in varying fullness. This style is often associated with short sleeve dresses, though some gowns with long, fitted sleeves may have a slight puff at the shoulder.

Spaghetti strap. Tiny straps over the shoulder. This sleeve treatment has been a hot fad recently.

Strapless/bustier. A strapless bodice has no sleeves at all. Since some churches or synagogues frown on these dresses, designers usually offer a matching jacket for the ceremony.

(These sleeve illustrations were reprinted from "How to Alter a Bridal Gown" by Susan Ormand. For more information on this book, see the earlier listing in Step 6 Alterations).

❖ *Trains* ....

There are three basic types of trains: A train that extends from the hemline is called a sweep. As you might guess, a waist train falls from the waist. The third train type is quite rare, but offers a unique effect: the watteau. The watteau extends from the shoulders, sort of like the dresses worn in medieval times (cone-shaped hat is optional).

Besides the position, trains come in various lengths. Here is a round-up of the various lengths names, which are measured from the waist to the train's end:

Brush/sweep. This is the shortest train. Floor-length evening gowns of the 1920's often had a slight brush trains.

Cathedral. Perhaps the most common train length, cathedral trains extend two and a half yards from the waist line.

Chapel. A chapel-length train extends about one and a third yards from the waist.

Court. Not often seen these days, a court train is shorter than a chapel train but longer than a brush (about a yard long).

Detached. Not actually a train length, this term refers to those removable trains that are popular today. Detachable trains usually have snaps or buttons that hold the train on at the waist.

Royal. The longest of all trains, this version extends three or more yards in length.

❖ *Headpieces* ....

What's the best-selling headpiece design? Designers tell us crowns and headbands make up more than half their business. The next most popular options are backpieces and wreaths, followed by sprays. What do these styles look like? Here's an overview, with pictures from the Betty Wales Bridal Veil company (call 212-279-8895 for a dealer near you):

Crowns. A fabric, lace or bead covered circlet that sits high atop the bride's head.

Crescents/headbands/bandeaus. A fabric or bead-covered strip that arcs over and fits close to the head.

V-bands. Usually a thin, beaded band that encircles the top of the bride's head and dips down to a V over the forehead. It may have fabric flowers or lace at the back of the band.

Backpieces. Most often a bow or cluster of flowers (such as fabric roses) that attach to the hair at the nape of the neck. Veiling flows from the bottom of the bow.

Halos/wreaths/garlands. Less formal than crowns, wreaths are also circles that sit on top of the head. For a more informal look, some wreaths are made of silk or real flowers.

Sprays. Composed of beading and flowers, sprays are smaller, less ornate headpieces that do not include veiling. Sprays typically clip to the hair.

Tiaras. This very formal style sits tall on a brides head in the same position as a headband.

Caps. A headpiece that is fitted closely to the bride's head. A cap is either positioned forward on the forehead or placed back on the rear of the head (also called a Juliet cap).

Picture hats. This type of hat has a very wide brim that may have lace, flowers and tulle surrounding the crown. Picture Scarlet O'Hara in *Gone With the Wind*.

❖ *Veils*..

Veils can be just as varied as the headpieces they're attached to. Some are plain, while others have satin ribbon edging, scattered pearls or even lace appliqués. Most bridal veils are described by their length. Here's a breakdown:

Blusher/illusion. In addition to the main veil, a blusher is a short, chin-length veil. It is pulled over the bride's face when she walks down the aisle, then pushed back during the wedding ceremony by the groom or father of the bride.

Pouf. In the '80's this was an incredibly popular veil style. A pouf veil rises up from the bride's head at least six inches and is usually worn with a longer veil in back.

Fly-away. Shoulder-length veil.

Fingertip. The most common length, this one reaches to your fingertips.

Ballet/waltz. Extends to knee length.

Sweep. This style is the same length as the dress skirt.

Chapel. 1.5 feet long from waist.

Cathedral. 2.5 feet long from waist.

Royal. A veil three or more feet long from the waist, matching the length of a cathedral train.

✦ INDEX ✦

HOW TO REACH THE AUTHORS
❖ *Have a question about the Bridal Gown Guide?*
❖ *Want to make a suggestion?*
❖ *Discovered a great bargain you'd like to share?*
Contact the Authors, Denise &Alan Fields in one of five ways:
1. By phone: (303) 442-8792.
2. By mail: 436 Pine Street, Suite G, Boulder, CO 80302.
3. By fax: (303) 442-3744.
4. By electronic mail: adfields@aol.com
5. On our web page: http://www.windsorpeak.com
(If you're having problems accessing our home page,
call our office at 1-800-888-0385).

OTHER PUBLICATIONS FROM WINDSOR PEAK PRESS   405

→JOIN OUR←

"Preferred Reader" List!

We've got lots of new books and special reports coming out over the next few years! Just jot down your name and address below, mail in the coupon and we'll keep you up-to-date!

Best of all, we have "early bird" DISCOUNTS especially for BRIDAL GOWN GUIDE readers!

Name_____

Address_____

City_____ State_____ Zip_____

Wedding Date _____

How did you hear about our book?_____

_____

What was your favorite section or tip? _____

_____

How can we improve this book? _____

_____

_____

_____

_____

_____

Mail to:

BRIDAL GOWN GUIDE
436 Pine Street, Suite G
Boulder, CO 80302
or fax to *(303) 442-3744*
or e-mail this info to adfields@aol.com